THE POOR
AND THE
PERFECT

THE POOR
AND THE
PERFECT

THE RISE OF LEARNING
IN THE FRANCISCAN
ORDER, 1209–1310

Neslihan Şenocak

CORNELL UNIVERSITY PRESS
Ithaca and London

First published 2012 by Cornell University Press

Printed in the United States of America

Library of Congress Cataloging-in-Publication Data

Senocak, Neslihan, 1972–
   The poor and the perfect : the rise of learning in the Franciscan order, 1209–1310 / Neslihan Senocak.
      p. cm.
   Includes bibliographical references and index.
   ISBN 978-0-8014-5057-0 (cloth : alk. paper)
   1. Franciscans—History—To 1500.   2. Franciscans—Education—History—To 1500.   3. Learning and scholarship—History—Medieval, 500–1500.   I. Title.
   BX3606.3.S46   2012
   271'.3—dc23   2011051734

Cornell University Press strives to use environmentally responsible suppliers and materials to the fullest extent possible in the publishing of its books. Such materials include vegetable-based, low-VOC inks and acid-free papers that are recycled, totally chlorine-free, or partly composed of nonwood fibers. For further information, visit our website at www.cornellpress.cornell.edu.

Cloth printing   10 9 8 7 6 5 4 3 2 1

To my parents,
Nevin and Erdoğan Şenocak,
and
to Alessandro and Devrim

❧ CONTENTS

✄ ACKNOWLEDGMENTS

When a Turkish engineer in Ankara, who had never been inside a church until the age of twenty-three, decides to write a book on medieval Franciscans, the list of people deserving thanks becomes necessarily very long. On top of this list is Paul Latimer, who in the capacity as a mentor, editor and friend made an enormous contribution both to this book and to my formation as a medievalist. He and Cadoc Leighton, Ord. Praem., with their brilliant English and Glaswegian humor, superior powers of reasoning, and vast erudition taught me more about medieval church and life at our legendary lunches at Bilkent than any other book or person. It was the Vatican scholarship in 1999–2000 that Cadoc facilitated that turned my career from that of an industrial engineer to one of a historian of the Middle Ages. To Paul and Cadoc, I owe a debt that can never be paid.

A number of institutions have been pivotal in the completion of this work. I thank the trustees of Bilkent University, Ankara, and everyone at its Department of History for creating and maintaining the first, and still the only, institution in Turkey where one can specialize in the history of medieval Latin West. I am grateful to the chairman of the history department at Bilkent, Mehmet Kalpaklı, for offering me a space at Bilkent as a visiting scholar in 2010–2011, where I completed the final revision of this book. The Pontifical Council for Interreligious Dialogue granted me thrice a scholarship to conduct research in Rome, which allowed me to put down the backbone of this book. I am grateful to the Bibliographical Society of UK for a generous grant to study the Franciscan manuscripts in Italy and to the Clarisse Sisters in Todi, who offered me not only hospitality but a warmest and long-lasting friendship. One of my most fruitful periods of study was spent at the Erasmus Institute at the University of Notre Dame—sadly, no longer in existence—which fostered an excellent scholarly environment. I give many thanks to the Pontifical Institute of Mediaeval Studies and Società Internazionale di Studi Francescani.

Because of this book, I have had the good fortune of knowing a great many exceptional people. David d'Avray and Brenda Bolton have been guiding examples of goodwill, generosity, erudition, and scholarly brilliance. Both of them read parts of the book and made valuable suggestions for its improvement. Many thanks also to William J. Courtenay, Guy Geltner, and Sylvain Piron, who kindly read sections of the book and made useful comments. I am indebted to Alvaro Cacciotti, OFM, the director of the School of Higher Franciscan Studies at the Pontificio Ateneo Antonianum in Rome during my sojourn there in 1999 and 2000, and his successor Pietro Messa for making me welcome in Rome's Franciscan community. There, I have had the good fortune of studying with many scholars, two of which, Paolo Vian and the late Father Cesare Cenci, both exceptional scholars, deserve particular thanks for their assistance to me over the years. Bert Roest was so kind to provide me with many sources and discussions when I first ventured into studying the history of the Franciscans. His work on Franciscan education provided a solid base upon which to construct. I give heartfelt thanks to John Howe and Sheila Campbell.

My colleagues at Columbia University have been wonderfully generous with their scholarly and professional assistance. I thank Susan Boynton, Tricia Dailey, Martha Howell, Joel Kaye, Adam Kosto, Pamela Smith, Bob Somerville, and particularly Betsy Blackmar, who was kind enough to read the entire manuscript in its final stage and made many suggestions that improved the book. Karen Green, the librarian of medieval history at Columbia, swiftly provided me with anything I needed.

Perhaps only rarely is an author as infatuated with readers' reports as I have been, and from them learns how to improve not only the manuscript but also one's own scholarship. The reports of David Burr and John van Engen, the readers for Cornell University Press—who have so kindly waived their anonymity and allowed me to consult with them further—did exactly that. This book owes its final shape to their meticulous reading and brilliant insights, for which I am infinitely grateful.

The professionalism of Peter J. Potter, Susan Specter, and the staff at Cornell University Press has been absolutely exceptional. I am much indebted to them for the care and attention with which they have approached this project from beginning to end.

Friendship certainly deserves the centrality in one's life that the wise philosophers of old attested to. I thank my friends Bill Duba, Aslıgül Gök, Francesca Grauso, Brette A. Jackson, Marilyn Keenan, Çağlar Kıral, Daniel A. Madigan, Patrick Nold, Caterina Pizzigoni, Mai Salmenkangas, and the late John B. Whelan, who have contributed to the making of this book in ways ranging from assistance with paleography and provision of photocopies to sharing jokes and alleviating troubles. My brother and sister-in-law, Erhan and Aysun Şenocak, have also provided constant support at many levels.

The medieval Franciscans left their mark on defining moments of my life. I met my husband Alessandro while studying the Franciscan manuscripts in

Todi and we celebrated our wedding in the garden of the Franciscan friary of Scarzuola in Montegiove, founded by Francis himself. Ale bore my demands for research travel with a saintly patience and listened to me talk endlessly about medieval Franciscans, and he has been a firm and compassionate support during the entire process. Our son Alessio Devrim, born during the writing of the first draft, showed me unexpectedly that writing an academic book is, after all, not such a big deal compared to minding a two-year-old.

My parents, Nevin and Erdoğan Şenocak, have shown grace in dealing with the unusual change of life this book instigated and bore with patience and good humor my prolonged absences from Turkey. It is to them that I dedicate this book.

❧ ABBREVIATIONS

Journals and Series

AF	*Analecta Franciscana,* 12 vols. (Quaracchi: College of Saint Bonaventure, 1885–1983)
AFH	*Archivum Franciscanum Historicum*
ALKG	*Archiv für Literatur- und Kirchengeschichte,* 7 vols. (Berlin, 1885–1900)
BF	*Bullarium Franciscanum, Romanorum pontificum, constitutiones, epistolas ac diplomata continens tribus ordinis S.P.N. Francisci spectantia,* vols. 1–4, ed. H. Sbaralea (Rome, 1759–1768)
CF	*Collectanea Franciscana*
CUP	*Chartularium Universitatis Parisiensis,* 2 vols., ed. Heinrich Denifle and Emile Chatelain (Paris: Ex Typis Fratrum Delalin, 1889–1891)
FS	*Franciscan Studies*
MF	*Miscellanea Franciscana*

Major Medieval Franciscan Texts

I Celano, x	Thomas de Celano, *Vita Prima S. Francisci* in *AF* 10 (1927), 1–117 (x indicates section number)
II Celano, x	Thomas de Celano, *Vita Secunda S. Francisci* in *AF* 10 (1927), 127–268 (x indicates section number)
Eccleston	*Fratris Thomae vulgo dicti de Eccleston tractatus de adventu Fratrum Minorum in Angliam,* ed. A. G. Little (Manchester, 1951)
Jordan of Giano	*Chronica Fratris Jordani,* ed. H. Boehmer (Paris, 1908) (numbers in notes indicate section numbers)
Narbonne-Assisi-Paris	"Statuta Generalia Ordinis edita in Capitulis generalibus celebratis Narbonae an. 1260, Assisii an. 1279

	atque Parisiis an. 1292," ed. M. Bihl, *AFH* 34 (1941): 13–94, 284–358.
Pre-Narbonne	"De fratrum minorum constitutionibus Prenarbonensibus," ed. C. Cenci, *AFH* 83 (1990): 50–95
RB	"Regula bullata Sancti Francisci Assisiensis," in *Opuscula Sancti Patris Francisci Assisiensis,* ed. Kajetan Esser (Rome, 1978), 226–38
RNB	"Regula non bullata Sancti Francisci Assisiensis," in *Opuscula sancti patris Francisci Assisiensis,* ed. Kajetan Esser (Rome, 1978), 241–94
Salimbene	Salimbene de Adam, *Cronica,* ed. O. Holder-Egger, in *Monumenta Germaniae historica: Scriptores,* 32 (Hanover, 1913)

THE POOR
AND THE
PERFECT

Prologue

The Challenges to the Historian

In the mid-thirteenth century, Matthew Paris, an English Benedictine monk, wrote about the early Franciscans:

> [They] carry constantly their books, indeed libraries, in sacks hanging from their necks. In time they built schools, afterward houses and cloisters, next large and lofty churches and offices, with the nobles bearing the expense.... Then, establishing schools of theology within their confines, lecturing and disputing, and preaching to the people, they carried much crop to the barn of Christ, "where the harvest is rich, but the laborers are few [Matt. 9:37]."[1]

Evidently, when he wrote these lines, Matthew Paris did not particularly object to friars carrying books, opening schools, and lecturing and disputing.[2] For

---

1. "Libros continue suos, videlicet bibliotecas, in forulis a collo dependentes baiulantes. Tandem scolas edificaverunt, deinde domos et claustra, denuo, magnatibus sumptus sufficienter administrantibus, ecclesias et officinas amplas et excelsas fabricaverunt.... Tandem scolas theologie infra septa sua constituentes, legentes et disputantes et populo predicantes, fructum ad horrea Christi, quia messis multa et operarii pauci fuerant, non modicum reportarunt." *Matthei Parisiensis historia Anglorum*, in *Monumenta Germaniae historica: Scriptores*, 28 (Hannover, 1888), 397.

2. This quotation is from the earliest entry on the Friars Minor in Matthew Paris's chronicle. In later entries, he seems to have had a change of heart and criticizes certain practices of the friars, although he still maintains a favorable view of many individual friars, often those engaged in scholarly activities. For Matthew Paris's view of friars and his increasing frustration with them, see Williell R. Thomson, "The Image of the Mendicants in the Chronicles of Matthew Paris," *AFH* 70 (1977): 3–34.

the modern scholar, this is an unexpected image when contrasted to that of Francis, who founded the Order of Friars Minor (OFM) in 1209. It is difficult to imagine Francis or any of his early brothers going around with a sack of books hanging from their necks. The sources at our disposal portray this most popular saint as a man strictly devoted to evangelical poverty, so much so that his followers were not allowed to have anything other than a tunic and a breviary. A sack of books, quite expensive items in the Middle Ages, was out of the question, as were permanent convents, money, and a school education.[3] The Francis we know was literate but not highly educated in theology, nor did he want to be. He respected theologians but was clear that his brotherhood was one of joyful minstrels of the apostolic life, not of well-educated schoolmen. Nevertheless, within only thirty years, his movement evolved into a Europe-wide order with hundreds of permanent houses, schools, and libraries, an order that produced some of the finest theologians and philosophers of all time. Its members were to be seen on the highways of Europe, walking from their friaries to distant schools, and carrying a sack of books, as Matthew observed. This did not seem to trouble Matthew, as he refers to the friars approvingly as laborers carrying crops to the barn of Christ. It did, however—and still does—trouble modern scholars. The image of Franciscan friars carrying books and listening to lectures in a classroom is problematic for us in a way that it was not for Matthew Paris, or many other religious men of the Middle Ages, who associated the pursuit of education and learning with respectability and pastoral duties.

Taking this apparent discrepancy between medieval and modern perspectives on the Franciscans' intellectual pursuits as a point of departure, this book deals with the questions of why and how the Franciscans, despite having their origins in a simple and predominantly lay brotherhood, embraced scholastic learning. Why did they open schools, establish libraries, and eagerly seek out and produce books? Why did they move to university towns and compete with the Dominicans to enroll scholars and masters? When did this "scholastic" transformation take place and under what conditions? Was it criticized within and outside of the Order, and if so, what was the nature of this criticism? How did the learned Franciscans reconcile their intellectual activities to their Franciscan identity? What were the consequences of making education a part of the Franciscan life? This book is not a comprehensive history of Franciscan education in the way Bert Roest's *A History of Franciscan Education (c. 1210–1517)* is, nor of Franciscan intellectual activities and theology. Instead, it is essentially a story of how and why learning became part of the Franciscan way of life, and the consequences of this integration.

---

3. Even though the modern meaning of the word convent is the house of nuns, here and throughout the book I use the word "convent" (*conventus*) as a synonym for the word "friary."

These questions cannot be answered only with reference to the Franciscan sources. It is imperative to understand this story within the larger medieval context, to keep in mind the changes in thirteenth-century religious and intellectual life at large with a view to establishing the outside influences on the friars and how these influences became instrumental in the transformation of the Order. This larger context is all the more powerful and influential in the case of the Franciscans because many of them did not shun society like hermits or monks. Instead they mixed in and with it, many living among the townspeople of Europe, serving the people as preachers, confessors, and *fidecommissarii*. In doing so they exposed themselves to contemporary social and moral values, and these in turn further shaped the way the Order evolved.

Four major issues vitiate our understanding of the Franciscans' relationship to learning in the Middle Ages. First, there is considerable difficulty, because of the uncertain or disputed dates of composition and authorship, involved in using and interpreting some of the narrative sources for the Order with respect to questions about learning and education. Second, historians, until recently, used these Franciscan narrative sources of uncertain origin and date to construct a view of the Order that presumes a split into two major parties: the "Spirituals," the friars who wished to observe the Rule strictly, and the "Community," indicating the rest of the friars. This split, it has usually been claimed, had started already in Francis's lifetime, worsened over the course of thirteenth century, and culminated in the fourteenth century when the Order was officially divided in two. This view of thirteenth-century Franciscan history has affected the arguments about learning, education, and books for a long time, because many scholars presumed these matters to have constituted one of the main issues between the two "parties." Although contested by recent historians, this view nevertheless permeated not just the histories of the Franciscan Order but also the intellectual and religious histories of the Middle Ages, making the use of secondary sources particularly difficult. The third issue that at times impedes a fresh study of the Franciscan history is the use of Dominican evidence and data, even Dominican history itself, to understand and explain developments in Franciscan history. Finally, few historical works contextualize Franciscan aspirations and activities such as preaching, governance, or papal service within the larger trends of the medieval world, making it difficult to situate the intellectual and educational activities and aspirations of the Franciscan Order. If the present undertaking fails to respond to all the questions the reader might have, or appears to be hesitant about forcefully pushing certain arguments, it is in part due to these difficulties.

Before starting to look at why and how Franciscans aspired to become an order of learned men, we need to consider how the writing of Franciscan history has affected our understanding of the Order's involvement in learning with respect to the issues mentioned above, and the stand of the present undertaking with regard to this historiographical state of affairs.

The Franciscan Narrative Sources and the "Franciscan Question"

Francis himself left a small corpus of diverse short texts as his written legacy. Although these are reasonably sufficient for the purpose of understanding his religious aspirations and desires, they give limited information about actual practices in the early days of the Order or about how he and his companions lived; nor is there much to be found in them with regard to attitudes toward learning. The rules of 1221 and 1223, which will be discussed in detail in chapter 1, are no exception. Francis died in 1226, and was canonized in 1228. That year the pope ordered a Franciscan friar named Thomas of Celano to compose a vita of the saint. The result of this commission, known as the *First Life* (*Vita prima*), was the first work to be written on Francis, and it remained the principal source for Francis's life until 1247.[4] Because he was writing on the occasion of Francis's canonization, Thomas aimed largely to make a case for the holiness of the saint manifested in his extraordinary life, his stigmata, and his miracles. Since it says very little about the first Franciscans, the *First Life* cannot serve as an account of the early Franciscan movement and is not a very useful source for its study. Nor does it have a solid grasp of what kind of an order Francis envisaged. In 1232–1235, a German friar named Julian of Speyer wrote a new vita, known as the *Life of Saint Francis of Assisi*, based on Celano's *First Life*, and primarily intended as a liturgical piece. In 2007 Jacques Dalarun showed that, in 1237–1239, Thomas of Celano wrote another short work, seemingly for liturgical purposes, the *Umbrian Legend*, which borrows from the *First Life* and Julian of Speyer's *Life of Saint Francis of Assisi*.[5] None of these works add to the limited information we have from the *First Life*.

The Franciscan General Chapter of 1244, under the direction of the newly elected general minister, Crescentius of Jesi, decided that a new vita of Francis was necessary, one that would include more detailed information on Francis's

---

4. For the most recent Latin edition of the *First Life* and for all subsequent Franciscan narrative sources mentioned in this chapter, see Enrico Menestò and Stefano Brufani, eds., *Fontes Franciscani* (Assisi: Porziuncola, 1995). Similarly, for the English translation of the Franciscan corpus mentioned here, see the three volumes edited and translated by J. A. Wayne Hellman, Regis J. Armstrong, and William J. Short, *Francis of Assisi: Early Documents*, 3 vols. (Hyde Park, NY: New City Press, 1999).

5. Jacques Dalarun, *Vers une résolution de la question franciscaine: La légende ombrienne de Thomas de Celano* (Paris: Fayard, 2007). See also the contributions of Michael Cusato and Jacques Dalarun in "'The Umbrian Legend' of Jacques Dalarun: Toward a Resolution of the Franciscan Question, Introduction to the Roundtable," *FS* 66 (2008): 479–508.

life.[6] The task was once again given to Thomas of Celano, and the result was the *Remembrance of the Desire of a Soul*, traditionally referred to as the *Second Life* (*Vita secunda*). In his prologue, Thomas wrote that he had incorporated new material regarding Francis's life and deeds previously unknown to him. The *Second Life* is considerably longer than the *First Life* and is rich in detail about Francis's intentions, his life, and, to a lesser degree, about the developments in the early Franciscan Order. The reader gets the distinct feeling that Thomas of Celano writes from the point of view of someone who has lived through a transformation. He has his own doubts and misgivings about the evolution of the Order, and is sometimes quite frank in voicing them.

What was the nature of this new material Thomas of Celano used? Who wrote it? These have become intriguing and difficult questions for historians of the Franciscan Order. Scholarly consensus suggests that among this new material were the memoirs of three companions of Francis, Leo, Rufino, and Angelo, and that parts of these memoirs have survived in various redactions in a number of fourteenth-century manuscripts and in works known as *The Legend of Three Companions* and *the Assisi Compilation*.[7] Evidently, reconstructing the material sent by the companions to Thomas of Celano has been a priority for the historians of the Order, since the testimonies of these companions are a gateway to Francis's mind and provide a historical context for us to understand and interpret the Franciscan Rule.[8] Furthermore, there are several medieval references suggesting that Leo was Francis's confessor, which would give his writings enormous authority: as Francis's confessor he would be most likely to know Francis's thoughts and intentions.

For the majority of the medieval Franciscans, the *Second Life* remained the major source on Francis for nineteen years. The General Chapter of 1260

---

6. The Franciscan General Chapter was the major legislative body of the Order and was convened every three years. It comprised the general minister of the Order—i.e., its executive head—the provincial ministers, and two other representatives from each province. In 1217, the Order divided the entire geographical area of the Franciscan settlements into eleven provinces. This number had increased by 1232, at which time the general minister Elias of Cortona designated thirty-two provinces. A province was further divided into custodies headed by a friar custodian. A custody would correspond to a major urban area that was likely to have more than one convent.

7. There is a tremendous amount of literature about and many editions of these manuscripts. The reader is advised to see the introduction to works such as *The Legend of Three Companions* and *The Assisi Compilation*, as well as *Second Life* in *Francis of Assisi: Early Documents*, 2. The most recent French edition of texts on Francis suggests that *The Assisi Compilation* was written by Leo of Assisi himself, and that most of it dates from 1246. Sylvain Piron, "Les écrits de frère Léon: Introduction," in *François d'Assise: Écrits, vies, témoignages*, ed. Jacques Dalarun, 1:1165–84 (Paris: Le Cerf-Editions franciscaines, 2010). See also the introduction by Jacques Dalarun to *Second Life*, ibid., 1:1429–1458.

8. In 1970 Rosalind B. Brooke published one such reconstruction of the body of texts produced in 1246 by these three companions, together with later texts by Leo himself, in *Scripta Leonis, Rufini et Angeli, Sociorum S. Francisci: The Writings of Leo, Rufino and Angelo, Companions of St. Francis.* (Oxford: Clarendon Press, 1970).

commissioned yet another vita of Francis, and this time from none other than Bonaventure of Bagnoregio, the minister general of the Order at the time and a famous theologian. In 1266, the new vita, titled the *Legenda major*, was finished and the General Chapter summoned that year declared it to be the official vita of Francis. It was furthermore announced that all the previous vitae of the saint were to be destroyed. What prompted the decision in favor of this new vita is unknown. In the prologue to his work, Bonaventure says that in preparation for this undertaking, he visited and interviewed the early companions of Francis, whose words, he says, can be trusted without doubt because of their proven virtue. A shorter version of this *Legenda*, known as the *Legenda minor*, was also commissioned for liturgical purposes.

In the early fourteenth century Franciscan historiography entered a new phase. In 1309–1310, a century after the founding of the Order of Friars Minor, a serious sense of inner conflict developed in the presence of two representative parties during the preparations for the Council of Vienne. Under the leadership of an Italian friar, Ubertino da Casale, a group of friars complained to the pope about many corrupt practices in the observance of the Rule and the Order's statutes. The other group, which included representatives from the Order's contemporary administration, generally denied the allegations of abuses and corruption, and defended the legitimacy of the current state of affairs. In fact, already from 1294 onward, in some provinces of the Order—notably Umbria, Ancona, and southern France—some friars were in rebellion against the provincial administrations on the issues of right observance. Some tried, with papal permission, to separate their convents and start the Franciscan observance anew. Friars fiercely disagreed over the observance of poverty: what exactly Franciscan poverty meant, how this poverty was or should be related to apostolic poverty as found in the Bible, and exactly how much poverty the Franciscan Rule prescribed.[9] More complication ensued when, in 1328, Pope John XXII entered the dispute and, rather than pursuing a reconciliatory attitude, widened the gap between the groups in conflict. During the course of the fourteenth century, the Order split irreversibly into Observants, the friars who claimed to observe the Rule strictly, and the Conventuals. Since this gradual fallout was over the question of correct observance, which was often understood to be the way Francis and the first companions lived, quite a few friars of the late thirteenth and fourteenth century composed short but vividly narrated works filled with many moving anecdotes of the life of Francis and his companions, emphasizing their strict, lovable simplicity and poverty, and accentuating now and then how the present Order had

---

9. The best source for the story of internal dissent in the medieval Franciscan Order is David Burr, *The Spiritual Franciscans: From Protest to Persecution in the Century after Saint Francis* (University Park: Pennsylvania State University Press, 2001). See in particular chaps. 1–4.

failed to fulfill Francis's legacy. Their content leaves no doubt that the friars who were displeased with the current state of the Order authored them.

The most important among these fourteenth-century works of anonymous authorship are *A Mirror of Perfection (Speculum perfectionis)* of 1317 or 1318, and *The Deeds of Blessed Francis and His Companions (Actus beati Francisci et sociorum eius)*, written sometime between 1328 and 1337. Both of these works use prophecy as a narrative tool: numerous times Francis informs the friars around him of the later tribulations and failures of his Order. These prophecies of Francis were aimed at impressing on the reader a sense of how far the Order had failed to live up to the spirit of its founder and first brothers and how the beauty of the sincere, simple, and holy lives of Francis and his companions was only a distant memory, not a legacy cherished and protected by the friars. The friars' preoccupation with learning is shown to be one of the reasons for the Order's spiritual decline.[10] Both of these works have come down to us in two different editions. Paul Sabatier published the first edition of *A Mirror of Perfection* in 1898.[11] He initially believed it to have been written in 1228 by Francis's companion Leo. Three years afterward, Leonard Lemmens, OFM, published a different and shorter version of the same work, which he dated post-1277 and titled *A Mirror of Perfection, Rule, Profession, Life and True Calling of a Lesser Brother.*[12] Compelled to revise his dating, Sabatier compiled a new edition based on forty-five extant manuscripts, which was published posthumously in 1928, entitled *A Mirror of Perfection of the Status of a Lesser Brother.*

The twentieth century witnessed the gradual discovery and publication of these fundamental texts concerning the medieval Franciscan Order. And as they are interdependent in their content, and a secure dating and authorship cannot be provided by using the manuscript evidence, a myriad of scholarly works have made conflicting claims on their dating and on the question of who borrows from whom. This controversy is known as the "Franciscan Question" (*Quaestio Franciscana*), and it remains to this day not fully resolved, even though progress has been made in establishing some scholarly consensus with regard to the Leonine corpus.[13] The "Franciscan Question" is about which sources give the most accurate and reliable picture of Francis and early Franciscan life. The

---

10. Armstrong, Hellman, and Short, *Francis of Assisi*, 3:110.

11. Paul Sabatier, ed., *Speculum perfectionis; seu, S. Francisci Assisiensis legenda antiquissima auctore fratre Leone* (Paris: Fischbacher, 1898).

12. The edition known as the Lemmens Edition is based on a single manuscript, the MS. 1/73 of the library of the friary of the Irish Franciscans in Rome, Saint Isidore. Leonhard Lemmens, ed., *Documenta antiqua franciscana* (Florence, 1901).

13. The bibliography on the "Franciscan Question" is immense. The reader is advised to look at the first chapter of the 2007 work on this subject, Dalarun, *Vers une résolution*, 21–43, and Dalarun, *La malavventura di Francesco*. See also Raoul Manselli, *Nos qui cum eo fuimus: Contributo alla questione francescana* (Rome: Istituto storico dei cappuccini, 1980).

construction and maintenance of the historiographical notion of two principal parties within the Order—the Spirituals who tried to be faithful to Francis and the early Franciscan spirit, and the Community who introduced novelties to the Order that contradicted the early Franciscan spirit—have largely been fueled by the complex nature and interdependency of the Franciscan narrative sources. As the introduction of education and learning, with its concomitant need for books beyond a breviary, was one of those "novelties," the understanding of the emergence and sustenance of the Spiritual-Community controversy in the Franciscan historiography becomes particularly relevant for the present study.

The Spirituals versus the Community and the Problem of Learning

It is tempting to write the history of the thirteenth- and early fourteenth-century Franciscan Order as a tragedy since the conflicts among the friars led to the Order's eventual split in the late fourteenth century. It is, after all, a story with an unhappy ending. This long and painful split and the fourteenth-century works that accompanied or even fueled it had a tremendous influence on the historiography of the Franciscan *Duecento*. Because of this traumatic experience, Franciscan history has often been read backward, as the knowledge of the fourteenth-century split affected the scholars' vision of the thirteenth-century Franciscan history. The teleological approach to history writing beyond what is necessary to form a narrative, which starts with the end and traces back the steps that led to it, always carries with it a significant danger, namely, the tendency to discount the variety of other possibilities at every step. In Franciscan historiography, the major question has often been how the Order came to the point of splitting in the fourteenth century.[14] As the question concerns a division, which self-evidently suggests two separate, uncompromising factions within the Order, the histories have, for a long time, tended to be dualistic in nature. If we can trace the origin of this historiographical approach, and put our finger on the misperceptions and misinformation that triggered it, then we would be in a better position to see how and why this historiographical tradition affected the way we have understood the nature of Franciscan involvement in learning, and why subsequently I have chosen to present a history of the thirteenth-century Order that consciously rejects this tradition as far as possible.

---

14. David Burr's *Spiritual Franciscans* opens with a similar account. After a brief mention of the burning of four Franciscans in Avignon in 1317, Burr asks, "How did Saint Francis's order manage to work itself into this situation? That is a very complex story and will take a long time to tell. It is essentially the story of a movement that grew up within the Order." Burr, *Spiritual Franciscans*, 1.

It would not be wrong to say that it all started with the publication of the groundbreaking *Vie de S. François d'Assise* by Paul Sabatier, a Protestant French historian.[15] This was not the first major biography of Francis. Karl A. von Hase and Léopold de Chérancé had already published earlier biographies, but it was Sabatier's work that became the turning point for scholarly interest in the life and deeds of Saint Francis.[16] Sabatier's impact has been such that as late as 2002 an entire conference was dedicated to his influence on Franciscan historiography.[17] *Vie de S. François* is a book of masterful rhetoric written with unwavering enthusiasm and devotion, a page-turner to say the least. It is difficult to find another history book where the style of narrative fits so perfectly to the story told, making such a powerful appeal to the reader's emotions. Sabatier's story is by and large a tragedy. It is the moving story of a saint, whose faith in Jesus Christ shines through the many beautiful anecdotes. It is also the story of his struggle to keep the Order he founded on the path of evangelical poverty and simplicity. Sabatier is brilliant in depicting the saint's self-imposed isolation, alleged bitterness, and disillusionment. Only a few of his followers are after his own heart; the rest either do not get the message in full or, worse, choose to ignore it.[18] The popes are culprits in disguise, manipulating Francis and his brotherhood to pursue their own agenda, ruthlessly destroying the genuine spirit of the Franciscan movement. Sabatier's critics were quick to point to the way his Protestant faith fed his allegedly ideological account. There is, however, no good reason to suspect any religious bias, though it is possible—given the way Sabatier dated and interpreted the historical sources, his Francis could not really be otherwise.

In the *Vie de S. François* Sabatier included a critical study of the sources for the life of Francis. A reading of this chapter reveals the origins of a circular argumentation that has persisted in Franciscan historiography in various forms to this day and that triggered the Franciscan Question. Sabatier starts with a preliminary note intended to give the reader a context for the documents on

15. Paul Sabatier, *Vie de S. François d'Assise* (Paris, 1894). For the English edition, see Sabatier, *Life of St. Francis of Assisi*, trans. Louise S. Houghton (London: Hodder and Stoughton, 1902).

16. Léopold de Chérancé, *Saint François d'Assise (1182–1226)* (Paris: Poussielgue, 1886); Karl A. von Hase, *Franz von Assisi, ein Heiligenbild* (Leipzig: Drud und Berlag von Breitkopf & Härtel, 1856).

17. For the argument concerning Sabatier's impact, see John R. H. Moorman, *The Sources for the Life of S. Francis of Assisi* (Manchester: Manchester University Press, 1940), 2; Società internazionale di studi francescani, *Paul Sabatier e gli studi francescani: Atti del XXX Convegno internazionale; In occasione del centenario della fondazione della Società internazionale di studi francescani (1902–2002); Assisi, 10–12 ottobre 2002.* Atti dei convegni della Società internazionale di studi francescani e del Centro interuniversitario di studi francescani, 13 (Spoleto: Fondazione Centro italiano di studi sull'alto Medioevo, 2003). The lasting effect of this influence is discussed in Raoul Manselli, *Francesco e i suoi compagni* (Rome: Istituto storico dei Cappuccini, 1995), 21–23.

18. Andrew G. Little delivered a wonderful lecture to the British Society of Franciscan Studies in 1929 on Sabatier titled "Paul Sabatier, Historian of St. Francis," published in Little, *Franciscan Papers, Lists, and Documents* (Manchester: Manchester University Press, 1943), 179–88.

the life of Francis. According to this context, already in Francis's lifetime there was a tripartite division in the Order: the *zelanti*, who were keen on observing the Rule most faithfully; the moderate party, largely made up of non-Italian friars, who admired Francis and wished to reform the Church, although they unfortunately lacked the poetic Umbrian spirit; and finally, the "liberals" in Italy, who were "men of mediocrity to whom the monastic life appeared the most facile existence."[19] "We can understand without difficulty that documents emanating from such different quarters must bear the impress of their origin," Sabatier writes, and he goes on to accuse the seventeenth-century Franciscan historian Luke Wadding and the Jesuit Bollandists, who published the *Acta sanctorum*, of not paying attention to the origins of the documents.[20] There was a very serious problem with this approach. The origins of these documents and their context can only be established from these documents themselves. No documents emanate from non-Franciscan circles, apart from the papal bulls, that can help establish a genuine and informed context for the Franciscan material. By assigning the origin of each document to one of the three Franciscan "parties" that Sabatier perceived from his reading of the sources, and interpreting the documents accordingly, he provided support for his notion of this tripartite division in the early thirteenth century. In the later historiography, the *zelanti* are often considered the forerunners of the "Spirituals," and the moderate and liberal parties are made into a single group named the "Community," thus largely reducing Sabatier's tripartite view of the Order to a dualism.

One of the greatest influences on Sabatier's dramatic vision was a work written around 1320 at the height of the conflicts within the Order, which in its style and content stands apart from all the sources mentioned thus far. This is none other than the *History of the Seven Tribulations of the Order of Brothers Minor* (*Historia septem tribulationum ordinis minorum*, published also under the title *Liber chronicarum; sive, Tribulationum ordinis minorum*) written by Angelo Clareno, who, together with Ubertino da Casale, is unanimously considered by modern scholars to be a major spokesman for the "Spiritual" Franciscans.[21] Angelo had a troubled existence in the Order.[22]

---

19. Sabatier, *Life of St. Francis of Assisi*, 361.

20. Ibid., 361–62.

21. Angelo Clareno, *Liber chronicarum; sive, Tribulationum ordinis minorum*, ed. G. M. Boccali (Assisi, 1999); *Historia septem tribulationum ordinis minorum*, ed. O. Rossini (Rome, 1999). Angelo also wrote a commentary on the Rule, *Expositio super regulam fratrum minorum*, ed. G. M. Boccali (Assisi: Edizioni Porziuncola, 1995). See the translation into English: Angelo Clareno, *Angelo Clareno: A Chronicle or History of the Seven Tribulations of the Order of Brothers Minor*, trans. David Burr and E. Randolph Daniel (St. Bonaventure, NY: Franciscan Institute, 2005). Burr and Daniel's translation places the dating at the 1320s, whereas Sylvain Piron places it at 1317. See Piron's introduction in Dalarun et al., *François d'Assise*, 2: 2565–76.

22. Angelo Clareno is a highly interesting character. The most thorough sources on him are *Angelo Clareno francescano: Atti del XXXIV Convegno internazionale; Assisi, 5–7 ottobre 2006* (Spoleto, 2007); Gian

He had in fact petitioned and managed to convince Celestine V to accept his plea of absolution from his Franciscan vows. He and his friends then started a new Order, known as the Poor Hermits of Celestine. A change of pope and papal policy forced Angelo into exile and more personal tribulations followed. So when he decided to write his chronicle he was already more than thirty years into his struggle against the administration of the Franciscan Order. It is in this historical context of bitterness and disillusionment that Angelo penned his story. "I have dwelt particularly on this document because its value appears to me not yet to have been properly appreciated," wrote Sabatier.[23] Despite the fact that Angelo had a long history of troubles with the Order, Sabatier's confidence in the trustworthiness of Angelo's evidence did not waver. He acknowledged that this was a work composed in 1330, its author a Joachite and partisan, but this made him only fonder. "It is indeed partisan," wrote Sabatier, but "the documents of which we must be most wary are not those whose tendency is manifest, but those where it is skillfully concealed."[24]

Angelo's chronicle borrows from *The Words of Saint Francis*, the *First Life* and *Second Life* of Thomas of Celano, Francis's *Testament*, and the Rule.[25] Along with works like *A Mirror of Perfection* and *The Deeds of Saint Francis and His Companions*, it is one of the essential culprits behind the present state of the dualist understanding of Franciscan history, as it reads Franciscan history as a tragic battle between the friars who wished to observe the Rule literally and those who persecuted them for their faithfulness.[26] The *History of the Seven Tribulations* is in many ways the story of the Order's gradual decline from the holy aspirations of the founder toward a state of thorough corruption and earthliness. "Angelo presents the suffering of the Spiritual Franciscans in his own day at the hands of their leaders as one more episode in a long series of persecutions stretching back to the beginning."[27] Within this history, Angelo gives some men a heroic status by identifying them as those who wished to honor the ideals of Francis and to maintain the Order's observance in its primitive purity, while demonizing others. In fact, it is mostly from this chronicle that modern scholars have derived the membership of the supposed two parties of "Spirituals" and the "Community." David Burr rightly casts doubt on the reliability of Angelo's work in the creation of the

---

Luca Potestà, *Angelo Clareno: Dai poveri eremiti ai fraticelli* (Rome, 1990); and L. v. Auw, *Angelo Clareno et les spirituels italiens: Uomini e dottrine* (Rome, 1979).

23. Sabatier, *Life of Francis of Assisi*, 414–15.

24. Ibid., 415.

25. Angelo Clareno, *Chronicle or History*, vii–x.

26. See David Burr, "History as Prophecy: Angelo Clareno's Chronicle as a Spiritual Franciscan Apocalypse," in *Defenders and Critics of Franciscan Life: Essays in Honor of John V. Fleming*, ed. M. F. Cusato and G. Geltner (Leiden: Brill, 2009), 119–38; Burr, *Spiritual Franciscans*, 11.

27. Burr, *Spiritual Franciscans*, 11.

historiographical categories of Spirituals and the Community in the conclusion of *The Spiritual Franciscans:*

> Was there a spiritual Franciscan movement at all, though? Or is the spiritual movement about which historians write essentially a trick played on us by Angelo Clareno? Certainly that movement attained its clearest outlines and greatest coherence in the pages of Angelo's Chronicle, where it became an old and honorable tradition running from Francis and his companions through Angelo himself. Once we turn from Angelo to the evidence, the contours of the movement blur. It is hard to trace any definable movement before the 1270s, and from then on we see different individuals and groups with notably different agendas.[28]

Apart from Angelo's *History of Seven Tribulations,* Sabatier was also influenced by *The Legend of the Three Companions, A Mirror of Perfection,* and *The Deeds of Blessed Francis and His Companions.* They helped create and power his history of the Franciscan Order, a history filled with betrayal and conspiracies that attempted to suppress the "real" Francis. As Sabatier tried to explain the thirteenth century using either explicitly fourteenth-century texts or sources of unknown authorship, which either belonged to the fourteenth century or survive only in fourteenth-century versions with serious questions hanging over their reliability and context, he tended to confuse and conflate fourteenth-century phenomena and terminology with those of the thirteenth century. He hailed *The Legend of Three Companions* as "the first utterance of the Spiritual Franciscans," which he thought to be the original work of Leo and Francis's other companions, thus linking the early companions of Francis to a fourteenth-century phenomenon that was itself historically complex and problematic. Sabatier showed a distinct lack of trust in the works written by Thomas of Celano and Bonaventure, the so-called official vitae.[29] He believed that these works covertly but consciously distorted the picture of Francis and the early Franciscans to reflect what the ministers wanted the friars to know about Francis and Franciscanism.

Unfortunately, Sabatier's mapping of Franciscan history took hold, and the term *Spirituals,* which is a distinctly fourteenth-century term, used for the first

---

28. Ibid., 310.

29. "Il Sabatier tendeva a risolvere in una tendenziosità delle fonti ufficiali—le due *Vite* di Tommaso Celano e la *Legenda maior* di san Bonaventura—e invece una esaltazione delle fonti non ufficiali, a cominciare del ben noto *Speculum perfectionis.*" Manselli, *Francesco e i suoi compagni,* 22. See also John R. H. Moorman, *A History of the Franciscan Order: From Its Origins to the Year 1517* (Chicago: Franciscan Herald Press, 1988), 20–31.

time by Ubertino da Casale in the period 1310–1312,[30] has often been used to designate all thirteenth-century friars who were critical in any way of the changes in the Order. Although we come across the phrase *spiritual man* or *spiritual observance* in documents throughout the thirteenth century, the term was never used to signify a certain group of friars with one well-defined standpoint opposed to another group within the Order. As a historical category the Spirituals are elusive. One can define them easily enough as those in favor of a strict observance of the Rule, but once we turn from theory to practice, it is unclear which historical figures fit this definition. We have a handful of names that have come down to us in texts such as those of Angelo Clareno or Ubertino da Casale, but each of these thirteenth-century men identified with the Spirituals defended opinions and stances that quite drastically disagree with the attributes of the Spirituals that historians have defined. And once we go beyond this handful, who were the rest of the Spirituals? The term has a mystical obscurity, which is largely the problem with any conspiracy theory. In this case, the Order's administration is said to have conspired against the Spirituals and the true intentions of Francis. This obscurity has prompted scholars to define and redefine the term. The best example of this problematic is the published collection, mostly of Franciscan authors, with the telltale title "Chi erano gli Spirituali?"[31] In a valuable contribution to this subject, Michael Cusato has made a case for moving beyond the disputes on poverty in Franciscan scholarship to determine the nature of the Spirituals-Community conflict. The questions he poses highlight the difficulties associated with looking at the Franciscan history through a divided lens.

> Whence "the Community"? That is: when, where and why does this group begin to enter onto the scene of history? For indeed, historians often use the term without explaining where its usage actually began. It is my contention that, once we have answered that question, we will then be able to ask an even more important question: who was "the Community"? That is: what did they represent in Franciscan history (especially when compared and contrasted with the Franciscan Spirituals)?[32]

While creating his tripartite view of thirteenth-century Franciscan history, Sabatier also set out the supposed major points of conflict between the parties

---

30. "[Fratres] qui spirituales dicuntur," Ubertino da Casale, *Rotulus iste*, in "Zur Vorgeschichte des Councils von Vienne no. 4 Vorarbeiten zur Constitution Exivi de Paradiso vom 6. Mai 1312," ed. F. Ehrle, *ALKG* (1887) 3: 101.

31. Società internazionale di studi francescani, *Chi erano gli spirituali: Atti del III Convegno internazionale: Assisi, 16–18 ottobre 1975* (Assisi: Società internazionale di studi francescani, 1976).

32. Michael Cusato, "Whence the 'Community'?" *FS* 60 (2002): 41.

in the Order, the subject of books and learning foremost among them. "He [Francis] believed his sons to be attacked with two maladies, unfaithful at once to poverty and humility; but perhaps he dreaded for them the demon of learning more than the temptation of riches."[33] Ten years after the first publication of *Vie de St. François*, Hilarin Felder, a Capuchin friar, published *Geschichte der wissenschaftlichen Studien im Franziskanerorden bis um die Mitte des 13. Jahrhunderts*, opposing Sabatier and ignoring all fourteenth-century sources, or sources of uncertain origin. Sticking only to the "official" vitae of Thomas of Celano and relying heavily on Bonaventure, Felder argued that the Order's involvement with study was a natural consequence of the pursuit of apostolic life.[34] On the other hand, the late Anglican bishop of Ripon, John R. H. Moorman, under the influence of Sabatier, held strongly to the view that the developments in the Order after the death of Saint Francis betrayed the founder's holy aspirations, a view that permeates Moorman's *History of the Franciscan Order*. Moorman regarded the Order's commitment to learning one such departure and therefore something that the Spirituals allegedly opposed. He wrote in 1940:

> The main *casus belli* between what came to be called the "Conventuals" and the "Spirituals" were these. First, what precisely was meant by Absolute Poverty? This question would include two very important issues: the problem of Building, which had been greatly intensified by the erection of the Basilica at Assisi; and the problem of Learning, which raised the question of whether or not a friar could legitimately possess any books.[35]

Moorman's view—that the Spirituals opposed learning and books, and that this was one of the issues that led to the split—has prevailed in discussions of the role of learning in medieval Franciscanism.[36] While describing the three divisions among the medieval Franciscans—strict, moderate, and relaxed—Duncan Nimmo, who authored one of the most substantial contributions to Franciscan history, followed Sabatier's tripartite division, and wrote that the moderate and relaxed friars favored "wholehearted commitment to learning and the

---

33. Sabatier, *Life of St. Francis of Assisi*, 277.

34. Hilarin Felder, *Geschichte der wissenschaftlichen Studien im Franziskanerorden bis um die Mitte des 13. Jahrhunderts* (Freiburg im Breisgau: Herder, 1904), 15.

35. Moorman, *Sources*, 102. See also Moorman, *History of the Franciscan Order*, 51–52, and Duncan Nimmo, *Reform and Division in the Medieval Franciscan Order: From Saint Francis to the Foundation of the Capuchins* (Rome: Capuchin Historical Institute, 1987), 3. Moorman studied under A. G. Little, who worked in collaboration with Sabatier. Sabatier's postcards to Little were kept by Moorman, who evidently collected them. They can be seen among the notes and papers of Moorman in the Flintshire Record Office, Hawarden, Wales.

36. Nimmo, *Reform and Division*, 3. Bert Roest, *A History of Franciscan Education (c. 1210–1517)* (Leiden: Brill, 2000), 1n, provides a small bibliography of historians who defended this view.

performance of episcopal functions."[37] Nimmo himself thought that the trans-formations in the thirteenth century disregarded the founder's understanding of humility.[38] This stance in Franciscan historiography influenced also the general historiography of thirteenth-century intellectual history. For example, Beryl Smalley suggested that Bonaventure was primarily interested in the spiritual interpretation of the Bible because he needed to justify the study of the Bible to some members of his Order.[39] Gordon Leff wrote that the Order's pursuit of learning was one of the problems raised during Saint Francis's lifetime and was at the heart of questions over Franciscan poverty.[40]

The view of thirteenth-century Franciscan history as an arena of a tragic inner conflict is made even more problematic because modern historians writing about the Order have been drawn to support one of the alleged parties, the Spirituals, which has had a considerable effect on histories of the Order.

> It is a striking point that non-Franciscan writers have had no more success than the Franciscans in emancipating themselves from the division of opinion in the order, which existed in the thirteenth century and continues in a modified form to trouble it to this day. The excess of polemic in this field is partly, but not entirely, explained by the ardent nature of Sabatier himself, whose errors were on the same generous scale as his discoveries, and who aroused a series of equally combative researchers, determined to rectify his exaggerations.[41]

Malcolm Lambert, quoted here, demonstrated how English historians dealing with Franciscan history, notably A. G. Little, Father Cuthbert, G. G. Coulton, and J. R. H. Moorman, were all sympathizers of the Spiritual tradition.[42] Duncan Nimmo has made a similar remark:

> The historians' difficulty is that, explicitly or implicitly—usually the latter—they have tended to take the side of any of the three main views on observance, and condemn the other two; the tendency has perhaps been particularly marked among those historians who are themselves Franciscans.[43]

---

37. Nimmo, *Reform and Division*, 3.

38. Ibid., 53.

39. Beryl Smalley, *The Gospels in the Schools, c. 1100–c. 1280* (London: Hambledon Press, 1985), 202.

40. Gordon Leff, "The Bible and Rights in the Franciscan Dispute over Poverty," in *The Bible in the Medieval World: Essays in Memory of Beryl Smalley*, ed. Katherine Walsh and Diana Wood (Oxford: Blackwell, 1985), 226.

41. Malcolm Lambert, *Franciscan Poverty: The Doctrine of the Absolute Poverty of Christ and the Apostles in the Franciscan Order, 1210–1323* (London: S.P.C.K., 1961), 2–3.

42. Ibid., 1.

43. Nimmo, *Reform and Division*, 4–5.

All this certainly makes it very difficult to write a fresh history of this subject, as both the sources and the historiography necessitate more than the usual amount of caution.

There were disputes and conflicts in the Order already in the thirteenth century, and one objective of this book is to study those conflicts related to learning on their own terms without reference to any group or groups. After all, one of the best studies on the subject of the Spirituals finds that the term is "largely a construct of modern historians and that for the thirteenth and early fourteenth centuries it is impossible to talk of a single united group of critics in the Order who had the same agenda."[44] Another book that approaches this dualism with skepticism is the erudite study by Michael Robson, OFM Conv., called *The Franciscans in the Middle Ages*. Robson prefers to use the term "reformers" instead of "Spirituals" when referring to Ubertino da Casale and Angelo Clareno.[45]

A study of the rise of learning in the Franciscan Order needs to be on guard against the tendency to explain the transformation of the Order in the thirteenth century in terms of a deviation from the Order's ideals and to attribute any related criticism of learning and books to such a deviation. It also needs to be wary of recourse to the elusive categories imposed on us by men of passion like Sabatier or Angelo Clareno. Therefore, throughout this book, I will use the terms "*zelanti*," "Spiritual," and "Community" only to signify historiographical categories, not historical ones, and therefore always in quotation marks. To abstain from using such categories is not to reject the existence of criticism and concerns in the Order with regard to the introduction of learning as part of the Franciscan mission. It is necessary, however, to be very careful in specifying the nature of that criticism, which is one of the preoccupations of this book.

The Influence of the Dominican History

While the historiographical "Spiritual-Community" controversy has complicated the question of the reception of, and attitude toward, learning in the medieval Franciscan Order, the persistent use of Dominican evidence has confused our understanding of the Franciscan education system. To compensate for the relative lack of Franciscan evidence, Dominican statutes and practices have often been used to paper over the cracks in the historical reconstruction of the building of the Franciscan educational system. Franciscan and Dominican educational organizations have been treated in common, by virtue of the fact that both orders were mendicant orders. This was the general approach at the

---

44. Burr, *Spiritual Franciscans*, viii. For further discussion of the term *Spiritual*, see vii–x and 39–41. Burr suggests that the term might as well be used, though with necessary caveats.

45. Michael Robson, *The Franciscans in the Middle Ages* (Woodbridge: Boydell Press, 2006), 119.

1976 conference on mendicant schools in Todi, Italy.[46] Giulia Barone asserted that "all those who have passed to history as the student orders have imitated the model of Dominicans in their school organization."[47] Marian Michèle Mulchahey, working on the Dominican educational structure, likewise suggested that "the Franciscans in particular copied the dispositions made by the Order of Preachers." She argued that the Dominicans "devised most of the common-sense solutions to educational challenges, and the Franciscans, and others, readily absorbed their lessons."[48] The same idea seems to have governed the 2002 conference on mendicant schools.[49] In 2003 Grado Merlo suggested that in the beginning of the 1220s, the two orders found a point of convergence in the recruitment of students and masters. Merlo cited Jordan of Saxony's depiction of the Dominican Order as a place of study and preaching, and then suggested that this combination of studying and preaching be as valid for Franciscans as it was for the Dominicans.[50] Dieter Berg's *Armut und Wissenschaft*, published in 1977, stands out in this early period by avoiding a "mendicant" story and dedicating separate chapters to Franciscan and Dominican educational developments.[51] Similarly, Bert Roest's book on Franciscan educational organization between 1210 and 1517 draws attention to this tendency and is admirable in its effort to use the Franciscan sources alone.[52] The strength of historians' conviction that the Dominican model may be used for the Franciscans is surprising, since so far no study has performed a thorough comparison of the two orders' educational organizations. The question here is whether there is any real evidence at all to justify an argument that the two orders shared a common system of education. Not only the structure of educational organization but also the reasons why both orders moved to schools, studied, and taught have been treated in common. Since Dominicans were from the beginning the more "scholarly" order, historians attributed the Franciscan move to schools to Dominican motives and aspirations.[53]

---

46. The papers presented at this colloquium are published in *Le scuole degli Ordini mendicanti (sec. XIII–XIV)*, Convegni del Centro di Studi sulla Spiritualita Medievale, 17, Todi 11–14 ottobre 1976 (Todi: Presso l'Accademia tudertina, 1978).

47. Giulia Barone, *Da frate Elia agli Spirituali* (Milano: Biblioteca francescana, 1999), 130.

48. Marian Michèle Mulchahey, *"First the bow is bent in study…": Dominican Education before 1350* (Toronto: Pontifical Institute of Mediaeval Studies, 1998), xi.

49. Alfonso Maierù, "Formazione culturale e tecniche d'insegnamento nelle scuole degli Ordini mendicanti," in *Studio e studia: Le scuole degli ordini mendicanti tra XIII e XIV secolo; Atti del XXIX convegno internazionale* (Spoleto: Centro italiano di studi sull'alto Medioevo, 2002), 11.

50. Grado Merlo, Nel nome di San Francesco: storia dei frati Minori e del francescanesimo sino agli inizi del XVI secolo. (Padua: Editrici Francescane, 2003), 113.

51. Dieter Berg, *Armut und Wissenschaft: Beiträge zur Geschichte des Studienwesens der Bettelorden im 13. Jahrhundert* (Düsseldorf: Schwann, 1977), 142–43.

52. Roest, *History of Franciscan Education*, 1.

53. See, for example, the article by Jacques Verger, "Studia mendicanti e università," in *Il pragmatismo degli intellettuali: Origini e primi sviluppi dell'istituzione universitaria*, ed. Roberto Greci (Torino: Scriptorium, 1996), 153. Verger poses the question "Did the mendicant orders have a scholastic vocation?" He then

It is true that the orders had a lot in common: they both started around the same time; both aimed at the *cura animarum;* and both preached, lived in towns, and went to schools. Despite having these things in common, however, the two orders were quite distinct from each other in their raison d'être. Learning and education was one of the pillars on which the Dominican Order was founded, since the Order principally aimed at fighting heresy through preaching. Already by 1228, the backbone of the educational organization of the Dominicans was established in the Order's constitutions. The surviving Dominican constitutions of the thirteenth century devoted much more space to decrees concerning study, and went into much more detail than the Franciscan constitutions. The organization of studies occurred within quite a different context in the Dominican Order. There was no change or evolution in the role of learning because it was integral and prominent among the Dominicans from the very start. There are examples of other significant differences between the two orders, which one might expect to affect the organization of their studies. By 1290, the Dominicans had a total of only six *studia generalia,* and constitutionally each Dominican province was allowed to have only a single one.[54] By the same date, the Franciscans had thirty-two provinces, and while some provinces had more than one studium generale—a school where the highest level of education is given—some did not have any until the late fourteenth century.

Another difference emerged from the settlement policies and patterns of the orders. Although the Dominicans had an approved Rule by 1215 and swiftly moved to the university cities, their general spread and settlement was much slower than that of the Franciscans. John Freed's detailed study on the settlement of Franciscans and Dominicans in Germany points to three differences. The first difference was due to the number of convents founded. By 1300, Franciscans had established approximately two hundred convents, whereas the Dominicans had only 111. The comparison includes sixteen Polish and one Italian Dominican priory, which would have been considered German under the Franciscan provincial structure.[55] It seems that the Franciscans tried to reach any town they could find, without any criteria of selection, while the Dominicans chose the major urban centers.[56] Freed also observed that the Franciscans usually arrived

---

goes on to cite P. Mandonnet's work on the Dominicans, without distinguishing the motives of the Dominicans and Franciscans. In fact, more than once when Verger refers to mendicants, he cites only Dominican evidence.

54. Mulchahey, *"First the bow is bent . . . ,"* 351, 355n. There are a total of seven by the end of the century. See Marian Michèle Mulchahey, "The Dominican Studium System and the Universities of Europe in the Thirteenth Century," in *Manuels, programmes de cours et techiques d'enseignement dans les universités médiévales,* ed. J. Hamesse (Louvain-la-Neuve: Pontifical Institute of Mediaeval Studies, 1994), 301, n. 70.

55. John B. Freed, *The Friars and German Society in the Thirteenth Century* (Cambridge, MA: Mediaeval Academy of America, 1977), 51.

56. Ibid., 51–52.

in a city before the Dominicans: "By 1300 there were 71 cities which possessed both Dominican and Franciscan houses. The Franciscans definitely arrived first in 43 of these cities, the Dominicans only 25."[57] The difference in the number of convents prompted a different strategy in the organization of studies, as well as the administration. While the Franciscans were holding a General Chapter every three years—most likely since it was difficult to summon such a large number of ministers—Dominicans held their General Chapter annually. When in 1241 Franciscans tried to experiment with the idea of a chapter of diffini-tors, a chapter of elected officials from each province that convened before the General Chapter and determined the crucial issues for legislation—and essentially a Dominican institution—there was such a reaction that the idea had to be abolished immediately and no such other chapter was ever convened. This is indicative of the differences between the two orders.

Admittedly, the existence of such differences does not mean that Franciscans never borrowed or adapted Dominican ideas, but perhaps they did not do this to the extent that has been assumed so far. Even if the Franciscan leaders wanted to emulate the Dominican system, the administrative structure of the Franciscan Order, the ideology embodied perpetually in the spirit of Francis, and the Rule itself would have made such an enterprise impossible without substantial modifi-cations. It is not known to what extent the two orders were in contact, or if the administrators ever exchanged ideas on how to educate their friars. Indeed, the unfriendliness that members of the two orders showed toward one another from time to time probably diminished contact. Rosalind Brooke's observations about Albert of Pisa, one of the most influential figures in the institutionalization of the Order, point in the same direction:

> The little that we know about his attitude towards the Dominicans is instructive in view of the later approximation of the two institutes. He was appreciative but detached. He tried, as a Franciscan should, to encourage friendly feeling between the two, but he was far from regarding the Dominicans as a model that the Minors would do well to copy.[58]

At present there is much less need for the use of Dominican evidence to fill the gaps in the Franciscan evidence. In the course of the twentieth century, the number of Franciscan constitutions that have been discovered and edited has steadily increased. In 1904, when Felder wrote his *Geschichte*, only Ehrle's

---

57. Ibid., 52. Freed notes, however, that this ratio could become fifty-two Franciscan convents to fourteen Dominican convents if the alleged foundation dates of Franciscan convents are substituted for the first definite reference in a document or chronicle to a Franciscan friary.

58. Rosalind B. Brooke, *Early Franciscan Government: Elias to Bonaventure* (Cambridge: Cambridge University Press, 1959), 192.

edition of the Narbonne constitutions had been edited and published. At the time when Brlek published his *De evolutione iuridica studiorum in Ordine Minorum* in 1942, thirteen sets had become available.[59] Since then, seven more sets of constitutions have been discovered and published, five appearing after 1982. These include the pre-Narbonne constitutions, which consist of those that date before 1260.[60]

All of these new publications, which contain hitherto unknown information on the educational organization in the Order and the treatment of books, make possible a rough reconstruction of the educational organization of the medieval Franciscan Order, as well as a delineation of its evolution. Chapter 5 of this book, which is devoted to such a reconstruction of the Franciscan educational program, uses only the Franciscan evidence from the thirteenth and early fourteenth centuries. The resulting picture is rather different from Bert Roest's, which relies on evidence combined from three centuries.

Contextualization

One might argue that all history is historiography. The attitudes of scholars toward a particular historical topic and the questions that interest them, changing over time as they do, help determine the shape of that history, and it is the current state of historiography that makes it quite difficult to examine the relationship of the Franciscan Order with education and learning. The Order's history has not been studied homogeneously. Certain topics, such as Saint Francis, Bonaventure, Franciscan poverty, the Franciscan Question, and the related Spiritual-Community controversy, have attracted a considerable investment of scholarly energy for over a century, while other topics remain underexamined— for example, the interaction of the Franciscans with urban society, their relationship with the local clergy, Franciscan involvement in medieval European politics, and the Order's financial affairs, the latter a subject that would throw significant light on the reasons for internal disputes within the Order. Historical monographs that examine Franciscan topics within a wider historical context are few.[61] This pattern, not an uncommon one with respect to the histories of

---

59. Michael Brlek, *De evolutione iuridica studiorum in Ordine Minorum (ab initio usque ad annum 1517)* (Dubrovnik: Jadran, 1942).

60. Pre-Narbonne. Other constitutions are published in the following: Cesare Cenci, ed., "Costituzioni della provincia Toscana tra i secoli XIII e XIV," *Studi Francescani* 79 (1982): 369–409, and *Studi Francescani* 80 (1983): 171–206; Cenci, ed., "Ordinazioni dei Capitoli Provinciali Umbri dal 1300 al 1305," *CF* 55 (1985): 5–31; Cenci, ed., "Le Costituzioni Padovane del 1310," *AFH* 76 (1983): 505–88; Cenci, ed., "Fragmenta priscarum Constitutionum Praenarbonensium," *AFH* 96 (2003): 289–300.

61. Examples of such monographs include Giacomo Todeschini, *Ricchezza francescana: Dalla povertà volontaria alla società di mercato*, Intersezioni 268 (Bologna: Il mulino, 2004); Stanislao da Campagnola, *Francesco e francescanesimo nella società dei secoli XIII–XIV*, Medioevo francescano, Saggi (Assisi: Porziuncola, 1999); and, to a limited extent, Daniel R. Lesnick, *Preaching in Medieval Florence: The Social World of*

medieval religious orders, results in part from the fact that many of the scholars who study medieval Franciscans are themselves Franciscans. Understandably, this can lead them to focus on historical questions that have a direct bearing on Franciscan identity and spirituality, often with an emphasis on the Franciscan documents and sources.

The enthusiasm for and organization of education in the Franciscan Order should not be seen through a distorting lens that presumes a long-running conflict between Spirituals and the Community, in the form the so-called proto-spirituals or *zelanti* versus the administration, nor can it be understood with reference to the Dominican case. We need to understand how and why an order starting off as a predominantly lay brotherhood was so eager to make itself educated and respectable. What was the role of Francis or the Franciscan Rule in bringing about this transformation? Was there any inevitability in this story, and if so, where? How do the institutionalization and clericalization of the Order relate to this transformation? The first chapter of this book will seek answers to such questions and serve to present the reader with the nuts and bolts of this transformation, strictly keeping track of chronology. It will stop at the end of the minister generalship of Haymo of Faversham in 1244, since pre-Narbonne constitutions clearly show the educational system was well in place by that date.

The second chapter investigates the integration of learning into Franciscan life and identity. How exactly was this new identity constructed, and what were reactions to it, if any? Joachitism had a particularly strong influence in the way that learned Franciscans perceived and took pride in their Franciscan identity, as the Joachite prophecies circulated by means of written texts among the learned friars. Quite a few historians have regarded learning as a departure from the ideas of Francis, but how well did the friars of the early thirteenth century, particularly those who had never met Francis or who had entered the Order away from Italy, know what Francis's ideas and wishes were? What we know today about the early days of the Order is not necessarily what an ordinary new

Franciscan and Dominican Spirituality (Athens: University of Georgia Press, 1989). The annual conferences organized by Italian institutions such as Societá Internazionale di Studi Francescani and the publication of their proceedings have remedied this gap to some extent. A relatively recent series, Vita regularis, under the direction of Gert Melville, brings together, in German, original research and excellent scholarship on a variety of subjects concerning the mendicant orders. Still, such volumes of collected works usually span various geographies and time frames and do not fully satisfy the need for monographs that give a coherent picture drawn against the medieval religious and social background. See Michael Robson and Jens Röhrkasten, *Franciscan Organisation in the Mendicant Context: Formal and Informal Structures of the Friars' Lives and Ministry in the Middle Ages* (Berlin: Lit Verlag, 2011); Gert Melville and A. Kehnel, eds., In proposito paupertatis: *Studien zum Armutsverständnis bei den mittelalterlichen Bettelorden* (Münster: Lit Verlag, 2001); Gert Melville and Jörg Oberste, eds., *Die Bettelorden im Aufbau: Beiträge zu Institutionalisierungsprozessen im mittelalterlichen Religiosentum* (Münster: Lit Verlag, 1999). An excellent monograph on Franciscan–papacy relations is Patrick Nold's *Pope John XXII and His Franciscan Cardinal: Bertrand de la Tour and the Apostolic Poverty Controversy* (Oxford: Clarendon Press, 2003).

recruit, who entered the Order in the 1230s in a corner remote from Assisi, would have known. Could it have ever occurred to such a friar that by establishing a network of schools and engaging in the study of theology, his Order was going against the wishes of their founder? After suggesting answers to these questions, the second chapter also includes a discussion of the commentary on the Rule written by the four Franciscan masters of theology in order to examine what the friars representative of the new identity understood of Franciscanism.

The Franciscans' involvement in the intellectual world of the Middle Ages has generally been explained in terms of the needs of the medieval Church and papacy for a workforce to carry out preaching and other pastoral activities. Bert Roest wrote in *A History of the Franciscan Education* that preaching was "the highest calling of a priest, and therefore a main objective of all religious learning."[62] When medieval authors made such statements, it was mainly to convince and influence a rather reluctant audience of clergy. The practical evidence contrasts with Roest's statement—learned clergy often despised preaching to the laity and looked down on pastoral care with contempt. That was something that many prelates were aware of, and they had difficulties in persuading the priests sent to the schools to resume pastoral work in the parishes. Medieval Franciscans engaged in the study of theology and philosophy to varying degrees, and certainly not always with a view to preaching. While some of the ministers encouraged the friars' study of theology to develop their potential as preachers, the followers of Francis went down the path of schooling and studying for other reasons as well. The third chapter attempts to understand these reasons. Why did the friars embrace scholastic learning specifically rather than looking toward the older tradition of monastic learning? Why did they go to universities and, once there, proceed to acquire teaching chairs? Was all the investment in learning really only to aid in preaching, or to train preachers or those who would hear confessions? How do we account for the stunning success with which the mendicant orders recruited students and masters in university towns? Should we understand this only in terms of a spiritual attraction to the mendicant way of life, or were there some other expectations and promises? To provide the answers it is necessary to move the focus away from the Order's internal dynamics toward the rise of universities, of scholasticism, and of the glorification of learning in medieval society.

The first three chapters, chronologically parallel, all deal with aspects of the rise of learning in the Order. The fourth, a sequel, jumps in chronology to 1310 and investigates the accusations with regard to learning and books presented to the pope by the Franciscan party headed by Ubertino da Casale

---

62. Roest, *History of Franciscan Education*, 272.

at the preparations for Council of Vienne. Ubertino and his fellow friars complained that friars abused the permission to use books and saw studying as a
means of rising to administrative positions in the Order. The raison d'être of
this chapter is historiographical as well as historical. It aims to examine how
Ubertino da Casale, who is considered a major spokesman for the "Spirituals"
by historians, approached the subject of learning, and whether his criticism of
the abusive practices in the Order was well-founded.[63] Was learning and the
presence of books a point of difference between two distinct Franciscan identi-
ties of "Spirituals" and "Community" by 1310? Was learning shunned by one
party and embraced by the other? This chapter primarily tries to understand
which aspects of learning, or of the mentality exalting it, were being criticized,
and whether this criticism concentrated on practical points such as clear violations of the Order's constitutions, or whether it represented an essentially different reading of the Franciscan Rule, one that regarded the presence of learning
and books as alien to it. Rather than supporting the idea of an Order-wide group
protesting against innovations to the Rule, or relaxations from it, evidence from
the thirteenth century shows that many sensible friars were concerned about
illegitimate deviations from the Rule and from the constitutions of the Order.
Several components of the Franciscan education system, such as the selection of
students, appointment of lectors, and circulation of books, abounded in dubious
practices—dubious since, on the one hand, they could be regarded as at odds
with the basic tenets of Franciscanism, yet on the other hand they were hardly
avoidable in a culture that cherished learning. Chapter 4 makes much use of the
evidence coming from men such as Angelo Clareno and Ubertino da Casale,
friars who are traditionally cast in the "Spiritual" category. Their claims, which
are indeed independently verified in many cases, reveal controversial practices,
of which the general administration of the Order was often aware and tried to
combat by issuing statutes.

Complementing the fourth chapter's analysis of the criticism of activities related to learning and books in the Order, the fifth aims to provide a
description of the state of the Franciscan education system at the time Ubertino wrote his complaints. Bert Roest's *History of Franciscan Education* does an
impressive job of revealing the basic workings of the Franciscan educational
organization, but because it treats material from three centuries, it is not always
easy to understand the structure of the system at any given time. Chapter 5
seeks an understanding of the education system around 1310; I have disregarded
evidence from after this time. The chapter investigates the state of the system,

---

63. As late as 2000, Bert Roest wrote that "the Spirituals condemned the unlimited use of distinc-
tions and verbal concordances as a departure from the original Franciscan *simplicitas*," referencing to
Ubertino's criticism. Ibid., 282.

not by charting legislative developments as one can find in Roest's book, but by looking at how it worked for a clerical friar who entered the Order and wished to have an intellectual career, tracing his steps on the educational ladder from novitiate all the way to becoming a master in Paris. New evidence that has come to light in the last decades renders such a narrative more feasible now than before.[64] This evidence necessitates revision of the description of some components of the Franciscan educational structure.

This book is not a history of Franciscan education but the story of a community of men that faced the tough challenge of realizing an otherworldly ideal of perfection in an imperfect world, their desperate search for a means, their conflicting opinions regarding that means, and their shared frustration. Is learning a means to achieve that perfection, or is it rather an obstruction? This is certainly not a question for a historian; it interests us only insofar as it interested the Franciscans. The question for historians, however, is why some medieval Franciscans thought learning to be the means to achieve their ideal, and how they succeeded in making it official for the entire community through legislation and effective discourse that incorporated studying into the evangelical ideal. The story of the rise of learning in the Franciscan Order is part of the story of the rise of learning in thirteenth-century Europe, particularly of the transformation of the clerical culture where learning, already a source of prestige, came to be increasingly associated with sanctity. It is also part of the story of mankind, in which men of education, by assuming positions of authority, succeeded in imposing learning on their respective communities as an ideal to strive for and as a criterion by which to judge the value of an individual. That story becomes all the more intriguing and ironic when looked at through the lens of a community formed around a man who loved to call himself simple and ignorant.

---

64. Bert Roest rightly accentuated the need to revise the history of Franciscan education in order to give the prime share to the pre-Narbonne constitutions published in 1990, where the older histories and even some new ones regarded the 1260 Narbonne constitutions a watershed. Roest, "The Franciscan School System: Re-Assessing the Early Evidence (ca. 1220–1260)," in *Franciscan Organisation in the Mendicant Context: Formal and Informal Structures of the Friars' Lives and Ministry in the Middle Ages*, ed. Michael Robson and Jens Röhrkasten, 253–79 (Berlin: LIT Verlag, 2011). See also Berg, *Armut und Wissenschaft*, 73.

❧ CHAPTER 1

The Formative Years, 1219–1244

In September 1219, Brother Pacifico[1] arrived at the gates of Paris hoping to find a place in that city for his brothers in religion, the Friars Minor.[2] This arrival marks the beginning of a history to be told in these pages, the history of the rise of learning in the Order of the Friars Minor. The Friars Minor originated in central Italy, made up largely of laymen in pursuit of a penitential life in apostolic poverty and simplicity. Had Paris been just another settlement of this evangelical fraternity in France, perhaps Pacifico's journey would not have special significance, but it was one of the earliest settlements in France, and one of the earliest settlements outside Italy. What could Paris, a large and growing city in the process of becoming a true capital of the kingdom of the Franks, and the seat of what was already the most famous university in Christendom, offer to these poor, semi-eremitical Italians that all other towns on the way from Italy to northern France did not? What brought Pacifico so far from home?

---

1. Also known as Guglielmo di Lisciano, a famous *versificator* and composer of songs in the Marches of Ancona. See II Celano, 106; Brooke, *Scripta Leonis,* 23.

2. For the date of arrival at Paris, see Laure Beaumont-Maillet, *Le Grand Couvent des Cordeliers de Paris: Étude historique et archéologique du XIIIe siècle à nos jours* (Paris: H. Champion, 1975), 10. See also Francesca Joyce Mapelli, *L'amministrazione francescana di Inghilterra e Francia: personale di governo e strutture dell'Ordine fino al Concilio di Vienne (1311)* (Rome: Pontificio Anteneo Antonianum, 2003), 112 and 395.

The Friars Minor were formed around the holy man known as Francis of Assisi. In 1209, when Francis had a dozen followers, he had written a simple Rule for them to follow, known as *Regula Primitiva* or *protoregula*.[3] The text of this earliest Rule does not survive, but it is believed to have been very short and based on quotes from the Bible, summarizing the basic tenets of the evangelical life.[4] Francis, quite firm on remaining obedient to the Church, took his Rule to Pope Innocent III (1198–1216), who sanctioned it orally and informally.[5] According to Francis's medieval biographer, Thomas Celano, Innocent simply said, "Go with the Lord, brothers, and as the Lord will deign to inspire you, preach penance to all."[6] Innocent may well have consulted with Guido, bishop of Assisi, then at the Curia, and learned that Francis and his brothers were harmless penitents[7] who had been living in the vicinity of Assisi for two years.[8] The pope could not really disapprove of Francis's Rule, since it was simply a summary of the *vita apostolica* as described in Acts 4:22: the brothers would earn the means of their existence by the work of their hands or by begging; all things were to be used in common; they would renounce money and all property; and they would preach repentance.

The arrival of the Franciscans in Paris in 1219 is generally believed to have been the very first settlement of the Order in Gaul. As far as we know, Francis himself had originally wished to lead this French expedition.[9] Some twenty

---

3. Laurentius Casutt, *Untersuchungen zur Regula Prima sine Bulla* (Graz: Verlag Styria, 1955), 11–62, established that Francis definitely produced a written Rule sometime in 1209 or 1210. See also Kajetan Esser, *Anfänge und Ursprüngliche Zielsetzungen des Ordens der Minderbrüder* (Leiden: E. J. Brill, 1966), 25–26.

4. For the reconstruction of the *Regula primitiva*, see Dominik Mandić, *De Protoregula Ordinis Fratrum Minorum* (Mostar: Ex Typ. croatica Franciscanae provinciae, 1923), and *De legislatione antiqua Ordinis Fratrum Minorum,* vol. 1, *Legislatio francescana ab an. 1210–1221* (Mostar: Ex Typ. croatica Franciscanae provinciae 1924).

5. Since Innocent's approval was verbal, we know it only through chronicles and later references. See I Celano, 32. Pope Honorius III's letter, *Solet annuere* of November 29, 1223, describes the Franciscan Rule as "regula, a bonae memorie Innocentio Papa praedecessore nostro, approbata" (*BF,* 1:15). The chronicler of the Franciscan settlement in Germany, Jordan of Giano writes, "Regulam authenticam utpote a sede apostolica confirmatam" (Jordan of Giano, 4). Leo, Angelo, and Rufino, Francis's three companions, date the approval of the first Rule to the Lateran Council of 1215. Brooke, *Scripta Leonis,* 204. For the argument that in *Solet annuere* Honorius referred only to the oral approval of 1209–1210, see James M. Powell, "The Papacy and the Early Franciscans," *FS* 36 (1976): 254–55. The extent to which oral approval can be regarded as canonical is, however, debatable. The appointment of Cardinal Hugolino as Cardinal Protector c. 1218–1219 supports the thesis that Francis had official recognition for some sort of way of life or Rule prior to the *Regula non bullata* and *Regula bullata* of 1221 and 1223 respectively. In any case, the canonical position of the Franciscan Order between 1210 and the confirmation of the Rule in 1223 is not clear.

6. I Celano, 33.

7. On the rural penitents, see Gilles G. Meersseman and Edvige Adda, "Pénitents ruraux communitaires en Italie au XIIe siècle," *Revue d'Histoire Ecclesiastique* 49 (1954): 343–90.

8. See I Celano, 32.

9. I Celano, 74: "Beatus Franciscus, non multos adhuc fratres habens et volens ad Franciam ire, devenit Florentiam."

months earlier, the Pentecost Chapter of 1217, made up of Francis and his fellow friars, decided that they ought to embrace their fellow Christians and Saracens alike beyond central Italy, particularly those whose need for Christ's message was greatest. Outside the Italian peninsula, five destinations—Germany, Spain, the Holy Land, southern France, and northern France—were named as areas especially appropriate in which to proselytize.[10] What was it about these territories that the Franciscans directed their attention to them at this early stage? Within Germany, the Rhineland was a hotbed of heresy.[11] Spain was divided between Christians and Muslims, and the Church in the Christian kingdoms of Leon, Castile, and Aragon was in dire need of reform, with heresy widespread.[12] In the Holy Land, the city of Jerusalem remained in Muslim hands, while the period 1217–1219 was one of intense crusading activity, both to the Holy Land itself and to Egypt.

Francis's interest in leading the expedition of *Francia* arose out of his devotion to *Corpus Domini*. Therefore, for northern France he targeted Liége, a center of that devotion, rather than Paris.[13] It is unclear whether a mission was also launched to the Languedoc.[14] This was a territory just as challenging as the Muslim lands, overtaken as it was by the Cathar heresy—even while the friars were sitting at the chapter of 1217, the armies of the Catholic Simon de Montfort were fighting the forces of the Count of Toulouse, Raymond VII (1197–1249), a convert and protector of Cathars living on his lands.

Francis himself took on the mission to northern France. Setting off for France from Assisi, he had only proceeded as far as Florence when he met Cardinal Hugolino.[15] Hugolino discouraged him from continuing with the planned journey, perhaps fearing that the Order would collapse in confusion and possibly heresy should its leader absent himself. Invited to stay in Italy as the head of his Order, Francis complied with this request. He, in turn, asked Hugolino to become cardinal protector of the Order. This was quite an interesting request as

---

10. Moorman, *History of the Franciscan Order,* 31.

11. Robert Ian Moore, *The Formation of a Persecuting Society: Power and Deviance in Western Europe, 950–1250* (Oxford: B. Blackwell, 1987), 9, 21–22.

12. Peter Linehan, *The Spanish Church and the Papacy in the Thirteenth Century* (Cambridge: Cambridge University Press, 1971), 5–11.

13. II Celano, 201. See here the note of the Quaracchi editors on the connection of Liége to Corpus Domini. Celano uses the word *Francia* to mean a territory including modern Belgium. Alcantara Mens, "L'ombrie italienne et l'ombrie brabançon: Deux courants religeux parallèles d'inspiration commune," *Études franciscaines,* Supplement 17 (1967): 45.

14. Moorman argues that France was envisaged as two provinces, north and south. The southern mission, initially a failure, appears to have been entrusted to John Bonelli. Moorman, *History of the Franciscan Order,* 65.

15. For Hugolino, see Werner Maleczek, *Papst und Kardinalskolleg von 1191 bis 1216,* Publikationen des Historischen Instituts beim Österreichischen Kulturinstitut in Rom, i/6 (Vienna: Verlag der Österreichischen Akademie der Wissenschaften, 1984), 126–33.

there had never before been a cardinal protector of any religious order. Such a move might indicate that Francis felt more comfortable with the papacy actively and officially involved in the affairs of the Order.

After Francis's withdrawal, the Gallic mission was reassigned to Brother Pacifico.[16] The problem of language was solved when a French-speaking brother, Louis of Lens, a *socius* of Francis, joined Pacifico for this mission.[17] Thus assuming the commission in place of Francis, Pacifico and Louis crossed the Alps in a northwesterly direction. Their first stop was Vézelay, whose great abbey accommodated many pilgrims and served as a natural break on the journey between Italy and Northern France. There are no certain records of any Franciscan settlement in northern France before Pacifico's arrival at Paris in 1219.[18] In short, settlement at Paris seems to have been the priority of the mission to northern France.

The choice of Paris, as apparently the earliest settlement in France, is something of a puzzle. Why should a predominantly Umbrian, penitential fraternity have hastened to settle at Paris? Of course, Paris was by the early thirteenth century a large and important city, already what one might call the capital of the French kingdom. However, the Franciscans had no particular business with the French court; they were not in the habit of asking privileges or assistance from local powers. Also, there were many other substantial towns and cities on the way to Paris from Italy. Should we not be surprised that, when the Franciscans settled at Paris, not a single settlement had yet been made in southern France, where such a great need for orthodox preachers had already clearly manifested itself?

The sources are completely silent on the reasons for choosing Paris. It was not a center for pilgrimages, it was not threatened by Muslims, nor was it particularly troubled by heretics. It would be difficult, in fact, not to think that the settlement at Paris, one of the earliest outside Italy, is best explained by the presence of the university there, and the major source of potential educated recruits that it could provide. As such, it marks the beginning of the story that will unfold in the rest of this book. This is so, even while as yet there was no official policy of the Order with regard to recruiting the educated, and, as will

---

16. I Celano, 75.

17. As a general rule, Franciscans traveled everywhere in pairs, the *socius* being the companion to an older friar or to one holding office in the Order. For the provision never to travel alone, see I Celano, 29: "Per universum mundum bini et bini dividuntur." Jacques de Vitry, *Lettres de Jacques de Vitry (1160/1170–1240), évêque de Saint-Jean-d'Acre,* ed. R. C. B. Huygens (Leiden: Brill, 1960), 132, letter 6.

18. Callebaut suggests that it was founded in 1219. André Callebaut, "Les provinciaux de la province de France au XIII siecle," *AFH* 10 (1917): 356. However, John R. H. Moorman, *Medieval Franciscan Houses* (St. Bonaventure, NY: Franciscan Institute, 1983): 259, suggests that there is "nothing certain before 1259" when the convent of Lens is mentioned in a will.

be discussed later, contemporary observers were struck by the total absence of any official recruitment policy.

When Francis Was Away...

The Paris settlement took place in August 1219 while Francis was away in the East. He had left in his place two vicars to take charge of his Order—Gregory of Naples and Matthew of Narni.[19] It is not known why these two men specifically were selected for this important job. They are not mentioned anywhere as Francis's companions or close friends. In fact, we hear nothing about them prior to their appointment as vicars. About Matthew of Narni we know absolutely nothing. His name is mentioned only in connection with this vicariate. Gregory of Naples, however, continues his historical presence in the capacity of provincial minister of France from 1223 to c. 1233, and quite an influential one at that.[20] It may well have been Gregory who made Paris a priority in the Franciscan plans for France and it is significant that the Parisian expedition took place under his vicariate. During the ten years of his residence in Paris, he worked very hard to attract scholars to the Order and was the architect of the integration of the Franciscan convent in Paris with the theology faculty at the University of Paris. This would provide support for the notion that Paris was chosen because of the university and presence of scholars there. Also, as soon as Gregory took up his Paris appointment, he organized the English expedition and the subsequent settlement there.[21] This settlement, too, favored towns with universities and important schools, and in a very short time the English province boasted the best educational network anywhere in the Franciscan lands.[22]

The Paris settlement was not Gregory of Naples's only initiative that has a bearing on the Order's future involvement in studies. During his vicariate, in 1219, the provincial minister of Lombardy, John of Stacia, built the first permanent Franciscan house in Bologna, home of the second-greatest university of the Middle Ages. Francis was very upset to find out about this on his return from the Holy Land, and ordered the friars to evacuate the house immediately.[23] The same story is narrated differently by the author of the *Actus beati Francisci*: Peter (John) of Stacia had built the new house with the intention of founding

---

19. Jordan of Giano, 11.

20. On Gregory of Naples and his work as the provincial minister of France, see Callebaut, "Les provinciaux de la province," 295–332.

21. Eccleston, 5.

22. See below. See also Neslihan Şenocak, "In the Pursuit of Knowledge: The Franciscan Settlement in England, 1224–1240," *Frate Francesco-Rivista di cultura Francescana* 71 n.s. (2005): 131–48, where I have argued that this settlement was organized with a view toward establishing a scholarly network.

23. II Celano, 58.

a school, and Francis reproved the minister, saying: "You want to destroy my Order! For I want my friars to pray more than to read, according to the example of my Lord Jesus Christ."[24]

The vicariate during Francis's absence in the East revealed also other tensions over the direction of the Order. The vicars imposed on the friars total abstinence from all types of meat in an echo of the prescriptions to be found in certain monastic rules and heretical movements.[25] Jordan of Giano describes Francis's fury on discovering this instruction when he returned, and his immediate annulment of it.[26] Most likely, the two vicars wished to impose some discipline on these loose bands of wandering friars to make them resemble more a respectable religious order like the Benedictines, Cistercians, or canons regular whose members were from the upper classes of society. To add to these troubles, during this vicariate a certain friar named Giovanni da Conpello gathered around himself a great number of lepers, both men and women, and subsequently withdrew from the Order. Conpello had composed a new Rule and went to the Curia for its confirmation. Francis managed to revoke this Rule on his return with the help of Cardinal Hugolino.[27]

Clearly, things did not go as smoothly as Francis might have expected when he left for the East. To say the least, Francis and his vicars disagreed on how the friars were supposed to live. Should we suspect the vicars' sincerity of intention, imagine them as "plotting" against Francis, and going deliberately and consciously against his wishes? That is what a Franciscan friar of the late thirteenth–early fourteenth century, Angelo Clareno, wants us to believe—that the vicariate government was the first tribulation of the Order.[28] Whatever the vicars' intentions were, there is something that Angelo Clareno does not seem to take into consideration—or at least, if he does, he does not mention it. In 1219, Francis and his followers were a penitential fraternity, which was growing at a tremendous speed in diverse parts of Europe, yet without a Rule and statutes that would offer detailed practical guidance. There was no supervision of the activities of the friars, no clear and consistent definition of Franciscan *religio*. Even if

---

24. There is no mention of a school in Celano. The school appears in Paul Sabatier, *Actus beati Francisci et sociorum ejus* (Paris: Fischbacher, 1902), 183–84.

25. Concerning this incident and its ties with "*monasticizzazione*," see Luigi Pellegrini, "Dalla fraternità all'Ordine: Origini e primi sviluppi del francescanesimo nella società del secolo XIII," in *I Francescani nelle Marche secoli XIII–XVI,* ed. Luigi Pellegrini and Roberto Paciocco (Milan: Arti Grafiche Amilcare Pizzi, 2000), 20; Malcolm Lambert, *Medieval Heresy: Popular Movements from the Gregorian Reform to the Reformation* (Cambridge, MA: B. Blackwell, 1992), 36; R. I. Moore, *The Birth of Popular Heresy* (London: Edward Arnold, 1975) 19.

26. Jordan of Giano, sections 11–13.

27. Ibid., sections 13–14.

28. Angelo Clareno, *Liber chronicarum; sive, Tribulationum ordinis minorum,* ed. G. M. Boccali, Pubblicazioni della Biblioteca francescana Chiesa nuova, Assisi 8 (Santa Maria degli Angeli, Santa Maria degli Angeli (Perugia): Porziuncola, 1999), 169–75.

such a definition could be said to exist in the person of Francis himself, how was he to transmit such a definition to the next generation of Franciscans, as no proper orientation of new recruits existed? In fact, up until 1220, the period of the novitiate was only three months. It was Honorius III who demanded it be prolonged to a year by his bull, *Cum secundum* of 1220.[29] The organizational structure consisted simply of Francis as the head of the Order, a handful of ministers appointed as executive heads of the friars to certain regions, and an annual chapter meeting that the ministers and Francis attended.[30] This provided the ministers with insufficient guidance on how to face the problems that inevitably arose in caring for and organizing quickly growing numbers of friars.

"Fratres Non Habeant Libros"

At the annual chapter of 1220, Francis chose to withdraw from the Order's administration. Perhaps the problems of organizing the Order or the disappointments of the vicariate overwhelmed him and made him decide that he would best serve the Order as a spiritual rather than executive leader. His invitation of Hugolino to become cardinal protector, his choice of two vicars who do not seem to have sufficiently understood the spirit of Francis's movement, and finally his own voluntary withdrawal from the leadership all point to a degree of unease as an administrator. "From now on, I am dead to you, but here is Brother Peter Caetani, whom you all and I should obey."[31] Thus he announced his decision to the chapter, which then continued under the direction of Brother Peter. The choice of Peter Caetani implicitly expressed Francis's dissatisfaction with the two vicars he had appointed earlier. Peter Caetani was one of the first men to join Francis, and had traveled with him to the East.[32] Three decrees survive from the chapter of 1220: first, that friars were not to have books; second, that novices were not to keep a psalter with them and were not allowed to make their religious profession before a year was up;[33] and third, that goods possessed by novices should not be used on any pretext whatsoever.[34]

---

29. "Auctoritate itaque vobis praesentium inhibemus, ne aliquem ad professionem vestri Ordinis, nisi per annum in probatione fuerit, admittatis....Inhibemus etiam, ne sub habitu viate vestrae liceat alicui extra obedientiam evagari et paupertatis vestrae corrumpere puritatem" (*BF,* 1:6, n. 5).

30. The Order was divided into administrative regions known as provinces. Francis particularly favored the word "minister" instead of the Dominican "prior" to refer to the provincial heads as minister meant essentially a servant rather than a man of power or privilege.

31. "Amodo sum mortuus vobis; sed ecce frater Petrus Cathanii, cui ego et vos omnes obediamus"; Brooke, *Scripta Leonis,* 272. On Caetani's assignment, see also Brooke, *Early Franciscan Government,* 76–77.

32. Marion A. Habig, ed., *St. Francis of Assisi: Writings and Early Biographies; English Omnibus of the Sources for the Life of St. Francis* (Chicago: Franciscan Herald Press, 1972), 1:566, n. 84.

33. This echoes the papal bull of the same year mentioned above, *Cum secundum.*

34. "Capitulum generale Assisii. Anno 1220. Petrus Cataneus. Leges. Item I. Fratres non habeant libros 2. Novitii non retineant apud se Psalterium, nec emittant professionem ante annum. 3. Novitiorum

Fratres non habeant libros. If we leave aside the fury of Francis toward the house in Bologna, which may have been directed against the innovation of a permanent house for the friars rather than at any educational activities inside it, the 1220 ban on books is the first "official" policy that has a bearing on learning. The prohibition against having books does not necessarily reflect hostility toward learning, even though in effect it crippled any intellectual activity of the friars. Most probably, this decree was passed to guard the cornerstone of Franciscan movement—the pursuit of an evangelical, apostolic life in all its simplicity and poverty. The other two decrees aimed at preparing novices specifically for such a life, requiring them to do without the psalter, which at least clerical novices might have been used to having at their fingertips, and indeed to do without the use of any goods that they, as novices, might still technically possess. The latter decree might also be designed to prevent the friars in general from benefiting from the possessions of novices. Given the very high price of books in the Middle Ages, it would seem odd for an order devoted to the strictest kind of poverty to cherish and keep books. The brothers of Francis were to be, or at least strive to be, poorer than the poorest member of society.[35] How could they possibly convert people to the apostolic life if they walked around with valued items such as books? Books and apostolic poverty were irreconcilable.

When asked by a friar why he had withdrawn from the administration of the Order, Francis, according to the testimony of Celano, replied as follows: "There are some prelates who draw them [the friars] to others, proposing to them the example of the ancients, and caring little for my admonitions."[36] By "prelates" he probably meant the provincial ministers of the Order, who were now administering the brothers in various parts of Christendom. As we have already seen with the two vicars and their decree on abstinence from meat, some ministers wanted to bring the Order into line with the more traditional monastic orders, hence the "ancients." Embracing the monastic tradition meant establishing permanent houses, holding property in common,[37] and abandoning undignified practices such as begging or wandering around. Since the inception of his penitential fraternity, Francis had made up his mind not to embrace the monastic life. His way was to be very different from that of the established

---

bona non serventur quocumque praetextu"; *Codex redactus legum Fratrum Minorum in synopism cum indice copioso. Ex literis Joannis Cervantes Cardinalis S. Petri ad vincula legati a latere ad XXXVI. Capitulum generale Assisii habito lectis anno MCDXXX. die XXI. Junii in eodem capitulo,* ed. Aloysius Perego Salvioni (Rome, 1796), 1.

35. Kenneth B. Wolf, *The Poverty of Riches: St. Francis of Assisi Reconsidered* (New York: Oxford University Press, 2003), 20–25.

36. "Nam sunt quidam de numero praelatorum, qui eos ad alia trahunt, antiquorum eis proponentes exempla, et parum mea monita repunantes. Sed quid agant, in fine videbitur" (II Celano, 188).

37. See the discourse by Leo on the insistence of some ministers to hold property in common. Brooke, *Scripta Leonis,* 284–85.

religious orders and the new Order of Dominicans. He believed that God had entrusted him with a very special mission: the literal enactment of the Gospel to the glory of God and for the edification of others. Until Judgment Day should come, he and his brothers were to be the animated images of Christ, the quintessential actors of the faith, reminding people constantly of how the incarnate God had lived in this life within the human flesh. A task as significant as this could not be compromised in any way. But then, what could a man who did not and could not believe in coercion—seemingly so contrary to the way of Christ—do in practice against those who objected? From this there must have seemed to be no escape. In fury, Francis would say, "Who are these, who have snatched my *religio* and that of my brothers from my hands? When I go to the General Chapter, I will show them what my will is!"[38] Indeed, to reach out to the body of simple friars, and to demonstrate to them the founding principles of the Order of Lesser Brothers, the most efficient means might have seemed to summon a General Chapter.

Yet there was another way, one that involved writing a new and more detailed Rule and obtaining official approval from the pope, thereby, at least, imposing a canonical liability on the friars to follow Francis, the way Francis wanted to be followed. By this time, the Order had greatly expanded, and the first Rule was not sufficient to regulate the behavior of the friars. There was a need for a new Rule that would correct the orientation of some of the ministers, and that would stand as the timeless, authoritative guide for the friars in their journey through this life. Francis withdrew to the solitude of the mountains so that he could allow himself to be possessed by God and have the Rule dictated to him. His retreat, however, was briefly interrupted by the death of his vicar, Peter Caetani, in 1221. Francis asked Brother Elias of Cortona, who had also been with him to Egypt, to replace Peter.

Francis was not alone in his retreat. He was accompanied by Leo of Assisi, who, around 1244–1246, wrote his memoirs of Francis and the early Order. Through his testimony, we learn that the rumors of a new Rule to be presented to the Curia made the provincial ministers anxious about their future canonical liabilities. It was obvious that anything that Francis might set down was bound to reflect his superhuman zeal and bind the friars to follow it unconditionally. Some ministers convinced Brother Elias, the new vicar, to join them and appeal to Francis to stop writing a new Rule on his own. "We have heard that this Brother Francis is making a new Rule. We are afraid that he may make it so severe that we will not be able to observe it. We want you to go to him and tell him that we do not want to be bound to that Rule. Let him make it for himself

---

38. "Qui sunt isti qui religionem meam et fratrum de meis manibus rapuerunt? Si ad generale capitulum venero, tunc eis ostendam qualem habeam voluntatem" (II Celano, 188).

and not for us!" they said to Elias.[39] The opposition was in vain; Francis replied that those friars who were not willing to obey should leave the Order.[40]

Francis summoned to the next General Chapter in 1221 not just the ministers, as was the custom, but all the brothers of the Order. This extraordinary chapter is known as the Chapter of Mats, for some 5,000 friars were sitting on mats in and around the Portiuncula in Assisi.[41] Apparently here, too, some friars attempted to push for a monastic Rule, this time using the cardinal protector Hugolino as agent. The friars requested that Hugolino persuade Francis to adopt one of the known Rules, by Benedict, Augustine, or Bernard. It is likely that they reminded the cardinal of the thirteenth canon of the Fourth Lateran Council of 1215 that forbade the foundation of any new orders and instructed all new religious institutions without one to adapt an existing and approved rule.[42] The Friars Preachers founded by Dominic Guzman had adapted the Rule of Saint Augustine in 1216, and Hugolino was present at that event.[43] Francis, however, rejected the offer, saying:

> My brothers,...I do not want you to name any other Rule to me, neither Saint Augustine's, nor Saint Bernard's, nor Saint Benedict's. The Lord said to me that he wished me to be a new *pazzus*[44] in the world. God did not want to lead us by any way other than this kind of learning [*per istam scientiam*]; however, through your learning and wisdom [*scientiam et sapientiam*] God will confound you.[45]

The Franciscan Rule

The Rule composed in 1221 reads almost like a gloss to the most popular biblical passages that had formed the basis of Christian ascetic life for centuries. If,

---

39. Leo witnessed the conversation between Francis, the ministers, and Elias. Translation in Brooke, *Scripta Leonis,* 285. Other sources give different versions of this story. See Brooke, *Early Franciscan Government,* 94.

40. Brooke, *Scripta Leonis,* 286–87.

41. Ibid., 286–88. It is impossible to ascertain the actual date of this big chapter. Scholars have also suggested 1219 and 1222. See, for example, Theophile Desbonnets, *From Intuition to Institution: The Franciscans* (Chicago: Franciscan Herald Press, 1988), 42, which suggests 1219. We know that the Rule was discussed in the Chapter of Mats, and since the *Regula non bullata* was written in 1221, it is more likely that the Chapter of Mats was summoned with all friars in the Order for the discussion and announcement of the Rule. Desbonnets gives no explanation why he thinks the Chapter of Mats took place in 1219. However, 1219 fits the way he constructs the story, which is based on his conviction that Francis's disillusionment and clash with the ministers in this chapter led to him to resign in the next chapter of 1220.

42. Josepho Alberigo et al., eds., *Conciliorum oecumenicorum decreta* (Basel: Herder, 1962), 218.

43. Francisco Gaude, ed., *Bullarium diplomatum et privilegiorum sanctorum Romanorum pontificum* (Turin: Seb. Franco et Henrico Dalmazzo, 1858), 3:309–10.

44. Colloquial Italian for "madman, wild man, lunatic; someone who is strange, odd, eccentric." Some manuscripts use *insanus* or *stultus,* meaning "stupid" and "idiot." As this is significant, I have left it untranslated, but clearly it shows that Francis regarded himself as eccentric.

45. Brooke, *Scripta Leonis,* 288 (my translation).

however, we depend on the testimony of Jordan of Giano, it was the other way around: the Rule was written first and then handed over to a learned brother, Caesar of Speyer, so that he could adorn it with passages from the Bible.[46] This Rule contains not a single line about the pursuit of scholarly learning as such. Indeed, education was rendered practically impossible by a series of prohibitions against the holding of property;[47] the acceptance of money, even for the purpose of buying books;[48] the possession of any books save those which served the Divine Office;[49] and the ownership of any dwelling.[50] Furthermore, these prohibitions were expressed with blatant clarity—even the most subtle of the exegetes would be unable to carve from this Rule any sort of legitimacy for a learned career.

In a mysterious way—no source tells us why—this Rule of 1221, known as the *Regula prima* or *Regula non bullata,* did not become the official Rule.[51] Two years later, with the bull *Solet annuere* of 1223, Honorius III formally approved a revised version, known today as *Regula bullata.* The differences between the two Rules are considerable in style, which translates somewhat also to content.[52] The revised Rule does not, for example, mention books. The *Regula bullata* is also stripped of the quotations from the Bible and written with great economy of words. Yet it seems that despite the resistance from within the Order, Francis had been able to extract papal approval for the essential elements of his way of life. The acceptance of money and the acquisition of any property remained forbidden.[53] The importance of begging, without shame, was firmly stated in the Rule.[54]

The only place where anything related to learning is mentioned is the tenth chapter: "Those who do not know their letters, should not strive to learn them."[55] Francis does not here use the term "lay brothers" (*fratres laici*) but

---

46. Jordan of Giano, 15.

47. RNB, chap. 1.

48. Ibid., chap. 8.

49. "Et libros tantum necessarios ad implendum eorum officium possint habere" (Ibid., chap. 3).

50. Ibid., chap. 7.

51. Leo speaks of a lost Rule, handed by Francis either to the ministers or to Elias; Brooke, *Scripta Leonis,* 113. But whether this is the Rule of 1221 is dubious. After all, if the only copy of it had really been lost, its text would not exist today.

52. For a full discussion of the general difference between the two Rules, see Nimmo, *Reform and Division,* 28–34. He argues that the two Rules were vastly different; in particular, that the later one was spiritually weaker and unable to transmit adequately Francis's ideals.

53. RB, chaps. 4–6.

54. Ibid., chap. 6.

55. "Non curent nescientes litteras litteras discere" (RB, chap. 10). For an exposition of this sentence, see Pietro Maranesi, "San Francesco e gli studi: Analisi del 'Nescientes litteras' del X Capitolo della Regola Bollata," *CF* 69 (1999): 15. Maranesi proposes that while Francis did not actually oppose the intellectual development of the Order, he nevertheless strongly "advised" a simple and lowly life, particularly for those who had not yet begun their studies. See also Maranesi, "L'intentio Francisci' sul rapporto tra minorità e studio nel dibattito del primo cinquantennio dell'Ordine Francescano," in *Minores*

"those who do not know their letters" (*nescientes litteras*). Medieval authors used the words *clericus* and *laicus* with a great deal of flexibility.[56] The dichotomy between *clericus* and *laicus* could indicate the difference between literate and illiterate, often in Latin specifically, or it could point to the canonical difference between someone in holy orders—a clergyman—as against someone who was not—a layman. *Clericus* could also mean someone ordained to one of the major holy orders (priest, deacon, subdeacon), above all, a priest, as opposed to someone who had taken only minor holy orders.[57] A man who had taken one of the minor holy orders could leave the clerical life if he wanted to, whereas those in the major holy orders could not. In the *Regula non bullata* of 1221, where Francis refers to lay brothers, he makes it clear that he refers to their canonical position, not their degree of literacy. In the third chapter of this Rule, he allows "the lay brothers who could read" to have a psalter.[58] This is to be expected, as by the thirteenth century laymen with some degree of literacy in Latin were not that uncommon, perhaps especially in Italy. Surely, among the early Franciscans, there were noblemen, merchants, or notaries who had an adequate knowledge of Latin. For these, the path to taking holy orders and becoming *clericus* in the canonical sense was open.

On the other hand, it is quite clear that Francis did not think it useful or important for an illiterate person who wanted to pursue the apostolic life to spend time and effort to become literate. This much can also be deduced, in fact, from everything else Francis did and said. Writing about what true "simplicity" meant to Francis, Celano states that "this is the simplicity that chooses to act rather than to learn or to teach."[59] Learning letters was in many ways a waste of one's time, as Christ could be served in many other ways, above all by living a humble life, and thereby being an example to others.

What is the stance of the Rule of 1223 toward the pursuit of learning for those who were literate? There is no straightforward answer. As expected, this Rule envisages something quite different from life in one of the traditional monastic orders. It champions both personal and institutional poverty, and insists

---

et subditi omnibus: Tratti caraterizzanti dell'identità francescana, ed. Luigi Padovese (Rome: Edizioni Collegio S. Lorenzo da Brindisi, 2003), 273–304. Here, Maranesi similarly argues that there is a certain degree of uncertainty and ambiguity in Francis's stance toward learning. Francis is not enthusiastic about learning, but neither does he condemn it. See Maranesi, "L'intentio Francisci," 285.

56. See Michael T. Clanchy, *From Memory to Written Record, England, 1066–1307* (Cambridge, MA: Harvard University Press, 1979), 177–81; and Giles Constable, "The Orders of Society in the Eleventh and Twelfth Centuries," in *Medieval Religion: New Approaches,* ed. Constance H. Berman, 68–94 (New York: Routledge, 2005), which examines the interplay between the various orders of society.

57. On this, see Stephen J. P. Van Dijk, and J. Hazelden Walker, *The Origins of the Modern Roman Liturgy: The Liturgy of the Papal Court and the Franciscan Order in the Thirteenth Century* (Westminster, MD: Newman Press, 1960), 192–98.

58. RNB, chap. 3. See Desbonnets, *From Intuition to Institution,* 37.

59. II Celano, 189. My translation.

on begging as a spiritual exercise, while encouraging and regulating missionary activity among the unfaithful. Learning, however, is not something with which the Rule concerns itself. The Rule of 1223 does not support or encourage the pursuit of learning, though nor does it explicitly reject it. It rather advises the illiterate not to waste their time learning letters. There is nothing that forbids reading books or sitting in a classroom and listening to lectures, but it requires creative thinking to suggest that a friar who promises to observe this Rule can make a career in theology. One obstacle was the lack of any permanent residence, made impossible by the prohibition on property. Someone might offer hospitality to the friars for a time, but they could be summarily ejected at the will of the owner. There were, of course, the hermitages and the mountains, where one might perhaps dwell continuously, but these were nowhere near established schools. There is also the problem of books. If the friars were to have neither money nor any property, then they could not possess books, except the Psalter. They could, however, accept things that served their temporal needs.[60] If one could classify books as a "temporal need," which is perhaps taking the analogy a little too far, then perhaps accepting a book donation could be made legitimate. Even then, one could hardly frequent a school while depending on donations. Franciscanism, with all the limitations imposed by the Rule of 1223, has some room for an individual friar to engage in study, but in 1223 the idea of an organized educational network was practically inconceivable. This was, however, soon going to change.

The Franciscan Mosaic in 1223

"Regula et vita Minorum Fratrum haec est, scilicet Domini nostri Jesu Christi sanctum Evangelium observare vivendo in obedientia, sine proprio et in castitate." This is the opening line of the Rule of 1223.[61] The essential feature of this basic creed of Franciscan life is its potential for multiplicity. One can, after all, observe the Gospel life in many different ways, and make many claims as to what that life really is. In the works of great scholars of the past, such as Chenu, Grundmann, and Meersseman,[62] it has been sufficiently demonstrated that long before Francis came along, monks, canons regular, and numerous lay confraternities of the twelfth century perceived themselves to be the true followers of the life specified in the Gospel. In a way, the Franciscan Order was a microcosm that

---

60. RB, chap. 5.

61. "The Rule and Life of the Friars Minor is this: to keep the Holy Gospel of Our Lord Jesus Christ by living in obedience, without any property, and in chastity" (RB, chap. 1).

62. There were many fraternities at this time in Europe and Italy, and their nature has been extensively investigated in a pathbreaking study by Gilles G. Meersseman and Gian Piero Pacini, *Ordo fraternitatis: Confraternite e pietà dei laici nel Medioevo*, 3 vols. (Roma: Herder, 1977).

incorporated all these various interpretations of the apostolic life. The challenge for the Order was, in fact, to maintain that diversity while also maintaining some sort of unity among all the followers.

In the early days before a formal Rule was presented to the Roman Curia for approval, the nature of this rapidly growing band of brothers gathered around Francis had the characteristics of a penitential fraternity (*fraternitas*).[63] Francis himself referred to the community of his followers as a *fraternitas,* and never actually used the term *ordo.*[64] Some of the characteristics of medieval fraternities observable in the early Franciscan Order are the use of the word *"frater,"* the communality of spiritual and material resources, and the simultaneous presence of laity and clergy, as well as of men and women.[65] With the Franciscans, we need further to remember that in the beginnings, the lines between what is today called the three Orders—namely, the First Order consisting of unmarried clergy and laity, the Second Order of cloistered nuns, and the Third Order of laymen who continue their normal life in the world—were quite blurred.[66] The story of the foundation of the female wing of the Franciscan Order, today known as the Poor Clares, or Clarisse sisters, is well known. In 1212, hearing the preaching of Francis at Assisi Cathedral, a young noblewoman from Assisi, Clare Favarone, left her home and asked Francis to allow her to follow the Franciscan "vita."[67] Francis suggested Clare take up the cloistered life while remaining loyal to the essential precepts of the evangelical life, above all poverty. He was probably aware that one of the characteristics of heretical groups was the mixing of men and women within them.[68] As such, it was essential that the females who wished to join his movement live as respectable nuns. Francis later wrote a *forma vivendi* for Clare and the other women who joined her, thereby effectively starting what is known to this day as the Second Order of Franciscans. The Franciscan way of life, with its emphasis on humility, chastity, penance, and voluntary poverty, was also adapted by many married people. They too responded to the magnetic spirit of this movement and asked Francis how they could join his penitential fraternity without abandoning their wives and husbands.[69] Francis was certainly keen on

---

63. Desbonnets, *From Intuition to Institution,* 57–82, contains a very illuminating discussion.

64. Ibid., 81.

65. Ibid., 63.

66. Meersseman and Pacini, *Ordo fraternitatis,* 1:359–60.

67. On Saint Clare, see the excellent biography, by Marco Bartoli, *Chiara d'Assisi* (Rome: Istituto storico dei cappuccini, 1989), and Joan Mueller, *A Companion to Clare of Assisi: Life, Writings, and Spirituality* (Leiden: Brill, 2010).

68. As evident in the testimony of a Premonstratensian monk Burchard of Ursperg, who calls it a scandalous and most shameful practice that in the Poor Men of Lyons (Waldensians), men and women walked together, and often stayed in the same house. Hellman, Armstrong, and Short, *Francis of Assisi,* 1:594.

69. "Similiter et viri uxores habentes dicebant: Uxores habemus, quas dimitti se non patiuntur. Docete ergo nos quam viam tenere salubriter valeamus. At illi ordinaverunt ipsis ordinem qui poenitentium

the idea of welcoming every willing and fitting soul on earth to the apostolic life. Once again, he wrote a sort of *forma vivendi* for the married in 1221, and created what has become the Third Order of Franciscans.[70] In the first two decades of the Franciscan movement, probably these three "orders" of the followers of Francis's *religio* seemed a single entity, since the canonical status of the Second and Third Orders was not clarified until the later thirteenth century. This tripartite nature of the early brotherhood was not, however, a novelty, as the same phenomenon can be observed also in the Humiliati, who were reconciled to the Church in 1201.[71]

Looking back at the religious history of the eleventh and twelfth centuries, and browsing the history of movements such as the Carthusians, Cistercians, or Premonstratensians, Christopher Brooke rightly poses the question of what Francis had to offer "which no earlier order or group or founder had conceived?"[72] Three particular characteristics of this brotherhood come to the forefront: the diversity of people who joined the movement and the diversity of the apostolic *lives* they pursued after they joined; the explosive growth of the brotherhood in a relatively short time; and the rejection of communal property in addition to the more usual rejection of private property. Although perhaps each on their own did not constitute originality, together they created one of the most intriguing phenomena of the Middle Ages.

The diversity of the people who joined the brotherhood in the early years is remarkable. The only criterion for recruitment into the Order in these early days seems to have been the possession of the zeal to follow naked the naked Christ. Other than that, one's social status, education, age, or even the kind of religious life that inspired the candidate did not make any difference. A hermit and a wandering preacher could just as well become fellow Franciscans. Likewise could a schoolmaster or an illiterate teenager, a substantial landowner or a peasant.[73] We know that the Order attracted clergy, nobility, and a variety of other laymen.[74] Some of these laymen were no doubt illiterate and from low social positions. As the Bolognese professor of rhetoric Boncampagno of

---

vocatur, facientes hoc a summo pontifice confirmari"; *Anonymus Peruginus,* Acta sanctorum, Oct, II, 600, 291. Cited by Meersseman and Pacini, *Ordo fraternitatis,* 1:360.

70. Kajetan Esser published this under the title *Epistola ad fideles* (*Exhortatio ad fratres et sorores de poenitentia*). K. Esser, ed., *Opuscula sancti patris Francisci Assisiensis* (Grottaferrata: Editiones Collegii S. Bonaventure Ad Claras Aquas, 1978), 107–12.

71. See the excellent work of Frances Andrews, *The Early Humiliati* (Cambridge: Cambridge University Press, 1999), particularly 60–63.

72. Chistopher N. L. Brooke, *The Age of the Cloister: The Story of Monastic Life in the Middle Ages* (Mahwah, NJ: Hidden Spring, 2003), 224.

73. Robson notes the robbers of Borgo San Sepolchro, men of higher social status like Leonard of Assisi, two Benedictine abbots, and four bishops, though his evidence is from the 1240s onward. Robson, *Franciscans in the Middle Ages,* 22–23.

74. I Celano, 56–57.

Signa remarked: "The Friars Minor are in part young men and boys. If they are inconstant and prone to influence due to the flexibility of their age, this is not unnatural, but these have already reached the level of extreme insanity, since they wander around in the cities, towns, and solitary places bearing many horrible things and inhuman martyrdom."[75] Uneducated laymen continued to join the Order in great numbers until 1239, as a case study on the social origins of the German friars has shown.[76] When the Order was mainly engaged in spreading throughout Europe, finding houses in which to live, the lay friars played an active part. The early settlements of the Order included a good number of lay friars, that in England beginning with four clerics and five lay brothers. Among the clerics, the level of the holy orders held by each does not seem to have created a hierarchy: for example, Agnellus of Pisa, while still only a deacon, became provincial minister and the administrative superior of priests and preachers such as Richard Ingeworth.[77] Similarly, in the German settlement of 1221, eleven clerics and fifteen laymen took part. Jordan of Giano speaks about the involvement of many laymen in the settlements and administration.[78]

The diversity of the recruits, matched by the diversity of lives led by them, all combined under the principles set out by Francis—simplicity, humility, obedience, and poverty—characterized the originality of Francis's brotherhood. We find those who aspired to live like monks such as Gregory of Naples and John Stacia, wandering preachers like Anthony of Padua, missionaries like Elias, hermits like Leo of Assisi, women like Clare of Assisi, together with married men and women of the Third Order, and many simple lay brothers wandering around in poverty, begging, and doing manual work. This multiplicity of recruits and ways of life in the Order was the distinguishing success of Francis, probably better noticed and appreciated in the Middle Ages than now. He managed to inspire different followers in different ways, but then united all through his own life, itself combining several different religious lifestyles and philosophies. The *Regula* of the Order was one, but the *vitae* many. Francis's relentless inclusiveness went even beyond the human species. In well-known tales he tried to reach out to birds, wolves, and nature in general.[79]

---

75. "Fratres minores ex parte sunt iuvenes et pueri; unde si iuxta aetatum suarum flexibilitatem sunt mutabiles et proclives, non est contra naturam; ipsi autem iam ad extremam dementiam pervenerunt, quia per civitates et oppida loca solitaria sine discretione vagantur horribilia et inhumana martiria tolerando." From *Rhetorica antiqua,* ed. A. Schönbach, "Beiträge zur Erklärung altdeutscher Dichterwerke," in *Sitzungsberichte der Wiener Akademie der Wissenschaften, philos.-histor. Klasse* 145 (1902): 68.

76. Freed, *Friars and German Society,* 126–28.

77. Eccleston, 4.

78. See, for example, Jordan of Giano, 25, 37, 40, 41, 44, 45; Freed, *Friars and German Society,* 126.

79. I Celano, 58. See also, on Francis's care of the members of the animal kingdom in his apostolate, I Celano, 59–61a, 80.

One look at the face of Francis would make it clear to any medieval man that they were in the presence of a new kind of religious. This was not a man who fashioned himself as a monk or a cleric, for he had a beard; nor was he an ordinary layman for he had a tonsure. In most medieval pictorial depictions, Francis always has a beard and a small tonsure. As such, his closest physical resemblance would be to a *conversus* in the Cistercian sense. The *conversi*, lay Cistercian brothers, had a small tonsure—like the one given to Francis by Innocent III—but to be easily distinguished from the clean-shaven choir monks, they wore a beard.[80] They were considered inferior to choir monks, but they represented a hybrid, a union of two worlds that were increasingly pushed apart by the institutional Church and its reforms. It is quite consistent with all that Francis did and said that he fashioned himself as a bridge between these two worlds divided by canonical status, hence a new *pazzus*. In following Christ, clergy and lay were one.[81]

Francis had gone through stages in his pursuit of an evangelical life. In the beginning, his inclination was toward eremitism. "When he was rebuilding the said church, [Portiuncula] he was in the third year of his conversion. At that time, he was wearing a habit almost like a hermit's, girded with a belt, carrying a staff in his hand, and shoes on his feet."[82] Only after hearing the Gospel did Francis cast aside his staff and shoes, exchange the belt for a cord, and design a new tunic for himself in the shape of a cross.[83] However, he did not completely cast aside the eremitical life, but instead integrated it into the apostolate of the wandering penitential preacher.[84] "During the day they go into the cities and villages, giving themselves over to the active life in order to gain others; at night, however, they return to their hermitage or solitary places to devote themselves to contemplation," wrote Jacques de Vitry in 1216.[85] This was the hybrid life led by Francis until he withdrew in 1220 almost exclusively to an eremitical life with his early companions in the valley of Rieti, practicing a form of religious life that scholars today term community-eremitism.[86] This

80. Christopher N. L. Brooke, "Priest, Deacon and Layman, from St. Peter Damian to St. Francis," in *Churches and Churchmen in Medieval Europe* (London: Hambledon Press, 1999), 246.

81. Ibid., 252–53 also stresses the idea that by opting for the small tonsure Francis made a gesture toward lay brothers, although Brooke does not mention Francis's beard. He does invite attention to, and finds quite symbolic, the fact that Francis took the order of deacon, which is a high order of clergy.

82. I Celano, 21.

83. Ibid., 22.

84. See Pietro Messa, *Frate Francesco: tra vita eremitica e predicazione* (Assisi: Porziuncola, 2001).

85. "De die intrant civitates et villas, ut aliquos lucrificiant operam dantes actione; nocte vero revertuntur ad heremum vel loca solitaria vacantes contemplationi"; Jacques de Vitry, *Lettres*, no. 1, 75–76, writing from Genoa to his friends in Liège. Translation from Hellman, Armstrong, and Short, *Francis of Assisi*, 1:579.

86. Grado G. Merlo, "Eremitismo nel francescanesimo medievale," in *Eremitismo nel francescanesimo medievale: Atti del XVII Convegno Internazionale, Assisi, 12–13–14 ottobre 1989* (Assisi: Università degli

was then a flourishing lifestyle among the ascetically inclined inhabitants of Italy, above all of Umbria. In this new type of eremitism, small groups or fraternities lived an eremitical life together.[87] The two other mendicant orders, which came into being after the Dominicans and Franciscans, namely, the Carmelites and the Augustinian hermits, were the products of this religious movement.

Community-eremitism was quite prominent in the early Franciscan Order. It was practiced not only by Francis and his immediate circle of friends but by a good many other Franciscans in various parts of Europe. Groups gathered around friars such as Cesario da Spira or Simone da Collazzone, living in hermitages in the valley of Spoleto, or individual friars like Giles cut themselves off from their communities to live the life of a hermit.[88] In the Marches of Ancona, a community of friars lived in a solitary place called Soffiano.[89] Numerous Franciscan hermitages in Italy are standing testimonies to this. Only four miles away from Assisi, in Monte Subasio, is the Eremo dei Carceri, where one can see the cell of Francis and his early companions. Other early Franciscan hermitages were the Portiuncula in Assisi, Celle di Cortona, Greccio, Verna, Fonte Colombo, Sant'Urbano, and the Island of Trasimeno.[90]

In fact, the number of friars that took up the eremitical life compelled Francis to set down a *forma vivendi* for them, called *De religiosa habitatione in eremis* (Concerning the Religious Life in the Hermitages) between 1217 and 1221.[91] In this Rule, he urged the friars to live in threes or fours, taking turns to contemplate and deal with practical matters such as begging for alms. Ministers and custodians were to visit the friars in the hermitages. That this phenomenon was not just an Italian one but practiced in other parts of Europe is evidenced in a story related by Celano. A Spanish friar informs Francis that the brothers in Spain are living in poor hermitages, taking turns contemplating and seeking alms, and that one of these brothers has risen to sanctity. Francis rejoices greatly in the news, and praises God for the example of these brothers.[92] When Thomas of Celano lamented bitterly that some friars living in the hermitages favored

Studi di Perugia Centro di Studi Francescani, 1991), 29–50; Luigi Pellegrini, *Insediamenti Francescani nell'Italia del Duecento* (Rome, 1984), 57–81 (chapter titled "L'eremo: Una specifica esperienza insediativa nel primo francescanesimo"). See also Jean François Godet-Calogeras, "Illi qui volunt religiose stare in eremis: Eremitical Practice in the Life of the Early Franciscans," in *Franciscans at Prayer*, ed. Timothy J. Johnson, 307–31 (Leiden: Brill, 2007).

87. Giovanna Casagrande, *Religiosità penitenziale e città al tempo dei comuni* (Rome: Istituto Storico dei Cappuccini, 1995), 24.

88. Merlo, "Eremitismo nel francescanesimo medievale," 33.

89. *The Little Flowers of Saint Francis,* in Hellman, Armstrong, and Short, *Francis of Assisi,* 3: 566–658, chaps. 46, 47.

90. For references to these places in the two vitae of Celano, see Pellegrini, *Insediamenti Francescani,* 72.

91. Kajetan Esser regarded this as a Rule and titled it *Regula pro eremitoriis data.* For its critical edition, see Esser, *Opuscula Sancti Patris Francisci Assisiensis,* 295–98.

92. II Celano, 178.

idleness and worldly pleasure, he wrote, "But this is not true for everyone, because we read that the saints, while they were living in the flesh, had a wonderful living in the hermitages. We know also those fathers who preceded them were like solitary flowers."[93] Clearly Celano is referring to the first-generation Franciscans, particularly the early companions of Francis such as Leo, Angelo, Rufino, and Giles. These men had embraced this eremitical life, both before and after Francis's death. We hear a lot about them in the fourteenth-century sources, where the early identity of the Order is very much associated with this community-eremitism.

While Francis and his early companions displayed strong eremitical tendencies, other early recruits had monastic tendencies. As seen with Gregory of Naples and Matthew of Narni, some friars in the Order felt more comfortable with a monastic discipline of refraining from meat. Francis himself had complained about the friars showing him "the example of the ancients" and of the propositions to adapt an existing monastic Rule. The existence of a Rule, which was presented to and approved by the papacy, itself can be considered a step toward a monastic character, and so were some of the relatively early changes in the Order, such as the establishment of permanent convents. Peter (John) of Stacia's attempt to found a permanent house in Bologna, which attracted Francis's ire, was a precursor of this trend.

In 1209 there were only twelve friars; by the time of the Chapter of Mats in 1221 there were at least five thousand.[94] This phenomenal growth was puzzling even for contemporaries: "They have multiplied in a short time to such a degree that there is no Christian territory that lacks a few Franciscans," wrote Jacques de Vitry in 1223. It is this growth after all that made Franciscans so influential and world-historical to use a Hegelian term; this is why today we study this particular medieval order more than any other. The inclusivity of the various forms of contemporary religious life, the acceptance of people of all status, and the brotherhood's decision to expand outside of Italy propelled successive recruitment. No doubt the diversity of envisaged lifestyles within the Order and its exceptionally explosive growth drawing from many different sources of recruits fed off each other.

A constellation of favorable external factors also aided the process. In the beginning of the thirteenth century, the urbanization and the increasing wealth and welfare in Europe created conditions where begging communities could survive.[95] On the papal throne sat a series of popes, Innocent III, Honorius III,

---

93. Ibid., 179.

94. Desbonnets, *From Intuition to Institution,* 80.

95. This point was made by Lawrence Landini in connection with why the Church did not endorse the apostolic movements before the thirteenth century. Lawrence C. Landini, *The Causes of the Clericalization of the Order of Friars Minor, 1209–1260, in the Light of Early Franciscan Sources* (Chicago: Pontificia Universitas Gregoriana, 1968), 12.

and, afterward, the cardinal protector of the Franciscans himself, Gregory IX, who did not feel threatened by the Franciscans' dedication to voluntary poverty and who were all sympathetic to such penitential fraternities pursuing the apostolic life.[96] They were convinced that assimilating these religious groups rather than isolating or suppressing them was the name of the game, and that the presence of such groups as a legitimate part of the institutional Church would strengthen the Church's position among the laity in the face of competition from heretical institutions such as the Church of the Cathars. From the early years of the Order onward, the popes' blessing and endorsement of the Franciscan fraternity allowed it to flourish without effective opposition from local secular clergy. Finally, there was the mesmerizing charisma of Francis of Assisi himself as the founder of this movement and its effective leader until 1220. One can only imagine what power of attraction this diminutive figure of a man had, as he, in equal measure, charmed and astonished popes and cardinals, learned and simple folk. The few witnesses we know of, who had the chance to hear Francis's sermons, testify to his extraordinary hold on people. Jacques De Vitry, who was at the crusading camp at the same time as Francis, wrote the following in a letter to his friends:

> The head of these brothers, who also founded the Order, came into our camp. He was so inflamed with zeal for the faith that he did not fear to cross the lines to the army of our enemy. For several days he preached the word of God to the Saracens and made a little progress. The Sultan, the ruler of Egypt, privately asked him to pray to the Lord for him, so that he might be inspired by God to adhere to that religion which most pleased God. Colin, the Englishman, our clerk, also had joined this Order, as well as two more of our company, namely Master Michael and Lord Matthew, to whom I had committed the care of the Church of the Holy Cross. I am having a difficult time holding on to the cantor and Henry and several others.[97]

Franciscan Poverty

No doubt today to the student of medieval religious history, the most obvious difference between the Franciscans and other religious orders of the Middle Ages is the former's commitment to apostolic poverty. There is an enormous and growing literature on Franciscan poverty,[98] hence I will emphasize here only

96. See on this the excellent article by Brenda Bolton, "Tradition and Temerity: Papal Attitudes to Deviants, 1159–1216," in *Innocent III: Studies on Papal Authority and Pastoral Care* (Aldershot: Variorum, 1995), no. 12.

97. Hellman, Armstrong, and Short, *Francis of Assisi* 1:581.

98. Lambert, *Franciscan Poverty;* David Flood, ed., *Poverty in the Middle Ages* (Werl/Weštf.: D. Čoelde, 1975); David Burr, *Olivi and Franciscan Poverty: The Origins of the Usus Pauper Controversy* (Philadelphia: University of Pennsylvania Press, 1989).

a few key points. The foremost characteristic of Franciscan poverty was the rejection of communal property in addition to the more usual rejection of individual property. This was not exactly a novelty since the Order of Grandmont in southern France had also adopted a strict communal poverty long before the Franciscans appeared on the scene.[99] The Franciscan poverty was *voluntary* in the sense that the idea was not "to live without property"—which the many poor of the Middle Ages did anyway against their will—but "to want to live without property." The concept of voluntary poverty is prone to be misunderstood, as one might be inclined to think that to embrace voluntary poverty, one needed to start off with some property at least and renounce it in the process. However, someone who was poor to start with could also embrace voluntary poverty if he rejoiced in his poverty. Francis and his companions linked poverty inextricably to the idea of the apostolic life. No possession was allowed except for a tunic and a psalter. Contemporaries observed the strictness of Franciscan poverty as practiced by the early friars with awe and admiration. Jacques de Vitry wrote:

> These poor men of Christ carry on their journey neither purse nor pouch nor bread, nor money in their belts; they possess neither gold nor silver nor do they have shoes on their feet. Indeed, no brother of this Order is allowed to possess anything; they have no monasteries or churches, no fields nor vineyards, no animals, no houses, nor any other possessions, and they have no place to lay their heads.... If anyone out of kindness should donate something to them, they do not hold on to it for future use.[100]

The problem, of course, with this kind of very strict communal poverty was that it had an almost heretical connotation: some apostolic communities that got into trouble with the Church had also opted for such absolute poverty and had the word "Poor" in their names, such as Waldensians, commonly known as the Poor Men of Lyons, and the Poor Lombards. Francis felt the need to stress his obedience to the papacy, lest his absolute poverty were deemed threatening and seen to be undermining the structure of the property-holding institutional Church. He put obedience to the papacy alongside the term *"sine proprio"* in the opening sentence of his Rule. One contemporary witness even asserts that the name Franciscans chose for themselves was in reality an effort to distinguish themselves from the other "Poor" religious groups.

> In place of these [Waldensians] the Lord Pope approved certain others then on the rise who called themselves "Poor Minors." These rejected

---

99. On the Order of Grandmont, see Carole A. Hutchison, *The Hermit Monks of Grandmont,* Cistercian Studies Series (Kalamazoo, MI: Cistercian Publications, 1989).

100. Hellman, Armstrong, and Short, *Francis of Assisi,* 1:583.

the above-mentioned superstitious and scandalous practices, but traveled about both in winter and in summer absolutely barefoot; they accepted neither money nor anything else besides food, and occasionally a needed garment that someone might spontaneously offer them, for they would not ask anything from anyone. However, later on these men realized that their name could possibly lead to self-glorification under the cover of great humility and that, as many bear the title "poor" to no purpose, they could boast in vain before God; therefore, obedient to the Apostolic See in all things, they preferred to be called Lesser Brothers instead of Poor Minors.[101]

In the earliest phase of Franciscan history, the particular nature of Franciscan poverty, communal, voluntary, and absolute, was certainly a practical impediment to any kind of intellectual undertaking. As discussed above, the presence of books except for a psalter was quite incompatible with the way Franciscan poverty was defined. As we will see in the next chapter, however, this same apostolic poverty of the friars evolved from being an impediment to becoming a substantial justification for the friars' involvement in studies, as Franciscan scholars claimed to be better teachers in comparison with those who did not live in apostolic poverty.

One point is worth making here. The unique nature of the early Franciscan Order and its Rule, with its diversity, its throngs of recruits, and communal poverty, does not really allow for its historical treatment under the umbrella name "mendicant orders" as we often find in current scholarship. Although the foundation of the Dominicans dates to 1215, their differences from the Franciscans in the early decades of the thirteenth century were too great to place them both in the same category. The Rule of the Friars Preachers was based on that of Saint Augustine and therefore allowed for communal property, even though it should be noted that they did impose many limitations on their possessions and tried to be as poor as possible without compromising their status as an Order devoted to rigorous intellectual and spiritual training.[102] An even greater difference was that the Dominicans were a primarily clerical order from their inception, and the members did not pursue a variety of lives; they were all to be trained as preachers. Dominic, the founder, was a cleric who had preached during the Albigensian Crusade; his major aim was to preach Catholic doctrine among the heretics, so naturally the Order was dedicated to the education of its friars concerning both the scriptures and other knowledge that could be used

---

101. Testimony of Burchard of Ursperg written around 1228–1230. Ibid., 1:594.

102. William A. Hinnebusch, *The History of the Dominican Order.* (Staten Island, NY: Alba House, 1966), 145–54.

against the heretics. No Dominican lived as a hermit; instead, the Order was predominantly urban, living in the convents that they either owned or rented.[103] However, while in the beginning there were fundamental differences of mentality and *religio* between the Franciscans and the Dominicans, one could perhaps start to speak of mendicant orders as a category starting from the second half of the thirteenth century, by which point the Dominicans and Franciscans had converged to an extent.

The Rule, the Ministers, and Diversity

In the Rule of 1221, Francis made it clear that no hierarchy was to be observed in the Order.[104] Yet if the many different types of men and religious lives that coexisted within the Order were to be held together and given equal place, each to be allowed to flourish without one group lording it over another, then the Franciscans needed administrators who shared this vision. This was going to be difficult when, in spite of all the divergent forms of religious life that existed in contemporary society, "there was a contrary tendency, very well known to all who have studied the religious movements of the twelfth century, towards assimilation between the different modes,"[105] as Christopher Brooke observes. Besides, by the thirteenth century, laymen in religious orders were coming to be regarded as indisputably inferior to clerics through the working out of the implications of a Church reform movement that stressed the separation and elevation of clerical status.

These tendencies could scarcely fail to have an effect on the Franciscan Order. Would it be possible for the learned scholars and illiterate laymen to coexist with equal rights and respect, when outside of the Order they could not? Could a poor wandering hermit and a nobleman find ways of appreciating each other and call each other "brother"? Would their enthusiasm for Francis's *religio* survive the prejudices and values they could be expected to hold in general? Anyone who reads the Italian Franciscan Salimbene's famous chronicle written in the 1280s would know that this, at least in part, did not turn out to be the

---

103. The difference between the two orders was observed by contemporary witnesses. See, for example, the account of the Premonstratensian canon Burchard of Ursperg (d. 1230), who describes the Friars Minor simply as "those who went really barefoot both in the summer and winter, and received neither money nor anything else but food," and "who did not ask anything from anybody," whereas the Dominicans "constantly occupied in study, and reading the Sacred Scriptures, had no other occupation than that of writing books[,] . . . teach[ing] and commend[ing] the statutes of the Church." Edward Peters, ed., *Heresy and Authority in Medieval Europe: Documents in Translation* (Philadelphia: University of Pennsylvania Press, 1980), 179–80.

104. RNB, chap. 5. "Similiter omnes fratres non habeant in hoc potestatem vel dominationem inter se."

105. Brooke, "Priest, Deacon and Layman," in *Churches and Churchmen,* 240.

case: Salimbene of Adam was the son of a well-to-do family with complete contempt for his fellow lay friars, openly calling them *"inutiles."*[106] Francis himself, a man of considerable insight, was well aware of the difficulty, according to his biographer, Thomas of Celano:

> His constant wish and watchful concern was to foster among his sons the bond of unity, so that those drawn by the same spirit and begotten by the same father should be held peacefully on the lap of the same mother. He wanted to unite the greater to the lesser, the join the wise to be simple brother in affection, and to hold together those far from each other with the glue of love.[107]

Perhaps if the Rule of 1223 had facilitated the selection of provincial ministers and minister general from any of the groups within the Order, whatever their canonical status, whatever their level of education, there may have been some hope of maintaining egalitarian relationships among the different groups and different forms of religious life. However, the way the Rule described the duties and responsibilities of the ministers required them to have at least some knowledge of canon law and theology: "If anyone is willing to accept this life and come to our brothers, they should be sent to the provincial ministers, who alone—and no one else—have license to receive brothers. Let the ministers examine them carefully concerning the Catholic faith and the sacraments of the Church." Should a friar sin, the provincial minister should impose the penance; if the minister were not a priest, then he had to commission a priest to do so. No one was to preach unless examined and approved by the general minister. The ministers were charged with correcting and admonishing the brothers. They were to grant permission to those friars who wished to go to preach to the Saracens and nonbelievers.[108] Could an illiterate provincial minister, even with the best of intentions, satisfactorily test a postulant on the sacraments of the Church? How could a minister general, who had never studied theology, examine a preacher on the orthodoxy of his sermons? If theoretically such difficulties could be circumvented by providing uneducated ministers with clerical assistance, in practice this does not seem to have happened. The chronicles concerning the early years of the Order often add the words "lawyer, preacher, or a man of great learning" after the names of provincial ministers. In short, those who were making the decisions in the Order were drawn from the more educated friars.

---

106. Salimbene, 141. "Porro secundus defectus fratris Helye fuit quia multos inutiles recepit ad Ordinem. Habitavi in conventu Senensi duobus annis, et vidi ibi XXV fratres laycos."

107. II Celano, 191. Hellman, Armstrong, and Short, *Francis of Assisi,* 2:369–70.

108. RB, chaps. 2, 7, 9, 10, 12.

We know, for example, that the companions of Francis, friars such as Leo, Rufino, and Angelo, did not play an active role in the Order's administration, despite calling themselves "we who were with him" (*nos qui cum eo fuimus*) and having some claim to knowing Francis's true mind. It would have been useful to know whether this was a conscious choice on their part, whether they were elbowed away, or whether it was simply impractical for a friar staying in a hermitage to function as a provincial minister. The crucial point is that other friars like them, those who pursued the eremitical life, were not really represented at the administrative level. As a result, after the death of Francis the general chapters were deprived of their contribution and they were unable to check the practices emerging in the Order that they deemed against the Franciscan spirit.

The equality among a varied membership that seemed to characterize the very early Franciscan brotherhood was in effect replaced with a hierarchy that placed ministers of at least some education on top. It is true that Francis envisaged them as servants of the other friars[109] and chose the word *minister* rather than *master*. However, there was and is no escape from the fact that serving as a minister conferred a position of authority and privilege. As if to confirm this, Thomas of Celano writes that Francis resigned the office of general minister to preserve his humility.[110] Similarly, Celano observed that some brothers were eager to hold offices and wanted to place themselves over their fellow friars and that Francis saw such an attitude as incompatible with being a Friar Minor.[111] Francis both wrote and spoke frequently about humility, and repeated several times that ministers were servants, that holding office ought not to be a source of pride, and that office holders should be able to renounce their positions easily.[112]

Francis was aware of the great difficulty of finding friars fit to be ministers for an Order that embraced such different groups and people. Toward the end of his life, he was approached by a friar to name a successor as minister general. He responded that he saw no one "who would be capable of being the leader of an army of so many different men and the shepherd of so large a flock." And he went on to describe in detail his ideal minister.

> He must be a very dignified person, of great discernment, and of praiseworthy reputation....He must be someone who does not create sordid favoritism toward persons, but will take as much care of the lesser and simple brothers as of the learned and greater ones. Even if he should be allowed to excel in gifts of learning, he should all the more bear in his behavior the image of holy simplicity, and nourish this virtue...as the head of a

---

109. I Celano, 104; II Celano, 145, 188.
110. II Celano, 143.
111. Ibid., 145.
112. I Celano, 104; II Celano, 145, 188.

poor religion, offering himself to others as someone to be imitated, he must never engage in the abuse of using any money pouch. For with his needs…a habit and a little book should be enough, and, for the brothers' needs, he should have a pen case and seal. He should not be a book collector, or too intent on reading, so he does not take away from his duties what he spends on his studies.[113]

From this it would seem that the minister that Celano's Francis had in mind was one who was learned, but who, on becoming a Franciscan, would be ready to relinquish any further interest in study or in reading books, instead giving himself fully to the affairs of all the different kinds of brothers. As such, the issue of learning was ultimately tied to the issue of governance in the early Franciscan Order. The kind of learning that was concerned here might essentially be modest, the kind absolutely required of ministers: a working knowledge of Latin, a basic understanding of the creed and of canonical norms. However, once the value of a learned administrator was appreciated, it was perhaps difficult then not to go on to say the more learned, the better.[114]

The association between learning and a ministerial position in a religious order of the thirteenth century was not peculiar to the Franciscans and needs to be understood within its proper medieval context. Everywhere in Europe, men of bureaucracy and business increasingly both produced and depended on written material for the government of their affairs, a process that stretched over several centuries but had become quite pronounced by the early thirteenth century. There is nothing extraordinary in the fact that once transformed into an *ordo* that functioned under the auspices of papacy, Franciscans too formed an administrative class of clerics that possessed at least a moderate degree of education. The surviving corpus of Franciscan statutes and letters points to a considerable degree of written activity at the administrative level. Provincial ministers routinely communicated through the written word with the custodians in their province, other provincial ministers, and the minister general as well as with bishops and abbots in their province concerning various business matters of the Order, but also to exchange civilities on major saints' days.[115] Hence, Francis's allusion to a "pen case and seal."

---

113. II Celano, 185. Translation in Hellman, Short, and Amstrong, *Francis of Assisi,* 2:365.

114. This theme, the relation between learning and administrative offices, will be explained in more detail in the fourth chapter.

115. The best source highlighting this immense activity is a surviving Franciscan formulary edited by Giuseppe De Luca, "Un formulario della cancelleria francescana e altri formulari tra il XIII e XIV secolo," *Archivio italiano per la storia della pieta* 1 (1951): 219–393. Franciscan provinces were divided to smaller administrative divisions known as custodies. Heads of the custodies were called custodians. See glossary.

A notable phenomenon of the first three decades of the Order was that it was basically governed by a fixed set of provincial ministers, particularly in the provinces outside Italy. Some of the early provincial ministers did not leave office for many years, while others simply rotated among the provinces. Gregory of Naples served as the minister of the French province from 1223 to 1232–1233. Agnellus of Pisa was minister of England from the first settlement in 1224 until his death in 1236. Albert of Pisa, with an extraordinary record of mobility, was provincial minister of Tuscany (1217–1221), of the province of Saint Francis (1221–1223), of Germany (1223–1227), possibly of Spain (1227–1230), of Bologna (1230–1232), of Hungary (1232–1236), and of England (1236–1239). Finally, in 1239, he was elected minister general, but died a few months later. By the time of his death, he had acted in a ministerial position for twenty-three years, nine of them in Francis's lifetime. John of Piancarpino was minister of Germany (1228–1230), of Spain (1230–1232), and of Saxony (1232–1234), following the division of Germany into the two provinces of Saxony and the Rhine. John Parenti, who was the minister general from 1227 to 1232, had been minister of Spain in 1219.[116] Thomas of Celano seems to think that Francis was angry that some ministers lingered in their office so long and at the way they used their office:

> He was asked by that friar: "Why not change those provincial ministers who have abused their liberty for so long?" And father, groaning, gave this frightful reply: "Let them live as they like. After all, the damnation of a few is less important than the loss of many!" He did not mean these words for all but for those who seemed to have claimed the superior position by hereditary right on account of having performed it for a very long time. To all kinds of superiors of the Order, he commended above all the following: not to change their habits (mores) unless for the better, not to ask favors, not to exercise power, but to fulfill the requirements of their office.[117]

It is difficult to overestimate the influence of this first group of ministers in the promotion of learning in the Order and the recruiting of learned men.[118] It was Agnellus of Pisa, as minister of England, who asked Robert Grosseteste to teach in the convent school at Oxford, thereby founding one of the most important studia in the Order. Gregory of Naples, through his preaching, did his best to provide a stream of university masters from Parisian circles. John of Piancarpino assigned the first lector of the German province, an English scholar

---

116. Brooke, *Early Franciscan Government,* 125.

117. II Celano, 188. My translation.

118. On the significance of the early ministers in the clericalization of the Order, see also Merlo, *Nel nome di san Francesco,* 110.

from Paris suggested to him by Gregory of Naples. The General Chapter of 1239 that elected Albert of Pisa as minister general went on to issue the first major set of constitutions of the Order, among which were many statutes regulating the Order's educational activities. It was these men who made the decision to introduce theology teaching into the Order, and who implemented this and the constitutions.

The personal convictions of members of this group were given currency through their office. Naturally, in provinces like England and France, where one man remained in power throughout these formative years, a certain continuity, even a tradition, was created. Similarly, the rotation through different provinces of a minister such as Albert of Pisa must have contributed to a degree of stability and uniformity in the Order. Both the Rule and the Testament gave power over recruitment to the provincial ministers, and the decision to settle in Paris at an early date indicates that they were making an effort to recruit learned men. These ministers also gave the first instruction to novices, or to men who approached them with a view to joining the Order. What instruction did they give on the subject of learning? This is something to be explored in more depth in the next chapter, while the reasons behind the shaping of a Franciscan educational network will be examined in the third chapter. It should suffice to say here that one can hardly imagine these men advising against study at the same time as they were making an effort to recruit and appoint lectors. At this point though, we should consider the events that enabled these ministers to make and implement decisions with respect to the introduction of theology teaching into the Order.

The Paris Convent and the English Settlement

The story of the rise of learning in the Franciscan Order certainly took a decisive turn when the very learned started to enter the Order in the university towns. On April 12, 1224, four Parisian scholars, all from England, assumed the Franciscan habit in the Benedictine Abbey of Saint-Denis, where the Franciscans had been given a place by the monks within the abbey's estates.[119] It is quite likely that at the time the friars had another convent within the walls of Paris on Mont Saint-Geneviève in the so-called English quarter of Paris, which may explain why so many Englishmen joined the Order.[120] Perhaps the English were inspired

---

119. Eccleston, 27; Eccleston calls them "*magistri,*" but the term is often used for learned men as well. It is doubtful whether all of these were actually teachers at the university. Beaumont-Maillet, *Le Grand Couvent*, 15–16.

120. For the existence of this second convent in the English quarter, see John Harding, *Agnellus of Pisa 1194–1236: The First Franciscan Provincial in England (1224–1236)* (Canterbury: Franciscan Study Centre, 1979), 3; André Callebaut, "Essai sur l'origine du Premier Convent des Mineurs à Paris," *La*

by the emotive sermons of Gregory of Naples, by then provincial minister of France.[121] The four English were Haymo of Faversham, Simon of Sandwich, Bartholomeus Anglicus, and Simon Anglicus.[122] It seems unlikely that these four Paris scholars were the first scholars to join the Order, but this event is of particular historical importance, as it marks the beginning of a tradition through which the Paris convent served as the source for the earliest lectors in the Order. Many Englishmen, university scholars at various levels of their education, entered the Order in the Paris convent.[123]

Four months after the profession of the four English masters at Paris, a group of nine Franciscans from the Paris convent landed at Dover in September 1224. Perhaps seeing the four Englishmen in the gray habit convinced the provincial minister of France that the Order would have a good chance of success in England, a territory into which it had not yet ventured. Agnellus of Pisa, the Italian guardian of the Paris convent, headed the group that included three Englishmen and a mixed band of Frenchmen and Italians. The settlement policy of Agnellus and his group in England tells us a lot about the young Order's interest in schools and recruitment of the learned.[124] Within two months of their arrival in England, the friars had entered the town gates of Oxford, having settled previously in Canterbury and London. Canterbury was the metropolitan see, and London by far the greatest and most crowded city of England; hence these two cities were natural settlement points. The choice of Oxford, however, as the third location seems less straightforward since the town did not have a large population—its real importance lay in its nascent university and in the existence of a small group of Dominicans.[125] There, the Dominicans at first received the Franciscans, who soon afterward rented a house from a layman, Robert le Mercer.[126] When some bachelors of the university and other

---

France Franciscaine 11 (1928): 189; Beaumont-Maillet, *Le Grand Couvent,* 13. There is no certain proof for the existence of this second house. For a discussion of the various standpoints, see John C. Murphy, "The Early Franciscan *Studium* at the University of Paris," in *Studium Generale: Studies Offered to Astrik L. Gabriel,* ed. L. S. Domonkos and R. J. Schneider (Notre Dame, IN: Medieval Institute, University of Notre Dame, 1967), 164–66.

121. "Quis enim Gregorio [de Neapoli] in praedicatione vel praelatione in universitate Parisius vel clero totius Franciae comparabilis?" (Eccleston, 29)

122. Beaumond-Maillet, *Le Grand Couvent,* 16, using Jordan of Giordano's chronicle, suggests that Bartholomew Anglicus and Simon Anglicus were the masters called from the Paris convent to teach in Germany.

123. Eccleston, 29–30.

124. For a detailed discussion of the English settlement, see Şenocak, "In the Pursuit of Knowledge."

125. On Oxford University, see Alan B. Cobban, *The Medieval English Universities: Oxford and Cambridge to c. 1500* (Aldershot: Scholar Press, 1988).

126. Eccleston, 9. For a detailed history of the Franciscan settlement in England, see Andrew G. Little, *Grey Friars in Oxford* (Oxford: Clarendon Press, 1892), 1–28.

noblemen joined them, they rented a larger house.[127] Other settlements made in 1225 were Northampton and Cambridge. Like Oxford, Northampton was renowned for its schools, which had almost achieved the status of a *studium generale* in the twelfth century.[128] Cambridge was the site of a fast-developing university.[129] The three settlements that followed within the next three years, namely, Norwich, Worcester, and Hereford, were cathedral cities, and two of them, Norwich and Hereford, had notable cathedral schools. These settlements became the sites of the provincial schools in the Order. It is not known how these decisions were made, and the sources do not give the reasons for choosing these places. It is plausible, however, to suggest that these cities were likely chosen for being centers of learning.

After Francis—The Coming of Lectors

By the time the English settlements were being made, Francis had already withdrawn to hermitages in central Italy and had practically abandoned the government of the Order. Approximately one year after the approval of the Rule, on the Feast of the Holy Cross on September 14, 1224, he spent a whole night outside praying. Toward morning, he experienced a vision of the seraphim and following this, he discovered wounds similar to the stigmata of Christ appearing on his hands and feet and in his side.[130] Although Francis carefully hid these wounds, they were witnessed by a few brothers while he still lived, and were publicly announced by Brother Elias on his death on October 3, 1226.[131]

Shortly before his death, Francis felt that his days were numbered and undertook a task that anyone in his condition might do: he wrote a testament. Of course he had no property to distribute, but he did have enormous spiritual wealth to pass on to his friars. The Testament represents one of the most significant documents in Franciscan history.[132] Some scholars have valued it even more than the Rule, accepting it as an authentic statement of the ideals of Francis and as a revelation of the true Franciscan spirit. Other scholars have taken a more

---

127. Eccleston, 22.

128. Cobban, *Medieval English Universities,* 29. See Herbert G. Richardson, "The Schools of Northampton in the Twelfth Century," *English Historical Review* 56 (1941): 595–605.

129. For the Cambridge settlement, see John R. H. Moorman, *The Grey Friars in Cambridge, 1225–1538* (Cambridge: Cambridge University Press, 1952), 6–12; and for the medieval university there, see Cobban, *Medieval English Universities,* 50–53.

130. Moorman, *History of the Franciscan Order,* 60–61. I Celano, 94–96.

131. II Celano, 135–38.

132. Francis of Assisi, "Testamentum" in *Opuscula Sancti Patris Francisci Assisiensis,* ed. Kajetan Esser (Grottaferrata, 1978), 305–17. Kajetan Esser wrote his dissertation (later published) on the authenticity and meaning of Saint Francis's Testament. Kajetan Esser, *Das Testament des Heiligen Franziskus von Assisi: Eine Untersuchung über seine Echtheit und seine Bedeutung* (Münster: Aschendorff, 1949).

moderate view, claiming it to be simply an expression of Francis's last wishes.[133] Some have even gone so far as to call it an autobiography.[134] Lambert, agreeing with Goetz, observes that the style of the Testament is rough, and the sequence of thoughts loose, supporting the notion that the Testament was composed directly from the saint's words.[135]

In his Testament Francis asked the friars to respect the priests of the Roman Church; not to preach without their permission; to honor theologians as much as priests; to earn their living by honest work, begging for alms when not paid for work; not to receive churches and dwellings that defied the standard of Franciscan poverty; not to ask privileges from the Roman Curia; to obey the guardians and ministers; and not to place any gloss on the Rule. The Testament only strengthened what the Rule had initiated—if the lawful inheritors of Francis's Testament were the friars, its *fidecommissarii* were the ministers: "And let the general minister and all the other ministers and custodians be bound through obedience not to add to or take away from these words. And let them always have this writing with them together with the Rule. And in all the chapters which they hold, when they read the Rule, let them also read these words."[136] With these words, the responsibility of making the contents of the Testament— with no addition or subtraction—available and known to the friars was left to the ministers. If, as most of the recent scholarship does, one considers the Testament a significant document in the friars' understanding of Francis's will, then the ministers were the ones who could actually have control over whether the friars followed Francis's will or not.

In the period following Francis's death, we see the continuation of the existing trend with regard to the election of ministers: some degree of learning was considered an essential prerequisite to filling the office of minister. In May 1227, the first chapter summoned after the death of Francis was faced with the task of appointing a minister general. Until then, Brother Elias, whom Francis had appointed as his vicar, governed the Order. Instead of appointing Brother Elias minister general, the chapter elected as head of the Order the provincial minister of Spain, John Parenti, a lawyer.[137] The first task of the new minister general was to appoint a new provincial minister for Germany. On this, he took the advice of Gregory of Naples, the provincial minister of France. Gregory recommended Simon Anglicus, one of the four English scholars who had joined the Order

133. For a discussion of various standpoints on the Testament's meaning, see Lambert, *Franciscan Poverty*, 21–22.

134. Moorman, *History of the Franciscan Order*, 77.

135. Lambert, *Franciscan Poverty*, 21. Walter W. Goetz, "Die Ursprünglichen Ideale des hl. Franz von Assisi," *Historische Vierteljahrschrift* 6 (1903): 19–50.

136. Hellman, Armstrong, and Short, *Francis of Assisi*, 1:127.

137. *Chronica XXIV Generalium* in *AF* (1897), 3:210; Jordan of Giano, 51.

in 1224 at the Parisian convent.[138] The preference for this total outsider, an Englishman from the Paris convent, over any of the many friars in the German convents who would have had a better knowledge of the language and customs of Germany, is a point worth reflecting on. Here we see clear favor being given to a university-trained minister. However, the ministership of Simon lasted only a year:

> In the year 1228, . . . Brother John Parenti, the minister general, hearing that Germany had no *lector* in theology, discharged Brother Simon from being the minister of Germany, and appointed him lector, and made Brother John of Piancarpino minister of Germany.[139]

Although Jordan of Giano wrote this in 1262, there seems little doubt from the text that *lector* had long before become an office in the Order. If we are to trust Jordan's memory, 1228 is the earliest we hear of a lector anywhere in the Order. "Then Brother John of Piancarpino, wishing to honor and exalt Saxony, sent the first lector, Brother Simon, to Magdeburg, and with him good, distinguished, and learned men, the brothers Marquard of Mainz, and Conrad of Worms, and many others."[140] If a province did not have any lector at all, the minister general was responsible for providing one for it. The provincial minister made the appointment of lectors present in the province to custodies and convents.

How and when was this office of lector introduced into the Order? And what exactly did a lector do? Francis never mentions the word *lector,* and if there was such an office in his lifetime, either he would have mentioned it in his writings, or the sources concerning Francis's life would have recorded at least one anecdote where a lector is involved. The office must have been created at a Chapter General after the death of Francis, in 1227 or 1228.

John Parenti had assigned Simon Anglicus as lector because Germany had no lector. One might infer from this that at least some other provinces had lectors. In fact, it is quite possible that even before the office of lector was formally introduced into the Order, some learned friars had started teaching theology to other friars. The first evidence of a friar teaching theology to other friars comes from a letter written by Francis to Anthony of Padua. A famous preacher, and today one of the most popular saints in the Catholic Church, Anthony had joined the Order after 1220, and quickly achieved a legendary reputation through his sermons. Apparently he wrote to the founder for permission to

---

138. Jordan of Giano, 52.

139. "Anno Domini 1228 . . . frater Johannes Parens minister audiens, quod Theutonia lectorem in theologia non haberet, absolvit fratrem Symonem a ministerio Theutonie et lectorem instituit et fratrem Johannem de Plano Carpinis ministrum Theutonie destinavit" (Jordan of Giano, 54).

140. Jordan of Giano, 54.

teach theology to the friars, and Francis replied with a brief letter: "It pleases me that you teach sacred theology to the friars, provided that you do not extinguish the spirit of prayer and devotion, as it is said in the Rule."[141] This letter, however, does not constitute sufficient evidence to argue for the existence of organized teaching of theology in the Order in Francis's lifetime.

Since no description of what the office of lector entailed survives from the early sources or constitutions, we can make only educated guesses by extrapolating from later information. It can be safely assumed that it was primarily introduced to give the friars some theological training. Unless stated otherwise, a Franciscan lector was a lector in theology, and until the introduction of arts into the educational curriculum in the late 1250s, a typical *lectio* in practice meant the reading and explanation of parts of the Bible. The lector and the friars would meet in a designated room in the convent, called the *studium,* at regular times. Friar Salimbene of Adam tells us that he attended the *lectiones* of Humilis of Milan on the Book of Isaiah and Gospel of Matthew in the 1240s.[142] Often lectors used the lectures of other, more famous lectors in the Order. An English lector named Stephen carried with him the *Lectura super Genesim* of the lector of the Oxford convent, Adam Marsh, and lectured to the friars from this text.[143] Throughout the thirteenth century, we find numerous examples of a friar being appointed to the office of lector for a few years, then chosen as guardian, or custodian, or provincial minister, and after a few years reverting to the office of lector. That suggests that the qualification once gained to become a lector was deemed permanent, but not necessarily the office itself.

Perhaps the most important question here is why the office of lector was introduced. Remarkably, the sources are completely silent on this point. Both Jordan of Giano and Thomas Eccleston, in whose chronicles we find much information about the earliest lectors, do not say anything about when, how, or why this particular office was created. They all seem to assume that it was part of the normal growth of the Order. Certainly, the introduction of this office did not create any tumult or controversy in the Order that caught the attention of these chroniclers.[144] A simple explanation for the creation of this office would be that the Franciscans decided to imitate the Dominicans, who had instituted the office of lector into their Order's structure much earlier. Even though no

---

141. Esser, *Opuscula Sancti Patris Francisci Assisiensis,* 94–95. This letter was known to Celano, who mentions it in the *Second Life;*see II Celano, 163. See also *Chronica XXIV Generalium,* in *AF* 3:132.

142. "Et audivi primo anno, quo intravi ordinem, in scolis theologie Ysaiam et Matheum, sicut frater Humilis legebat ibidem" (Salimbene of Adam, 277).

143. "Habebat optima scripta, scilicet fratris Adae de Marisco, cuius lectura super Genesim audivi ab eo" (ibid., 296).

144. Dieter Berg also suggests that the introduction of studies was supported by "strong forces" within the Order. Berg, *Armut und Wissenschaft,* 68.

direct evidence can be cited to support this point, it is nevertheless possible. Dominicans had often given hospitality to Franciscans on the arrival of the latter in the university towns, and this way Franciscans would have had a chance to observe firsthand the educational activities of the Dominicans. Yet why did the Franciscans wait until 1227 to imitate the Dominicans in instituting the office of lector? There is no denying that there was some convergence between the two Orders during the course of the thirteenth century, but it is important to mark the steps of this convergence and to determine whether similar initiatives were introduced for the same reasons. As we know well, the two Orders retained otherwise distinct administrative structures. So why was this particular office imitated by the Franciscans? This question about the office of lector in the Franciscan Order is clearly one of the central questions this book attempts to answer, and it would not do the question justice to accept imitation alone as a sufficient explanation.

The settlement by Franciscans in Paris in 1219 was a step on the road to the creation of the office of lector. In the years that followed, the English recruits from the University of Paris seem to have been the major source for the provision of lectors. Haymo of Faversham, one of the four university scholars who joined in 1224, served in the Order as lector for a number of periods, although the specific dates of his tenures of the office are not known. The English chronicler Eccleston tells us that Haymo was appointed first as the custodian of the Paris convent, and afterward took the post of lector at Tours, Bologna, and Padua.[145] When Simon Anglicus, the first lector in Germany, died in 1230, the ministers of the two German provinces of Saxony and the Rhineland demanded a new lector from the minister general. Again, the appeal was referred to the French Province. The minister general asked the provincial minister of France to send Bartholomeus Anglicus as lector to Germany.[146]

It is possible that the entry of Parisian scholars into the Order slowed down in 1229, since the University of Paris entered a period of turmoil that year. A great number of masters and students left Paris as a result of a dispute with the townspeople and dispersed throughout Europe. Some of them left for the new studium generale in Toulouse, initiated by none other than Gregory IX, who offered competitive wages to scholars who would take up teaching posts there.[147] Quite a few Parisian scholars went to England at the invitation of the king, Henry III, some to the University of Oxford and others to Cambridge. By the beginning of

---

145. Eccleston, chap. 6.

146. It is almost certain that this Barthelomeus Anglicus is identical with the author of *De rerum proprietaribus*. See Thomas Plasmann, "Bartholomaeus Anglicus," *AFH*, 12 (1919): 68–109. See also Murphy, "The Early Franciscan *Studium*," 167–68.

147. Hastings Rashdall, *The Universities of Europe in the Middle Ages*, 3 vols., ed. Maurice Powicke and Alfred B. Emden (Oxford: Clarendon Press, 1936), 1:163.

1231, the University of Paris had almost ceased to exist.[148] In these years, there-fore, there must have been a particular shortage in the provision of lectors. This crisis may explain why, sometime around 1229–1230, Agnellus of Pisa, the provincial minister of England, instead of requesting a suitable lector from the Parisian convent, asked Robert Grosseteste, a famous regent master in theology at the University of Oxford, to teach in the Franciscan convent of Oxford.[149] Grosseteste accepted the invitation and became the first lector of the Oxford convent.[150] This practice of employing a secular lector continued in the Oxford convent for almost fifteen years until the assignment of the first homegrown Franciscan lector, Adam Marsh.[151] Technically, it would be wrong to call such outsiders lectors, since they could not receive this office officially without being friars. Apart from the English province, we have no other evidence for outsid-ers being employed to teach the friars. Once the Order embraced all levels of intellectual activity, slowly a system of education evolved, which produced homegrown lectors. The lectorship developed into a career, starting after the novitiate and leading on to the schools of Paris and Oxford.

Doubts about the Rule and Gregory IX's Response: *Quo Elongati*

Francis had stated in his Testament that the Rule was not to be interpreted.[152] The Rule was perhaps clear on certain principles, but as a regulating text it did not, and could not, deal with every contingency; nor could it provide a ready answer to every question about the legitimacy of a particular course of action. Soon questions and doubts arose over how to understand certain parts of the Rule.[153] Yet no one in the Order, not even the minister general or the General Chapter, had the jurisdiction to be able to offer an official interpretation on a Rule that bore the seal of papacy. Therefore, John Parenti, himself trained in law, appointed formal delegates to seek from the pope a settlement of some prob-lematic points in the Rule.[154]

---

148. Ibid., 1:335–38.

149. "Ampliato loco, ubi principale studium florebat in Anglia, et ubi universitas scholarium con-venire consuevit, fecit frater Agnellus scholam satis honestam aedificari in loco fratrum, et impetravit a sanctae memoriae magistro Roberto Grosseteste, ut legeret ibi fratribus." (Eccleston, 48).

150. Richard W. Southern, *Robert Grosseteste: The Growth of an English Mind in Medieval Europe,* 2nd ed. (Oxford: Clarendon Press, 1992), 75.

151. Eccleston, 50.

152. "Testamentum," 316.

153. "Tempore istius Generalis, ut dicit frater Bonaventura de Balnoregio in quodam sermone, insurrexit inter fratres multiplex dubitatio de his quae in regula continentur" (*Chronica XXIV Generalium,* in *AF* 3:213).

154. "Sane constitutis nuper in praesentia nostra Nunciis, quos vos filii Ministri misistis, qui eratis in Capitulo generali congregati et te, fili Generalis Minister, personaliter comparante, fuit nobis expositum,

The man who sat on the papal throne in Rome in 1230 was none other than the former Cardinal Hugolino, who had by now assumed the pontifical name of Gregory IX. Having been involved in the Order's affairs for a long time both as cardinal protector and as Francis's friend, Gregory IX was an ideal choice as an authority to approach on questions concerning the Rule. One of the first items on the friars' agenda was the Testament. Francis had made certain demands of the friars in the Testament that were not in the Rule, such as not seeking papal privileges and not interpreting the Rule. Were the friars under any canonical obligation to follow the stipulations of the Testament? "No," said the pope. Canonically speaking, the Testament had no binding power on the friars. It was only the Rule that carried with it the legal status conferred by the papal bull that contained it. The Testament was not part of the Rule, so its observance was only a matter of conscience.[155]

Furthermore, concerning the issue of the material needs of friars and their lodgings, the Pope gave his permission for the friars to have recourse to "agents," that is, some of the secular faithful, *amici spirituales,* who could receive money from donors and buy with it necessities for the friars. Though repeating the prohibition on communal and private property that was contained in the Rule, the pope allowed the "use" of necessary things, including books among those necessities. The use of these items by individual friars was to be at the discretion of the ministers.[156] For the purposes of the pursuit of learning, this decree was very important, since it removed a serious obstacle to educational activities by allowing the use of necessary materials such as parchment, ink, and books.

The Pope: The Usual Suspect?

In his Testament, Francis had referred to Gregory IX as both the "Protector" and "Corrector" of his Order. His firm trust in the pope's judgment is not, however, matched by some of the modern historians. Quite a few scholars have interpreted *Quo elongati* as a relaxation to the Rule, the bull standing as the ultimate proof that the papacy was using the Franciscans for its own ends and thereby destroying the true legacy of Francis, turning the friars from simple holy men into a privileged clerical order.[157] In 1987, concerning Gregory's assertion that

---

quod in regula vestra quaedam dubia et obscura quaedam intellectu difficilia continentur" *(BF,* 1, no. 56, p. 68); see also Eccleston, 66.

155. *BF,* 1, no. 56.

156. "Dicimus itaque, quod nec in communi, nec in speciali debeant proprietatem habere; sed utensilium, ac librorum et eorum mobilium, quae licet habere, eorum usum habeant" *(BF,* 1, no. 56, p. 69).

157. See Moorman, *History of the Franciscan Order,* 90–91. Etienne Gilson argued that Cardinal Hugolino made Elias an instrument of the papal Curia and promoted university studies; Gilson, *The Philosophy of Saint Bonaventure,* trans. I. Trethowan and F. J. Sheed (New York: Sheed & Ward, 1938), 47. For Sabatier, the papal plans had started even before *Quo elongati.* Concerning the bull of privileges on

the Testament was not legally binding, Nimmo wrote as follows: "No-one will deny that, in practical terms, it was justified. At the same time it drove such a wedge between the friars as by itself, perhaps, made certain the fraternity's future disintegration. It is sobering indeed to find the springs of the Franciscan tragedy set in motion hardly four years after Francis's death, and by the man who had been his friend and counselor, and had pronounced his canonization."[158]

It is not the canonical status of the Testament, but the discussion concerning the use of movable goods that is the compelling issue in *Quo elongati*. The introduction of the possibility of material support from "spiritual friends" was a significant compromise of Franciscan poverty. It meant that in practice the friars now had the chance of getting whatever they needed without relying on someone to donate it at the actual time of need. Also, the specific inclusion of books among the movable goods that Franciscans could use certainly cleared the obstacles that lay between the friars and the schools. Yet it would be going too far to presume papal initiative on either of these points. Gregory's judgment was given in response to appeals by the Franciscan delegates. It was not that the bull encouraged study by the friars, but it made it a more practical possibility.

What were the pope's reasons for allowing the friars the use of books? There is a complex story here. Gregory IX stands in a unique position in relation to the Order's development. In 1218, shortly after his encounter with Francis, he was appointed as the cardinal protector at the express wish of the saint.[159] This is quite interesting as Francis himself in the Testament insisted that no special privileges were to be ever asked from the papacy. Did he not consider having a cardinal protector in the Roman Curia a special privilege? Cardinal protectors at the curiae of particular kings and nations were not unprecedented.[160] However, no religious order before the Franciscans had possessed such a special representative. It is also worth noting that the powers, and the limits of the authority of cardinal protectors, were never juridically defined.[161] After 1227, in his capacity as Pope Gregory IX, Hugolino had become the protector not only of the

---

March 22, 1222, and the Franciscans' involvement in the papal mission to Lisbon with the bull *Ex parte* of March 29, 1222, Paul Sabatier argued that "la papauté, activant de toutes ses forces ces transformations.... Le fait que le pape donnait aux frères le soin de choisir eux-mêmes les mesures à prendre, prouve combien on était pressé à Rome d'oublier le but dans lequel ils avaient été créés, pour les transformer en chargés d'affaires du Saint-Siège"; Paul Sabatier, *Vie de S. François d'Assise*, 9th ed. (Paris: Librairie Fischbacher, 1894), 313. From a similar perspective but with a positive tone, Hilarin Felder argued that the popes demonstrated a zeal in attracting the mendicant orders to the universities, that the pope himself assigned a "scientific mission" to the mendicant orders; Felder, *Geschichte*, 113.

158. Nimmo, *Reform and Division*, 56.

159. Moorman, *History of the Franciscan Order*, 47. The first bull addressed to Hugolino about the funds for building the houses of the Poor Clares is dated August 27, 1218.

160. Stephen L. Forte, *The Cardinal-Protector of the Dominican Order*, Dissertationes Historicae, Fasc. 15, Institutum Historicum FF. Praedicatorum (Rome: ad A. Sabinae, 1959), 9.

161. Ibid., 15.

Franciscans but of the whole of Christendom. In 1230, when the Franciscan delegation came up with their questions, heresy was one of the major issues on the pope's agenda. He was deeply disappointed with the inability of the bishops and other local prelates to deal with the spreading heresies, and was trying to design new approaches, which culminated the next year in the formation of the Inquisition.[162]

Scholastic learning and universities constituted another issue that confronted the pope. The theology faculties were prone to ideas that verged on, or even sometimes toppled over into, heresy. Indeed, Innocent III, while pursuing the dream of a well-educated clergy who could explain Christianity and the scriptures to the laity, had had some doubts about the university theology faculties as proper replacements for the cathedral schools of old as centers of study of the *sacra pagina*. This much we can tell from the provisions on the education of the clergy of the Fourth Lateran Council. It is likely that the pantheistic heresy of 1206–1210 at the University of Paris contributed to Innocent III's suspicions.[163] Gregory IX, on the other hand, believed in the universities, despite the challenges they presented, regarding them as representing a great opportunity to advance the education of the clergy. Gregory himself was an alumnus of the University of Paris, and like his predecessor, Honorius III, saw the universities as potential weapons in the battle against heresy, as long as the Church could maintain a degree of control over what was taught. Gregory IX supported the cause of the university masters in 1231 during the dispersion of the University of Paris, despite the dissent of the papal legate.[164]

Popular heresies had much to do with the growing lay interest in the Bible. Largely *illiterati*—that is, unable to read Latin—laymen in various parts of Europe sought to have the Bible translated into the vernacular.[165] Peter Waldo, founder of the Waldensians, for example, commissioned a scribe and a translator

---

162. Albert C. Shannon, *The Popes and Heresy in the Thirteenth Century* (Villanova, PA: Augustinian Press, 1949), 24–25.

163. See on this J. M. M. H. Thijssen, "Master Amalric and the Amalricians: Inquisitorial Procedure and the Suppression of Heresy at the University of Paris," *Speculum* 71 (1996): 43–65. In 1210, the Synod of Paris condemned the works of Aristotle on natural philosophy, declaring his commentaries to be heretical and forbidding them to be read publicly or privately for three years until they were checked for errors. "Librorum Aristotelis, qui de naturali philosophia inscripti sunt, ante paucos annos Parisiis coeceperunt lectitari: interdicta est tribus annis, quia ex ipsis errorum semina viderentur exorta." Giovan Domenico Mansi, *Sacrorum conciliorum nova amplissima collectio* (Florence, 1759), 22:804.

164. Rashdall, *The Universities,* 1:337–38. For the championing of universities by Honorius III and Gregory IX, see ibid., 2:163.

165. Innocent III's response to a letter from the bishop of Metz: "Sane significavit nobis venerabilis frater noster Metensis episcopus per litteras suas quod tam in dioecesi quam urbe Metensi laicorum et mulierum multitudo non modica tracta quodammodo desiderio Scripturarum, Evangelia, Epistolas Pauli, Psalterium, moralia Job et plures alios libros sibi fecit in Gallico sermone transferri, translationi hujusmodi adeo libenter, utinam autem et prudenter, intendens, ut secretis conventionibus talia inter se laici et mulieres eructare praesumant, et sibi invicem praedicare." *Patrologia Latina,* vol. 214, col. 0695C,

to translate the gospels, some parts of Bible, and the books of the Church Fathers into the vernacular.[166] Rather than confronting the considerable difficulties of providing vernacular translations based on sound Catholic exegesis, the papacy preferred to try to satisfy lay interest through the preaching of clerics specially trained for the task. By the time the Albigensian Crusade drew to a close in 1229, Romano Frangipani, the papal legate, had published forty-five decrees at the Council of Toulouse, among which was a decree prohibiting the possession of the New and Old Testament by the laity; in future, only the possession of the Psalter, Breviary, and the Hours of the Holy Virgin was allowed. It was also forbidden to have these books translated into the vernacular.[167] Perhaps to compensate for these prohibitions, the pope founded the first papal university in 1229 at Toulouse in the heartlands of Albigensian heresy.[168] Universities were to be bastions of sound Catholic doctrine and of its promotion through education.

A pope who was so convinced of the utility of university learning as to establish a university himself was unlikely to discourage the friars' interest in studying theology by severely limiting their use of books. It is also quite possible that he feared that this fast-expanding order—now that its saintly founder was dead—could fall into the pit of heresy if not protected. Many uneducated, simpleminded laymen had joined the Order who could easily be convinced of heretical opinions. Should heresy begin to spread among the Franciscans, a great disaster would ensue. It was natural that the pope would be inclined to allow those friars who were capable to receive a proper theological training, if they chose to do so, if only so that they could then instruct and guide the rest. As stressed above, the pope did not prescribe formal, advanced education; rather, he removed the obstacles to it. Under the circumstances, it would have been highly surprising had he discouraged it.

There is insufficient evidence to conclude that the papacy deliberately interfered with the development of the Franciscan Order so that it could use its members as preachers and inquisitors. In fact, the papacy began to use the Franciscans for pastoral care only after the Order had firmly placed itself on the path of learning. In 1230, too much was unclear about the nature of the Order. The Dominicans, who were fully determined to become "free lances of pastoral care," to use Leonard Boyle's term, seemed much more immediately suitable for

http://www.documentacatholicaomnia.eu/01p/1198-1216,_SS_Innocentius_III,_Regestorum_Sive_Epistolarum_[AD_1198-1202],_MLT.pdf.

166. Brenda Bolton, "Poverty as Protest: Some Inspirational Groups at the Turn of the Twelfth Century," in *Innocent III: Studies on Papal Authority and Pastoral Care,* Variorum Collected Studies, vol. 490 (Aldershot: Variorum, 1995), 1–11.

167. Charles-Joseph Hefele and H. Leclercq, *Histoire des conciles d'après les documents originaux* (1907–1952)(10 vols., Paris, 1913), 5:1498.

168. For the championing of universities by Honorius III and Gregory IX, see Rashdall, *Universities of Europe,* 2:163.

the many purposes of the papacy.[169] Such papal hesitation with regard to the Franciscan Order is reflected in the papal treatment of both orders in matters concerning pastoral care and the Inquisition.[170] In spite of Gregory IX's partiality for the Franciscans, it is remarkable that he appointed only a single Franciscan bishop, whereas he elevated thirty-one Dominicans to episcopal sees. It is only during the pontificate of Innocent IV (1243–1254) that the Franciscans begin to catch up, twenty-four of them then becoming bishops.[171] Similarly, while Dominicans, by 1227, were permitted to hear confessions generally of those outside of their Order, the Franciscans received a more limited permission to hear confessions of those attending their sermons in 1237, and confessions generally only in 1250.[172] Dominicans received general rights to perform burials in 1227. At that time the Franciscans were permitted to bury only their own friars, receiving general rights to perform burials much later, in 1250. Furthermore, Dominicans acted as inquisitors from the foundation of the Inquisition in 1231. The first papal mandate sending Franciscans on a inquisitorial mission together with Dominicans dates from 1237, while the general mandate of Innocent IV to the Franciscans with regard to inquisition came as late as 1254.[173]

Often cited by scholars as papal encouragement of the Franciscans to work against heretics, the papal letter of 1227 to the friars of Marches of Treviso, giving consent to the friars to preach against heresy, has been shown in a 2005 study to be a response to a request made by the friars themselves, encouraged by Bishop Ziliberto of Vicenza, rather than a papal initiative.[174] Certainly, papal confidence in the Franciscans was gradually increasing; while in 1230 Gregory IX restricted the right to accept or reject novices to the provincial ministers of the Order, by 1241 he was allowing guardians and custodians to do so, and this extension was made with the convents in the university towns particularly in

---

169. Leonard E. Boyle, "Robert Grosseteste and Pastoral Care," in *Pastoral Care, Clerical Education and Canon Law, 1200–1400* (London: Variorum Reprints, 1981), 12, where he actually uses this term for both Franciscans and Dominicans, initially applying it to the Dominicans.

170. This gap with regard to concessions is pointed out in Andrews, *Early Humiliati,* 222; Andrews offers an explanation in terms of "the relative clericalization of the two orders, as well as the prohibition in the Testament of Francis in requesting privileges from the Roman Curia."

171. Paul R. Oliger, *Les évêques reguliers: Recherche sur leur condition juridique depuis les origines du monachisme jusqu'a la fin du Moyen Age* (Paris-Louvain: Desclée de Brouwer, 1958), 128–34. See also Williell R. Thomson, *Friars in the Cathedral: The First Franciscan Bishops 1226–1261* (Toronto: Pontifical Institute of Mediaeval Studies, 1975), 11–12.

172. Andrews, *Early Humiliati,* 222. Franciscans, however, received the concession to listen to the confessions of the people who attended their sermons in 1237.

173. On the Franciscans and the Inquisition, see Holly J. Grieco, "Pastoral Care, Inquisition, and Mendicancy," in *The Origin, Development, and Refinement of Medieval Religious Mendicancies,* ed. D. Prudlo (Leiden: Brill, 2011), 133–35.

174. Andrea Piazza, "Alle origini del coinvolgimento dei Minori contro l'eresia: I frati di Angarano nella Marca di Ezzelino da Romano," *Bullettino dell'Istituto storico italiano per il Medio Evo* 107 (2005): 210–12.

mind.[175] On the issue of preaching, Gregory IX waited until 1237 to issue the bull *Quoniam abundavit iniquitas,* which addressed all secular prelates, recommending the Friars Minor as suitable preachers.[176] This bull was based on a papal bull with the same name and similar content issued to Dominicans in 1221.[177] In Germany, the papacy in the early 1230s seems to have preferred to employ Dominicans rather than Franciscans to preach a crusade, probably because the Franciscans were predominantly lay and uneducated, largely belonging to the lower social strata and therefore thought less effective at influencing the ministerials, patricians, or local authorities.[178]

Nevertheless, a picture emerges: until the late 1230s the papacy looked quite differently on the Dominicans and Franciscans. While papal confidence in the Dominican Order seems to have been total from the beginning, the Franciscans were viewed with some hesitation and uncertainty as to whether the Order was ready to enjoy certain privileges, or whether it was ready to be employed by the papacy in certain aspects of pastoral care. This comes as no surprise—the papacy was well aware of the sui generis nature of the Franciscan Order, with its diversity of men and forms of religious life. The early Dominican Order, with its fully clerical membership all settled in urban convents and receiving a solid formation in theology, was so much more attuned to fulfilling the duties of pastoral care than the Franciscans, a mix of lay and cleric, learned and ignorant, living in the countryside as well as the cities. That the hesitation and uncertainty over the Franciscans started to be overcome by the second half of the 1230s is readily understandable. If at least some lectors were in place by 1228, it was in the course of the 1230s that some flesh began to be put on the bones of an educational organization to train Franciscan friars.

Elias of Cortona

In 1232, the minister general John Parenti died, and the General Chapter faced the challenge of appointing a suitable successor. Elias of Cortona, friend of Francis and former vicar of the Order, had been bypassed in 1227, possibly so that he could take full charge of the project of constructing a basilica in Assisi. By 1232, however, he appeared to be the best candidate, and was finally elected as minister general. Historically, Elias is a difficult figure to deal with since the medieval perception of him shows a striking change

175. "Praecipue in locis, ad quae Ecclesiastici seculares, et laici diversarum nationum conveniunt scientiae litteralis obtentu" (*Gloriantibus vobis, BF,* 1.344.298). Landini, "Causes of the Clericalization," 67.

176. *BF,* 1.214.224.

177. Landini, "Causes of the Clericalization," 66. Michael Tangl, *Die päpstlichen Kanzleiordnungen von 1200–1500* (Inssbruck: Verlag der Wagnerschen Universitäts), 285.

178. This is what John B. Freed argued quite convincingly. See Freed, *Friars and German Society,* 128.

within a period of eleven years.[179] While the *Vita prima* of Thomas Celano written in 1228 shows Elias very sympathetically,[180] and as a close friend of Francis, by 1239 the General Chapter deposed him in his absence for the offensive way he ruled the Order. He fled to the imperial court of Frederick II and was subsequently excommunicated. Works composed after 1239, such as the chronicles of Thomas of Eccleston and Salimbene de Adam, present him as nothing less than the devil on earth. He was favored neither by the leading clerics of the Order, who orchestrated his deposition, nor by later dissenters such as Angelo Clareno.

Let us first deal with the question of whether Elias, as minister general, fostered or prevented the advance of learning within the Order. As I will discuss in depth in the next chapter, at the time of his deposition in 1239, the basic framework of the educational organization had already been formed. This makes the years of Elias's ministry, stretching from 1232 to 1239, a crucial period for the consolidation of learning within Franciscan practice. For Salimbene, the only good that ever came from Elias was his support for the progress of the study of theology in the Order.[181] He appointed an English scholar, Samson, as lector to the convent of Parma. In Fano, Salimbene studied with a lector called Humilis of Milan, who had studied in Bologna under Haymo of Faversham.[182] Fano was probably one of the convents of study for the province of the Marches of Ancona. Eccleston tells us that Elias appointed Philip of Wales and Adam of York as lectors to Lyon.[183] Lyon was most probably the designated convent of study for the province of Burgundy, a province that Elias himself created. Soon after accession of Elias, lectors were found not just in each province but often in each custody of a province. According to Eccleston, Albert of Pisa, on his election as the provincial minister in 1236, appointed lectors to London and Canterbury.[184] The enlisting as a Friar Minor of Alexander of Hales in 1236, a regent doctor of theology in Paris, was an event of great significance that took place during Elias's time as minister general. It contributed greatly to the popularity of the Franciscans within scholarly circles in Paris, since Alexander was famous, and also enabled Franciscans to follow the lectures of a professor holding a chair in Paris.

---

179. For divergent opinions on Elias, see Moorman, *History of the Franciscan Order,* 96–104; Brooke, *Early Franciscan Government,* 137–67; Barone, *Da frate Elia,* 29–86.

180. For discussion of Celano's positive treatment of Elias, see Barone, *Da frate Elia,* 36–39.

181. "Nam hoc solum habuit bonum frater Helyas, quia ordinem fratrum Minorum ad studium theologie promovit" (Salimbene, 104).

182. Ibid. See also 277.

183. Eccleston, 49. Probably these lectors were appointed at different times. As there was a shortage at this time, it is unreasonable that one convent should have had two lectors.

184. Ibid.

Salimbene wrote that one of the greatest evils of Elias was his appointment of lay brothers to high administrative posts. It would seem that Elias, while encouraging the education of friars, did not at all aspire to create a clerical order on the model of the Dominicans. Rosalind Brooke argues that the ministers were not pleased with Elias's evenhanded approach to laymen and clerics, preferring to see the Friars Minor coming more into line with the older, predominantly clerical, orders.[185] Whatever the reason for the dissatisfaction with Elias might be, Elias does not seem to have tried to displace the established group of long-serving provincial ministers. When he was elected, Agnellus of Pisa remained as provincial minister of England, John of Piancarpino became minister of Saxony, and Albert of Pisa took the ministry of Hungary. Among the long-serving provincial ministers, only Gregory of Naples seems to have been removed from the office of provincial minister, a certain Brother Bonaventura being assigned instead to the post and holding this office until 1238.[186] However, Gregory's removal from office appears not to have been the result of personal conflict between him and Elias but of a papal bull issued against Gregory in 1233. When Agnellus of Pisa died in 1236, apparently not allowing the provincial chapter to choose its own candidate, Brother Elias appointed Albert of Pisa to England.[187] The provincial ministers had other reasons to be annoyed with Elias. During his seven years in office, he appears to have summoned only one General Chapter, that of 1233, from which no decrees have survived.[188] He was grossly unpopular for the visitations that he orchestrated, during which the visiting friars came to be seen as spying for Elias on the affairs of the provinces.[189]

Apart from Salimbene's remarks, one other event suggests negative sentiments existed between Elias and the learned clerics.[190] At the General Chapter, the Englishman Haymo of Faversham, a notable Paris-trained scholar, criticized Elias. A personal dislike may have existed between the two men. Eccleston tells us that Haymo of Faversham was custodian of Paris, and later lector of Bologna, Padua, and Tours.[191] The importance of Paris needs no comment, while Bologna was one of the most important study-convents. It was probably after 1227 that Haymo was assigned there as lector. By 1230, he was in the delegation

---

185. Brooke, *Early Franciscan Government*, 161.

186. According to *Cum ordinem* of June 28, 1233, Gregory of Naples is referred as *olim quidam Minister in Francia, videlicet Fr. Gregorius;* Antoine de Sérent, "Bulla inedita Gregorii IX contra Fr. Gregorium Neapolitanum quondam provinciae Franciae ministrum data 28 Iunii 1233," *AFH* 26 (1933): 6. The accession of Gregory's successor, Bonaventura, to the ministry of France is known again from his surviving letters from the years 1234 and 1238. Ibid., 23–24.

187. Eccleston, 78. The date of the Agnellus's death is not exactly known.

188. Moorman, *History of the Franciscan Order*, 98.

189. Brooke, *Early Franciscan Government*, 193.

190. Ibid., 67–68.

191. Eccleston, 28.

sent by John Parenti to Gregory IX, which prompted the bull *Quo elongati*.[192] Under the ministry of John Parenti, the province of Lombardy was divided into three as Bologna, the Marches of Treviso (Saint Anthony), and Genoa.[193] Padua would then have been the usual choice of study-convent for the province of the Marches of Treviso, since the city hosted a growing university. If the Order adhered to its rule of assigning a lector for each province, Haymo might have been sent to Padua sometime after 1230. Elias, however, appointed Haymo as lector to the small province of Tours, newly created by Elias, presumably after Haymo's return from a papal mission to the East to negotiate with the Eastern Church around 1234. Tours had no university, its province consisting of only a few convents formerly divided between the larger provinces of France and Provence.[194] Such an appointment would seem to represent a demotion for Haymo, or even a deliberate move by Elias to exclude him from Italy, placing him in a province where his influence in the government of the Order would be minimal.[195] In fact, after Elias's deposition in 1239, his successor, Minister General Albert of Pisa, immediately promoted Haymo of Faversham as the new provincial minister of England.

Haymo of Faversham and the Beginning of a New Franciscanism

The General Chapter of 1239 that deposed Elias and elected Albert of Pisa as the minister general went on to issue the Order's first general set of constitutions or statutes. Salimbene tells us that the constitutions issued on this occasion were "many in number," and that Bonaventure later put them in order.[196] Until 1990, the Narbonne constitutions of 1260 were the earliest extant constitutions known to scholars.[197] However, in 1990, Cesare Cenci published the discoveries he had made at Rome of some *membra disiecta* under the title of the

---

192. Ibid., 67.

193. Golubovich, *Biblioteca bio-bibliografica*, 2:228.

194. Ibid., 2:229.

195. Eccleston, 86–87. This scheme depends on the hypothesis that each province was assigned a lector. Haymo was commissioned by the pope for an Eastern visit around 1233–1234. On this mission see ibid., 200–201. Thus, it might have been on his return that he was appointed lector of Tours. Roest, on the other hand, argues that Haymo was lector in Bologna between 1233–1238 and that he was appointed to Padua before he was elected minister general; Roest, *History of Franciscan Education,* 45, 58n. However, before his election as minister general, Haymo of Faversham was provincial minister of England. See Eccleston, 85–86.

196. "Et in illo capitulo facta est maxima multitudo constitutionum generalium, sed non erant ordinate; quas processu temporis ordinavit frater Bonaventura generalis minister, et parum addidit de suo, sed penitentias taxavit in aliquibus locis" (Salimbene, 158–59).

197. Brooke (*Early Franciscan Government,* 210–46) tried to recover the 1239 constitutions by searching through later documents and chronicles.

pre-Narbonne constitutions, which are likely to have been made in the general chapters held between 1239 and 1254. Relying on Salimbene's evidence, Cenci also suggested that the majority of these constitutions must have been made in the General Chapter of 1239. After the discovery of the fragments of an older set of constitutions in Todi dating from 1239–1241, he revised the dating of the pre-Narbonne constitutions and suggested that the bulk of the constitutions must have been made at the 1242 General Chapter.[198] Among these pre-Narbonne constitutions, we find quite a few that address the educational activities of the Order: the Paris convent was to be visited every year by a special *visitator* chosen by the minister general, and any insolent students were to be sent away. A studium is mentioned as a part of the convent, like the refectory or dormitory. Two students from each province were to be sent Paris. The constitutions also contained regulations concerning the writing and the procurement of books.[199] These regulations leave no doubt that the Order kept and used books, and that the Paris studium was intended to train lectors, who were then sent to the provinces to teach friars. In broad terms, the backbone of the Order's educational structure was well established already by 1242, and parts of that structure perhaps even before that. Later constitutions elaborated and dealt with more technical and logistical detail, and the Narbonne constitutions of 1260 presented the constitutions in an orderly way.

When Albert of Pisa died in 1240, the General Chapter summoned by Gregory IX elected Haymo of Faversham as minister general.[200] Even though Haymo of Faversham ruled only for four years, from 1240 to 1244, his term in office is marked with so many "firsts" that it signals a new era in the history of Franciscanism. Haymo was the first minister general educated in Paris. After him, this became the norm. Almost all of the Franciscan minister generals of the Middle Ages after Haymo were theologians, who not only had studied but had often taught in Paris. Haymo was also the first minister general from the northern side of Alps. A practical reason for the minister generals to be predominantly from Italy was that half of the provinces were Italian, and Italy was represented by a clear majority at the general chapters. However, the election of Haymo was not that surprising for several reasons. He had served as lector in Bologna, Padua, and Tours, and by this time probably some of his former students were serving as ministers and custodians in Italy, and were therefore part of the General Chapter that elected him. The pope had a high opinion of him, having sent him in 1233 to the East for negotiations with the Eastern Church. However, Haymo was also

198. Cenci, "Fragmenta priscarum," 290, n. 6.

199. Pre-Narbonne, 75, no. 29, 52, 82, 76–81, 84.

200. For the life of Haymo of Faversham and his activities as a Franciscan, see Brooke, *Early Franciscan Government*, 195–209, and Van Dijk and Walker, *Origins,* 280–91.

the first minister general who had not had personal contact with Francis; he had made his Franciscan profession in Paris in 1225 and Francis had died in 1226.

With the exception of the bull *Quo elongati* in 1230, the making of which Haymo had influenced, it was during his term of office that the papacy began to issue bulls that modified certain items in the Franciscan Rule. Within the first seven months of Haymo's reign, no less than nine bulls were issued that gave certain privileges to the Order, or relaxed the Rule to make the life of friars easier.[201] Only a month after Haymo's election, on December 12, 1240, Pope Gregory IX issued *Prohibente regula vestra*. With this bull, the authority to examine preachers, which had belonged solely to ministers general according to the Rule, was delegated to provincial ministers. The specific wording of the bull said that in each province friars were to be examined by those "learned in sacred theology" when the diffinitors were gathered in the provincial chapter.[202] In June 1241, a similar bull, *Gloriantibus vobis,* relaxed the article in the Rule concerning the reception of postulants.[203] According to the Rule, only the minister general or provincial ministers could authorize the entry of new friars into the Order. By 1230, this particular statute in the Rule was still so strictly enforced that not even the vicars of the provincial ministers were allowed to accept novices when the ministers were away.[204] *Gloriantibus vobis,* however, permitted the provincial ministers to delegate the authority to receive postulants to custodians and guardians alike. On June 6, 1241, Gregory IX issued another bull, in which he gave provincial ministers the power to absolve the friars who had suffered excommunication before or after their entry to the Order.[205] The bull indicated the presence of "your *fratres discreti,* who are literate and God-fearing," who were to take part in the process of absolution.[206] ("*Fratres discreti,*" or simply "*discreti,*" as they are referred to in many late thirteenth-century documents, were friars elected from among the learned and respectable friars of a convent, custody, or province for the purpose of assisting the guardian, custodian, or provincial minister in the process of decision making.) These bulls on the one hand reveal the growing papal confidence in the

---

201. Brooke, *Early Franciscan Government,* 206.

202. *Prohibente regula vestra,* December 12, 1240, *BF,* 1:287, no. 325. "Ut singuli vestrum in suis Provinciis cum Diffinitoribus in Provincialibus Capitulis congregatis Fratres in sacra pagina eruditos examinare, ac approbare, & eis officium praedicationis, deum habendo prae oculis, committere valeant."

203. *Gloriantibus vobis,* June 19, 1241, *BF,* 1:298, no. 344.

204. In the famous papal bull *Quo elongati* (1230), Pope Gregory IX responds strictly in the negative to the question of the Franciscan delegation as to whether vicars of the ministers can accept postulants. He further reminds the delegation that even the ministers themselves need to be authorized by the general minister to accept postulants. *BF,* 1:68–70, no. 56.

205. *Licet ad hoc fratrum,* June 6, 1241, *BF,* 1:295–96, no. 341.

206. "De conscientia discretorum fratrum vestrorum, qui litterati sint et Deum timentes, impertiri valeant absolutionis beneficium" (ibid).

Franciscan Order, but on the other hand signal a papal assumption that the friars who were to fill the ministerial offices, such as the *discreti,* guardians, and custodians, would be learned enough to perform these new duties and responsibilities of their office, which clearly required some theological training. Education was becoming more and more a prerequisite to hold any kind of administrative office in the Order.

Another "first" during Haymo's tenure is the composition of the first commentary, known as the Commentary of Four Masters (*Expositio regulae quatuor magistrorum*) by four friar-scholars from the Paris convent. We learn from Eccleston that "in his days [i.e., during the ministry of Haymo of Faversham] a mandate was issued by the chapter ordering that each province of the Order should elect friars, who would write down any points of doubt concerning the Rule and send them to the minister general."[207] Presumably, friars confronted the provincial ministers with many questions concerning how to understand the Rule, and the ministers needed an authoritative guide for settling such questions, doubts, and confusions. The solution found was to collect questions and doubts and to attempt to explain them. In England, the task of compiling doubts about the Rule was entrusted to educated friars. "For this purpose, in England, Brother Adam Marsh, Brother Peter, the custodian of Oxford, Brother Henry of Boreford, and some others were elected."[208] Adam Marsh was quite famous; a well-connected and erudite friar, he had studied under the famous master Robert Grosseteste at the Franciscan convent of Oxford, and had become the first Franciscan lector to teach there. Peter of Tewkesbury had served as guardian of London, *custos* of Oxford, and provincial minister of Cologne.[209] The English team responded to this mandate by sending a simple note that asserted that the Holy Spirit had dictated the Rule to Francis, and thus it should not be changed.[210]

Scholars have generally suggested that the French province responded to this mandate by submitting a full commentary on the Rule, written by the four Parisian masters who had become Franciscans.[211] I believe this to be an erroneous

---

207. "In diebus suis venit mandatum a capitulo, ut eligerentur fratres per singulas provincias ordinis, qui dubitabilia regulae annotarent et ad ministrum generalem transmitterent" (Eccleston, 71).

208. Ibid., 71.

209. Moorman, *History of the Franciscan Order,* 173.

210. Eccleston, 71.

211. This was suggested by the editor of this commentary, Livario Oliger, and the view has been subsequently adopted by the scholars. Oliger wrote that while the notes of the English province did not survive, the response of the French province was the *Expositio.* "Dum igitur Fratrum Anglicorum notae ad nos non pervenerunt, superest responsum quod eadem occasione Magistri Parisienses Provinciae Franciae nomine dederunt scil. Quatuor Magistrorum super Regulam Expositio." Livarius Oliger, ed., *Expositio quatuor magistrorum super Regulam Fratrum Minorum* (Rome: Edizioni di storia e letteratura, 1950), 12–13. Moorman, *History of the Franciscan Order,* 117.

interpretation. The confusion on this subject seems to have arisen from a paragraph in the fourteenth-century *Chronicle of Twenty-Four Generals,* which says:

> To this general's mandate, the illustrious masters of theology, excelling in theology, knowledge, and religion, Alexander of Hales, John of Rupella, who at that time were shining as two great luminaries together with brothers Geoffrey, the custodian of Paris, Robert of Bastia, Odo Rigaldi, and other many distinguished and erudite brothers, have written a very useful work on the Rule, which they have sent to the minister general and the other diffinitors.[212]

Identifying the "general's mandate" in this paragraph as the one mentioned in Eccleston, scholars suggested that the commentary was written as a response of the French province to the call for the submission of doubtful points. However, it rather seems to be the case that the General Chapter had specifically commissioned these masters to offer explanations to the controversial points in the Rule that had been raised by friars from all of the provinces. In the prologue to their commentary, the masters state that, after a decision in the General Chapter, they had been instructed to undertake the task in the Provincial Chapter.[213] Ubertino da Casale, writing around 1310–1312, offers us testimony on the nature of this commission, which, although it was known to Oliger, seemingly did not influence his construction of the history of this commentary. According to Ubertino, Haymo of Faversham, on behalf of the General Chapter, asked these four masters to write something to make the Rule clearer.[214] While Eccleston in the paragraph cited above says that the General Chapter asked all friars to write down any point of doubt, Ubertino instead says that the minister general asked four masters specifically to write a clarification. These two mandates cannot be the same. Once friars from all

---

212. "Ad istius Generalis (Haymo of Faversham) mandatum praecellentes in theologia magistri, scientia et religione clarissimi fratres Alexander de Alis et Iohannes de Rupella, qui tunc mundo tamquam duo luminaria magna fulgebant, habita collatione cum fratribus Gaufrido, Custode Parisiensi, Roberto de Bastia, Rigaldo et aliis pluribus discretis et eruditiis fratribus, scriptum valde utile super regulam ediderunt, quod dicto Generali et aliis Definitoribus ad generale capitulum transmiserunt" (*Chronica XXIV generalium,* 247–48).

213. "Judicio et examinationi discretionis vestrae referimus ea quae, Domino docente, circa intellectum regulae nostrae iuxta paupertatis nostrae modulum percepimus, secundum iniunctam nobis obedientiam in provinciali capitulo, iuxta hoc quod in praecedenti diffinitorum capitulo fuerat ordinatum" (Oliger, *Expositio quatuor magistrorum,* 123–24).

214. "Quod verbum et multa alia verba regule exposuerunt IIIIor magistri Parysienses scilicet frater Alexander de Alis, frater Johannes de Rupella, frater Robertus de Bastia, frater Rigaldus, qui fuit postea episcopus Rotomagensis, rogati a fratre Aymone, qui quartus a beato Franciscus generalis magister rogavit eos ex parte generalis capituli, quod aliqua verba regule declararent"; Ubertino da Casale, *Responsio* in "Zur Vorgeschichte des Councils von Vienne no. 4 Vorarbeiten zur Constitution Exivi de Paradiso vom 6. Mai 1312," ed. F. Ehrle, *ALKG* (1887), 3:55.

provinces had sent in their doubts and questions about the Rule, Haymo handed them all to the four masters and asked them to write a text that would answer the friars' questions.

The fact that this commentary survived intact in twenty-seven manuscripts and partially in nine manuscripts—a sign of its considerable circulation within the Order—supports this theory.[215] If this text were simply the response of the French province to the General Chapter's call for *dubitabilia,* it would be difficult for us to explain why it was copied so many times. Whereas, if Haymo asked the four masters to produce answers concerning the points of doubt, he may well have also arranged for all provinces to have a copy of this commentary, and this would explain the high number of extant copies. Moreover, the style of the commentary makes it clear that its authors were not intent on raising a new series of questions on the Rule. Instead they were answering questions. The commentary often assumes a question-and-answer format, but it was not quite the scholastic model commonly seen in university treatises, where the questions were used as a dialectical tool. The questions to which the commentary responds were those genuinely posed by the friars of the Order.[216]

This commentary was sent to the Chapter of Bologna in 1242, where it was probably approved, thereby enjoying great authority in the succeeding years.[217] Later on, Hugh of Digne, Peter John Olivi, and Ubertino da Casale all referred to this text when they commented on the Rule. The fact that the interpretation of the Rule had been entrusted to friars who were scholars from the university circle is noteworthy. Even if this document did not have the status suggested, that of an officially commissioned commentary on doubtful points, it is not disputed that the commentary circulated extensively in the Order and was subsequently cited by other friars. This demonstrated the considerable degree of importance attached to this clarification of the Rule, one made by friars who had entered the Order relatively recently, who were not connected with Francis or his companions, and who had not had the chance to observe the primitive Franciscan movement. Even though it might be suggested that Haymo wished simply to elucidate the text of the Rule rather than reconstruct Francis's intentions in writing the Rule, in reality the four masters were evidently concerned with Francis's intentions because in some places they cite the Testament in

---

215. For the manuscripts, see Oliger, *Expositio quatuor magistrorum,* 37–72.

216. For example, "Hic quaeritur si licet fratri minori habere duas tunicas vel plura vestimenta. Ad quod videtur dicendum, quod habere duas tunicas." "Sequitur: Finito vero anno probationis, recipiantur ad obedientiam. Hic quaeritur an guardiani et custodes possint recipere fratres ad obedientiam." Ibid., 131–32.

217. On the authority of the text, see ibid., 35–36.

support of what they believed to be his intentions.[218] Further discussion of the contents of this commentary will be presented in the next chapter.

It is today generally accepted in the literature on the Franciscan Order that, in an unprecedented move, Haymo of Faversham barred lay brothers from offices in the Order. By "offices" in the Order we should understand ministers, custodians, and guardians, but also preachers, confessors, lectors, *visitatores, diffinitores,* and the *discreti* who served in the provincial and General Chapter.[219] The only evidence for this action by Haymo against lay brothers is from the *Chronica XXIV generalium* written in 1389.[220] Leaving aside doubts as to what exactly the author of this chronicle meant by *laici,* no thirteenth-century source supports the claim that Haymo banned laymen from Franciscan offices. The fact that Eccleston, to whom we owe most of our information about Haymo of Faversham, does not mention such an important detail raises questions about the chronicle's late testimony. Neither in the pre-Narbonne constitutions nor in any of the other medieval constitutions of the Order do we see a statute prohibiting lay brothers from taking an office in the Order.

Could Haymo of Faversham have decided on his own, without the consent of the General Chapter, to bar lay brothers from office? Legally, such a move would not be possible. Even if he had so decided, or even if he had consulted the General Chapter, without making a constitutional decree how could he actually ensure that this decision would be known about and carried out throughout the Order by the provincial ministers? Haymo does not come across as a minister general who wished to rule the Order single-handedly. Quite the contrary, he deliberately wished to limit his own power and that of the provincial ministers and custodians.[221] The papal bulls for the Order issued during Haymo's term concern above all the delegation of power from top to bottom. No doubt Haymo may have encouraged the provincial ministers to appoint guardians and custodians from among the clergy, and perhaps it is no more than this to which, nearly a century and a half later, the author of *Chronica XXIV generalium* refers. Given the way ministerial duties were coming to be delegated to lesser offices, it would have been surprising if Haymo had done otherwise.

Finally, one major contribution of Haymo was in the domain of liturgy, and here perhaps we have an insight into Haymo's self-identification with his Order. He set himself the task of composing a new ordinal, one that would

---

218. See, for example, the discussion in the fifth chapter concerning provisions for the friars to do work; ibid., 149.

219. Michael Bihl, ed., Narbonne-Assisi-Paris, chapter 7, no. 9.

220. "Hic Generalis Frater Haymo laicos ad officia Ordinis inhabilitavit, quae usque tunc, ut clerici, exercebant" (*Chronica XXIV generalium,* 251).

221. Brooke, *Early Franciscan Government,* 241.

be particularly "Franciscan."[222] The breviary and the missal that were in use by the friars until then had errors and presented the friars with difficulties. Haymo's new ordinal contained three self-sufficient, exclusive orders of service: for the Breviary, for graces at meals, and for the Mass. The latter was particularly useful to the growing number of priests in the Order who wished to celebrate private masses.[223] In this new ordinal, Haymo set the feast dates to be celebrated throughout the Order. These were the feast and translation of Saint Francis, and the feasts of Saint Anthony of Padua, Saint Elizabeth of Hungary, Saint Dominic, and Saint Catherine of Alexandria.[224] The inclusion of the latter saint was a significant symbolic gesture. The cult of Catherine of Alexandria was associated in Haymo's day particularly with the University of Paris, as she became the patron saint of the university sometime after 1230.[225] Haymo's vision of Franciscanism certainly contained a significant element of scholarship and learning.

When we look at all Haymo's actions, we see a man who quite clearly believed in the value of being learned and educated, not surprisingly so since he himself was a theologian from arguably the best university in Christendom. He commissioned university masters to write a clarification of the Rule. He petitioned the pope for regulations that would have enabled the quicker acceptance into the Order of scholars in the university towns. He took it on himself to reshape the Order's liturgical activity. Even if he did not officially bar lay friars from offices in the Order, he probably encouraged the assignment of learned friars to those official positions. As we will see in the next chapter, he certainly did discourage the recruitment into the Order of ignorant and unlettered laymen. However, despite being a man vastly different from Saint Francis, he was a friar who was quite sure and proud of his Franciscan identity, which he essentially understood as a life of penitence and strict poverty. Eccleston describes Haymo sitting at the far end of the refectory in provincial chapters, wearing always a very poor and patched habit.[226] He visited the provinces on foot. Haymo of Faversham was the first minister general who united in himself the three essentials that defined the new Franciscan leadership: priesthood, university education, and strict adherence to poverty. His Franciscanism was that of respectable, well-educated priests worshipping God in perfect liturgical harmony, embracing a life of penitence in poverty. This was to take hold.

---

222. Ibid., 208–9.

223. See Van Dijk and Walker, *Origins,* 292–312.

224. Brooke, *Early Franciscan Government,* 208; Van Dijk and Walker, *Origins,* 378ff.

225. Van Dijk and Walker, *Origins,* 387–88.

226. Here, Eccleston probably refers to the times when Haymo of Faversham was the provincial minister of England. Eccleston, 86.

❧ Chapter 2

Studying as Evangelical Perfection

The story told in the preceding chapter shows that by the time the leadership of the Order passed from Haymo of Faversham to Crescentius of Jesi in 1244, the backbone of an educational framework and the formation of an administrative culture that favored the pursuit of learning as a good and useful activity was complete. This speedy change in the value system as well as daily routine was not welcome to the entire Order. Feelings ranging from skepticism to bitterness were expressed in the written texts of the period after 1244: learning was compromising the quintessential Franciscan virtue of simplicity.

A New Policy of Recruitment

The front flyleaf of MS 106 in the Biblioteca Comunale Lorenzo Leonii of Todi contain some statutes written in faded ink in a thirteenth-century Umbrian script.[1] They contain some of the oldest statutes of the Franciscan Order, made either at the General Chapter of 1239 or at the first and last Chapter of

---

1. Todi, Biblioteca Comunale, 106ir–iv. I have had the chance to examine personally these two folios. They are edited by Cesare Cenci in "Fragmenta priscarum."

Diffinitors that was summoned on May 19, 1241.[2] Among these statutes we find the following curious entry that regulates admission to the Order:

> No one is to be received into our Order unless he is such that has taught in arts or [illegible]... in medicine or canon law or civil law or he is a solemn *responsor* in theology, or a very famous preacher, or a very famous and commendable lawyer, or he has taught grammar laudably in famous cities and fortified towns, or he is a cleric or layman of the sort whose entry shall bring renown and edify people and clergy alike.[3]

The Rule had left the reception of the postulants to the discretion of the ministers, and this remained so until 1241. On June 19, 1241, only a month after the Chapter of Diffinitors, Pope Gregory IX amended the Rule in order to allow ministers to delegate to guardians and custodians their authority to receive new recruits.[4] Gregory issued the bull to facilitate the reception of new members in the convents located in the university towns. The pope specifically referred in the bull to "the various parts of the world and chiefly in the places to which secular churchmen and laymen of diverse nations come in order to obtain the knowledge of letters."[5] However, he added a caveat: "Admit only those who are useful to the Order, and who can edify others by the example of their conversion."[6] Just like Gregory, the friars sitting at the Chapter of Diffinitors must have had in mind the setting of the university towns, since the disciplines mentioned in the statute cited above—arts, medicine, canon and civil law, and theology—constituted the four typical faculties that could be found in a medieval university.

Francis had no recruitment policy, nor did he make one while composing the Rule. This statute is remarkable in its specificity: a friar desirable to the Order is one who teaches, or who is a notable preacher, or who knows law or Latin really well. These qualifications are unmistakably reminiscent of the skills

---

2. The chapter had met on Whitsun 1241, which corresponds to May 19. Since it excluded provincial ministers, it created a scandal in the Order and was abolished altogether in the General Chapter of 1242, in Bologna. See Eccleston, 70. The fragments in Todi 106 contain statutes regulating the Chapter of Diffinitors, whence it can be safely assumed that they must have been written before the General Chapter of 1242.

3. "Item, nullus recipiatur in ordine nostro nisi talis qui rexerit in artibus, vel qui [illegible]... aut rexerit in medicina, in decretis aut legibus, aut sit sollempnizatus responsor in theologia, seu valde famosus predicator, seu multus celebris et approbatus advocatus, vel qui in famosis civitatibus vel castellis laudabiliter in gramatica rexerit, vel sit talis clericus vel laycus, de cuius ingressu esset valde celebris et famosa edificatio in populo et clero" (Cenci, "Fragmenta priscarum," 298).

4. *Gloriantibus vobis,* June 19, 1241, *BF,* no. 344, 1:298. Cf. RB, chap. 2.

5. *Gloriantibus vobis, BF,* no. 344, 1:298. See Landini, "Causes of the Clericalization," 67.

6. "Ita tamen, ut non passim admittantur converti volentes, sed illi soli, qui et Ordini utiles, et alii aedificari valeant suae conversationis exemplo" (*Gloriantibus vobis, BF,* no. 344, 1:298).

required for the Order's offices. Those who could teach were to serve as lectors, those who could preach were to act as preachers, those who knew the law and Latin well could fill the administrative offices as ministers, custodians, and guardians. This statute reveals that the Order was looking for candidates who could fill its offices, and the major prerequisite was that the candidates should be educated. But there is more. The statute has a preference for men of distinction and fame among both clerical and lay candidates. It is hard not to notice that there is a concern with the prestige of the Order. The friars who made this statute had little interest in seeing among their fellow brothers ordinary priests or simple laymen. They probably thought that there were already enough such brothers around, remnants from the days of Francis, when simple laymen constituted the majority.

Perhaps the wording of the statute sounded too ambitious, as it repeatedly uses the words *"famosus"* and *"celebris."* It was revised sometime between 1241 and 1254, most likely in the General Chapter of 1242,[7] and replaced by a toned-down version:

> No one is to be received into our order unless he is a cleric competently educated in grammar or logic or medicine or canon law or civil law or theology, or unless he is a cleric or layman of the sort whose entry will bring renown and edify people and clergy alike.[8]

This new version has a diminished emphasis on fame. Being educated, even without any implication of teaching experience, was good enough. The emphasis on the university faculties is still there, though the mention of preachers specifically is not. As in the previous statute, lack of education was to be overlooked only in those cases where the recruit, whether cleric or layman, would clearly add to the prestige or effectiveness of the Order.

A question arises as to whether the words *laicus* and *clericus* were used in the sense of canonical status or in terms of literacy. Looking at Franciscan constitutions in general, it would seem that, where the use is reasonably clear, these terms are used in the canonical sense. For example, in the Todi fragments mentioned above, a decree regulates the tonsure by stating that both clerical brothers and lay brothers should be tonsured above their ears.[9] It is difficult

---

7. Brooke, *Early Franciscan Government*, 243–44.

8. "Nullus recipiatur in ordine nostro nisi sit talis clericus qui sit competenter in gramatica instructus vel logica vel medicina vel decretis vel legibus vel theologia, aut nisi sit talis clericus vel laicus, de cuius ingressu esset valde famosa et celebris edificatio in populo et in clero" (Pre-Narbonne, 75). After having edited the "Fragmenta," Father Cenci revised the dating of the previously edited pre-Narbonne constitutions to suggest that they must have been written sometime between the general chapters of 1242 and 1260. See Cenci, "Fragmenta priscarum," 290, n. 6.

9. "Tonsuram desuper aures tam clerici quam layci facere procurent, et fiat temporibus hiis" (Cenci, "Fragmenta priscarum," 299, no. 45).

to imagine that here the words *lay* and *clerical* could be used in the sense of literacy. Nor, without good reason, should we think that in some decrees these words indicated literacy while in others they stood for canonical status. Would, therefore, the statute on recruitment under discussion here mean that any laymen in the faculties of medicine or civil law would be turned down? Probably not, because in such cases laymen could be accepted on the grounds that their recruitment could be an edifying example to others.

The major conclusions to be drawn from the evidence above are the following: first of all, a more complex story of clericalization exists here than has so far been acknowledged. Scholars have termed the transformation of the Order in the thirteenth century as "clericalization," that is, the process of domination of the Order—both in terms of numbers and administrative power—by clerical as opposed to lay friars.[10] As seen in the statute above, the Order does not simply legislate toward allowing clerical recruits and forbidding the recruitment of laymen. There is a clear interest in recruiting men from university circles, those with a distinction in scholarly erudition. Furthermore, the interest was not only in "religious" disciplines such as theology or canon law, which would be useful in pastoral and other ecclesiastical functions, but also in medicine and civil law. This prompts us to revise the traditional theory of the clericalization of the Franciscans advocated by Landini and Manselli. Landini, at the end of his study of the clericalization of the Franciscan Order, concluded that the external force leading the Order toward clericalization was the pastoral need of the medieval Church, and that this clericalization was inevitable and absolutely necessary if the Order wished to survive.[11] Similarly, Raoul Manselli saw the clerical transformation of the Order as largely orchestrated by the Church, in particular as a result of papal policies designed to suppress heresy and to organize a task force for pastoral care, with Bonaventure bearing the highest responsibility for the process.[12] However, if the objective of the papacy or indeed of the ministers who made these statutes was to find clerical men to serve as pastoral caretakers, there would be no need to aim particularly at men excelling in the university disciplines. Men of moderate literacy would be good enough to satisfy the needs of the Church.[13] The insistence on recruiting from among university scholars cannot be explained simply in terms of clericalization or of a push by the papacy toward pastoral activity. Popes from Gregory IX onward supported the

---

10. The most cited work on the application of this term to Franciscan history is Landini's *Causes of the Clericalization*.

11. "The choice which confronted the Friars Minor was either to clericalize their Order or perish as a distinct way of life in the Church" (ibid., 143).

12. Raoul Manselli, "St. Bonaventure and the Clericalization of the Friars Minor," trans. P. Colbourne, *Greyfriars Review* 4 (1990): 84–87.

13. For a fuller exposition of the link between schools and pastoral care, see chap. 3.

universities and the theology education there, but there is no evidence that they specifically wanted the Dominicans and the Franciscans to be the spearheads of the scholastic movement of the thirteenth century.

Second, the preference for university-educated men might have more to do with raising the Order's prestige and reputation than with pastoral purposes directly. This thesis is supported by the fact that the Order was interested in recruiting laymen from prominent local families, noble or mercantile, or in admitting those whose entry was championed by some high-ranking ecclesiastical or secular personages—for example, the nephew of a cardinal or son of a local baron. This is at least what the anonymous Franciscan author of the *Determinations concerning the Rule of the Friars Minor* tells us, who wrote that recruits should be accepted into the Order on consideration of four factors:

> First, out of compassion if the person can hardly be saved outside the Order; second, for the progress of the Order on account of their diligence and learning, the honesty of their character and their reverence; third, if they are famous personages that their entry into the Order will create interest among the public, and inspire others to follow the lead, and fourth, if they or some other people on their behalf are so relentlessly insisting on their acceptance that it would be impossible to deny it.[14]

Third, perhaps the most important point here concerns the diversity in the Franciscan Order that was explored in the first chapter. The statutes concerning the reception of postulants demonstrate the effort on the part of the ministers to increase the number of "respectable" men in the Order with a view to balancing the larger population of illiterate laymen. In this respect, education was regarded as the key, the only feasible way to make up for the huge differences in social status other than recruiting from the higher classes of society, which admittedly was quite a challenge for a new Order that emphasized voluntary poverty and mendicancy. The previously cited case of the Franciscans in Germany who predominantly recruited from the lower classes of society, as opposed to the Dominicans who attracted the higher classes, is a case in point. The remedy for the Franciscans was to further educate the barely literate clerical

---

14. "Una est compassio perditionis eorum qui vix extra Ordinem in saeculo salvarentur.... Secunda, propter profectum Ordinis, qui ex scientia et industria, morum honestate et reverentia quorundam futurus praesumitur. Tertia, propter aliorum aedificationem, ut multi de talium conversione, qui aliquo modo sunt famosi in saeculo, emendentur et eorum incitentur exemplo. Quarta, propter precum instantiam, quam ipsi faciunt pro se et alii pro eis, nimia importunitate obtinent, aliquos recipi, quibus denegari non potest" (ps.) Bonaventure of Bagnoregio, *Determinationes quaestionum circa Regulam Fratrum Minorum,* in *Opera omnia,* ed. PP. Collegii S. Bonaventurae (Florence, 1898), 8:347, Quaestio 15. Even though *Determinations* has been published within the *Opera omnia* of Bonaventure, scholarship now contests this attribution. See Ignatius Brady, "The Writings of Saint Bonaventure regarding the Franciscan Order," *Miscellanea Francescana* 75 (1975): 107.

friars, so as to increase their respectability and to enable them to perform functions such as preaching, and to limit the entry of ignorant, poor laymen in the future. A friar who could perform a function was a "useful" friar. To see how this concept of "usefulness" and "uselessness" played out in the everyday rhetoric of the Order, let us look at an undated thirteenth-century formulary letter by the *visitatores* reporting back to the provincial chapter on the conduct of their minister:

> We are visiting our minister because he multiplied in our custody the useless reception of many useless people into the Order. . . . He receives many young people who are of poor condition in the world, despicable in person, having no education and almost illiterate, entirely unable to progress both in the knowledge of the Scriptures and in ecclesiastical chant, revealing an unconquerable ignorance according to the judgment of many who judge with discretion.[15]

To be of use, therefore, a postulant had to be able to progress in the knowledge of the Scriptures or ecclesiastical chant, which are both related to activities of a distinctly clerical culture. At the same time, this letter suggests that the reception of such uneducated laymen had not really ceased. As in the case of many other statutes of the Order, the statute concerning admissions was often observed at the discretion of the ministers. The difference between the adopted norm and practice signals the presence of ambiguity, tension, and unease in the Order, and a conflict between the general administration, which materialized itself in the General Chapter, and the individual provincial ministers.

Even though we surely see a policy with an underlying mentality that favored educated men and consequently implies clericalization, it would be wrong to assume that by 1260 the clerics outnumbered the laymen, as some scholars have suggested.[16] Literate men were rare in medieval Europe, and even rarer were those who were knowledgeable beyond elementary Latin. Outside the university towns, of which there were only a few, it was difficult to find men who were educated in the academic disciplines, let alone teaching them. Furthermore, for the enrollment of such prized candidates, Franciscans had to compete with Dominicans, other religious orders, and with conscientious bishops who

---

15. "Visitamus Ministrum nostrum, quia multiplicavit in Custodia nostra inutiles receptiones multarum inutilium personarum. . . . Plures recepit iuvenes parve condicionis quoad seculum, despicabiles in personis, ignaros scientie et quasi illecteratos, omnino inabiles ad proficiendum tam in scientia Scripturarum quam in cantu ecclesiastico, ignorantiam invincibilem, iudicio plurium discrete iudicantium, prebentes" (De Luca, "Un formulario di cancelleria," 237). The formula cited above is titled "a letter to the Provincial Chapter about the excesses of the minister."

16. Landini, "Causes of the Clericalization," 119, suggests that by 1260 there must be more clerics than laity, but he admits that there are no such statistics and suggests it as a hypothesis.

were intent on appointing educated men to pastoral positions. In their Rule commentary of 1242, the four Parisian Franciscan masters observed that only a few convents in the Order had student-friars.[17] We cannot be sure if or when the number of clergy in the Order caught up with the number of laymen. The letter of the *visitatores* shows that some ministers continued to receive illiterate laymen into the Order in violation of the statute of reception. Also, it was not solely a question of a policy of clericalization, to whatever extent that was successful. The statutory evidence itself suggests that laymen of high social status were gladly being received into the Order. The problem seems to have been particularly with the illiterate men of lower social status. However, thanks to the recent discoveries of Cesare Cenci, we know that even before the constitutions of 1260, sometime between 1239 and 1257 the Order legislated that the laymen in the Order should not become clerics.[18] Illiterate or lowly laymen and clerics lived side by side in the Order for the better part of the thirteenth century, in a setting that did not always make their coexistence a felicitous one. During the course of the thirteenth century, the number of illiterate brothers must have gone down steadily as the friars of the first generation died, and the entry of such men into the Order must have been slowed down, if not stopped altogether, by the barrier erected in the constitutions. However, it is clear that from the 1240s onward at least, if not before, there was a hierarchy of superiority and inferiority.[19] Categorizations such as "useful" and "useless" among the men who were supposed to live as brothers embracing each other with fervent love and zeal were bound to be painful. The documents produced in the Order after 1242 reflect this internal tension and the discontent of their authors.

Franciscan "Simplicity": From Absence or Renunciation of Learning to Humility

The administration of the Franciscan Order of the 1240s adopted an official strategy to create a community of learned and respectable men, living more or less an urban, semimonastic life, and turning away from the early Franciscan tradition of wandering friar-hermits. It is precisely in this strategy that we see a divergence from the original *religio* of Francis, who aspired to preserve and cherish the coexistence of poor and rich, ignorant and learned in the same Order and in full equality. For most ministers sitting in the general chapters of 1239 and 1242, this aspiration was unrealizable in view of the "institutionalization" of the Order, which can be roughly understood in terms of the friars taking on certain

---

17. Oliger, *Expositio quatuor magistrorum,* 138.
18. Cesare Cenci, "Vestigia constitutionum Praenarbonensium," *AFH* 97 (2004): 92, no. 108.
19. Salimbene, 141, refers to the lay friars as the "useless" (*inutiles*).

"functions" within and outside the Order. By the term *simple friars,* as Francis had used it, we understand those who were uneducated, illiterate or barely literate, and who had nothing to commend them by way of social status, wealth, or practical merits, as well as those who embraced a simple life of quiet devotion and prayer in spite of being educated or coming from respectable families.[20] It was with them that Francis chose to associate rather than with the learned clerics. He referred to himself as *"ignorans et idiota"* and *"homo inutilis,"* precisely a "useless man," in a letter he sent to the entire Order.[21] His own education did not go beyond an elementary knowledge of Latin.[22] Celano quotes Francis as saying to the man who shaved his head, "Be careful not to give me a large tonsure.... For I want my simple brothers to have a share in my head."[23] His first companions were probably literate like him, since many of them belonged to the socially upward families of Assisi, but they nevertheless fashioned themselves as simple laymen, not as learned men. There was nothing respectable about the appearance of Francis and his companions. An eyewitness described Francis thus: "His habit was filthy, his whole appearance contemptible, and his face unattractive."[24] Young women trembled and ran away when they encountered these men in wretched habits.[25] There is, however, a point worth making here. From the point of view of the friars, who would have knowledge of the background and family status of the friars with whom they lived, there must have been a difference between their regard for friars coming from wealthy or respectable families, like Francis and some of his early companions, and their opinion of those who were the real simpletons and ignoramuses. It was one thing to act the simpleton and quite another actually to be one. It is not surprising that many friars shunned the latter and praised the former.

Francis, however, saw the simple friars to be the driving force of the Order's central mission: to preach by example. After all, the friars were called *Fratres*

---

20. What follows has some overlaps with my article, Şenocak, "Voluntary Simplicity: Attitudes to Learning in the Medieval Biographies of Francis," in *The Cambridge Companion to Francis of Assisi,* ed. Michael Robson, 84–100 (Cambridge: Cambridge University Press, 2011).

21. *Epistola toti ordini missa,* in Menestò and Brufani, *Fontes Franciscani,* 103, lines 39 and 47; *Testamentum,* 19. A valuable contribution to the subject of Francis's education and his self-fashioning as a simple and ignorant brother is Oktavian Schmucki, "St. Francis's Level of Education," trans. P. Barrett, *Greyfriars Review* 10 (1996): 153–70. On Francis's level of literacy, see also Attilio B. Langeli, "Gli scritti da Francesco: L'autografo di un 'illiteratus,'" in *Frate Francesco d'Assisi: Atti del XXI Convegno internazionale, Assisi, 14–16 ottobre 1993.* 1st ed, *Atti dei convegni della Societa internazionale di studi francescani e del Centro interuniversitario di studi francescani nuova ser. 4* (Spoleto: Centro italiano di studi sull'alto Medioevo, 1994), 101–59.

22. See Schmucki, "St. Francis's Level of Education," 168.

23. II Celano, 193. "Volo enim, quod fratres mei simplices partem habeant in capite meo."

24. The eyewitness was Thomas of Split, who recorded in 1250–1265 his memory about Francis's sermon in 1222. Armstrong, Hellman, and Short, *Francis of Assisi,* 2:808.

25. *The Legend of Three Companions,* ibid., 2:88.

Minores for a reason, a name that indicated simplicity and humility. One of the meanings of the word *minores* in the Middle Ages was in fact "laypeople."[26] By *simplicity,* we understand living in a childlike purity by way of true or adopted ignorance. The way the term is used in the Franciscan context refers to an *ad litteram* imitation of Christ, much like a child imitating a parent, without any reserve, inhibition, or thought. Understanding the concept of simplicity, and the initially central role of the simple, illiterate friars in the early Franciscan movement is necessary if we wish to understand the position of learning and the learned in the Order.[27] The decline of the simple and the rise of the learned go hand in hand. The role of simplicity in the apostolic life is essentially founded on the fact that the apostles of Christ were simple fishermen. For Francis, they were fishermen who became apostles, for many others they were apostles who happened to be fishermen. Francis saw a divine reason why the apostles were chosen from among the simple folk, so he rejoiced when simple men joined him in the pursuit of apostolic life. Once he was dead, and his early companions had retreated to the hermitages of central Italy rather than taking an active part in administering the Order, doubts about the potential for holiness in the simple friars started to appear in the statutes.

The statutes concerning reception of the postulants leave no doubt that by the time we reach the early 1240s, simple friars were "not wanted" in the Order. The poor and the illiterate were being denied the coarse gray habit. This change did not go unnoticed within the Order, so much so that a section titled "Holy Simplicity" made its way into the *Second Life* of Thomas of Celano written around 1245–1247.[28] The general argument of this section is to show how much Francis cherished the simple friars and how he had certain worries about whether the learned would make good Franciscans, and under what conditions. Prior to the composition of the *Second Life,* a general call was made to friars to write down their memories related to Francis, and Celano used the resulting collections from the friars when he wrote the *Second Life* of Francis in 1247. Hence, we can assume that some of the anecdotes and parables told in this section were communicated to Celano by the friars. It is clear that Thomas of Celano takes sides, that he is critical of the recent developments and attitudes in the Order. He does not shy away from pointing out to his reader that simplicity

---

26. In a sermon preached in Paris around 1230–1231, the Franciscan Jean of Blois said: "Hoc est contra quosdam magnos qui nolunt minoribus praedicare, scilicet laicis, sed clericis praedicant." Marie-Madeleine Davy, *Les sermons universitaires parisiens de 1230–1231: Contribution à la histoire de la prédication médiévale* (Paris: J. Vrin, 1931), 376.

27. See also Achim Weisjohann, "Simplicitas als franziskanishes Ideal und der Prozeß der Institutionalisierung," in *Die Bettelorden im Aufbau: Beiträge zu Institutionalisierungsprozessen im mittelalterlichen Religiosentum,* ed. Gert Melville and Jörg Oberste (Münster: LIT, 1999), 107–67.

28. II Celano, 189–95.

and wisdom must exist together, just as the lay and learned brothers should coexist peacefully in the Order. The section opens with a chapter titled *"Quae sit vera simplicitas?"*

> She [Holy Simplicity] was what the most holy father demanded in the brothers, learned and lay; not believing she was the contrary of wisdom but rather, her true sister, though easier to acquire for those poor in knowledge and more quickly to be put into use. Therefore in the Praises of the Virtues which he composed, he says 'Hail, Queen Wisdom! May the Lord protect you, with your sister, holy pure simplicity.'[29]

In general, simplicity is taken to be the attribute of the unlettered and ignorant, the absence of learning and wisdom. For Francis, however, wisdom and simplicity are not necessarily in conflict—a wise man can become simple. In the *Praise of Virtues,* Francis distinguishes between the "holy" wisdom that fights against the tricks of Satan and the wisdom of the world, which can be overcome by "holy simplicity." The wisdom of this world is a vice, which the simple men naturally do not have.

In the next tale, Thomas narrates the story of one such simple man, John the Simple. This is a tale that was communicated to Celano by Francis's companions.[30] John was a very simple farmer who left his plow to follow Francis. He imitated the saint literally in everything to the degree of ridicule. He coughed when Francis coughed and spat when the saint spat.[31] Francis rejoiced at the man's simplicity and remembered him as Saint John when he passed away. Celano ends the tale customarily with the lesson to be drawn:

> Note that it is typical of holy simplicity to live by the norms of the elder and always to rely on the example and teaching of the saints. *Who will allow human wisdom* [Job 6:8; 1 Cor. 2:4] to follow him now reigning in heaven, with as much care as holy simplicity conformed herself to him on earth! What more can I say? She followed the saint in life and went before the saint to Life.[32]

The message of the tale is fascinating. Since the simple men lack intellectual training (and perhaps a lower capacity for reflection and analysis is implied in John's simplicity), they follow the examples of saints rather than inventing new paths on their own. They do not decide for themselves what to imitate and

---

29. Ibid., 189. I have slightly revised the translation of Armstrong, Hellman and Short, *Francis of Assisi,* 1:368. Celano quotes Francis accurately; see the *Salutation of Virtues* in Armstrong, Hellman, and Short, *Francis of Assisi,* 1:164.

30. See the longer version of the tale in Brooke, *Scripta Leonis,* 118–22, no. 19.

31. II Celano, 190.

32. Ibid; translation in Armstrong, Hellman, and Short, *Francis of Assisi,* 1:369.

what not, but imitate thoroughly and sincerely without getting distracted by the acquired wisdom of the world, without having second thoughts or inventing modifications. It is this pure and absolute imitation that leads them to holiness. It is, after all, exactly this kind of *ad litteram* imitation that Francis himself wished to do with regard to Christ, and admonished his friars to do. "The Rule and the Life of Friars Minor is to observe the Holy Gospel of our Lord Jesus Christ." This is the very first line of the Franciscan Rule. Learned wisdom can be a hindrance to the literal imitation of Christ; therefore the wise of the world cannot imitate as perfectly as the simple do.

What was expected from the learned was that they shed their learning on entering the Order, along with other possessions. What Francis demanded was a "renunciation" of learning, and an embrace of voluntary simplicity.

> Once he said that if an "eminent cleric" were to join the Order, he should in some way renounce even learning, so that having renounced even this possession, he might offer himself naked to the arms of the Crucified. "Learning," he would say, "makes many hard to teach, not allowing them to bend something rigid in them to humble disciplines. And so I wish an educated man would first *offer* me this *prayer:* 'Look, Brother; I have *lived* for a long time *in the world* and have *not* really *known* my *God*. Grant me, I pray you, a place removed from the noise of the world, where *I may recall my years in* sorrow and where I may gather the *scattered bits of* my *heart* and turn my spirit to better things.'"[33]

This story supports the message of the previous tales of Thomas: learning is at best still an obstacle to following Christ. A learned friar after Francis's own heart does not look for God in books and schools.

Thomas of Celano's *Second Life* is remarkable in its clear position that simple friars, not the learned, are intended to be the driving spirit of Francis's Order. The point about the simple friars and their importance in the Franciscan movement was not just based on the argument that simplicity combined with piety and zeal leads to holiness. Francis thought the simple friars vital for maintaining his Order in balance; they were to serve as an apostolic model for the learned brothers. This is the lesson of one of the most beautiful and illuminating stories in the entire *Second Life* of Celano.[34] It deserves to be cited in full.

> He [Francis] once presented a moral parable, containing no little instruction. "Imagine," he said, "a general chapter of all the religious in the Church. Because the literate are present along with those *who are unlettered,*

---

33. II Celano, 194; translation in Armstrong, Hellman, and Short, *Francis of Assisi*, 2: 371.

34. This story does not come from the Leonine tradition, as we have it.

the learned, as well as those who, without learning, have learned *how to please God,* a sermon is assigned to one of the wise and another to one of the simple. The wise man, because he is wise, *thinks to himself:* 'This is not the place to show off my learning, since it is full of understanding scholars. And it would not be proper to make myself stand out for originality, making subtle points to men who are even more subtle. Speaking simply would be more fruitful.'

"*The appointed day* dawns, *the gathering of the saints gathers as one,* thirsting to hear this sermon. The learned man comes forward *dressed in sackcloth,* with *head sprinkled with ashes,* and to the amazement of all, *he spoke briefly,* preaching more by his action. 'Great things have we promised,' he said, 'greater things have been promised us; let us observe the former and yearn for the latter. Pleasure is short and punishment is eternal; suffering is slight and glory infinite. *Many are called; few are chosen,* all are repaid.' The hearts of the listeners *were pierced,* and they *burst into tears,* and revered this truly wise man as a saint.

"'What's this?' the simple man says *in his heart.* 'This wise man has stolen everything I planned to do or say! But *I know what I will do.* I know a few verses of the psalms; I'll use the style of the wise man, since he used the style of the simple.' The next day's meeting arrives and the simple brother gets up, and proposes a psalm as his theme. Then, inspired with the divine Spirit, he preaches by the inspired gift of God with such fire, subtlety and sweetness that all are *filled with amazement* and say: 'Yes, *He speaks with the simple!*'"

The *man of God* would then explain the moral parable he told: "Our religion is a very large gathering, like a general council gathered together from every part of the world under a single form of life. In it the learned can draw from the simple to their own advantage when they see the unlettered seeking the things of heaven with fiery vigor and those not taught by men knowing *spiritual things by the Spirit.* In it even the simple turn to their advantage what belongs to the learned, when they see outstanding men, who could live with great *honor* anywhere *in the world,* humble themselves to the same level with themselves. Here," he said, "is where the beauty of this blessed family shines; a diverse beauty that gives great pleasure to the father of the family."[35]

For Francis, the diversity of the friars, the inclusion in his Order of the simple illiterate men side by side with the wise and the learned was, far from being a problem, a necessary blessing. The learned needed to see how zealous faith was

---

35. II Celano 191–92; translation in Armstrong, Hellman, and Short, *Francis of Assisi,* 2:370–71.

sufficient for holiness, and how it was a "superior" way of "knowing" compared to bookish learning, as in the tale it is the simple friar's sermon that amazes the crowds. The simple, too, needed to see the learned humble themselves by choosing the Franciscan life of poverty, so that they would not stray from the perfection of lowliness, and would not be tempted to change their ways. This way all vices would be kept at bay. It was indeed a perfect recipe for both parties, and the only way to keep the Order united and serene.

The setting of the story of the simple and learned friar is precisely that of preaching. Even if we are uncertain about the actual source of this story, and how it came down to Celano, the fact that Celano chose to include it in the *Second Life* presents us with clues about Celano, who, himself as a Franciscan, lived through the transformation of the Order. The message of the story does not show any hostility to learning or the learned, but one senses a clear partiality for the simple friars: there is no need for the friars to be educated for the purpose of preaching, since the simple men could do it quite well, as well or even better than the learned. The detail concerning the sackcloth and ashes worn by the learned friar when he appears in front of his audience is quite significant. The sermon of the learned friar is all the more effective as he chooses the look of the simple and poor. The message of the story is a powerful one: having knowledge helps make a good preacher, but if not united with holy simplicity and poverty, learning alone will not render a sermon effective.

A similar defense of simple brothers is also found in Thomas of Eccleston's chronicle, which is by and large a tribute to the English friars. Writing around 1257, the English Thomas loves to depict the English friars as those who faithfully observe the Rule and remain true to the nature of the Franciscan Order.[36] As such, it is a perfect source for understanding which virtues he considers praiseworthy in the friars, and which not. There is no question that for Thomas the many learned friars of England were a source of pride, but he is also quick to point to their reverence for the simple friars. When Haymo of Faversham demands that all provinces note down questions and doubts regarding the Rule, the English province puts together a team that includes the lector Adam Marsh and the custodian of Oxford. That night one of the friars has a vision of Francis, who tells him that if the friars want the Rule to be explained, they should go to the lay brothers. After this incident, the elected friars simply scribble a few notes and send their response to the minister general, saying that the Rule should remain unchanged, as it was communicated to Saint Francis

---

36. This is the sense that the reader gets from the entire chronicle. For a specific instance, see Eccleston, 69–70, where Thomas says that the minister general Albert of Pisa praised the English for their zeal above all other nations.

through the Holy Spirit.[37] In common with the story given by Thomas of Celano, according to this vision the lay brothers are better equipped to understand the Franciscan life and mission. Yet the learned brothers too are after Saint Francis's heart, as they refuse to use their learning on the Rule and return a very simple response.

It is noteworthy, however, that Thomas of Eccleston does not say "simple brothers"; instead he says "lay brothers." That's because his understanding of *simplicitas* is essentially different from Celano's. Talking of the first English friars, Thomas of Eccleston says,

> Although the friars were striving exceedingly for perfect simplicity and purity of conscience, they were particularly fervent in listening to the scriptures and in scholastic exercises, so much so that they were going every day to the schools of theology, no matter how distant, with bare feet, not slowing down even in the deep mud and freezing cold.[38]

Clearly Eccleston applauds these friars' efforts to go to school barefoot in difficult conditions, and there eagerly learning the scriptures. This does not stop him, however, from believing that they strove for "perfect simplicity." Here, however, simplicity takes on the meaning of "humility." For Eccleston, a simple brother is not an uneducated brother, as it is for Celano. He can be a learned brother, eager to continue his studies, but his simplicity comes from his embrace of the humble, penitential life of poverty. This shift in the meaning of "simplicity" from designating an absence of educational formation to signifying humility and poverty is also found in Bonaventure's *Legenda maior.* There, Bonaventure writes that, having been asked whether he was pleased that some brothers wished to pursue theological studies further, the saint responded positively, saying, "I want my brothers to be Gospel disciples and so progress in knowledge of the truth that they increase in pure simplicity without separating the simplicity of the dove from the wisdom of the serpent."[39]

Eccleston's narrative, like Celano's, suggests that not all learned brothers had a low opinion of the lay brothers, and some of them did actually feel that the simple penitential life of lay brothers was a life of true virtue, even though their ignorance was frowned upon and despised in some learned circles of the

---

37. Eccleston, 71. Rosalind B. Brooke, *The Image of St Francis: Responses to Sainthood in the Thirteenth Century* (Cambridge: Cambridge University Press, 2006), 124, says that Eccleston here sounds like Leo, Rufino, and Angelo.

38. "Licet autem fratres summae simplicitati et conscientiae puritati summopere studerent in omnibus, in audienda tamen lege divina et scholasticis exercitiis ita fuerunt ferventes, ut scholas theologiae, quantumcumque distarent, adire quotidie nudis pedibus in frigoris asperitate et luti profunditate non pigritarentur" (Eccleston, 27).

39. Bonaventure of Bagnoregio, *Legenda maior,* chap. 11, sec. 1; translation in Armstrong, Hellman, and Short, *Francis of Assisi,* 2:612–13.

thirteenth century. They were able to discern that their learning made them respectable in this world, but not necessarily in the eyes of God. This is the message we get from an *exemplum* (an anecdotal piece used as preaching aid) in a thirteenth-century Franciscan collection of *exempla*. The story is narrated by a learned brother named Eustace, while he was a bachelor of theology at Paris. One night he has a vision, in which he enters the refectory and sees a most beautiful boy sitting among the friars. He inquires who the boy is, and the boy turns out to be Jesus Christ. The boy asks him for bread, and he runs to the kitchen of the Father to find bread, but no bread is good enough to give to Christ. At this point enters a certain Friar Oliverius, *simplex et despectus*. He tells Eustace to let him find the bread. And instantly he presents the boy with the most beautiful bread. The boy Christ then says to Eustace that those who are great and famous and learned in the eyes of men have hardly anything to offer God. Then Eustace understands that a man is nothing except what he is in the eyes of God.[40]

Another story recorded in an early fourteenth-century manuscript of Franciscan provenance reveals the ambivalence of the position of learning in the Order's life.

> In the convent of the Friars Minor at Salop a friar named Warenn South was sick to death, and another friar, Thomas de Qwytchirch, was serving him. As he was nearing his end and the cross was fastened up in front of him as is the custom with the sick, he looked up in terror and cried loudly for the lector of the house. The serving friar hurried to him and asked what he wanted with the lector. The sick man replied: "Countless devils have just come in by window and door and filled the house, and as I have very little learning they are posing me with hard questions on the Trinity and Catholic faith, so run and ask the lector to help me and answer for me." The serving brother hurriedly took the cross and put it into the hands of the sick man, and said, "Do not be afraid if you cannot answer; this will answer for you till I return," and he ran off for the lector. The sick man almost immediately broke into loud laughter, and the servitor, turning back in astonishment, asked the reason. The other replied, "As soon as you gave me this champion, all the devils took to flight and they are crowding out of windows and doors in such hurry and confusion that I think they are breaking each other's necks and backs."[41]

The author of this manuscript is a very learned English friar; he recognizes, however, that theological learning can be a way the Devil tempts the faithful,

---

40. Livarius Oliger, "Liber exemplorum fratrum minorum saeculi XIII," *Antonianum* 2 (1927): 216.

41. Andrew G. Little, *Studies in English Franciscan History* (Manchester: Manchester University Press, 1917), 145–46. Little's translation. The story comes from Eton MS 34, f. 17r; Bodl. 410, f. 15v.

and simple devotion to Christ, represented in this story by the cross put in the sick friar's hand, is a more effective way to salvation than learning.[42]

The sections cited above from the *Second Life* of Thomas of Celano, the chronicle of Thomas Eccleston, and the Franciscan *exempla* have one point in common: a strong belief that an uneducated simple brother can exceed a learned brother in the knowledge and understanding of God. They also reflect a conviction that the peaceful coexistence of the learned and the simple is the ideal way for the Franciscan Order. Simplicity must unite with learning, even though the two concepts seem irreconcilable in the medieval world. However, the crucial point is that the learned were to learn to be like the simple friars, rather than the simple to become learned. The following verses of Thomas of Celano explain it all very well:

> His constant wish and watchful concern
> was to foster among his sons the bond of unity
> so that those drawn by the same Spirit
> and begotten by the same father
> should be held peacefully
> on the lap of the same mother.
> He wanted to unite the greater to the lesser,
> to join the wise to the simple in brotherly affection
> and to hold together those far from each other
> with the glue of love.[43]

The learned and the simple could live together if only the learned could renounce their learning, but could the Order promote simplicity and the pursuit of learning at the same time? If we accept the meticulous work of Rosalind Brooke, and accept *Scripta Leonis* as, indeed, a collection of the original writings of Leo, Rufino, and Angelo, then it seems that to these men it appeared quite difficult for the Order to embrace both learning and simplicity at the same time. And if one of them had to go, it had to be learning, not simplicity. These three companions were not all simple laymen. Leo was a priest and Saint Francis's confessor.[44] Angelo, too, was a priest, for whom Francis acquired a Breviary.[45] Yet, in the tradition of Thomas Celano's *Second Life,* we find in the Leonine

---

42. Little observes the author of this manuscript to be a very learned man, since he cites a variety of authors from Seneca to Augustine and Thomas Aquinas.

43. II Celano, 191; translation in Armstrong, Hellman, and Short, *Francis of Assisi,* 2:369–70.

44. Brooke, *Scripta Leonis,* 14–15. Oliger, "Liber exemplorum," 239, has a story narrated by Leo, where he says that he was a priest. "Refert fr. Pe. sibi dixisse fratrem Leonem socium sancti. Cum novus, aiebat, sacerdos essem, protrahere solebam officum Misse, quando celebrabam. Sentiebam enim consolationes divinas et ideo iocundum mihi erat diutius immorari. Quadam die beatus Franciscus vocavit me et alloquens familiariter dixit: Fili, fr. Leo, facias quod dico."

45. Brooke, *Scripta Leonis,* 11.

corpus not only an exaltation of simplicity but also a suspicion of making learning into a Franciscan virtue:

> Not that he [Francis] condemned or despised holy knowledge: on the contrary he venerated most warmly those who were wise in religion and wise men in general. He himself bore witness to this in his Testament when he said: "We ought to honor all theologians and the ministers of the divine word and to revere them as the dispensers to us of spirit and life." But looking into the future he knew through the Holy Spirit, and even said many a time to the brothers, that "many other brothers on the ground of edifying others would put aside their vocation, that is to say pure and holy simplicity, holy prayer and our lady poverty."[46]

According to these companions, simplicity was the true vocation of the Franciscans, not learning. Here then we have almost a carbon negative of the mentality cherished by the ministers who made the statutes concerning reception. The unity of the Order is to be achieved through the embrace by all of simplicity not learning.

Just as in Thomas of Celano's *Second Life,* the writings of Leo and the companions refer to the significance of voluntary simplicity and the importance of the coexistence of simple and learned brothers to edify one another: "He [Francis] used to say: 'The ordinary brothers are greatly edified if their ministers and preachers devote themselves willingly to prayer and bow down and behave humbly, and help in the work and labour.'"[47] The companions are relentless in asserting in the strongest terms possible the central role of simplicity in the Franciscan movement. One time when Francis was upset about the behavior of some friars, he is consoled by God: "'I did not choose you as an educated and eloquent man over my family but I chose you as a simple man, that both you and others might know that I will watch over my flock. I put you as a sign to them, that the works which I work in you they ought to perceive in you, and [they should perform them].'"[48]

---

46. "Non ut contempneret et despiceret sanctam scientiam, ymo eos qui erant sapientes in religione et omnes sapientes nimio venerabatur affectu, quemadmodum ipse testatur in Testamento suo dicens: 'Omnes theologos et qui ministrant verba divina debemus honorare et venerari tamquam qui ministrant nobis spiritum et vitam.' Sed futura prospiciens cognoscebat per Spiritum Sanctum et etiam multotiens fratribus dixit, quod 'multi fratres sub occasione hedificandi alios dimittent vocationem suam, videlicet puram et sanctam simplicitatem, orationem sanctam et dominam nostram paupertatem'" (Brooke, *Scripta Leonis,* 210, no. 70; Brooke's translation). This story is found in the *Intentio regule,* section 7.

47. Brooke, *Scripta Leonis,* 213, no. 71.

48. Ibid., 239, no. 86. Brooke's translation. I have amended the translation in brackets. Original translation: "[do them]." The story is in the Assisi Compilation; also found in *Speculum perfectionis* and II Celano with some variations.

The companions see the incorporation of learning into the Order's mission as a major threat to the founding ideals of the Order because learning will threaten holy poverty, and because studying requires expensive books. On this particular point, the companions narrate a story in what Rosalind Brooke calls three acts,[49] in which Francis shows his displeasure with a friar who wishes to have a psalter.[50] After some internal struggle, Francis ultimately says that the true vocation of a Friar Minor is not to have anything except a tunic, a cord, and breeches.[51]

It was not only that learning distracted from prayer and threatened simplicity and poverty, but it was also conducive to the vice of pride. Pride or vanity is in general a Christian vice, but in the context of Franciscan ideals it was more than a vice. It was destructive and threatened the entire fabric of the brotherhood, which was based essentially on humility and brotherly love:

> He [Francis] used to say: "They are many who put all their efforts and their care day and night in learning, casting aside their holy vocation and devout prayer, and when they preach to a group or to the people and then see that some are edified or turned to penitence, they are puffed up and congratulate themselves on the works and profit of another: for those whom they believe they have edified or converted to penitence by their words, God has edified and converted through the prayers of saintly brothers, though they do not know it themselves. It is God's will that they should not observe it, lest they grow proud."[52]

The "saintly brothers" mentioned here are the brothers "who conceal themselves in remote and desert places that they may more diligently apply themselves to prayer and meditation, and weep over the sins of themselves and others."[53] They are, in other words, those who do not pursue intellectual activities. These are contrasted to the friars who spend their time studying instead of praying. There is a reason why both Celano and the companions of Francis are using specific examples related to preaching. As will be explained in depth in the next chapter, preaching around this time was becoming the major justification for the friars' involvement in study.

The friction within the Order with regard to the stand that should be taken toward the endorsement of learning is also reflected in a non-Franciscan

---

49. See a discussion of these stories concerning the friar requesting the Psalter in Brooke, *Image of St Francis*, 122–23.

50. On the subject of books and Francis's attitude to learning, see Brooke, *Scripta Leonis*, 206–17, no. 69–74. All of these stories are from *Intentio regule*, sections 5–12, repeated also in Sabatier's edition of *Speculum perfectionis*, sections 150a–152.

51. Brooke, *Scripta Leonis*, 217, no. 74.

52. Ibid., 211–13, no. 71. A similar warning about knowledge making men proud is in no. 72.

53. Ibid., 213, no. 71.

source. In a sermon he preached to the Franciscans, Jacques de Vitry demonstrates knowledge of the arguments within the Order that favored simplicity as a Franciscan virtue. His position is very much in line with the clerical culture of the thirteenth century, which viewed ignorance with abhorrence, particularly in the setting of a religious Order.

> Some, miserable and senseless, seeking an excuse for their laziness, say that they should not study, but that it is better for them to remain brothers in the humility of their simplicity, because *knowledge puffs up* and much learning makes them foolish. To them we can respond that the other virtues can also occasionally make one proud. In fact, without charity, none of them are profitable, but for the most part are an obstacle. For if they disdain to learn and fill themselves with the words of Scripture, how will they be able to ruminate?...
>
> If therefore a simple brother is not gifted with much cleverness, let him make up for his lack of brilliance with the ardor of study. Let him not be ashamed to beg the bread of the word of God where he can, and commit to memory each day at least one good passage. I have seen many who were slow in wit make more progress than those who presumed on their abilities and their intelligence, and refused to learn from others.[54]

Similarly, Eccleston reports the advice of the first theology lector of the Oxford Franciscans, the eminent scholar and churchman Robert Grosseteste, to an English friar, Peter of Tewkesbury, who served as the provincial minister of Germany. "He [Grosseteste] told him once that unless friars keep studying and make an effort to learn the divine law, they will for sure become like other religious orders whom we see with great sorrow to walk in the darkness of ignorance."[55] As Eccleston also tells us that Peter was taught by Grosseteste, one cannot but note how the mind of a provincial minister like Peter was shaped by his own studies under a famous man like Grosseteste who was certainly greatly in favor of the education of clergy. Friars who listened to Jacques de Vitry's sermon faced a similar pressure from another eminent churchman to make learning a part of their religious life.

These passages are evidence that there were tensions deriving from the coexistence within the Order of simple and learned friars, and of two mentalities competing with one another. Since the ruling group was formed of the learned

---

54. Armstrong, Hellman, and Short, *Francis of Assisi*, 1:587–88.

55. "Ipse speciali dilectione domini Lincolnias ditari meruit, a quo plura secreta sapientias frequenter audivit. Dixit enim ei aliquando, quod nisi fratres foverent studium et studiose vacarent legi divine, pro certo similiter contingeret de nobis, sicut de aliis religiosis, quos videmus in tenebris ignorantiae, proh dolor! ambulare" (Eccleston, 91).

brothers, who were representatives of a distinctly clerical culture, and many of whom came from intellectual circles, the simple were disadvantaged. In fact, in an insightful article, Pietro Maranesi suggested that these tensions might have dated even from the 1220s, and that perhaps it was the entry of the learned clerics into the Order that prompted Francis to add to the 1223 Rule the instruction that "those who do not know the letters, should not learn," in an attempt to protect and maintain the presence the simple friars.[56] This is quite a plausible assertion.

In the same article, Maranesi also wrote about what he called "the double stand" of Francis with regard to learning. On the one hand, we have Francis's statement in the Testament that he wanted all friars to revere and honor theologians;[57] on the other hand Francis did not want ignorant friars to study. Actually, if we are to believe the stories narrated by the companions, there is no contradiction or ambiguity in Francis. Precisely because he saw theologians as objects of reverence and honor, he did not want his own friars to become theologians or respectable men in general. In his mind, it was much better for the souls of the friars if they were held in contempt and despised by people. And they could save the souls of others precisely by responding to contempt and disdain with true joy, humility, and good deeds and prayers, setting out vividly thereby the example of Christ to others. This is best exemplified by a story communicated to the companions by an eyewitness. Once in Terni, when Francis had finished his sermon to the people in the presence of the bishop, the bishop took the stand and said to the people,

> "But now in this last time, he [God] has adorned her [the Church] with this poor, little, contemptible, ignorant man"—indicating St. Francis with his finger to the whole people—"on which account you are bound to love and honour God.". . . Then St. Francis bowed himself down before the bishop and threw himself at his feet saying: "I tell you in truth, lord bishop, that no man has yet done me such honour in this world as you have done me today. For other men say: 'This is a holy man', attributing glory and sanctity to the creature and not to the Creator. But you separated the precious from the worthless, like a wise man."[58]

There were, as we have seen, repercussions from the ministers' decision to rule out the reception of simple laypeople and to encourage the reception of the learned. The companions and Thomas of Celano both convey the idea of what

---

56. Maranesi, "L'intentio Francisci,'" 282–83.

57. "Et omnes theologos et, qui ministrant sanctissima verba divina, debemus honorari et venerari, sicut qui ministrant nobis spiritum et vitam" (*Testamentum,* 13).

58. Brooke, *Scripta Leonis,* 271, no. 103

can be termed "voluntary simplicity" as Francis's intention. Instead of wishing that simple friars imitate the learned by applying themselves to study, which was contrary to the Rule, they want the learned friars to make themselves "simple," just as they committed themselves to becoming "poor." Surely this did not mean that they should "unlearn," but that they should cease further study once they take the Franciscan habit, should not take pride in their learning, nor pose as elevated, respectable men, superior to the uneducated brothers, and that they should use their learning prudently. Thomas of Celano uses the setting of preaching to show how a sermon could become more effective if the learned brother chose simplicity, instead of using the pulpit as a place to show off his knowledge to a largely illiterate society. In this respect, Celano reflected Francis's intention accurately, as the Franciscan Rule of 1223 admonishes and exhorts the friars to keep their sermons chaste and short.[59]

The idea of voluntary simplicity in Thomas of Eccleston's chronicle is rather different. An Englishman, who most likely never met Francis and his early companions, Thomas uses *simplicity* as if it were almost synonymous with *humility* and respect for simple lay brothers. By refusing to use their learning to explicate the Rule, and not minding the poor conditions in which they studied, the learned English brothers voluntarily embraced simplicity.

The Formation of a New Franciscan Identity

Friars' Knowledge of Francis and the Early Franciscans

The introduction mentioned that learning came to be viewed in the historiography as a "problem area," a point of conflict between the so-called Spirituals and the Community. Since the "Spirituals" were fashioned as the "true followers" of Francis, their agenda and thoughts on the Franciscan mission were naturally regarded as being in line with those of Francis. As such, the establishment of Francis's will with regard to learning has become of particular importance to historians. For this reason, almost every study concerning the history of Franciscan education and learning, even the general histories of the Order, contains an account of Francis's approach toward learning. The question of whether Francis approved or disapproved of study has remained a constant debate in Franciscan historiography even now.[60] Questions that were particularly attractive to

---

59. RB, chap. 9.
60. Among Franciscan scholars, see Felder, *Die Geschichte der wissenschaftlichen Studien,* 1–31; Gratien de Paris, *Histoire de la fondation et de l'évolution de l'Ordre des Frères Mineurs au XIIIe siècle* (Paris, 1928), 83–96; Pietro Maranesi, "I commenti alla Regola francescana e la questione dello studio," in *Studio e Studia: Le scuole degli ordini mendicanti tra XIII e XIV secolo; Atti del XXIX Convegno internazionale* (Spoleto, 2002), 42–46. Notable contributions from non-Franciscan scholars are Bert Roest, *History of Franciscan*

modern Franciscan scholars, such as whether the Order's subsequent history was a betrayal of, or instead an adaptation of, the founder's ideals, have also fanned this keen interest in determining Francis's position with regard to learning. Francis, in his own writings, said very little directly on the subject of learning. While in his letter to Anthony of Padua, he endorsed studying theology, the sources at the center of the Franciscan Question, such as *The Legend of Three Companions, Intentio regule,* and *The Assisi Compilation,* exhibit clearly his concern about, even dislike of, the friars' pursuit of learning and the keeping of books, as indicated above. Views on this subject are generally expressed with considerable force in Franciscan historiography, ranging from regarding Francis as a fervent opponent of studies, as being neutral, or as adapting to the needs of the Church. Yet at the other extreme, others see him as an advocate of study.[61] To date, there is no scholarly consensus as to how Francis felt about the pursuit of learning in his Order.

Amid the many difficulties involved in trying to penetrate the mind of Francis, an essential question has been largely ignored, and discussed by only a few scholars: What could *the majority of the Franciscans of the thirteenth century,* who did not have direct access to Francis, know about his intentions and will concerning the pursuit of learning?[62] After all, if the assumption is that the founder's intentions were influential in the Order's development, then what matters is to try and establish what the majority of first generation Franciscans knew about or thought of Francis's intentions, rather than what those intentions actually were. It is irrelevant what we know and can know in the twenty-first century, with our access to all the fourteenth-century material that could spin the head of even such a great scholar like Sabatier, particularly when many historians have found themselves taking sides personally in the perceived conflict between the two parties in the Order. Today we have far more material on Franciscan history available to us than was available to an early thirteenth-century friar. What, then, was accessible to a literate or illiterate friar in the middle of the thirteenth century, should he wish to know about the intentions of the Order's founder and the early Franciscan way of life? Did the medieval

---

Education, 1–4; Dieter Berg, "Das Studienproblem im Spiegel der franziskanisher Historiographie," *Wissenschaft und Weisheit* 42 (1979): 13–16.

61. For a brief discussion of the various positions, see Maranesi, "San Francesco e gli studi," 15.

62. Dieter Berg, *Armut und Geschichte: Studien zur Geschichte der Bettelorden im Hohen und Späten Mittelalter,* Band 11, Saxonia Franciscana: Beiträge zur Geschichte der Sächsischen Franziskanerprovinz (Münster: Butzon und Bercker, 2001), 51–114. Berg tries to pin down the approaches to the study in the various pieces written on Francis. He fails, however, to treat the problem of how widely these works circulated within the Order. In 1983, images of Francis in history were discussed at a conference and the proceedings published in Servus Gieben, ed., *Francesco d'Assisi nella Storia: Atti del primo convegno di studi per l'VIII centenario della nascita di S. Francesco, 1182–1982,* 2 vols. (Rome: Instituto Storico dei Cappuccini, 1983). See also Nimmo, *Reform and Division,* 70–75.

friars, prior to the publication of the *Second Life* by Thomas of Celano, even consider that Francis's intentions might have been different from what is stated in the Rule, as Sabatier believed in the nineteenth century? By what means did the Franciscan friars form their opinions about their Franciscan vocation and identity? For the purpose of this book, the central question is whether the majority of the friars thought or could think that study and learning might be irreconcilable with the Franciscan vocation. Certainly, while their understanding of their identity, and the place of learning in it as religious men, was highly affected by conditions outside the Order, in this chapter we will look only to the sources that were produced within the Order, and only to those that were produced before 1239–1242. This latter period saw extensive legislation that, among other things, regulated educational activities in the Order. To this end, two questions need to be asked initially. What kind of material about Francis and the early Franciscans did the friars have access to before 1242, and what did this material say about Francis's attitude toward learning?

Surely one of the best ways to discover Francis's intentions, what he expected from the friars, and the manner in which the first friars lived was to gain direct access to the saint and to the first friars. This was, however, difficult for most friars outside Italy. The great expansion of the Order took place after 1217, when the friars decided to spread throughout Christendom. For those who joined the Order in various parts of Europe, outside of central Italy, in these years of expansion, meeting Francis and his early companions was not possible, unless they traveled to Italy: once Francis had returned from the East in 1220, he never again left Italy. Thus most friars beyond the confines of the Italian peninsula had no chance to meet the founder of the Order, with the notable exception of those present at the Chapter of Mats in 1221. Francis's worsening health in his last years kept him from traveling long distances.

Many of Francis's companions outlived him. Bernard of Quintavalle, who had been the first to join Francis, died in 1242, to be followed in 1258 by brother Angelo, Giles in 1261; and in 1278, both Rufino and Leo. Saint Clare, the founder of the Second Order, the female branch of the Franciscans, lived until 1253.[63] This core group of early Franciscans kept in close touch with one another, and younger friars wanting to know more about the early days of the Order frequently visited them.[64] Although most visitors were probably local Italian friars, evidently some friars from distant parts also had access to these "original" Franciscans at general chapters or on other journeys to Italy. The English chronicler Thomas of Eccleston mentions that Brother Leo spoke to Peter of Tewkesbury, the English provincial minister from 1254 to 1258, while

---

63. For these dates, see Nimmo, *Reform and Division,* 78–79.
64. Ibid., 79.

another English friar, Warin of Sedenfeld, wrote a story concerning Francis "from the mouth of Leo."[65] Possibly Peter had met Leo on one of his trips to Italy to participate in the General Chapter. Furthermore, Eccleston tells us that at the General Chapter of Genoa (1249 or 1251), the minister general John of Parma (1247–1257) had asked a companion of Francis, Bonitius of Bologna, to tell the friars the truth about the stigmata of Francis, since many around the world were in doubt about it.[66] Some other early companions seem to have spent time at various convents and talked to the friars there. As Salimbene himself saw, Bernard of Quintavalle, the first man to join Francis and his close friend, instructed the friars personally on the life of Francis at the convent of Siena.[67] The knowledge that this group had of Francis must have been considerably greater than what could be known through the Rule, the Testament, and Thomas of Celano's vitae. They might have had a good idea of what kind of an Order Francis wanted to have, and what the Franciscan Rule meant to him.

Stories about Francis and the early Franciscans did not circulate in the Order in written form,[68] but it is probable that they circulated more by word of mouth, and the reason why we come across the idea of Francis's preference for lay brothers in such an unlikely place as Thomas of Eccleston's chronicle might well be the power of oral communication. It is important to bear in mind the fact that it was only in 1244 that the General Chapter asked friars to write down their memories about Francis, as a consequence of which Leo and other companions of Francis wrote down their memories within the next two years. But this was after the statutes concerning reception. The Leonine corpus is, therefore, not perhaps a very safe indication of what Leo and others might have said to the friars who visited them in the years leading up to 1240. By 1246, they might either have adopted a different attitude toward learning or felt the need to emphasize Francis's concerns about it once they had seen that the emphasis on education, and books accumulating in the convent libraries, had diverted some friars from the path of simplicity and spirituality. It is also impossible to know in what context they told these stories, and what their audience exactly understood by them. In his written response to an unnamed Parisian master, Bonaventure told a story that he had heard from a brother who was with Francis. "And that you might appreciate how much the study of Holy Scripture

---

65. "Sed et frater Leo, socius sancti Francisci, dixit fratri Petro, ministro Angliae. . . . Ista scripsit frater Garynus de Sedenefeld ab ore fratris Leonis" (Eccleston, 75).

66. "Frater Johannes de Parma, minister generalis, in pleno capitulo generali Januae praecipit fratri Bonicio, qui fuerat socius sancti Francisci, ut diceret fratribus de stigmatibus suis veritatem, quia multi de hoc per orbem dubitabant" (ibid., 74).

67. Salimbene, 39.

68. The original parchment—written by Leo and others—was kept under lock and key in the Assisi convent. This is what Ubertino da Casale said in 1310. Ubertino, *Declaratio,* 168.

delighted him, let me tell you what I myself heard from a brother who is still living. Once a New Testament came into Francis's hands, and since so many brothers could not all use it at once, he pulled the leaves apart and distributed the pages among them."[69] Here, then, is a story that is obviously intended to support the idea that Francis encouraged learning, though perhaps not a love of books, but we do not know in what context it was told. Similarly, the context is missing in the often-cited words of Brother Giles, another close companion of Francis. His utterance "Paris, Paris, you destroyed the Order of Saint Francis" has been interpreted, rather naturally, as a lament over the Order's involvement in the scholastic world.[70] We might understand Assisi as a symbol of the true Franciscan spirit, but it is unclear what exactly "Paris" indicates here. Was it the Paris convent itself, which was so generously endowed, the scholastic theology embodied in the University of Paris, or the Order's commitment to learning embodied in the Franciscan studium in Paris?[71] It is also unknown who reported these words, and whether this source was trustworthy. While, based on strong evidence, Rosalind Brooke included the *Life of Brother Giles* in her compilation of *Scripta Leonis,* she refrained from considering the *Dicta,* which is the source of this lamentation, in the Leonine tradition.[72] Nevertheless, it is quite conceivable that Giles, like Leo, Rufino, and Angelo, was not pleased with the Order's new emphasis on learning.

Let us then deal with the material written down by or about Francis or any other Franciscans before 1242. What were these texts? To what extent did they circulate in the Order, and how can we interpret Franciscan identity as depicted in these sources? The decision of Francis and his Italian brothers in 1217 to make their brotherhood an international one was a turning point in their history. This was done with a lot of goodwill and idealism, but Francis did not have much experience as an administrator, particularly as one who would have to manage an international Order with members not in his physical presence. Being Francis, he put his full trust in his brother-ministers and did not envisage any other means of instructing the men recruited outside of Italy in Franciscan virtues. During the period between 1217 and 1223, the only document produced that could help the ministers in this serious responsibility or that the clerical recruits

---

69. *A Letter in Response to Three Questions by an Unnamed Master (1254–1255),* in Bonaventure of Bognoregio, *Works of Saint Bonaventure,* vol. 5, *St. Bonaventure's Writings concerning the Franciscan Order,* ed. and trans. Dominic Monti (St. Bonaventure, NY: Franciscan Institute, 1994), 51.

70. "Parisius, Parisius, ipse destruis ordinem sancti Francisci"; Aegidius Assisiensis, *Dicta beati Aegidii Assisiensis sec. codices mss. emendata et denuo edita,* ed. PP. Collegii S. Bonaventurae (Florence: Ad Clara Aquas, 1939), 91. The utterance owes its actual fame to the famous Franciscan poet Jacopone da Todi, who used it as well.

71. For the material support the Paris convent received, see chap. 5.

72. See Brooke, *Scripta Leonis,* 307–9.

could read for themselves was the *Regula non bullata* of 1221.[73] There was as yet no vita of Francis, no Testament, no liturgical pieces that could be sung in the choir or *legendae* to be read to friars at mealtimes. The primitive Rule, which has not survived, was nothing more than passages describing apostolic life from the Bible. The Rule of 1221 was completely silent on the issue of learning. It does, however, say that brothers who know a trade should continue to practice it. This gives some room for maneuver to an activity such as teaching. Theoretically, anyone who was a grammar teacher before joining the Order could continue teaching grammar. The decision in this respect seems to have been left to the discretion and knowledge of the ministers, provided, of course, that the problem of books could be solved by way of borrowing or receiving donations.

In 1223, a new Rule, the *Regula bullata,* was approved by the pope and distributed to the provinces. As discussed in chapter 1, this new Rule was not very helpful in explaining how the study of sacred scripture related to the Franciscan mission, particularly in the case of men who were already literate. What the Rule suggested was simply that the illiterate should not learn letters and that books seemed to be off limits since the friars were to have no possessions. There is no clause in the Rule prohibiting clerical members of the Order from pursuing the study of sacred scripture. On the other hand, there is nothing that either encourages it or suggests how the pursuit of studies could be made practical. If books were offered as a donation—for instance, by a bishop or other high ecclesiastic—were they to be turned down? Apparently not, as we know, for example, that the Paris convent was accepting book donations already in 1224. In that year a certain Bartolomeo de Bruyères left ten books to the Paris friars.[74] How then was the acceptance of this book donation justified? It is difficult to tell, particularly in view of the 1220 statute specifying that "friars shall not have books."

Let us consider the case of Haymo of Faversham. He entered the Order in Paris sometime in 1224, already a theologian and master at the University of Paris. As he would have had to spend a year as a novice, his profession must have been around 1225. Paris is not Umbria or anything like it. There were no hermitages dotting the hills where friars in their coarse, gray habits spent their days in the bosom of nature praising the Lord in a state of cheerful spirituality, not reading books, but living such lives that would become the subject of books. Haymo became a Franciscan while teaching at the University of Paris. In the days leading up to this decision to become a Franciscan, he must have met and

---

73. We know that this Rule had circulated in the Order as Francis mentions it in a letter he wrote to a minister: *Epistola ad quendam ministrum,* in Menestò and Brufani, "Fontes Franciscani," 95–96. It is dated to the period 1221–1223. Armstrong, Hellman, and Short, *Francis of Assisi,* 1:97–98.

74. Beaumont-Maillet, *Le Grand Couvent,* 12. This is the earliest book donation to a Franciscan convent that we know of.

spoken to Gregory of Naples, then the provincial minister of France, about what it meant to become a Franciscan, and what kind of a life he was to lead after he became a Franciscan. We can safely assume that Haymo had never met Francis, and it is unlikely that he made the trip to Umbria before Francis's death. Most of Haymo's knowledge about the Franciscans was received, then, from Gregory of Naples, the minister of France, or from observing how the Franciscans in Paris lived. In fact, tradition has it that he also spoke with the Dominican master general, Jordan of Saxony, before his decision.[75] It would be fascinating to know what impression about Francis and the Franciscan way of life these contacts had given Haymo. After all, Gregory of Naples was not exactly Francis's favorite minister, as his deeds during the vicariate, unwelcome to Francis and discussed in the previous chapter, reveal. Perhaps Haymo would have asked Gregory whether he had to abandon his books as well as studying and teaching after he took the habit, but it is difficult to imagine Gregory recommending him to do so, judging from the life Haymo lived after his profession as a Franciscan. He served as a lector for many years in the Order before becoming the minister general in 1240. As it was not possible for a lector to teach without having at least a Bible together with a commentary, it is possible Haymo brought his own books along to the Franciscan convent and made them available for common use. If Haymo wanted to learn for himself what Franciscanism was about, and how he was expected to live and behave after he became a Franciscan, there was nothing available to him to read except the Rule, where he would not find any prohibition against the study of sacred scripture.

In 1226 Francis died, leaving behind a new document, his Testament, which is rich in details about the kind of behavior he expected from the friars. It could serve as a good guide for Franciscan identity. Francis had ordered the Testament to be copied and kept with the Rule. However, the bull *Quo elongati* of 1230 declared that the Testament was not canonically binding, and so quite possibly after 1230 its circulation within the Order slowed down. The Testament, just like the Rule, does not make any mention of whether or not the brothers should make themselves knowledgeable about sacred scripture or not, but it does mention that theologians should be honored.

Francis did not write a great deal: nevertheless, in his own distinctive fashion he left behind a small corpus. This corpus includes two Rules, the *Regula non bullata* and the *Regula bullata;* one long text known as the *Admonitions;* ten letters; a note to Brother Leo with a benediction and praises to God; the *Canticle of the Sun;* two *Laudes* (*Exhortatio ad laudem Dei* and *Laudes ad omnes horas dicendae*); two *Salutationes* (*Salutatio beatae Mariae Virginis* and *Salutatio virtutum*); one *Expositio*

---

75. Eccleston, 27–28.

in Pater Noster; an *Officium passionis,* a prayer before the Cross; the Rule for the hermits; a *forma vivendi* for Saint Clare; his Testament; and a last wish addressed to Saint Clare. The writings of Francis that have been extracted from other works include short fragments of two benedictions, four letters, another Testament, and a short text on happiness. With the exception of the *Regula non bullata,* the *Regula bullata,* and the *Admonitions,* most of these writings average one or two book pages. This small corpus gives a fairly good idea of the most characteristic aspects of Francis's faith, namely, his concern with obedience, poverty, humility, and simplicity. However, a friar who wished to know something of the saint's standing with regard to the pursuit of learning would find no answer.

There is no evidence that these writings, with the notable exception of the *Regula bullata* and *Testament,* were widely circulated in the Order. From the thirteenth century only four manuscripts have survived that contain Francis's writings other than the *Regula bullata,* and none of these contains the entire corpus.[76] Also, works of Franciscan authors of the thirteenth century generally seem to be lacking in quotations from or references to the writings of Francis.[77] Thomas of Pavia, who served around the 1240s as lector in Bologna, Parma, and Ferrara, displays no familiarity in his *Distinctiones* with any of Francis's writings other than the *Regula bullata.*[78] The author of the Rule commentary attributed to Bonaventure shows familiarity only with the Primitive Rule, no longer extant, and the Testament.[79] In fact, this issue of the circulation and knowledge of Francis's writings requires closer historical attention. Some historians have suggested that this restricted circulation was a deliberate policy

---

76. Nimmo, *Reform and Division,* 72.

77. Bougerol mentions a quotation from Francis's *Admonitions* in a Dominican sermon dated July 15, 1231, and in the *Summa* of Alexander of Hales. Jacques-Guy Bougerol, "La teorizzazione dell'esperienza di S. Francesco negli autori francescani pre-bonaventuriani," in *Lettura biblico teologica delle fonti francescane,* ed. Gerardo Cardaropoli and M. Conti (Rome: Pubblicazioni dell'Istituto Apostolico, 1979), 248–49. The quotation in Hales's *Summa* is "obedience is to satisfy the will of the superior." As Bougerol says, Hales obtained this quotation not directly from a Franciscan source but from the *Summa de bono* of Philip the Chancellor. Bougerol then goes on to suggest that the original source for this quotation is the *Admonitions* 3 and I Celano, 45. However, what Francis says in *Admonitions* 3 does not agree with this citation. In fact, in *Admonitions* 3, Francis suggests that if a friar receives from a prelate a command against his conscience, he may not obey him, but he should not leave him either. It is only in I Celano, 45, that we find an expression close in meaning to the citation: "Si frater fratris praelati subditus non solum audiat vocem, sed comprehendat voluntatem, statim ad obedientiam totum se debet colligere ac facere quod eum velle signo aliquo comprehendet." Therefore, the circulating text here was not the *Admonitions* but the *Vita prima.* Bougerol then goes on to suggest that since Francis was canonized in 1228, his writings had become *auctoritates,* just as those of other saints such as Hugh and Richard of Saint Victor and Bernard. However, the quotation in Hales's *Summa* cannot stand as testimony of the circulation of Francis's *Admonitions* in Paris.

78. Ephrem Longpré, "Les 'Distinctiones' de Fr. Thomas de Pavie, O.F.M.," *AFH* 14 (1923): 28–33.

79. Nimmo, *Reform and Division,* 72. Nimmo does not mention the contested nature of the *Expositio super Regulam Fratrum Minorum* published in Bonaventure's *Opera omnia* (Quaracchi: Ad Claras Aquas, 1882–1902), 8:391–437.

of the Order's administration. It has also been suggested that, while the "Community" deliberately shied away from investigating and following Francis's ideas, "the Spirituals," on the contrary, treasured and cherished his writings.[80] If there were indeed such a deliberate, official policy of neglect, it is difficult to find out exactly when it started. One piece of evidence cited is the 1310 claim of friar Ubertino da Casale that in the province of Marches and in many other places the ministers had ordered the Testament to be burned.[81] If true, however, this seems more likely to have been something connected with the disputes of the early fourteenth century.

To summarize: in the period between the foundation of the brotherhood in 1210 and 1229 when Thomas of Celano composed the *First Life,* the only written material widely available on the Franciscan mission consisted of the *Regula bullata* and the *Testament,* which offered little that was useful in understanding the founder's stance toward the education of the literate and clerical friars of the Order. In fact, the very appeal of the friars in 1230 to Pope Gregory IX for clarification of certain points in the Rule is strong testimony that the ministers, with only the Testament and the Rule to guide them, did not feel adequately equipped to respond to questions from friars on the many day-to-day issues arising for the administration.

The first work written on Francis is by Thomas of Celano, commissioned by the pope in 1228 and completed sometime in 1229, known as *The Life of St. Francis,* or the *Vita prima.* Thomas wrote in the prologue that he used his own conversations with the saint and those of "trustworthy and respectable" witnesses.[82] The *First Life* consists of three books. The first book is an account of Francis's life starting from his early youth, followed by his conversion, the first brothers who joined him, his oral approval from the pope, his preaching, and anecdotes concerning his devotion to poverty, humility, simplicity, and obedience to the Church. The second book concerns the last two years of his life, with an emphasis on his stigmata and his death, while the third book addresses the canonization of Francis and the miracles he worked.

It was two years before his death that Francis received the stigmata, the wounds of Christ, on Mount La Verna.[83] To those who believed it—and that group certainly included the Franciscans—it was the ultimate sign that Saint Francis

---

80. Nimmo, *Reform and Division,* 72–73; Lambert, *Medieval Heresy,* 83–84. For Nimmo's evaluation of the knowledge of Francis from two different perspectives—that of the Community and the Spirituals—see Nimmo, *Reform and Division,* 70–95.

81. "In provintia Marchie et in pluribus aliis locis testamentum beati Francisci mandaverunt districte per obedientiam ab omnibus auferi et comburi" (Ubertino da Casale, *Declaratio,* 168).

82. I Celano, *Prologus.*

83. On this subject, see the excellent work of Chiara Frugoni, *Francesco e l'invenzione delle stimmate: Una storia per parole e immagini fino a Bonaventura e Giotto,* Saggi (Torino: G. Einaudi, 1993).

was not just another zealous Christian: God placed his ultimate seal of approval on Francis and his way of life by likening him to Christ. The stigmata deeply affected the perception of Francis by his brothers. Along with his miracles, his wounds became the central point of all the literature produced about Francis immediately after his canonization, particularly the early biographies of Francis, miracle treatises, and pictorial representations. In fact, it is only in the second half of the thirteenth century, with the writings of the companions and the *Second Life,* that the focus seems to shift more toward his life and deeds rather than his miracles and stigmata. The same change is reflected in the artistic representation of the saint as well. The images of Francis made after this date contain not only his miracles but also scenes from his life that demonstrate his virtues and the story of the foundation of the Order,[84] which probably is the consequence of the publication of the *Second Life.*

In the *First Life,* Thomas's account of Francis projects the image of Francis that comes across in Francis's own writings. Just as in his *Second Life,* in the *First Life,* too, Thomas is keen to voice Francis's self-representation as a "simple" man.[85] Side by side with this simplicity, however, we encounter the idea of wisdom granted as a divine gift to Francis and his early companions. While talking of Brother Philip, one of Francis's early companions, Thomas of Celano says that "the Lord touched his lips with the coal that cleanses, so that he might speak of Him in words that were sweet and flowing with honey. Understanding and interpreting the Holy Scriptures, although he had not studied, he became an imitator of those whom the Jewish leaders had considered ignorant and without learning."[86] Talking of Francis's preaching, Celano wrote that he preached "not in the persuasive words of human wisdom but in the learning and virtue of Spirit."[87]

Roughly three years after Celano's *First Life,* sometime between 1232 and 1235, a German friar from the Paris friary, Julian of Speyer, wrote another *Life of Saint Francis,* based on Celano's *First Life,*[88] along with a liturgical piece, a rhymed *Office of Saint Francis* (*Officium rhytmicum Sancti Francisci*). While Celano had no known connection to any university or center of scholastic learning, Julian of Speyer is exclusively associated with the friary at Paris. Our knowledge of him is fragmentary, and to a great extent constructed from allusions to him

---

84. Klaus Krüger, "Un santo da guardare: L'immagine di san Francesco nelle tavole del Duecento," in *Francesco d'Assisi e il primo secolo di storia francescana,* ed. Maria Pia Alberzoni (Turin: Einaudi, 1997), 153–54.

85. See, for example, I Celano, 27: "Nec vos deterreat mea vel vestra simplicitas."

86. I Celano, 25; translation in Armstrong, Hellman, and Short, *Francis of Assisi,* 1:204.

87. I Celano, 36; my translation.

88. Julian of Speyer, *Vita Sancti Francisci* in *AF* 10 (1941): 333–71.

in the medieval manuscripts of his work.[89] We know that he was German, and that he spent many years in the Paris friary as the *corrector mensae.* It is curious that only a few years after Celano, another friar attempted to write a new vita of Saint Francis without being commissioned to do so. It has been suggested that this was an apology extended by the friary at Paris for their pursuit of studies. By showing interest in Francis's life they were making the point that they were zealous followers of their founder.[90] Perhaps a more straightforward explanation is that the focus of this initiative was not the vita itself, but the Divine Office that was based on it. Julian was better at composing liturgical pieces than Thomas of Celano was. Before joining the Franciscans, he had held the prestigious post of the *magister cantus* at the court of the king of France. Perhaps for this reason, he was informally charged with composing pieces for the Divine Office for the feast of Saint Francis in the rhythmic tradition, a genre known as *officium rhythmicum.*

Even though Julian's *Life of Saint Francis* and the *Divine Office of Saint Francis* are based on Celano's *Vita,* Julian's own alterations and emphases can be distinctly observed, some related to the subject of learning. Julian is quite keen on making a case for Francis's special reverence for the educated and noble. In his Testament, Francis had written that the friars should revere and honor theologians and those who administer the Sacrament.[91] Julian neatly adds his own touch by suggesting that Francis had admonished that the *ordo sacerdotalis* should be held in the highest reverence, and that the doctors of divine law and *omnes ecclesiastici ordines* ought to be very much revered.[92] Elsewhere he says, "He stayed a little while at Saint Mary of the Portiuncula. At that time, too, he received certain educated men and nobles into the Order. These he treated with the care and decency they deserved and with that outstanding discernment he showed to others."[93]

It is in Julian's work that we observe strongly the depiction of Francis as a man of learning, only as one who did not receive his learning from any human teacher but directly from God. To trace the development of Franciscan identity, perhaps it is even more important to see how Julian depicted Francis in the *Divine Office,* as that was a piece that every friar must have heard on the feast of Saint Francis and throughout its octave. The opening antiphons for the first

89. Julian of Speyer, *Officio ritmico e Vita secunda,* in *Fonti agiografiche antoniane,* ed. Vergilio Gamboso (Padua: Edizioni Messaggero, 1985), 11–33.

90. Julian of Speyer, *Officio ritmico,* 263.

91. Julian of Speyer, *Vita Sancti Francisci,* 362.

92. "Hoc enim ipse . . . monuit, ut Romanae Ecclesiae fides inviolabiliter servaretur, et ob Dominici sacramenti, quod ministerio sacerdotum conficitur, dignitatem, in summa sacerdotalis ordo reverentia teneretur. Sed et divinae legis doctores et omnes ecclesiasticos ordines 'docebat summopere reverendos'" (ibid., 348).

93. Ibid., 352; translation in Armstrong, Hellman, and Short, *Francis of Assisi,* 1:395.

vespers emphasize Francis's loyalty to the Church, briefly giving the story of his relations with the popes. Julian then draws a picture of the saint as a prophet and miracle worker.[94] The critical point concerns his preaching: although he was not taught by any human being, he confounded the learned.[95]

In his *Life of Saint Francis,* Julian elaborated on the divine "wisdom" of Francis:

> What do you think he drank in of true knowledge, sweetness and grace in the sun, the moon, the stars and the firmament, in the elements and in their effects or embellishments? What, I ask, did he drink in when he contemplated the power, wisdom and goodness of the Creator of all in all things? Surely, I do not think that it would be possible for any mortal to express this in words. Since he traced all things back to their one first beginning, he called every creature "brother," and, in his own praises, continuously invited all creatures to praise their one common Creator.[96]

Even before Julian's works on Francis, the idea of Francis as a divinely inspired learned man circulated in Parisian circles. One of the earliest recorded sermons on Francis in the University of Paris, preached on October 4, 1230, the saint's feast day, belongs to a Parisian master named Guiard of Laon. The sermon is significant in that it marks the origin of the idea that Francis was learned, not through his own efforts, but by means of a divine gift. Guiard of Laon compares Francis to Saint Paul, declaring that Francis had been made learned by God, so much so that he could preach in front of the pope and the cardinals.[97]

Works composed after 1242, notably the *Second Life* of Thomas of Celano, the *Legend of Three Companions,* the *Assisi Compilation,* and the *Intentio regule,* can be read as reflections of the ideas and views of their authors, but they can also be read as the texts, insofar as they circulated and were read in the Order, that informed the opinion and identity of friars as Franciscans. As noted above, some of these texts, in particular the *Second Life* of Thomas of Celano and *The Legend of Three Companions,* contain stories and anecdotes that convey an incompatibility between Francis's intention for his fellow friars and the presence of books and the interest in learning. However, to use these as evidence of the mentality present in the earlier period is rather problematic, as these works likely reflect reactions to developments in the Order rather than being repositories of the

---

94. The Magnificat Antiphon: "In te signis radians, in te ventura nuntians, requievit spiritus duplex prophetarum" (*Officium S. Francisci, AF* [1897]: 3:377).

95. "Hic praedicando circuit et, quem non homo docuit, fit doctis in stuporem" (ibid., 3:383).

96. Julian of Speyer, *Vita Sancti Francisci,* 356; translation in Armstrong, Hellman, and Short, *Francis of Assisi,* 1:400–401.

97. "Sic beatus Franciscus doctus fuit a Domino solummodo et propter hoc coram Pape et cardinalibus ausus est praedicare" (Davy, *Les sermons universitaires,* 220).

ideas that shaped the Franciscan identity in the first three decades of the Order. In the cover letter attached to their notes, Leo and the other companions wrote that they had not only written their own memories about Francis but had also collected information from other friars who had been close associates of Francis or of Francis's companions.[98] "We were not content simply to narrate miracles, which do not create, but only demonstrate holiness; we wished to make known striking examples of his discourse and his holy will and pleasure, to the praise and glory of God and of our holy father Francis, and for the instruction of those who wish to follow in his footsteps."[99] The friars also state in this letter that they include stories that were unknown to the writers of previous *Legendae,* clearly a reference to Thomas of Celano and Julian of Speyer.[100] The contents of these texts were only partially available to the friars before 1247, and then only by way of oral communication, insofar as their authors voiced their opinions to other friars before they put them down in writing.

Visual images of Francis, though not a major source for the first half of the thirteenth century, also served to inform the brothers' perception of Francis. With the exception of Mary, Francis was, at least in Italy, the most represented saint of the thirteenth century.[101] This is quite significant when compared to the fact that there is only one image of Saint Dominic dating from this period.[102] Francis's extraordinarily rapid canonization, which took place only two years after his death in 1228, and his general popularity no doubt contributed to the spread of a "Francis" iconography. The earliest representations of Francis are in the form of panel paintings, such as those of San Miniato dated to 1228, Pescia to 1235, and Pisa to 1240. These simply represent, without exception, the miracles of the saint as depicted in the *Vita prima* of Celano. The two most recurrent scenes in these panel paintings are the stigmatization and the preaching to the birds. These miracles seem to have entered into the minds of the friars, since the Franciscan convent of Saint Omer in 1241 and the convent of Auxerre in 1243 both chose the image of Francis preaching to

98. "Pauca de multis gestis ipsius [i.e., of Francis] que per nos vidimus, vel per alios sanctos fratres scire potuimus, et specialiter per fratrem Philippum, visitatorem pauperum dominarum, fratrem Illuminatum de Arce, fratrem Masseum de Marignano, fratrem Iohannem, socium venerabilis patris fratris Egidii, qui plura de hiis habuit ab eodem sancto fratre Egidio, et sancte memorie fratre Bernardo, primo socio beati Francisci" (Brooke, *Scripta Leonis,* 86).

99. Translation by Brooke, *Scripta Leonis,* 87.

100. "Credimus enim, quod, si venerabilibus viris qui prefatas confecerunt legendas hec nota fuissent, ea minime preterissent, quin saltem pro parte ipsa suo decorassent eloquio et posteris ad memoriam reliquissent" (ibid., 88).

101. Krüger, "Un santo da guardare," 145. The following section is a summary of the main points of this article.

102. Henk W. van Os, "The Earliest Altarpieces of S. Francis," in Gieben, *Francesco d'Assisi nella storia,* 1:335.

birds as their convent's seal.[103] The preaching to the birds is a demonstration of the *"verbum simplex,"* the divine gift of Francis as a perfect preacher who communicates his message with such simplicity and clarity that even the birds are able to understand it. As such, Francis's preaching is itself a miracle.[104] A comparison with Dominic can be illuminating here. Klaus Krüger writes that, in contrast to Francis, the hagiographical tradition of Dominic represents him as an educated cleric, who is characterized by determination, intelligence, and hostility to heresies.[105] Of particular interest is the Bardi panel painting in Cappella Bardi, Santa Croce, Florence, dating from 1250–1255, where Francis is depicted as the *alter Christus,* who has received his mission directly from God.[106] As such, the visual representations of Francis reinforced the message of the sermons by depicting the saint as a miracle maker and, most important, by describing Francis's understanding and preaching of the Bible as a miracle in itself.

Two Saints, Two Men of Learning: Francis of Assisi and Anthony of Padua

The depiction of Francis as a simple man who had received the divine gift of learning, emphasized in Thomas of Celano's *First Life* and Julian of Speyer's *Life of Saint Francis,* was reiterated in the *Second Life* of Celano. "Although this blessed man was not educated in scholarly disciplines, still he learned from God wisdom from above and enlightened by the splendors of eternal light, he understood Scripture deeply."[107] In Celano's *Second Life,* Francis was not the only one who received the divine gift of learning. There are stories concerning other simple friars who preached impressively in front of a learned crowd. The possibility of acquiring divine learning through living a devotedly spiritual, impeccable penitential life of virtue was open to anyone, not just to Francis.

Bonaventure, minister general of the Order from 1257 to 1274, was not as optimistic as Celano. For him, Francis was "unique" in receiving the divine gift of learning. In fact, this gift was precisely the sign of Francis's closeness to the

---

103. For the most detailed discussions of these themes, see Klaus Krüger, *Der frühe Bildkult des Franziskus in Italien: Gestalt- und Funktionswandel des Tafelbildes im 13. und 14. Jahrhundert* (Berlin: Gebr. Mann, 1992), 102–3; Krüger, "Un santo da guardare," 152–53; Servus Gieben, "San Francesco nell'arte popolare," in Gieben, *Francesco d'Assisi nella storia,* 1:343.

104. Krüger, *Der frühe Bildkult,* 103, and Krüger, "Un santo da guardare," 153–54.

105. Krüger, *Der frühe Bildkult,* 143.

106. Krüger, "Un santo da guardare," 156.

107. II Celano, 102; translation in Armstrong, Hellman, and Short, *Francis of Assisi,* 2:314.

divinity, his sanctity: it was one of his miracles. Bonaventure's view is best illustrated by the following excerpt from a sermon he preached in 1255:

> One may well wonder at his teaching. How was he able to teach others what no man had taught him? Did he come to this knowledge of himself? Be assured he did not. The evidence of that is found in the account of his life. When he was instructed by another man or had to prepare something himself, he had absolutely nothing to say. In that, however, he is more to be praised and wondered at than imitated. Hence it is not without reason that his sons attend the schools. To arrive at knowledge without a human teacher is not for everyone, but the privilege of a few. Though the Lord himself chose to teach St. Paul and St. Francis, it is his will that their disciples be taught by human teachers.[108]

In the tale of John the Simple recounted by Thomas of Celano in his *Second Life,* the archetypal simple brother attains holiness precisely by imitating Francis *ad litteram,* not by being taught by a human or divine teacher. Bonaventure, however, seems to have a different position based on the "frequency" with which God bestowed learning on his disciples. It is extremely rare that God teaches one, so the history of mankind can produce only a few examples. For the rest, the only possibility for sacred knowledge is being "taught" by human teachers.

When Bonaventure preached his conviction that Saint Francis was divinely illuminated, and that this was an extremely rare miracle, he was borrowing the ideas of non-Franciscan scholars in the universities, such as William of Auvergne (d. 1249) and Robert of Grosseteste (d. 1253), who had enlarged the scope of the ancient theory of divine illumination. These scholastics were among the first proponents of the idea that some individuals could receive the divine light and thus acquire the knowledge of higher substances like the realm of angels and God.[109] In his 2001 book on the theory of divine illumination, Steven Marrone summarizes their position:

> Mind, and thus soul, could achieve cognitive perfection only if open to intelligible lights from above—most importantly the divine light. Since perfection was essential to beatitude, humankind could achieve its intended end only when illumined by God. With such illumination out of the question in the present life, soul depended upon faith and obedience for hope of salvation and upon the words of the Fathers and traditions of the Church for whatever specific higher knowledge was required. To be

---

108. Eric Doyle, *The Disciple and the Master: St. Bonaventure's Sermons on St. Francis of Assisi* (Chicago: Franciscan Herald Press, 1984), 64.

109. On this, see Steven P. Marrone, *The Light of Thy Countenance: Science and Knowledge of God in the Thirteenth Century* (Leiden: Brill, 2001), 1:98–104.

sure, there were direct divine revelations to a few privileged souls before death, though not always totally lucid and sometimes of modest cognitive content. According to Grosseteste, God showed himself this way only to individuals perfectly free of love of material things, perhaps just Moses, Paul and the Virgin Mary, while a more liberal William granted that melancholy might render one prone to such visions. Chief prerequisites for Godly revelation were in any case pure living and strong attachment to study, and William remarked that even some diligent philosophers of unsavory life had been given special insights by the divinity.[110]

Having been exposed to such ideas in Paris, Bonaventure should not have found it difficult to place Francis (who received the grace of stigmata) alongside Moses and Paul among the rare examples of the men who received the gift of divine illumination and to identify the Franciscan life as the life of perfection, devoid of material dependencies, the kind of life that was needed to accompany a mind in pursuit of higher knowledge. In this Bonaventure was also encouraged by the application of the prophecies of Joachim of Fiore to the Franciscan Order, as a result of which the Franciscan life came to be seen as the life of "evangelical perfection."[111] Equally important in this theory of divine illumination is the way in which one should seek divine illumination. As William of Auvergne stressed, "strong attachment to study" certainly led at least to a partial and imperfect illumination of the mind.

This was perhaps in the mind of the minister general John of Parma, himself a bachelor of theology in Paris in the 1240s, as he famously said that the Order rose on two columns: good life and learning. Bonaventure's famous treatise *The Journey of the Soul to God (Itinerarium mentis ad Deum)* is in fact based on this particular theory that intellectual efforts are a stage in the contemplation of God. Bonaventure's idea that Saint Francis was to be praised and wondered at but not imitated in the way by which he received his learning was probably also inspired by John of Rupella (d. 1245), the second regent master of the Paris studium. John appears to have been the first friar to preach on Francis in Paris.[112] His four sermons on Francis have been studied by Bougerol. All these

---

110. Ibid., 1:101.

111. On the particular association of evangelical perfection with Joachim's third status, see Marjorie Reeves, *The Influence of Prophecy in the Later Middle Ages: A Study in Joachimism* (Oxford: Clarendon Press, 1969), 176.

112. Jacques-Guy Bougerol, "S. François dans les sermons universitaires," in *Francesco d'Assisi nella Storia, secoli XIII–XV: Atti del primo Convegno di studi per l'VIII centenario della nascita di S. Francesco, 1182–1982, Roma, 29 settembre–2 ottobre 1981*, ed. Servus Gieben (Rome, 1983), 187; Jacques Dalarun, "Francesco nei sermoni: Agiografia e predicazione," in *La predicazione dei Frati dalla Metà del '200 alla fine del '300, Atti del xxii convegno internazionale, Assisi, 13–15 octobre 1994*, ed. Edith Pasztor (Spoleto: Centro italiano di studi sull'Alto medioevo, 1995), 361.

sermons borrow extensively from the *Vita prima*.[113] In one of these, John of Rupella stresses Francis's resemblance to the perfection of Christ in his human life and concludes that God created Francis in the image of the divinity of Christ and in the resemblance of his humanity.[114]

Although the central figure in early Franciscanism, Francis was not the only saint to shape the Franciscan identity, which speedily integrated learning. Perhaps more than Francis, Anthony of Padua made his mark on the learned Franciscans and how they identified themselves with the Franciscan movement. Today one of the most popular saints in the Catholic world, Anthony of Padua, the second Franciscan to be canonized, was actually an Augustinian canon regular in Lisbon before joining the Franciscans. He was very well educated and, after taking the Franciscan habit, became famous in a short time mainly through his very effective preaching. His fame was so well established in his own time that his canonization proceeded even more quickly than that of Francis. Anthony died in 1231 and he was canonized by Pope Gregory IX less than a year later in 1232.

The first work produced on Saint Anthony was an anonymous *Life of Saint Anthony (known as the Vita prima, or Assidua)* composed by a friar from the Paduan convent at the time of his canonization. Soon after, between 1232 and 1235, Julian of Speyer wrote a *Divine Office* for Anthony's feast day (June 13) based on *Assidua*. It was Julian's *Divine Office of Saint Anthony* and his life of Anthony, *Vita secunda,* that made the contents of the *Assidua* known to the friars of the Order.[115] It is therefore more important to investigate Julian's depiction of Anthony. Curiously, Francis is absent from the *Assidua.* However, Julian reinstates him into the life of Anthony by depicting Anthony as a loyal follower of Francis. Sometimes the relationship between the two men is alluded to as that of a father and son, and at other times that of a commander and his soldier.[116] Antonio Rigon refers to the "franciscanization" of Anthony, and this is of course quite significant, considering the fact that Anthony, with all his erudition, was not a "typical" follower of Francis, as he was quite different from Francis's original companions.[117] By emphasizing Anthony's link to Francis, Julian represents Anthony as the exemplary Franciscan. The *Assidua* records with enthusiasm Saint Anthony's erudition and his efforts at teaching theology to friars.[118] Julian picks up these parts and actually carves a new Franciscan role model. Anthony

113. Dalarun, "Francesco nei sermoni," 361–63.

114. Bougerol, "S. François dans les sermons universitaires," 189.

115. Julian of Speyer, *Officio ritmico,* 277.

116. Ibid., 106–7.

117. Antonio Rigon, *Dal libro alla folla: Antonio di Padova e il francescanesimo medievale* (Rome: Viella, 2002), 57.

118. Vergilio Gamboso, ed., *Vita prima di S. Antonio; o, Assidua (c. 1232),* Fonti agiografiche antoniane, vol. 1 (Padua: Edizioni Messagero, 1981), chaps. 4 and 10.

comes across as a friar whose wisdom and erudition were in perfect harmony with the mainstream Franciscan virtues of poverty and humility. There is certainly an emphasis on poverty and humility, but the prime virtue of Anthony is his wisdom and erudition.[119] Julian makes fifteen references to this theme in the Divine Office.[120]

"In the wise son, the father glorifies," writes Julian at the beginning of the Divine Office for the first vespers. "This is recommended suitably in Anthony."[121] In the *Vita secunda* we read:

> The Spirit, predicting the future, was pushing him to the study of sacred scripture. By meditating on it continually, he not only learned how to sow virtues in the fields of others and to root out vices—first improving himself with great care—but also he fortified himself with the strongest teachings of the Fathers and this way built on the norm of faith and confronted the errors.[122]

The "future" that is predicted by the Spirit is no doubt Saint Anthony's future life as a Franciscan. For Julian, then, the study of sacred scripture is a necessary part of Franciscan life, and it not only is useful for preaching but also makes one a "better" Christian by strengthening the knowledge of virtue and vice, and confronting heresies. In passages such as these, Julian displays conviction in a Franciscan identity of which the study of scripture is an essential part. Should we consider Julian as representative of the Paris convent or of the general tendencies in the Franciscan Order? There is no easy answer to this question. Neither in the *Assidua,* which was not a fruit of the Paris convent but that of Padua, nor in Julian's work is discussion of Saint Anthony's studies and erudition communicated in a "defensive" tone that could lead one to the conclusion that the authors were responding to some criticism, or were trying to make an argument against a general tendency. Instead, the figure of Anthony is represented as that of a learned friar embracing voluntary simplicity, an identity also promoted at a later time by Thomas of Celano, albeit not as an exclusive identity. It is quite interesting that when Anthony of Padua first entered the Order, instead of pursuing a life as a teacher or preacher, he petitioned the minister of Romagna to be able to live in the hermitage of Monte Paolo. Here he pursued a life of

---

119. See Julian of Speyer, *Officio ritmico,* 104–6.

120. Ibid., 105.

121. "Sapiente filio, pater gloriatur: hoc et in Antonio digne commendatur" (ibid., 176).

122. Ibid., 390–92 (*Vita secunda,* chap. 1, sentence 7). "Propellebat autem eum iam Spiritus, quodam futurorum presagio, ad divinarum studia litterarum, in quibus iugiter meditando, non solum qualiter in agro alieno vicia exstirpando virtutes insereret, semet ipsum sollicite primitus excolendo, cognovit: verum etiam qualiter fidei normam astrueret ac confutaret errores, firmissimis Patrum sententiis se munivit."

rigorous asceticism and prayer. Julian says: "Although he was filled with the gift of wisdom, he lived for a long time a simple life among the simple."[123]

> His *vilitas,* his simple innocence,
> His care for discipline prove his life
> His zeal joined with love,
> His truthfulness and his modesty
> Are the testimonies of his teaching.[124]

In his *Life of Saint Anthony,* Julian also draws the link between learning and usefulness that has been discussed above. The same rhetoric that was present in Gregory IX's bull concerning the delegation of authority with regard to the reception of recruits had already been employed by Julian around 1232–1235. At the end of the General Chapter of Assisi when, "as it is the custom," friars were being assigned to convents, Anthony was the only one whom nobody wanted, because he was not known and seemed "useless" (*inutilis*). Julian says that finally Anthony approached the minister of Romagna, Brother Gratian, without saying anything of his erudition or the other ways in which he could be useful.[125] We can conclude that an association between learning and usefulness, or a general preoccupation with the "usefulness" of friars, dates back to the 1230s. Anthony's silence about his erudition presents a good example of voluntary simplicity—he is a friar who does not boast about being learned.

Julian of Speyer's representation of Anthony as the learned man who voluntarily embraced simplicity seem to have influenced the sermons delivered by the friars on the feast of Saint Anthony. We have three sermons on Saint Anthony preached by the second regent master of theology in Paris, John of Rupella (1238–1245). John of Rupella knew both works of Julian of Speyer, the *Divine Office* and the *Life of Saint Anthony,* and cites these in his sermons.[126] The central focus and the objective of these sermons were to represent Anthony as the ideal example for the Franciscans. In him, efficient preaching on account of his learning is strongly united to his virtuous life and character based on the

---

123. "Sic igitur vir Dei Antonius, cum dono sapientie plenus esset, multo tempore simplicem inter simplices vitam duxit" Julian of Speyer, *Officio ritmico,* 404 (*Vita secunda,* chap. 3).

124. "Vitam probant vilitas, / simplex innocentia, / cura discipline; / zelo iuncta caritas, / veritas, modestia / testes sunt doctrine" (*Divine Office of St. Anthony,* 7, in Julian of Speyer, *Officio ritmico,* 204).

125. "Soluto igitur ex more capitulo fratribusque ad sua circumquaque loca dimissis, solus Antonius a nemine petebatur, qui, sicut erat ignotus, ita et inutilis videbatur. Nulla ergo de se vel litterature vel cuiuscumque alterius utilitatis habita mentione, ad fratrem Gratianum, qui tunc fratribus Romagniole preerat" (Julian of Speyer, *Officio ritmico,* 402, based on *Assidua,* chap. 7).

126. Gamboso demonstrated that John of Rupella knew Julian's works on Anthony well enough to cite them in his sermons. Julian Speyer, *Officio ritmico,* 58–61. See also Balduinus de Amsterdam, "Tres sermones inediti Joannis de Rupellae in honorem S. Antonii Patavini," *CF* 28 (1958), 40–41; Rigon, *Dal libro alla folla,* 57.

primary Franciscan virtues of humility and poverty.[127] In all three sermons, John of Rupella gives ample space to the learning of Anthony and its connection to his preaching. John praises the saint's preaching and compares it to that of other preachers of his day. Anthony uses the words of scripture instead of tricks and fables. His preaching corresponds to the intelligence of his audience. He does not strive to ornament his sermons with subtleties instead of useful things, like some do. He tries to reach out and preach to the sinners, whereas some wish to preach only to the good and the learned clergy.[128]

The third sermon is particularly crucial in understanding how a Parisian master like John of Rupella saw learning and teaching as an essential part of his Franciscan identity. There is nothing that resembles a justification or apology in this sermon. Rather, it is a subtle and powerful argument: if, indeed, the Rule of the Friars Minor is to observe the Gospel, then the friars ought to know and teach sacred scripture, because that is what Christ did on earth. This sermon takes as its theme Luke 6:40: "Everyone shall be perfect, if he were as his master."[129] The opening lines link all three figures, Anthony of Padua, Francis, and Christ. "The master of blessed Anthony was blessed Francis. Although the mastership in this sense belongs to Christ, nevertheless it can belong to Francis too....Blessed Anthony was perfect just as his master Christ." Anthony is represented as the perfect disciple of Christ and therefore the perfect disciple of Francis. The emphasis on such an association between Anthony and Francis is all the more remarkable when we consider the fact that Anthony of Padua himself never mentioned Francis in his sermons.[130] Servus Gieben has explained this oddity by suggesting that the surviving sermons of Anthony were from the time when he was still an Augustinian canon.[131]

In this third sermon, John says that the perfection of the mastership consists in the life and the teaching (*vita et doctrina*) of Christ. He finds eight conditions that bring about perfection in life, and similarly eight conditions for perfection in terms of teaching. All these conditions were present in Anthony, who was perfect like his master, Christ. The very first condition is *scientia*:

> For he who is a doctor ought to read sacred scripture and teach....He has to announce and teach the virtues, argue against the vices, chastise crimes,

---

127. de Amsterdam, "Tres sermones inediti," 36–37.

128. Ibid., 47.

129. "Perfectus autem omnis erit, si sit sicut magister eius" (ibid., 52).

130. I have searched through his edited sermons but found nothing about Francis. Beniamino Costa, Leonardo Frasson, and Giovanni M. Luisetto, eds., *S. Antonii Patavini sermones dominicales et festivi ad fidem codicum recogniti* (Padua: Centro studi antoniani, 1979).

131. Servus Gieben, "Preaching in the Franciscan Order (Thirteenth Century)," in *Monks, Nuns, and Friars in Mediaeval Society,* ed. Edward B. King, Jacqueline T. Schaefer, and William B. Wadley (Sewanee, TN: University of the South Press, 1989), 14.

instruct concerning the rewards and punishments. He ought to be learned and humble to teach the virtues, innocent, at an advanced age,[132] to argue against the vices, righteous, irreprehensible, in order to explain correctly the rewards and punishments.... And this is found easily in Christ. For he had knowledge, since *in Christ are hidden all the treasures of wisdom and knowledge* [Col. 2, 3], *and the Spirit fills him with wisdom and understanding* [Isa 11, 2].... But many are puffed up by their knowledge; therefore humility is necessary, which was utmost in Christ.[133]

After enumerating other virtues of Christ, John moves on to show that all these virtues are present in Anthony too. Therefore he was perfect just as his master Christ was:

He was perfect in knowledge, that is why he was called by the lord pope *Archa Testamenti*. In him, there was, just as in Christ, the treasury of knowledge. That is why we read about him that he was using his memory instead of books.... However, he was not puffed up by this wisdom, and in him the perfection of humility was united to knowledge. For although he was fit to teach, as we read about him, he would rather practice doing the dishes than reading books of *scientia*.... Therefore he was suitable to teach.[134]

John believes in the necessity of combining learning with humility, but there is more than that.[135] *Scientia*, which can be translated here as "learning," appears as a virtue of Christ, and consequently as a "Franciscan" virtue, since Franciscans set out to imitate Christ. We observe, then, a difference in the way John of Rupella and Thomas of Celano experienced Franciscanism. For Thomas, the simple zealous friar could be more saintly and preach better than a learned

---

132. The condition for old age is explained later in the sermon: Christ did not start teaching when he was a boy even though he was already *plenus sapientiae,* but at a manly (*virili*) age. Reference is to Luke (2:40) where it says Christ was almost thirty years old.

133. "Nam qui doctor est, oportet quod legat sacram scripturam ac doceat... Debet enim virtutes annuntiare et docere, arguere vitia, corripere de commissis, erudire de premiis et suppliciis. Oportet ergo ut sit sciens et humilis ad docendum virtutes, innocens, annosus ad arguendum vitia, iustus, irreprehensibilis ad corripiendum de premiis et suppliciis.... Et hoc in Christo facillime est reperire. Fuit enim sciens, nam *in Christo sunt omnes thesauri sapientie et scientie absconditi,* Col. II, *et replevit eum spiritus sapientie et intellectus,* Ysa VII.... Sed multi inflantur scientia, ideo necessaria est humilitas, que maxime fuit in Christo" (de Amsterdam, "Tres sermones inediti," 53).

134. "Perfectus fuit in scientia, unde et Archa Testamenti dicebatur a domino papa. Erat enim in ipso, queadmodum et in Christo, thesaurus scientie. Unde et de ipso legitur, quod memoria pro codicibus utebatur.... Sed non fuit hac sapientia inflatus, ideo perfectionem humilitatis habuit scientie coniunctam. Nam cum esset ad docendum ydoneus, tamen de ipso legitur, quod in abluendis coquine utensilibus magis quam exercendis scripturis scientie exercitior habebatur.... Ex hoc fuit ydoneus ad docendum" (ibid., 54).

135. Rigon, *Dal libro alla folla,* 58.

brother, even when the latter embraced humility. For John, learning is a virtue of Christ, so a perfect disciple of Christ should be learned. Francis received it directly from God, Anthony through human teachers.

A sermon of another Franciscan preacher, Nicholas d'Hacqueville, preached on the feast of Saint Anthony, possibly in Paris, presents Anthony as a Francis-like figure that the friars should look up to:

> God created two great lanterns, the bigger lantern is present during the day, and the smaller one during the night, and then he created the stars and placed them in the fixed sphere of Heavens so that they shine over the earth, and are present day and night. The bigger lantern is blessed Francis, and the smaller lantern is blessed Anthony. The stars, which are in the fixed sphere, are all other Friars Minor who have to shine over the earth as good examples.[136]

Studying as Perfection

Following in the tradition of John of Rupella and Bonaventure, in the late thirteenth century the baton of representing learning as a saintly activity passed to Peter John Olivi. In fact in Olivi, another designated "Spiritual," we find full exposition of the way that the study of sacred scripture and other auxiliary disciplines (it is particularly noteworthy that Olivi includes "studere in aliis scientiis" in the formulation of the question) became an integral part of the life of "evangelical perfection"—of Franciscan life, in other words. Following in the footsteps of Bonaventure, Olivi too left behind a series of questions titled *Questions on Evangelical Perfection* published in 1279. In the third question of his *Quaestiones de perfectione evangelica,* Olivi discusses the question of "whether the study of sacred scripture and other disciplines is a perfect activity in itself."[137] His discussion of this question possibly implies that doubts were being raised in his time, most probably from those outside the Order, concerning the appropriateness of study in an Order dedicated to evangelical perfection. For Olivi, study itself—not only of sacred scripture but also of other sciences where these were necessary for understanding the divinity—is a perfect activity under certain

---

136. "Fecit Deus duo luminaria magna, luminare majus ut praeesset diei et luminare minus ut praeesset nocti, et stellas, et posuit in firmamento coeli ut lucerent super terram et praeessent diei et nocti. Luminare majus est beatus Franciscus, luminare minus est beatus Antonius; stellae, quae debent esse in firmamento, omnes alii fratres Minores qui debent lucere super terram per bonum exemplum." Barthélemy Hauréau, *Notices et extraits de quelques manuscrits latins de la Bibliothèque nationale* (Paris: Klincksieck, 1891), 3:283.

137. Peter John Olivi, "An studere sit opus de genere suo perfectum," in *La dottrina dell'Olivi sulla contemplazione, la vita attiva e mista,* ed. Aquilino Emmen and Feliciano Simoncioli, *Studi Francescani* 61 (1964): 141–59.

conditions and circumstances.[138] He explains in detail what these requirements are: an activity is said to be perfect *ex suo genere* if it has a perfect end. Study of the divinity, since it has a perfect end, is an activity that is perfect *ex suo genere*:

> To know in which way studying is suitable to the perfect man one needs know what is necessary to perfection, what is useful and appropriate, what is superfluous and harmful. To study those things, the knowledge of which is necessary to man, is necessary for perfection and for grace. Second, beside the necessity, studying stimulates the mind and illuminates it more fully in the divinities and in those things that serve the understanding of the divinities, therefore it is perfect, useful, and proper; and it is necessary insofar as the fullness of perfection cannot be complete without the perfect illustration of the mind; and insofar as others cannot be led to perfection and maintained without great learning and understanding. Also, to want to lead others to goodness and to show care for men on this account is not less of a perfection. Again, since there are only a few, perhaps no one in this life, who can be constant in their fervor of devotion, and since laziness is worst, it is best and expedient for perfect men to be occupied in studying, at least for those who do not know how or are unable to occupy themselves with other things.[139]

Furthermore, Olivi suggested that studying contributes to perfection insofar as it keeps one's mind away from worldly things. Studying harms perfection only if a scholar studies not for the love of God or for his own edification or the edification of others, but out of curiosity.[140]

---

138. "Studere ergo in sacra Scriptura est perfectivum et viro perfecto competens, informatum conditionibus et circumstantiis supradictis; et etiam studere in aliis scientiis, quantum est necessarium et utile ad praedicta" (ibid., 151).

139. "Ut sciatur autem quomodo competat viro perfecto, sciendum quod aliquid est ad perfectionem necessarium, aliquid utile et accomodum, aliquid supervacuum et nocivum. Studere autem in illis, quae necessarie sunt homini scienda, est ad perfectionem et etiam ad gratiam necessarium. Secundum autem, quo ultra necessitatem in divinis et in his, quae ad haec intuenda valent, mentem exacuit et plenius illuminat, est perfectum utile et accommodum; et pro tanto necessarium, in quantum perfectionis consummata plenitudo sine intellectus perfecta illustratione esse non potest; et in quantum alii non possunt ad perfectionem per aliquem adduci et conservari sine magna scientia et cognitione. Velle autem alios ad bonum adducere et curam ad hoc pro viribus adhibere, non est modicae perfectionis. Cum autem pauci sint, qui in devotionis fervore possint esse continui, et forsitan in vita ista nulli, otiumque sit pessimum, et maxime viris perfectis, optimum est valde, et expediens, in studio pro tempore occupari, saltem illis qui in aliis occupare se nesciunt vel non possunt" (ibid., 150).

140. "Cum etiam studium valde mentem abstrahat a mundanis et a negotiationum tumultibus, et hoc summe expediat viro perfecto et ad perfectionum tendenti, optimum est, et valde expediens, ab istis per studium se abstrahere, saltem ei qui per alia vel non novit, vel non potest. Studere autem in quocumque, non referendo illud totaliter ad Dei amorem vel ad sui et aliorum aedificationem, sed potius propter sciendi curiositatem, aut propter popularis gloriae vanitatem, aut propter quaestus cupiditatem, est perfectioni nocivum et viro perfecto nullo modo competens" (ibid.).

Following the same line drawn by Bonaventure and Olivi, Matthew of Aquasparta, another important theologian and general minister of the Order, while he was a bachelor at Paris (c. 1268–1272) made a case in his *introitus* on theology for the significance of love of and dedication to learning as a step necessary for the acquisition of wisdom:

> The gift of wisdom is given only to those who fervently desire it and who abandon and despise everything for the love of it.... And for this reason Daniel, as he was a man of desires, received through revelation the understanding of the mysteries. Such deep understanding cannot be found except by scholars and those who investigate diligently.[141]

Matthew too, like other Franciscan scholars, was quick to add that a perfect scholar must have "simplicity" of intention and purity of heart:

> The third condition that makes man a suitable student of this science is the purity of the eye accompanied by the tranquillity of mind, so that the disciple of truth is saintly and peaceful and similarly he listens with great tranquillity and purity of heart.... It [the eye of the mind] is purified through the simplicity of intention; it strives for wisdom not out of a desire to please men but out of love of intellectual beauty. And this is the simple eye and pure heart: and likewise the pure heart is the simple heart.[142]

This openly expressed love of learning should not automatically put Matthew of Aquasparta in a category with those who intentionally harmed the Franciscan spirit, even though Dante considered him so.[143] Men like Bonaventure, Olivi, and Matthew of Aquasparta shared a love of learning as much as they shared an enthusiasm to remain true to the Franciscan spirit as they understood it. When Matthew of Aquasparta was elected the minister general of the Order, one of his first acts was to donate his substantial book collection to the convent libraries of

---

141. "Ideo donum sapientiae non datur nisi ferventer desiderantibus et prae eius amore omnia contemnentibus et despicientibus.... Et propterea Daniel, quia vir fuit desideriorum, accepit per revelationem intelligentiam mysteriorum. Quia autem profundissima, non invenitur nisi a studiosis et diligenter investigantibus." Matthew of Aquasparta, *Quaestiones disputatae: De fide et de cognitione,* ed. PP. Collegii S. Bonaventurae, 2nd ed. (Quaracchi, Florence: ex Typographia Collegii S. Bonaventure, 1957), 24).

142. "Tertia conditio, quae facit hominem idoneum auditorem istius scientiae, est puritas oculi cum mentis tranquillitate, ut videlicet discipulus veritatis sit sanctus et tranquillus, ita quod audiat cum magna tranquillitate et cordis munditia.... Ideo purificatur per intentionis simplicitatem, quo nullo studio placendi hominibus, sed solum amore intellectualis pulcritudinis studeret sapientiae. Et iste est oculus simplex et mundum cor: idem enim est mundum cor quod simplex cor" (ibid., 25).

143. Dante in *Paradiso,* canto XII, of the *Divine Comedy* says, "Ma non fia da Casal né d'Acquasparta, là onde vegnon tali scrittura, ch'uno la fugge e altro la coarta." This passage has been traditionally interpreted to mean that Matthew of Aquasparta relaxed the Rule, and Ubertino da Casale has been too rigid in its observance. Dante Alighieri, *Paradiso,* ed. and trans. Robert and Jean Hollander (New York: Doubleday, 2007), 298.

Assisi and Todi, probably obeying Francis's wish that a minister general should not be a book collector.[144] He was also responsible for the reinstatement of Olivi as a lector in Florence in 1287, then one of the most important studia in the Order, shortly after Olivi was cleared of charges of heresy.[145]

In this insistence by Franciscan scholars on purity of mind, humility, and simplicity of intention, we can see another powerful idea in action. Along with making the pursuit of learning into an element of the saintly life, Franciscan discourse introduced the claim that the Franciscan life was the ideal state in which learning could be pursued. Therefore, if anyone wished to dedicate themselves to the study of sacred scripture, it was best for them to study it while living the Franciscan life, at the heart of which lay the ideal of apostolic poverty.

"Those who do not and cannot have anything": Franciscan Scholars as Perfect Teachers

In the sermon of John of Rupella where he likened Anthony of Padua to Christ, a Christly virtue mentioned along with learning and humility was Anthony's choice of poverty, in particular Franciscan poverty. John of Rupella knew that Anthony was an Augustinian canon regular before joining the Franciscans, and that as such he had already embraced the poverty of the regular religious, that is, those who vowed to a Rule (*regula*) by entering a religious order. But the poverty that permitted common property did not constitute a state of perfection. According to John, the poverty of the Franciscans, where all property was denied, was the highest level of poverty, and thus the state of Christ. "The ultimate level of poverty is that of those who do not and cannot have anything. They give away what they own. This is the poverty of the Friars Minor, which he [Anthony] had and in which he persevered. That is why he is perfect and suitable to teach."[146] This sermon was preached sometime before John of Rupella's death in 1244. As such it is one of earliest texts that presents not the more common monastic poverty but Franciscan poverty as perfection, long before John's student, Bonaventure, elaborated on the subject in his questions

---

144. For the books of Matthew of Aquasparta, the best and most up-to-date study is Francesca Grauso, *I libri di Matteo d'Acquasparta,* Tesi di diploma in Paleografia Latina, Università degli Studi di Roma "La Sapienza," Scuola Speciale per Archivisti e Bibliotecari, corso di Diploma per Conservatore di Manoscritti, Anno accademico 2001–2002. For Francis's wish that minister generals should not collect books, see chap. 1, n. 117.

145. Roest, *History of Franciscan Education,* 47.

146. "Preterea est reperire alium gradum paupertatis, eorum scilicet, qui nihil habentes proprium possident in communi. Hec est paupertas religiosorum, quam beatus Antonius habuit, quamdiu beati Augustini regule subiacuit. Est etiam ultimus gradus paupertatis, eorum scilicet, qui nichil habent nec habere possunt; communicant proprium. Et hec est paupertas fratrum minorum, quam habuit et in qua perseveravit. Ideo perfectus et ydoneus est ad erudiendum" (de Amsterdam, "Tres sermones inediti," 56).

On Evangelical Perfection. There is more, however: Anthony's evangelical poverty makes him fit to teach. It is precisely in this link that we find an answer to the question of why so many learned men became Franciscans and clung to this identity, and why they did not choose the Dominican Order, which might have seemed better suited to the intellectually inclined.[147]

Even though today poverty appears to be the most essential feature of medieval Franciscanism, it might come as a surprise that in Francis's own writings, poverty does not have a dominant place. In his salutation of virtues, Francis praises six virtues in three pairs: wisdom and simplicity, poverty and humility, charity and obedience. There is no reason to think that for Francis poverty figured larger than the other virtues. In fact, in his small corpus, Francis gives the lion's share to reverence for the Eucharist, and to obedience and humility.[148] Nowhere does he clearly define what Franciscan poverty is about. In the sixth chapter of the Franciscan Rule is a clause that specifies that friars are not supposed to appropriate anything, followed by a sentence that probably inspired John of Rupella's sermon cited above: "This is the height of the highest poverty."[149] Elsewhere in his works, Francis is rather silent on the subject of communal property, as he is on the subject of learning. That which he wishes to condemn is rather "the property-owning mind" is the conclusion of Malcolm Lambert.[150] It is quite remarkable that in his Testament, which can be considered the most significant and authentic document reflecting his will, Francis does not mention poverty at all.[151]

Somehow, however, during the first half of the thirteenth century, poverty rose to a position of preeminence among all the virtues associated with Franciscanism. This rise can be observed in the attention given to poverty in the sermons, in the theological works, in the Rule commentaries, and in statutes produced in this period and beyond. Since all this written material exalting and cherishing Franciscan poverty was essentially the production of the "learned" brothers, there seems to be an organic link between the two phenomena, poverty and learning. Together they have come to define medieval Franciscanism. As the scope of this book is not to trace the rise of poverty but that of learning, the central question here is how exactly was poverty linked to the rise of learning in the Order?

---

147. The connections between poverty and learning in the discourse of medieval Franciscan scholars remain unexplored. It is difficult to do justice to such a complex subject in this book, since it requires a thorough investigation of all treatises and sermons focusing on Franciscan poverty, which are many in number. The present section will introduce ideas that I plan to examine in depth in the future.

148. Lambert, *Franciscan Poverty,* 43.

149. "Haec est celsitudo altissimae paupertatis" (RB, chap. 6).

150. Lambert, *Franciscan Poverty,* 51. See the entire analysis in pp. 31–67.

151. Menestò and Brufani, *Fontes Franciscani,* 1697, cite Esser, *Il testamento di San Francesco* (Milan, 1978), 99, as having noted this peculiarity.

Even though Francis, as a poor, little man with a giant faith, had energized so many, intellectually speaking, the rationality of Franciscan poverty could be challenged on many fronts. Poverty of this sort was a novelty for the official Church, its administrators, and for the learned men in it, who were mostly monks. There does not seem, in written theological discourses up until this time, to have been a precedent for absolute poverty being the highest virtue.[152] Since Saint Francis was credited with the doctrine of the absolute poverty—and of course he was no learned doctor but had the reputation of being an uneducated, simple man—the viability, credibility, and theological soundness of this doctrine was open to challenge. From a sermon preached by Bonaventure in 1255 we get a sense of the difficulties in this respect that the Franciscans in Parisian circles faced:

> Moreover, it pleased the Lord to endorse and confirm the teaching and Rule of St. Francis, not only by miraculous signs, but also by the marks of his own stigmata, so that no true believer could possibly call them into question on external or internal evidence.... His teaching could not have had its lasting character, in the eyes of others, from St. Francis himself, for he was an uneducated merchant and no learned doctor. Therefore, it was the Lord's good pleasure to confirm it by manifest signs in the form of an awe-inspiring seal from on high, so that none of the learned could dare despise his teaching and Rule as only the efforts of an uneducated man. This shows us clearly how we ought to marvel at the depth of God's judgments, which Christ indicates at the beginning of today's Gospel when he says: *thank you, Father, Lord of heaven and earth, that you have hidden these things from the wise and understanding and revealed them to little ones....*Consequently, anyone who doubts that the doctrine and Rule of St. Francis are a most perfect way to reach eternal life, when these have been confirmed by such great signs, must be exceedingly hard of heart.[153]

The discourse concerning Franciscan life and especially poverty produced by learned Franciscans can be read in two ways. In one sense, it gives us clues as to why learned men chose the Franciscan life—what they saw in it that they did not find in other religious vocations. However, it can also be taken to explain how learned Franciscans, in their capacity as preachers, lectors, and ministers, justified the life of poverty and mendicancy among the intellectual elite, advertised

---

152. See Lambert, *Franciscan Poverty,* 40, where he writes that the poverty of monastic Orders was incomplete and partial, and the closest followers of Franciscan poverty in the twelfth century are to be found among heretical sects like the Waldenses and Cathars.

153. Sermon 1 on Saint Francis, preached at Paris, October 4, 1255, *The Disciple and the Master: St. Bonaventure's Sermons on St. Francis of Assisi,* ed. and trans. Eric Doyle (Chicago: Franciscan Herald Press, 1984), 66.

their Order in the university circles for the purposes of recruiting scholars, and emphasized their difference from the contemporary Dominican Order.

The publication of several treatises by Franciscan masters defending poverty during the conflict between the secular and regular (clergy who were also members of a religious order) university masters in the second half of the thirteenth century might lead us to think that the justification of poverty and the Franciscan life was a late phenomenon. In reality, though, it started much earlier in the 1230s. The following is from a sermon by an anonymous Franciscan preached at the University of Paris on January 21, 1231. "The means to go to God is poverty, which is proved by the argument from opposites....If riches are the way to go to hell, then poverty is the way to go to paradise. And this is why the Philosopher calls poverty 'gold.'"[154] The preacher then alludes to those in university circles who despise poverty and stop others from joining the Franciscans, informing us of the impediments Franciscan recruiters encountered:

> Let us therefore be poor for the sake of Christ, because he made himself poor for our sake. But there are some who not only do not want to become poor, but they also prohibit others to become poor or to enter the cloister, and therefore whoever wishes to join the Order must beware of accepting counsel from those who are worldly and speak of the things of the world.[155]

Another sermon dating from April 7, 1231, warns further against the "enemies" of poverty:

> The plenitude of graces is acquired through poverty. Those who condemn poverty are so filled with temporal things that they cannot be filled with any spiritual good....Some say boldly that the apostle was rich...but he himself shows that he was not rich saying, "We have food, and some things to cover ourselves. We are content with these" [1 Tim. 6:8]....This is chiefly against those clerics who grasp riches with their hands. Therefore, relinquishing riches, you will love poverty, so that this way we shall be filled with grace now, and with glory in the future.[156]

---

154. "Medium autem eundi ad Deum est paupertas quod probatur per locum ab oppositis....Si divitae sunt medium eundi in infernum et paupertas medium erit eundi in paradisum. Et propter hoc Philosophus vocat paupertatem: auream" (Davy, *Les sermons universitaires,* 385).

155. "Simus igitur pauperes pro Christo quia et pro nobis factus est pauper. Sed sunt aliqui qui non solum nolunt fieri pauperes sed etiam prohibent aliis ne et ipsi pauperes sint, et ne intrent claustrum; et propter hoc qui vult intrare religionem caveat sibi ne consilium accipiat a talibus quia de mundo sunt et de mundo loquuntur" (ibid.).

156. "Primum est plenitudo gratiarum; haec autem plenitudo per paupertatem acquiritur....Sed sunt nonnulli qui paupertatem contemnerunt, ita pleni sunt temporalibus qui nullo bono spirituali possunt repleri....Sed forte dicet aliquis: Apostolus dives erat. Sed quod dives non fuerit ipsemet ostendit dicens:'Habentes alimenta et quibus tegamur: iis contenti sumus.'...Quod maxime est contra clericos qui

It looks like the objection in some clerical circles to the pursuit of poverty initially pushed the learned Franciscans to rise to its defense, thereby making it slowly the quintessential feature of Franciscanism that was constantly exposed, formulated, and reformulated in the intellectual discourse of the thirteenth and fourteenth centuries.

By the time John of Rupella preached his sermon on Anthony in the 1240s, Franciscan poverty was not just defended but was thought of as an indispensable attribute of "evangelical perfection," even though John does not use that term. It is from this perspective that we need to read *The Sacred Exchange between Saint Francis and Lady Poverty* (*Sacrum commercium s. Francisci cum domina Paupertate*), which is thought to have been written sometime after 1256.[157] *The Sacred Exchange* is a very rich and wonderfully imaginative allegory recounting a love story between Francis and Holy Poverty, who is personified in the story as a lady that lives in a high mountain retreat, reminiscent of Franciscan hermitages. This work presents the ambitious identification of Franciscanism—in fact, of Christian life in general—with poverty, all other virtues pushed into its shade. The primary aim of the author of *The Sacred Exchange* is to prove that the kind of poverty that Francis embraced is the foremost Christian virtue. It is to poverty that God has given the keys of the Kingdom of Heaven.[158] She also reigns over all other virtues.[159] Duane Lapsanski interpreted *The Sacred Exchange* as a pioneering text that placed poverty within the history of salvation, diverging from the twelfth-century movements that emphasized only the external and ascetic aspects of poverty.[160]

In the very beginning of this text, Francis is depicted going around asking people whether they have seen his love, Lady Poverty. After being scolded by the townspeople, he resolves to ask the wise, "who know the way of God." The learned also scold him saying that they have never heard any such teaching that exalted poverty and reply "We do not know anything better than to eat, drink and be merry as long as we live."[161] The incident makes Francis marvel at God's ways, in that such things

---

divitias manibus amplectentur. Propter hoc ergo divitias relinquentes diligetis paupertatem ut sic, boni in praesenti, et gratia repleamur et gloria in futuro" (ibid., 393–94).

157. The most recent edition of this work is S. Brufani, ed., *Sacrum commercium sancti Francisci cum domina Paupertate* (Assisi: Edizione Porziuncola, 1990). It is reprinted in Menestò and Brufani, "Fontes Francescani," 1693–1732. For the English translation, see Armstrong, Hellman, and Short, *Francis of Assisi*, 1:529–54.

158. Brufani, *Sacrum commercium,* prologue, sen. 12. See also Brufani's introduction, *Fontes Francescani*, 1697.

159. Brufani, *Sacrum commercium,* chap. 5, sen. 4.

160. See Duane V. Lapsanski, *Evangelical Perfection: An Historical Examination of the Concept in the Early Franciscan Sources* (St. Bonaventure, NY: Franciscan Institute, 1977), 263.

161. "'Ibo'—inquit beatus Franciscus—'ad optimates et sapientes et loquar eis. Ipsi enim cognoverunt viam Domini et judicium Dei sui....' Quo facto ipsi durius responderunt ei, dicentes: 'Que nova est

are kept hidden from the wise and prudent and revealed to the minors (*parvuli*).[162] By "learned men" the author refers most likely to the learned secular clergy, such as the university masters who have found a theology of poverty as evangelical perfection quite objectionable. The author of the *Sacred Exchange* himself was clearly a very learned man judging by the erudition he displays in this work and according to the testimony of Ubertino da Casale.[163] He does not criticize learning, but the "learned men who despise and refuse poverty."

In the absence of a reliable date or authorship, Stefano Brufani, the most recent scholar to work on this text, placed the composition of *Sacred Exchange* in the main period of the mendicant-secular controversy, that is, after 1256, based on the general assumption that the exaltation of Franciscan poverty must belong to the context of the defense of Franciscan life against the secular clergy.[164] This is reasonable, but, as indicated above, the intellectualization of poverty as a state of perfection, and the claim that Franciscan poverty was a higher state of poverty than that of other religious, started much earlier. In fact, it is more plausible to read the secular-mendicant controversy as a consequence of successful Franciscan propaganda concerning the importance of poverty within university circles and of Franciscan recruitment from among the university scholars, which threatened the established hegemony of the secular masters in the universities. The 1230s and 1240s are therefore as likely a date for the production of *The Sacred Exchange* as the period after 1256. Impressed by its author's absolute devotion to poverty, Sabatier suggested Francis's companion Leo of Assisi to be the author of the Sacred Exchange. However, Sabatier never took into consideration the fact that, at least in intellectual discourse, Franciscan scholars were fervent defenders of poverty. Editors of the 1999 English translation suggest the German theologian Caesar of Speyer as the possible author.[165]

By the 1250s, poverty looms larger than ever in the identity of Franciscan scholars. By then, *pauper* had become a synonym for a Franciscan. "Greetings and whatever can avail you the devotion of a *pauper* and the prayers of a sinner," wrote the Franciscan lector of Oxford Adam Marsh to an acquaintance in his letter in 1250.[166] In 1255, responding to the question of a secular scholar in

---

hec doctrina, quam infers auribus nostris?... Nihil enim melius cognovimus quam letari, manducare et bibere donec vivimus'" (Brufani, *Sacrum commercium*, chap. 1, sen. 6–7, 10).

162. Ibid., chap. 1, sen. 12.

163. Ubertino da Casale wrote that the author of the *Sacred Exchange* was a holy doctor. See Armstrong, Hellman, and Short, *Francis of Assisi*, 1:526.

164. Menestò and Brufani, *Fontes Francescani*, 1700. In earlier editions, *Sacred Exchange* was dated to 1227, since this was explicitly written in one of the manuscripts where the text is preserved. Brufani shows that this manuscript comes from the weaker branch and therefore is not reliable.

165. Armstrong, Hellman, and Short, *Francis of Assisi*, 1:526–27.

166. *The Letters of Adam Marsh,* ed. and trans. C. Hugh Lawrence (Oxford: Clarendon Press, 2006), 1:271. Lawrence's translation with slight modification.

Paris concerning the appropriateness of Franciscans teaching and being called masters, Bonaventure wrote:

> Who is more suited to the teaching of the Gospel than those who profess and keep it? For as the Gospel says: *He who does and teaches will be called great in the kingdom of Heaven.* Who in their right mind can say that the master and friar Alexander [of Hales] was bound to preach and teach *"Blessed are the Poor"* while he was rich, and that he ought to remain silent when he has become poor? Surely, if it is fitting that friars learn and ruminate on the divine word just as all other creatures of the world, and if they are self-sufficient in teaching it to themselves, who can be so stupid as to say that they should beg to learn the doctrine that they follow and teach from those who do not follow it?[167]

Of exactly the same mind we find Hugh of Digne, another influential Franciscan of the mid-thirteenth century. In his Rule commentary, written probably 1255–1256, Hugh discussed the question of studies in the Order.[168] "Can the friars study and take the chairs of masters?" "Of course they can," says Hugh. The Rule prohibits studies only to the illiterate.[169] He then goes on to quote Bonaventure almost verbatim: "Who is, after all, more suited to teach the Gospel, or to have the magisterial authority to teach the Gospel, than the Friars Minor who actually profess and keep the Gospel?"[170]

This discourse is also very much reminiscent of John of Rupella's sermon on Saint Anthony. In both Bonaventure and John of Rupella, the subjects,

---

167. "Quos enim magis decet docere Evangelium quam eos qui Evangelium profitentur et servant? Nam cum dicat Evangelium: Qui fecerit et docuerit, hic magnus vocabitur in regno celorum, quis sane mentis dicat ut magister et frater Alexander dives debuerit predicare et docere: Beati Pauperes, et pauper effectus debeat reticere? Certe si fratres adiscere decet et ruminare tanquam munda animalia verba divina et sibi ipsis sufficiunt in docendo, quis tam stultus est ut dicat quod doctrinam, quam decet eos facere et docere, debeant a non facientibus mendicare?" Ferdinand Delorme, "Textes Franciscains (Lettre de S. Bonaventure innominato magistro)," *Archivio Italiano per la storia della pietà* 1 (1951): 216.

168. See Lapsanski, *Evangelical Perfection,* 280–82, for Hugh's use of the term "evangelical perfection" in relation to the Franciscan Order.

169. "Numquid fratres studium litterarum et maxime cathedram magisterii possunt assumere? Possunt utique. Non sanctus regulae conditor litteratis sed laicis et illiteratis studium vetat...scientes litteras in litteris proficere non veluit." *Hugh of Digne's Rule Commentary,* ed. David Flood (Grottaferrata: Editiones Collegii S. Bonaventurae ad Claras Aquas, 1979), 186–87.

170. "Quod enim magis decet evangelium docere, sive docendi evangelii auctoritatem quae in magisterio datur habere, quam fratres minores qui evangelium profitentur et servant?" (ibid., 187). Roberto Lambertini has successfully shown strong parallels between Hugh of Digne's Rule commentary and some writings of Bonaventure, namely, his *Epistola de tribus questionibus* and his article on manual labor from *Questiones de perfectione evangelica.* These parallels are in the form of literal citations in certain cases, and Lambertini convincingly argues that it was Hugh who cited Bonaventure rather than the other way around. Since the earliest possible date of composition for the texts of Bonaventure is 1255, Lambertini dates Hugh's Rule commentary to the last months of 1255. Roberto Lambertini, *Apologia e crescita dell'identità francescana (1255–1279)* (Rome: Nella sede dell'Istituto Palazzo Borromini, 1990), 43–50.

Anthony of Padua and Alexander of Hales respectively, are better teachers for having chosen poverty. A voluntary subscription to the highest state of poverty validated their teaching and elevated them above secular teachers who did not live in a state of apostolic poverty. Following from these premises, a teacher or a scholar of the Gospel who lives the life of evangelical perfection is superior to one who does not. This argument, in various forms, can be traced back to the Franciscan sermons delivered in Parisian circles from the 1230s onward. There is irony here. For Francis, poverty was inextricably connected with humility. This much was known with certainty by all three of the Franciscans cited so far—John of Rupella, Bonaventure, and Hugh of Digne, all of them highly educated, intelligent, and influential. Surprisingly, these learned Franciscans used poverty or the apostolic life to assert the perfection of their own religious life, an argument that made them look often quite the opposite of humble. One would guess that this was a common thought among the secular masters.

If we wonder why so many scholars in the university circles chose the mendicant life and adopted poverty as part of their scholarly identity, it is in part because the first generation friars successfully argued for the necessity of poverty for a life of evangelical perfection. Dominicans, despite accepting communal property in their Rule, also expressed a love of Franciscan-like poverty.[171] Emphasis on poverty was present in the Dominican lectures taught and sermons preached in Paris in the early thirteenth century, though not to the degree that it was pursued by the Franciscans. In his study of the Postills of the Dominican Hugh of St. Cher, seemingly a compilation of lectures by Hugh's students penned in 1231–1236 in Paris, Robert E. Lerner observed that poverty is argued to be a necessary quality of a preacher. "The preacher practices poverty, for it is the first virtue the Lord names. The preacher must not be like those who 'preach poverty like a medicine but flee it like poison.'"[172] Even more, Lerner cites a passage in the Postills that assigns poverty a calling of the Dominicans.[173] A sermon preached by the Dominican master Gilbert of Brabant in the 1260s presents supporting evidence that Dominicans, just as Franciscans, chose to emphasize poverty as an essential companion of the pursuit of learning.

> A student asks a great theology master: "Master, how can I get a good prebend?" The master replies: "Put your hood up and be like a fox; let others see you behave devoutly; this way you will be able to get the prebend."

171. Lester K. Little, *Religious Poverty and the Profit Economy in Medieval Europe* (Ithaca, NY: Cornell University Press, 1978), 166.

172. Robert E. Lerner, "The Vocation of the Friars Preacher: Hugh of St. Cher between Peter the Chanter and Albert the Great," in *Hugues de Saint-Cher († 1263): Bibliste et théologien*, ed. L. J. Bataillon, G. Dahan, and P.-M. Gy (Turnhout: Brepols, 2004), 223.

173. Ibid., n. 32.

That's not how the good master Christ would respond to him; instead [Christ says]: "If you want to be perfect, then go and sell everything you have and give them to the poor, come and follow me: so you will have your prebend in Heavens." Elsewhere Christ said: "Unless someone renounces all he has, he cannot be my disciple." And in Luke: "If anyone comes to me and does not hate his own father and mother, etc." [Luke 14:26].... Therefore whoever loves his prebend or money more than the eternal life is not the disciple of Christ."[174]

The Perfection of Franciscan Teachers: Those Who Teach and Live the Gospel

Bonaventure's *Letter to the Unknown Master* and Hugh of Digne's commentary on the Rule mark the beginning of a new period in the intellectual history of the Franciscan Order. This was the time when Franciscans, along with Dominicans, embarked on a war of treatises with some of the secular masters at the University of Paris. In March 1256, a secular master at Paris, William of Saint-Amour, published a short treatise called *On the Dangers of Recent Times (De periculis novissimorum temporum),* a work that fumed with rage against the friars.[175] It was triggered by the publication of the *Introduction to the Evangelical Gospel (Introductio ad aeternum evangelium)* by a Franciscan scholar in 1254, who, under the influence of the writings of Joachim of Fiore, practically claimed the Franciscans to be the new saviors of mankind.[176] Claiming in return that the friars were pseudo-apostles who had unlawfully appropriated the priests' apostolic functions, William launched a theological attack on the Franciscans and Dominicans on three points: "the friars' right to observe a life of complete renunciation of temporal goods both in private and in common; the friars' obligation, as religious, to perform manual labor; and the friars' claim to the alms of

---

174. "Quaeritur aliquis scolaris a magistro aliquo magno in theologia. 'Magister quomodo unam bonam prebendam habere potero?' Forte diceret magister 'pone capucium tuum ex transverso et sumla te vulpem. Solum ostendas aliis conversationem religiosam. Sic poteris habere prebendam.' Non ita respondit ei bonus magister Christus 'sed si vis perfectus esse vade et vende omnia quam habes et da pauperibus et veni et sequere me. Sic habebis in celo prebendam.' Unde alibi docebat. 'Nisi renunciaverit aliquis omnibus que possidet non potest meus esse discipulus. alibi in Luca. Si quis venit ad me et non odit patrem aut matrem et cetera....Qui ergo plus diligit prebendam suam vel pecuniam quam vitam eternam non est discipulis Christi'" (Paris, BnF Ms lat. 14952, f. 186ra).

175. See the 2008 edition and English translation, William of Saint-Amour, *De periculis novissimorum temporum,* ed. and trans. Guy Geltner (Paris: Peeters Press, 2008). For the prominent role of this tract in the antifraternal literature of the Middle Ages, see the introduction of the above by Geltner, and also chapter 2 in Penn R. Szittya, *The Antifraternal Tradition in Medieval Literature* (Princeton, NJ: Princeton University Press, 1986), 62–122.

176. I will discuss this work and Joachimism in the next section.

the faithful."[177] William also touched on the question of studies. He hinted that the friars' preoccupation with studies was a sign of their secretly evil nature, as false apostles were always to be found among those bent on studies. He claimed that such men would never attain the knowledge of truth.[178]

To be sure, there were previous conflicts between the secular masters and the friars at the universities of Paris and Oxford.[179] However, these had largely been clashes over administrative issues and practices, such as whether a friar could receive a degree in theology without prior attendance at the arts faculty, or whether friars could teach when secular masters were on strike. *De periculis* pointed to the elephant in the room. It was not really about the status of the friars with regard to the university's administration, or about who represented a superior administrative authority, but instead it was about the form of religious life that Franciscans and Dominicans adopted.[180] Had the friars kept a low and humble profile, mendicancy would probably not have become a target. It was the friars' claim to perfection and superiority over the secular clergy, announced by way of sermons, and their recourse to papal privileges that exasperated men like William of Saint-Amour.

John of Parma, when minister general, had hushed an earlier conflict at Paris between the secular masters and friars through humble reconciliation.[181] But John's position was weakened because of the scandal that had erupted with the publication of the *Introduction to the Evangelical Gospel* and its condemnation as heretical in late 1255 by a commission of cardinals established at the insistence of a group of university masters headed by William of Saint-Amour.[182] The job of rising to the defense of the Order fell to the friar, who was second only to the minister general in prestige within the Order: the occupant of the chair of theology at Paris, Bonaventure of Bagnoregio. He was to become minister general within a year and would hold that office for a record period of seventeen years, which testifies to his immense popularity within the Order. His response to William of Saint-Amour was titled the *Disputed Questions on Evangelical Perfection (Quaestiones disputatae de perfectione evangelica)*.[183] Here he argued

177. Andrew G. Traver, "Thomas of York's Role in the Conflict between Mendicants and Seculars at Paris," *FS* 57 (1999): 180–81.

178. William of Saint-Amour, *De periculis novissimorum temporum,* 106.

179. For the mendicant defense against the secular masters in Paris, see Andrew Traver, "The Forging of an Intellectual Defense of Mendicancy in the Medieval University," in *The Origin, Development, and Refinement of Medieval Religious Mendicancies,* ed. Donald S. Prudlo, 157–95 (Leiden: Brill, 2011).

180. About this change, see Moorman, *History of the Franciscan Order,* 130.

181. Eccleston, 74.

182. Szittya, *Antifraternal Tradition,* 15.

183. For the English translation see Bonaventure of Bagnoregio, *Disputed Questions on Evangelical Perfection,* ed. and trans. Thomas Reist, O.F.M. Conv., and Robert J. Karris, O.F.M, Works of St. Bonaventure, vol. XIII (St. Bonaventure, NY: Franciscan Institute Publications, 2008).

for the perfection of Franciscan life, dealing with topics such as humility, poverty, manual labor, continence, and obedience. The overall aim was to prove the perfection of Franciscan life, but specifically a perfection that permeated all human attributes and activities, including wisdom and learning. His response was heavily influenced by the application of Joachite prophecies into Franciscan history, which will be discussed in detail below. Following Joachim's historicizing concordances between the Old and New Testaments, Bonaventure identified St. Francis as the Angel of the Sixth Seal and the herald of the "Seraphic order" of the last and seventh age.[184] In a similar exaltation of Franciscan life, Thomas of York entered the dispute with *Manus quae contra omnipotentem tenditur,* where he reiterated the Franciscan position that Franciscan poverty was the highest kind of poverty.[185]

All of these works were scholastic refutations of the arguments that had been put forward in the treatises of William of Saint-Amour.[186] The heart of the battle for Franciscans was about the friars' claim to evangelical perfection, particularly that absolute poverty was a necessary condition for it. Once they were convinced, the learned Franciscans were faced with the task of using all their force of argumentation not just to defend but to glorify poverty in order to make it a viable alternative for a respectable religious life. As has been mentioned before, the fact of Francis's stigmata was nothing but an incontestable sign of approval bestowed on the Franciscan life and on its associated poverty:

> So there is a poverty borne in patience that is good, a poverty that is desired and longed for which is better, and a poverty embraced with joy in which a person glories and rejoices, which is best of all. Poverty, therefore, is the reason why a person can be likened to the heavens, because it leads to the kingdom of heaven.... Take note that avarice casts a person into the depths. Poverty, on the other hand, uplifts a person to the state of heavenly life and, above all, that poverty in which a person glorifies and rejoices. You will not find anyone who embraced poverty like St. Francis, nor who gloried in it as he did. He refused to possess anything at all, either personally or in common, nor did he want his friars to own anything. The cross of Christ is the sign of poverty because on it he was reduced to the utmost poverty, not having had even an old rag with which to cover his nakedness. St. Francis also chose the highest poverty. It is fitting, therefore,

---

184. On the influence of Joachim's view of history on Bonaventure, see Joseph Ratzinger, *The Theology of History in St. Bonaventure,* trans. Zachary Hayes (Chicago: Franciscan Herald Press, 1989).

185. Thomas di York, *Manus,* 3.48, cited by Lambertini, *Apologia e crescita,* 82.

186. Decima L. Douie, "St. Bonaventura's Part in the Conflict between Seculars and Mendicants at Paris," in *S. Bonaventura 1274–1974,* vol. 2, *Studia de vita, mente, fontibus et operibus S. Bonaventurae* (Grottaferrata: Collegio S. Bonaventura, 1973), 589–90.

that the sign of the Son of man, namely, Christ's cross, should be found on St. Francis.[187]

In 1269, another secular master, Gerard of Abbeville, published his *Contra adversarium perfectionis christianae*. The book not only refuted the points made by Thomas of York but also dealt theologically with the question of poverty. The reply came once again from Bonaventure, who answered Gerard's claims with *The Apology of the Poor (Apologia pauperum)*.[188] This is regarded as the major work of the Bonaventuran doctrine of absolute poverty.[189] Between 1269 and 1271 the famous English Franciscan master of theology and later archbishop of Canterbury, John Peckham, wrote three treatises in response to the secular masters— *Treatise of the Poor Man (Tractatus pauperis), On Child Oblates (De pueris oblatis)*, and the disputed question of *Whether Evangelical Perfection Consists in Rejecting or Lacking Riches (Utrum perfectio evangelica consistat in renuntiando vel carendo divitiis)*. In the latter, Peckham engages in a powerful glorification of poverty, demonstrating under eight titles that poverty is indispensable to perfection. One of these titles reads "Poverty prevails in the search for wisdom" (*paupertas valet ad sapientiae inquisitionem*). Here Peckham offers a short but precise account of why learning must be accompanied by poverty. Quoting diverse authorities such as Seneca, Abu Ma'shar, and Bede, he argues that poverty is the necessary condition for a powerful intellect; that the desire for wisdom and intellect is contradicted by the desire for material goods and riches. The most learned fathers of the old times were the monks of greatest poverty.[190]

By the 1270s, the whole discourse of Franciscan life as evangelical perfection and the place of poverty and learning in it found a culmination in the writings of Peter John Olivi. His theory of poverty, while similar to his predecessors', had some novel elements or new formulations of old concepts. Around forty years after John of Rupella, Peter John Olivi was to elaborate on John's words concerning the perfection of "those who do not and cannot have anything." The vow a Franciscan took bound not only his present state but his future state

---

187. From the second sermon preached at Paris, October 4, 1262. Bonaventure of Bagnoregio, *Disciple and the Master*, 86–87.

188. Bonaventure of Bagnoregio, *Apologia pauperum*, in *Opera omnia*, 8:233–330.

189. Lambert, *Franciscan Poverty*, 126–34.

190. "Item, ad sapientiae inquisitionem. Hoc patet per factum, quia toti mundo mittunt doctrinam, quoniam omne hoc genus pauperum plus videtur in sapientia proficere. Seneca, *Ad Lucillum:* 'Si vacare animo vis, aut pauper sis oportet, aut pauperi similis. Non potest studium salutare fieri sine frugalitatis cura. Frugalitas autem est paupertas voluntaria'.—Item, Albumasar: 'Iupiter significat substantiam et hereditates; Mercurius sapientiam et intellectum'. Quoniam igitur concupiscentia substantiae et divitiarum opposita est concupiscientiae sapientiae et intellectus, horum signorum domicilia in oppositione ponuntur. Unde antiqui patres studiosissimi monachi erant pauperrimi." John Peckham, *Quaestiones disputatae*, ed. Gerard J. Etzkorn, Hieronymus Spettmann, and Livarius Oliger, Bibliotheca Franciscana scholastica Medii Aevi (Grottaferrata: Quaracchi, 2002), 285.

as well.[191] Being a Franciscan meant embracing, with a solemn vow, one's present state of poverty while simultaneously abandoning all hope for material gain, and it was precisely this voluntary abandonment of all future material hope that made Franciscan poverty "perfect." This is in fact quite similar to the argument for mendicant perfection formulated by Thomas Aquinas, who, in his *Quodlibet,* said:

> Therefore, those who preserve either voluntary poverty or chastity have indeed something preparatory to perfection but they are not said to have a state of perfection unless they obligate themselves to such a position by a solemn profession. Something solemn and perpetual is said to have a state, as is clear in the states of liberty, matrimony, and the like.[192]

Olivi's theory of Franciscan poverty differed from that of his predecessors in one significant aspect. In the ninth section of his *Questions on Evangelical Perfection,* he defined a theory of Franciscan poverty that was based not just on the rejection of property rights but also on the concept of poor use, *usus pauper.*[193] Everything that a Franciscan used had to be minimalistic. New had to be abandoned for old, expensive for cheap. This was a new formulation of the old Franciscan virtue of *vilitas,* and Olivi argued that *usus pauper* was indispensable for the perfection of Franciscan poverty. As David Burr said: "Olivi's approach was unique in that, by allotting a separate question to the issue of usus pauper and the vow, he concentrated scholarly attention on a problem that had lain dormant throughout the secular-mendicant controversy."[194] Olivi's formulation drew attention starkly to the implications and was also dangerously topical in that, by Olivi's time, the 1270s, abuses and material corruption in some of the provinces of the Franciscan Order had reached problematic proportions, and attempts by the general administration to curb them, particularly from Bonaventure onward, had been failing miserably.[195] Olivi, like Aquinas, constructed an organic link between the vow and evangelical perfection, and from this inferred that the Franciscan vow entailed *usus pauper.*[196] Concerning the indeterminacy of what

---

191. David Burr, "Olivi's Poverty," in *Poverty in the Middle Ages,* ed. D. Flood (Werl/Westf.: D. Coelde, 1975), 72.

192. Thomas Aquinas, *Quodlibetal Questions 1 and 2,* ed. and trans. Sandra Edwards, Mediaeval Sources in Translation 27 (Toronto: Pontifical Institute of Mediaeval Studies, 1983), 57–60, quoted in J. R. Shinners and W. J. Dohar, *Pastors and the Care of Souls in Medieval England* (Notre Dame, IN: University of Notre Dame Press, 1998), 10.

193. Peter John Olivi, *De usu paupere: The Quaestio and the Tractatus,* ed. David Burr (Florence: Leonardo S. Olschki, 1992). See also David Burr, *Olivi and Franciscan Poverty: The Origins of the Usus Pauper Controversy* (Philadelphia: University of Pennsylvania Press, 1989).

194. Burr, *Olivi and Franciscan Poverty,* 45–46.

195. This subject of abuses and material corruption will be examined in depth in the next chapter.

196. David Burr, "The Correctorium Controversy and the Origins of the *Usus Pauper* Controversy," *Speculum* 60 (1985): 332–33.

constitutes the standard of *usus pauper,* Olivi allowed for variation of practice within limits. Certain practices, such as ownership of goods, were clear violations of one's vow resulting in mortal sin; other practices might have meant an imperfect observance of the vow, hence a venial sin.[197] With the incorporation of the theory of *usus pauper* into the definition of Franciscan poverty as evangelical perfection, the gravitational center of the disputes over Franciscan poverty shifted. While before Olivi theories of poverty were formulated with a view to asserting Franciscan superiority over the secular clergy, now it became an internal problem, dividing the Order between those who supported and followed this doctrine and those who did not. What emerged was a controversy that went on for half a century, exacerbating the aggravation that already existed in the Order because of scandalizing practices and the abuse of papal privileges.

Poverty and Learning: The Rule Commentary of the Four Masters

The evidence presented above points to a rise to prominence of poverty in the intellectual discourse of the Order from the 1230s onward. Poverty loomed increasingly larger in sermons and in the vitae of saints, and it became the subject of a sui generis allegory in the *Sacred Exchange.* What attracted some learned men in Parisian circles to the Franciscan vocation seems to have been their conviction of the place of poverty in salvation history, and an understanding of it as a gateway to other virtues, thus a keystone for a life of evangelical perfection. In fact, contrary to the general understanding in the historiography, where the learned Franciscans are generally categorized as members of the "Community," the learned Franciscans of the 1230s and 1240s come across as staunch defenders of poverty. To be a Franciscan was for them first and foremost to live in poverty.

This perception of poverty as the central tenet of Franciscanism is also present in the commentary on the Rule produced by four Parisian masters in 1241–1242. The previous chapter presented evidence that Haymo of Faversham had asked four Parisian masters to explain the doubtful points concerning the Rule in 1242. The primary concern in this commentary is with poverty; more space is devoted to this issue than to any other.[198] The masters are quite careful to keep the poverty of Franciscans as absolute as possible, and are unwilling to accept even the papal relaxations that had been granted on this point. On the crucial question of accepting goods, the masters wish to interpret the revisions authorized by the bull *Quo elongati* in as limited a way as possible. They discuss the question of whether the friars could accept

---

197. Ibid., 335.

198. Brooke, *Image of St Francis,* 79–80, notes that the masters were concerned with the intention of the Rule. "When it came to money," Brooke says, "learned masters out-Francised Francis" (79).

raw materials to make goods to sell or exchange in order to acquire necessary items, such as parchment to make books or leather to make shoes.[199] Their answer is in the negative. If these were allowed, the friars could similarly accept gold or silver with which they could make money to buy necessities. Friars were allowed to accept into their possession only worthless material, like straw from which a basket could be woven to sell, the proceeds to be used to purchase necessities; they could not accept any skin, leather, or wool, however, since such a material had a value in itself.[200]

The masters have a cautious attitude toward profiting from the papal privileges given to the Order. This is best displayed in the discussion of the second and ninth chapter of the Rule, which concern, respectively, the reception of recruits and the examination of candidates for the office of preaching. In their comment on the ninth chapter of the Rule, which commands that only the minister general can examine the candidates for the office of preacher and confer the office, the masters seem to be nervous about the papal bull of 1240, *Prohibente regula vestra*. This bull had given permission to provincial chapters to approve candidates "to provide the salvation of the souls more easily, and to save the friars labor and dangerous travels."[201]

> Many, however, fear that, similarly, by other privileges procured, the high perfection of the Order can be relaxed in the future.... Besides, it does not seem safe to their consciences that they should be allowed to recede from the Rule to which they have vowed by some privileges obtained against the article concerning reception and preaching, unless by that relaxation nothing temporal or carnal is added to the Order, but only something purely and simply spiritual.[202]

---

199. "Circa partem istam quaeritur an, sicut fratres recipiunt libros et alia, quibus licet uti, possunt recipere materiam iuxta suum artificium, et ex ea operari aliquid quod postmodum darent pro corporalis necessitatibus acquirendis, ut pergamenum de quo faciunt libros, et corium de quo faciunt sotilares, et huiusmodi?" (ibid., 149–50).

200. "Quod si diceretur, possent similiter recipere aurum et argentum et metalla, de quibus fabricarent monetam et alia pretiosa, de quibus sibi necessaria compararent. Quibusdam indistincte videtur quod nullam materiam possunt in possessionem recipere, sed solum suum artificium in alterius materia pro habendis necessariis praestare" (Oliger, *Expositio quatuor magistrorum,* 150–51).

201. "Verum, cum pium sit, ut pro dictorum Fratrum laboribus, ac periculosis discursibus evitandis, necnon quod animarum salus possit provenire facilius, Apostolicae Sedis circumspectio super prohibitione huiusmodi opportunae remedium provisionis apponat." *Prohibente regula vestra,* December 12, 1242, *BF,* no. 325, 1:287.

202. "Timetur autem a multis, quod similiter per alia privilegia impetranda posset tota perfectio ordinis in posterum relaxari. Praeterea non videtur conscientiis securum a regula quam voverunt, recedere per aliqua privilegia impetrata contra articulum receptionis et praedicationis debeant tolerari, nisi quia per illam relaxationem, nihil carnale aut temporale religioni accrescit, sed solum est pure et simpliciter spirituale" (Oliger, *Expositio quatuor magistrorum,* 164). A similar warning about privileges is to be found in the discussion of reception of friars (ibid., 129–30).

Nowhere in the *Expositio* is there a discussion of questions concerning the Order's involvement in studies.[203] This probably means that whether or not friars could engage in educational and intellectual activities simply was not an important matter of dispute within the Order at the time the commentary was penned. This is not really surprising as the Rule never directly deals with learning. Questions concerning the legitimacy of learning or the collection of books surfaced only incidentally in discussion about friars' occupations and the prohibition of property. For example, in their discussion of the duty of clerical brothers to say the office, the four masters argue that the friars are more prone to laziness than to prayer, and that abbreviation of the Divine Office is not prescribed to anyone except the friars who study, and that those exist only in a few places.[204] The absence of fundamental questions about study and learning can be interpreted to mean that learning had been integrated rather smoothly into the friars' vocation and routine. Perhaps there were some *dubitabilia* in this respect, but the masters did not think them important enough to comment on.

Joachitism and Its Effect on Franciscan Identity

In the powerful and passionate defense of the Franciscan way of life by the learned Franciscans, their representation of this life as "evangelical perfection," a term that was not employed in theological discourse prior to being used by the Franciscans, has quite a lot to do with the diffusion of Joachite ideas among Franciscan lectors and scholars.[205] The vibrant period of 1240–1250, which is marked by the issue of several papal privileges, the publication of the first commentary on the Rule, and by Thomas of Celano's *Second Life,* also witnessed the rise of a historical phenomenon that left a very prominent mark on all the various perceptions of Franciscanism. Some fascinating prophecies that were derived from the books of a Cistercian monk called Joachim of Fiore took hold of the intellects and imaginations of the learned friars. The application of these Joachite[206] prophecies to Franciscan history had a significant impact on the

---

203. Brooke notes this as a "significant omission" (*Image of St Francis,* 80).

204. "Item cum levitas sit in nobis maxime reprobanda, et fratres multi proniores sint ad otium quam ad orationem, et in paucis locis comparatione partis residuae sint studentes…, mutatio facta officii multos gravat" (Oliger, *Expositio quatuor magistrorum,* 138).

205. Marjorie Reeves wrote that *status evangelicae perfectionis* was thought to be Joachim's third status. Reeves, *Influence of Prophecy,* 176. See also Lapsanski, *Evangelical Perfection,* who relates the term to Joachim's third status.

206. To use the convention of Sabine Schmolinsky and Bernard McGinn, the word *Joachimist* denotes a relation to the authentic works of Joachim, and the word *Joachite* covers a relation to all the changes and expansions that his followers introduced in his corpus. Sabine Schmolinsky, *Der Apokalypsenkommentar des Alexander Minorita: Zur frühen Rezeption Joachims von Fiore in Deutschland* (Hannover: Hahnsche Buchhandlung, 1991), 1, n. 1; Bernard McGinn, *The Calabrian Abbot: Joachim of Fiore in the History of Western Thought* (New York: Macmillan, 1985), 208.

friars' perception of their own Franciscan identity, and influenced tremendously the Order's subsequent history.[207]

Joachim of Fiore (1135–1202) was a zealous Cistercian monk who desired a stricter and more ascetic observance of the Benedictine Rule, which led him to found a new order—the Florensians at Fiore in Calabria.[208] His fame was rooted in a series of prophecies he made and his design of a new world history in his works *Concordia novi et veteris Testamenti, Expositio in apocalypsim,* and the *Psalterium decem chordarum,*[209] and in two works, titled *Expositio in Hieremiam* and *Expositio in Isaiam,* which were once thought to be authentic works of the abbot but may have been written between 1240 and 1266.[210] Scholars have even considered them to be of Franciscan authorship.[211] Joachim's eschatalogy comprised two views of history. In one view, Joachim divided human history into three phases—the ages of the Father, the Son, and the Holy Spirit—and he prophesied that in the third era, that of the Holy Spirit, a new order was to emerge that would be endowed with the evangelical spirit. This would be the age of the Eternal Gospel when pagans, Jews, and Greeks would be converted. The other view divided history into seven periods, based on a reading of the Book of Revelation, where the seventh period corresponded to the third era, the era of the Holy Spirit.[212] Joachim's Trinitarian theology, elaborated in *De unitate; seu, Essentia trinitatis,* now lost, was found to be in conflict with that of Peter Lombard and condemned posthumously at the Fourth Lateran Council in 1215.[213] Owing to the abbot's reputation for piety and his close ties with the

---

207. For bibliography concerning the diffusion of Joachimism in the Franciscan Order, see Morton Bloomfield and Marjorie Reeves, "The Penetration of Joachimism into Northern Europe," in *Joachim of Fiore in Christian Thought: Essays on the Influence of the Calabrian Prophet,* ed. Delno C. West (New York: B. Franklin, 1975), 1:107, nn. 2–3.

208. Some of the best works on Joachim of Fiore are Gian Luca Potestà, *Il tempo dell'Apocalisse: Vita di Gioacchino da Fiore* (Rome: Laterza, 2004); Alexander Patschovsky, *Die Bildwelt der Diagramme Joachims von Fiore: Zur Medialität religiös-politischer Programme im Mittelalter* (Ostfildern: Thorbecke, 2003); M. Rainini, *Disegni dei tempi: Il "Liber figurarum" e la teologia figurativa di Gioacchino da Fiore* (Rome, 2006); McGinn, *Calabrian Abbot.* See also the volume of reprinted articles from 1930 to 1971 by Delno C. West, ed., *Joachim of Fiore in Christian Thought: Essays on the Influence of the Calabrian Prophet* (New York: B. Franklin, 1975).

209. Joachim of Fiore, *Psalterium decem cordarum,* ed. Kurt-Victor Selge (Hannover: Hahnsche Buchhandlung, 2009).

210. Morton Bloomfield, "Joachim of Flora: A Critical Survey of his Canon, Teachings, Sources, Biography and Influence," *Traditio* 13 (1957): 251–52.

211. For a critical survey of Joachim's writings, see Morton Bloomfield, "Recent Scholarship on Joachim of Fiore and His Influence," in *Prophecy and Millenarianism: Essays in Honor of Marjorie Reeves,* edited by Ann Williams, 23–52 (London: Longman, 1980). For the claim of Franciscan authorship, see Bloomfield, "Joachim of Flora," 252.

212. See Robert Lerner, "Antichrists and Antichrist in Joachim of Fiore," *Speculum* 60 (1985): 558–59.

213. See Fiona Robb, "Did Pope Innocent III Personally Condemn Joachim of Fiore?" *Florensia* 7 (1993): 77–91; Robb, "Joachimist Exegesis in the Theology of Innocent III and Rainier of Ponza,"

papacy, his other works were allowed to circulate and maintained their popularity.[214]

Joachim was not the first in the medieval monastic apocalyptic tradition, but his significance and later fame lay in the "applicability of his hopes for the coming *viri spirituales* to the great orders of mendicants."[215] For many Franciscans, who had become familiar with the work of the Calabrian abbot, the Joachite exegesis appeared closely linked to the history of their Order. It was not too difficult to identify Francis with his stigmata as the *alter Christus* who bore the *signum Dei,* while Joachim's evangelical Order of *viri spirituales* became equated with the Franciscans in general.[216] Francis had said several times that his Rule had been written under the guidance of the Holy Spirit, which was the identifying "person" of Joachim's third era. The result was not surprisingly a very strong boost to the friars's self-identification with their Order. From being just another religious Order, they were transformed into Christ's very own, the saviors of the day.

Joachite ideas spread through the Order primarily through clerical and learned brothers, particularly through masters, lectors, and students of the Order. Salimbene of Parma, whose chronicle composed in 1282 is the sole source for the early development and diffusion of Joachite ideas in the Order, recounts several incidents associating lectors with Joachite writings. The first recorded instance in Salimbene's chronicle is dated to the 1240s.[217] Sometime between 1243 and 1247, while Salimbene was at the convent of Pisa, an abbot from Fiore—described by Salimbene as *vetulus* and *sanctus*—fearing that his monastery might be destroyed by Frederick II, brought all the manuscripts of Joachim's writings that had been preserved in his monastery to the Franciscan convent of Pisa for safekeeping. The lector of the convent, Rodolph of Saxony, who was, according to Salimbene, a great logician, theologian, and *disputator,* gave up the study of theology and dedicated himself to reading these manuscripts. In Salimbene's words, he became a *maximus Joachita.*[218] Another

---

Florensia 11 (1997): 137–52; Robb, "The Fourth Lateran Council's Definition of Trinitarian Orthodoxy," *Journal of Ecclesiastical History* 48 (1997): 22–43.

214. K. J. v. Hefele and H. Leclercq, *Histoire des conciles d'après les documents originaux,* part 2 (Hildesheim, 1973), 5:1327, canon 2; Reeves, *Influence of Prophecy,* 37.

215. Bernard McGinn, "Apocalyptic Traditions and Spiritual Identity in the Thirteenth Century Religious Life," in *Apocalypticism in the Western Tradition* (Aldershot, U.K.: Variorum, 1994), 2, 6.

216. For the early influence of Joachimism on the Franciscans through the prophecies of Joachim, see Francesco Russo, "Gioachimismo e Francescanesimo," in West, *Joachim of Fiore in Christian Thought,* 129–41; E. Randolph Daniel, "A Re-Examination of the Origins of Franciscan Joachitism," *Speculum* 43 (1968): 671–76. See also the chapter titled "Early Franciscans" in Reeves, *Influence of Prophecy.*

217. Salimbene, 236.

218. "Nam prius eram edoctus et hanc doctrinam audieram, cum habitarem Pisis, a quodam abbate de ordine Floris, qui erat vetulus et sanctus homo, et omnes libros suos a Joachim editos in conventu Pisano sub custodia collocaverat, timens, ne imperator Fridericus monasterium suum destrueret, quod

incident dates from 1247–1248, when Salimbene was residing at the convent of Provins.[219] Here he met two Joachite Franciscans, Bartholomeo Guisculus of Parma and Gerard of Borgo di San Donnino. These men had taught Latin grammar before they joined the Order, and had a thorough knowledge of Joachimist writings. They possessed a copy of *Expositio in Hieremiam,* the pseudo-Joachimist book, and many other books. Salimbene states that Bartholomeo went on to the convent of Siena, and Brother Gerard was sent to Paris to study theology on behalf of the province of Sicily where he had been brought up.[220] The mobility of lectors and students in the Order no doubt contributed to the diffusion of Joachimist ideas. One of the most influential and famous figures in the Order around the late 1240s and early 1250s was Hugh of Digne. In Salimbene's words, he was another *magnus Joachita* and disseminated Joachite ideas and teachings at the convent of Hyères, where a great number of notaries, judges, doctors and other learned people came to listen to him. He possessed all of Joachim's books,[221] and it was here that two Franciscans from the convent of Naples, Iohannes Gallicus and Iohanninus Pigulinus de Parma, came to listen to Hugh's Joachite teachings.[222] Perhaps it was these two friars who introduced the Joachite prophecies to John of Parma, the future minister general of the Order, when he served as lector at the convent of Naples. According to Salimbene, John was another great Joachite, who was sent to Paris to take up a position as a bachelor of theology. Before 1250, the interest in Joachite texts also reached England, where they circulated among prominent Franciscan scholars. The famous English lector Adam Marsh, in a letter of unknown date to Robert Grosseteste, wrote that he had received the works of Joachim from a friar, who had come from the other side of the Alps and demanded the bishop's opinion of them.[223] Hugh of Digne had a long-standing friendship with both Robert Grosseteste and Adam Marsh, and all three men were accustomed to exchanging not only works but also ideas.[224] Among other prominent names in the Order influenced by Joachite ideas

---

erat inter Lucam et civitatem Pisanam, per viam que vadit ad civitatem Lunensem. . . . Frater vero Rodulfus de Saxonia, lector Pisanus, magnus logicus et magnus theologus et magnus disputator, dimisso studio theologie, occasione illorum librorum abbatis Joachim, qui in domo nostra repositi erant, factus est maximus Joachita" (Salimbene, 236).

219. It is worth noting that Provins (Lat. Pruvinensis) is very close to Paris, in the custody of Champagne, France. Ibid.

220. Ibid., 237

221. "Erat enim magnus Joachita et omnes libros abbatis Ioachim de grossa littera habebat" (ibid., 236).

222. Ibid., 239.

223. Adam of Marsh, *Epistolae,* in *Monumenta Franciscana,* ed. T. Brewer, Rerum Britannicarum medii aevi scriptores, vol. 1 (London, 1859), letter 43, 146–47.

224. Salimbene writes that one of the greatest friends of Hugh was Grosseteste (Salimbene, 233). Southern suggests that Grosseteste had sent a copy of his new translation of Aristotle's *Nicomachean Ethics*

were John of Rupella, whose *postilla* on Saint Matthew bears traces of Joachite prophecies;[225] Bonaventure, who identified Francis with Joachim's "Angel of the Sixth Seal" in the *Legenda maior* and *Legenda minor,* with a fuller combination of Joachimist exegesis and Franciscan spirituality presented in *Collationes in Hexaemeron;*[226] and Peter John Olivi. Following Bonaventure, Olivi also identified Francis as the Angel of the Sixth Seal.[227] Some learned Franciscans such as David of Augsburg frowned on the Joachite prophecies. Thomas of Pavia regarded the prophecies as lies and foolishness.[228] Matthew of Aquasparta had borrowed Joachim's *Expositio in Apocalypsim* from the library of the Todi convent.[229] This manuscript, today preserved at the Biblioteca Comunale of Todi, contains annotations by three medieval hands, further proving the interest of the learned Franciscans.[230]

In 1254, Gerard of Borgo di San Donnino published the *Introduction to the Eternal Gospel (Introductio ad evangelium aeternum)*, an interpretation of Franciscan history according to Joachite prophecies. Gerard not only claimed the mendicants to be the spiritual men of Joachim's third era, but also implicitly suggested Joachim's writings to be the last Gospel, thus superseding both the Old and New Testaments.[231] An assertion of this magnitude could not go unnoticed by the heresy watchers. A papal commission, summoned in 1255 in Anagni, examined the orthodoxy of both Gerard's work and the original writings of Joachim.[232] They found the *Introduction to the Eternal Gospel* to be "*maxime vane glorie causa*" and highly offensive, since Gerard set his Order not only above all

---

to Hugh of Digne, whom he probably met at the Council of Lyon. For this and the influence of Joachimism on Grosseteste, see Southern, *Robert Grosseteste,* 290.

225. For a thorough treatment of the subject, see Southern, *Robert Grosseteste,* 183–86.

226. McGinn, *Calabrian Abbot,* 214–24. On the influence of Joachimist concepts on Bonaventure, see also Reeves, *Influence of Prophecy,* 67, 178–81.

227. For an excellent discussion of Francis's place in the exegesis of medieval Franciscan theologians, see David Burr, "Franciscan Exegesis and Francis as Apocalyptic Figure," in *Monks, Nuns and Friars in Medieval Society,* ed. Edward B. King, Jacqueline T. Schaefer, and William B. Wadley, 51–62 (Sewanee, TN: University of the South Press, 1989).

228. Reeves, *Influence of Prophecy,* 53.

229. This is attested by ASPerugia, Convento di S Fortunato di Todi, Pergamene, 20, which documents the act of borrowal of this book by Matthew of Aquasparta for a payment of 18 libre cortonense. "Item habuit idem dominus frater Matheus cardinalis expositionem Ioachim super apocalipsim scriptam in textu de cinabrio et in expositione (?) de in castro (?), quam frater bevegnate de marcellano emerat pro conventu tudertino et ipse dominus frater matheus acceperat a dicto fratre Bevengnate et solvit tum pro dicto libro idem dominus Matheus circa quantitatem (?) XVIII librarum cortonensium et dictum fuit tunc quod dictus liber debere esse conventus fratrum minorum de tuderto."

230. Todi, Biblioteca Comunale, 43. For the description and the three hands identified, see E. Menestò, *I manoscritti medievali della Biblioteca del Convento francescano di San Fortunato di Todi* (Spoleto: Fondazione Centro italiano di studi sull'alto Medioevo, 2009), 285–86.

231. For an account of the *Introduction to the Eternal Gospel,* see ibid., 59–70.

232. The report of the Anagni commission has been edited by Heinrich Denifle, "Protocoll der Commission zu Anagni," *ALKG* 1(1885): 99–142.

other Orders, but above the whole institution of the Church. The *Introduction to the Eternal Gospel* was found heretical, and Gerard himself was condemned to prison for life.[233]

The fate of Gerard and his book made the Order necessarily more cautious. Thus, the Narbonne constitutions of 1260 included precautions against potentially dangerous publications. No new writing was to be published outside the Order unless either the minister general or the provincial minister and the diffinitors of the provincial chapter had first examined it.[234] Moreover, no friar was to dare to assert or approve an opinion that had been reproved by the masters of the Order in unison, nor could friars defend anyone's suspicious opinion against faith and tradition. Any friar who acted otherwise was to be deprived of all his offices in the Order.[235] Interestingly enough, despite the shame Gerard's publication brought on the Order, no contemporary or later member of the Order, not even those among the fourteenth-century critics like Ubertino da Casale or Angelo Clareno, both of them strongly influenced by the Joachite prophecies, seems to have linked this shame to learning or to the circulation of books in the Order.

Franciscan poverty was already, for some of the learned Franciscans, a central faculty that made Franciscan life distinct from and superior to other forms of religious life. After the diffusion of Joachite prophecies, the conviction of the perfection of Franciscan life grew stronger and acquired a broader scope. There was new and more powerful zeal and enthusiasm to represent Franciscan life as the ultimate "evangelical life" and as such the "best" religious life in the contemporary medieval world, notably in defiance of the virtue most associated with Francis himself—humility. This new zeal is reflected in the written works produced in the Order after the 1240s. Disputed questions on "the perfection of evangelical life" became a Franciscan genre featured for the first time in 1255/1256 by Bonaventure, and reappearing with John Peckham and Peter

---

233. "Huc usque verba Joachim et fratris Girardi. Ex prenotatis videtur, quod iste novas et falsas opiniones confingat, et hoc maxime vane glorie causa, id est, ut exaltet huiusmodi ordinem incredibiliter et intempestive super alios ordines, immo super totam ecclesiam. Et ideo diligenter conferenda est hec difinitio Augustini de heretico in primo libro de utilitate credendi, ubi dicit: 'hereticus est qui alicuius temporalis commodi et maxime vane glorie principatusque sui gratia falsas ac novas opiniones vel gignit vel sequitur'" (ibid., 115).

234. "Item inhibemus, ne de cetero aliquod scriptum novum extra ordinem publicetur, nisi prius examinatum fuerit diligenter per glem Ministrum vel provlem et definitores in capitulo provli" (Narbonne-Assisi-Paris, 73, no. 21).

235. "Nullus frater audeat aliquam opinionem asserere vel approbare scienter, quae a magistris nostris communiter reprobatur, nec opinionem singularem cuiuscumque, suspectam vel calumniabilem, maxima contra fidem vel mores audeat defensare. Et qui contrafecerit, nisi, admonitus per Ministrum, resipuerit, ab omnis doctrinae officio sit suspensus" (ibid., no. 22).

John Olivi. Joachite ideas were transmitted by way of learned friars to the entire Order through sermons. On Francis, Bonaventure preached thus:

> Further, it was made necessary by the needs of the Church in these last times. At the beginning of the Church unbelief held sway; as it developed heresy reigned and at the end wickedness will prevail, for then *most men's love will grow cold.* So at the beginning of the Church, the Lord granted powerful miracles to drive out idolatry. Later on he endowed learned men with proofs of wisdom to root out heresy. In these latter times he bestowed the signs of goodness and mercy on St. Francis to enkindle love. And what are the signs of consummate love except the marks of the passion which God chose to endure for us out of measureless love?[236]

While the first chapter has shown the steps by which the Franciscan Order incorporated learning into its life, this chapter testifies to the rise of a new Franciscan identity that simultaneously exalted learning and absolute poverty, and—encouraged by the diffusion of Joachite ideas—saw their union as the height of evangelical perfection. This identity finds its first clear expression in the 1240s, when the ministers in charge of the Order legislated for a recruitment strategy directed toward admitting educated men into the Order and rejecting simple laymen. To see that not everyone in the Order agreed with this mentality there is no need to turn to the fourteenth-century texts or to Francis's companions. The twice official biographer of Francis, Thomas of Celano, did not refrain from pointing out Francis's confidence in the potential for holiness of simple and uneducated friars, his vision of voluntary simplicity as a value and lifestyle to be upheld by the learned brothers, and his desire to see his followers forming a mosaic of men from all social and intellectual levels, living peacefully in brotherly love, thereby establishing themselves as an ideal Christian microcosm, an ideal for all human communities to follow. Celano expressed these sentiments powerfully in his *Second Life* in 1247, which received the approval of the General Chapter and remained the official biography of Francis until 1266.

However, perhaps Thomas's efforts to express and defend Francis's will, as he understood it, were a little too late. *The Second Life* was completed in 1247, and perhaps a few years more passed before it was copied, circulated among, and read by members of the Order. Many of the friars who read or heard the *Second Life* during liturgical activities could not fail to feel the difference between Francis's desires, as expressed by Celano, and the ideals set out by the contemporary administration, particularly in terms of the relationship between learning and

---

236. Doyle, *Disciple and the Master,* 68.

simplicity. Until that time there had been no document circulating in the Order comparable to the *Second Life* as a source of information about Francis's life and his vision for the Order. For most friars, particularly for those who had entered the Order after Francis's death and in provinces far from Umbria, Francis was a holy man and a miracle worker. This minimal picture of him was conveyed and maintained by most of the sources of information available to the friars, such as the *First Life,* liturgical readings, and visual depictions. The *Second Life* certainly contributed to the survival of the idea of the "holy simple friar," as the chronicle of Thomas of Eccleston and the late thirteenth-century *Liber exemplorum* remind us. Simple friars continued to haunt the imagination of educated friars and preach to them in dreams and visions.

The absence of a good source of information about Francis and the life of early friars up until the composition of the *Second Life* therefore left the stage empty for the appearance and promotion of a new Franciscan identity. Here we run up against the principal problem of a historian. We can follow the construction of this new Franciscan identity only by way of the written texts of the thirteenth century, and those texts were almost invariably produced by the learned brothers, in fact by brothers who were in some capacity associated with the educational and intellectual center of the Order—the Paris convent. This chapter has quoted as evidence the vitae composed by Julian of Speyer, who was *corrector mensae* in Paris, and the sermons by anonymous Franciscans, John of Rupella, and Bonaventure. The latter two were masters of theology in Paris. Hence, we have in our hands inevitably the Franciscan identity constructed and adhered to by the Franciscans of higher learning. It is natural perhaps to expect these brothers to construct an identity that did not contradict or impede what they did, and wanted to continue to do, but there is no evidence for a conspiracy theory here such as Sabatier envisaged. We have no reason to think that the many scholarly friars who entered the Order in Paris ever encountered a written or oral exposition of Francis's ideas on simplicity, learning, and books. We will, of course, unfortunately never know how the multitude of friars, who did not engage with learning and writing, felt about being a Franciscan, and how they constructed their Franciscan identity.

We will also never really know the reasons why the majority of friars entered the Order, or why most men entered any religious order in the Middle Ages or later. What we can know is how some friars constructed and understood their identity afterward. Judging by the written testimonies they left after they became Franciscans, the learned friars indisputably saw learning, but above all teaching, as part of the perfection of apostolic life. The Franciscan vow to follow the apostolic life obliged them to engage in learning and teaching the Gospel. Francis's self-proclaimed simplicity was no obstacle to this construction, but only a token of his humility. He was understood to be a man of the highest learning, one that has been taught by God himself. The average friar, who could not presume on such direct instruction, had to set himself firmly on the path of study in order to follow Francis. This way he could open his mind to divine illumination, as the contemporary intellectual theories that influenced men like Bonaventure taught. In this new identity, Anthony of Padua rather than Francis of Assisi was the Franciscan saint to be imitated.

The new Franciscan identity, essentially a combination of absolute poverty and learning, was in many ways a unique product of the thirteenth century. The twelfth century had witnessed "a rise of poverty" as an attribute of Christ, as many lay fraternities and some of the heretical groups adopted this voluntarily, and in fact were known collectively as the Poor of Christ. But the twelfth century saw also the rise of learning, in particular scholastic learning, the learning acquired in the schools that prompted the rise of universities. When Franciscans moved to the towns with schools and universities, and attracted students and teachers to their ranks, their history partly converged with the history of learning in the thirteenth century. Insofar as learning penetrated into the everyday life of these Gospelmen, it has come to be emphasized as an attribute of Christ. The rise of learning in the Franciscan Order is, then, in part a consequence of the rise of scholastic learning, in this particular instance, among religious communities and institutions.

❧ CHAPTER 3

Beyond Preaching and Confession

The Franciscan theologians following John of Rupella had little trouble making a case for the advantages of study within the fulfillment of Franciscan vocation. However, these men had entered the Order at a time when it had already made the commitment to education and learning. An established intellectual culture awaited Bonaventure when he put on his Franciscan habit for the first time. Therefore their justifications for and defense of study cannot be accepted as the last word on why the Order had chosen to move toward the intellectual realm. The question of why the Franciscan Order, despite its lay origins, embraced learning at various levels is an intriguing one, and has the potential to reveal the dynamics of the general religious and intellectual life of the early thirteenth century through the lens of an emerging religious order. Historians' answer to this question entails by and large slight variations on two basic themes: either it was the result of the headlong pursuit of the Dominicans, who were the first to move to universities;[1] or the Franciscans were meant to preach, and this necessitated the education of the friars.[2] In

---

1. Mulchahey, "*First the bow is bent,*" xi; Louis Julius Lekai, *The White Monks: A History of the Cistercian Order* (Okauchee, WI: Cistercian Fathers, Our Lady of Spring Bank, 1953), 55.

2. See, for example, Maierù, "Formazione culturale," 11; Bert Roest, *Franciscan Literature of Religious Instruction before the Council of Trent* (Leiden: Brill, 2004), 4; Manselli, "St. Bonaventure and the Clericalization," 83–88; Gieben, "Preaching in the Franciscan Order," 9; Berg, *Armut und Wissenschaft,* 72–73. Grado Merlo in the most recent history of the medieval Franciscan Order also ties the pursuit of learning to the friars' undertaking of pastoral duties. Merlo, *Nel nome di San Francesco,* 109.

fact, the two explanations are interwoven, since the Dominicans are generally believed to have adopted schooling for the purposes of preaching and of serving the Church in areas that required theological training. Although both arguments seem plausible, certain objections must be raised.

The claim that the Franciscans imitated the Dominicans is a weak one, as there is no solid evidence to support this *post hoc ergo propter hoc* approach. Neither in the Franciscan nor in the Dominican documents can one find a single line suggesting that such an intention was ever present. In fact, substantial differences in the education system of the two Orders deprive such an assumption of any solid foundation, though that is not to deny that the Dominican experience—inasmuch as Franciscans knew of it—might have influenced individual friars or provincial ministers. Any similarities can also be explained by the fact that, having emerged at roughly the same time, both orders were subject to the same Zeitgeist and therefore sometimes made similar decisions.

The second argument, that Franciscans moved to universities and established an educational organization because they needed to preach, is a very popular and widespread argument among historians, taking on certain variations, such as the need to perform other aspects of pastoral care, or papal pressure on the Order to fulfill the need for preachers and confessors. The argument that education was to meet the needs of preaching draws on the authority of the medieval Franciscans themselves. In his letter to the unknown master written in 1254–1255, Bonaventure said that the Rule expressly imposed on the friars the authority and office of preaching. Since the friars had to preach not fables but the sacred word, they would need books from which they could read in order to preach. As the Rule allows the missal and the breviary, it also does not impede having books to preach.[3] Probably writing around the same time, the anonymous Franciscan author of the *Determinations of Questions concerning the Rule* listed the study of the sacred scripture as one of the four ornaments of the Franciscan Order, the others being an impeccable life, the authority to preach and listen to confessions, and a satisfying account concerning certain doubts of some people.[4] Why do friars study and have masters? Because the office of preacher and confessor are annexed to the Franciscan Rule, and these offices require knowledge of sacred

---

3. Delorme, "Textes Franciscains," 214.

4. "Cum inter alios Ordines Religiosorum Ordo Fratrum Minorum datus sit Ecclesiae ad aedificationem fidelium in fide et moribus per verba doctrinae et exempla bonae conversationis...ut eadem aedificatio afferat fructum ampliorem, necesse est, Ordinem ipsum quatuor ornamentis esse praeditum, sine quibus minus proficeret in aliis, licet forte quoad se aliquo illorum posset carere. Primum est vita irreprehensibilis, quae maxime sibimet prodest et alios aedificat. Secundum est scientia sacrae Scripturae, sine qua nec secure nec utiliter posset alios docere. Tertium est auctoritas praedicandi et confessiones audiendi, in quibus maxime prosunt fidelibus fratres. Quartum est ratio satisfactoria super quibusdam dubiis apud alios" (*Determinationes quaestionum,* 337).

scripture.[5] According to this text, one of the qualities needed by those who were to assume the office of preacher or confessor was "that he may be sufficiently instructed in Latin grammar and the Bible, and without error and confusion, he may know how to advocate the truth in front of the people and clergy, and competently give counsel to those who ask in cases of necessity and impose the right penance in confessions."[6] Historians of the Dominican Order have also given similar arguments for that Order's involvement in schools. Paul Mandonnet, in an outdated yet still influential article, suggested that Dominicans had taken upon not only the duty of pastoral care but also that of providing masters of theology to teach the clergy, since such masters were in short supply in the Middle Ages.[7] Michèle Mulchahey draws on medieval Dominican authorities such as the master general Humbert of Romans, who said that studying was not an end but a means to preach and to save souls.[8]

It is, however, risky to accept the arguments of medieval friars at face value. Bonaventure and Humbert were subject to the fashions and paradigms of their time; they took certain premises for granted, without necessarily feeling the need to make them explicit, and yet formed their ideas accordingly. As Alexander Murray put it, "Intellectual interest was invisible to many contemporaries, most of all to those best placed professionally to describe it."[9] Bonaventure and other like-minded Franciscan scholars might have explained the Order's pursuit of learning as a function of preaching and confession in certain contexts, but this apparently simple argument assumes not only that the Franciscans were to preach and to hear confessions but also that these two activities required systematic study of theology. Such an argument fails to explain the variety and sophistication of the friars' intellectual involvement, an involvement that produced a very diverse output on theological and philosophical matters, not all of which were really directed toward preaching and confessions.

Furthermore, the chronology also complicates our understanding of the initial reasons that made the Franciscans rush to schools. Bonaventure joined the Order around 1244, at a time when the Order had already made a commitment

---

5. "Respondeo. Cum, sicut dictum est, Praedicationis officium ex regulari professione Ordini annexum sit et confessionis, quae notitiam requirunt sacrae Scripturae, quae subtili indiget in plerisque locis expositione, ne ex imperitia errores pro veritate doceamus; necesse est, nos sacrae Scripturae habere studium et magistros" (ibid., 339).

6. "Sexto, quod sit saltem in grammatica et sacra Scriptura tam sufficienter instructus, quod sine errore vel confusione sciat coram populo et clero proponere veritatem et in consiliis competenter satisfecere requirentibus de causis necessariis et in confessione de poenitentiis iniungendis imponendis" (ibid., 360).

7. Pierre Mandonnet, "La crise scolaire au début du XIIIe siècle et la fondation de l'Ordre des Frères Prêcheurs," *Revue d'histoire ecclesiastique* 15 (1914): 43. Verger, "Studia mendicanti e università," 154–55.

8. Mulchahey, "*First the bow is bent*," 5.

9. Alexander Murray, *Reason and Society in the Middle Ages* (Oxford: Clarendon Press, 1978), 237.

to learning. His expressed views and his works date from after 1254. At that time, the Franciscans were already well into their role as preachers and confessors. It is therefore understandable that he or any other Franciscan joining the Order after around 1244 would explain the Order's involvement in learning in terms of the preaching apostolate, which truly might have seemed to be the case. Moreover, the years running from the publication of the *Introduction to the Eternal Gospel* in 1254 to the issue of the papal bull *Exiit qui seminat* in 1279 represent a tumultuous period in Franciscan history, a time when Franciscan scholars found themselves on the defensive against the secular masters in the universities. They had to defend not just their position in the university but quite a few of the major principles on which their Rule was based. If, therefore, in the face of the charges laid at their door and the questions as to why they studied and strived to become masters in the schools, they increasingly employed a rhetoric that emphasized their work as preachers and confessors and as such their "usefulness" to the Church at large, this should come as no surprise. However, these explanations and justifications were subsequent to the integration of study into the Franciscan vocation, and I would suggest that we need to look to earlier times to explain that integration. Therefore, this chapter examines the period 1219–1242, the formative years in which the Franciscans moved to the university towns and made their commitment to study. The use of evidence after 1242 is hard to avoid, since more texts and documents have come down to us from the second half of the thirteenth century, but while employing this later evidence, the rapidly changing historical context needs to be taken into account.

To determine whether Franciscan interest in study and in the recruitment of the learned in the early period arose out of an interest in preaching, the usual place to start is the Franciscan Rule. Both Bonaventure and the anonymous author of the *Determinations* traced the friars' involvement in studying to the preaching mission of the Order inherent in the Rule. Yet both the earlier and the later Franciscan Rules are not terribly helpful in establishing the precise status of preaching in the friars' apostolate. In the earlier Rule of 1221, Francis urged all friars to exhort people to do penance for their sins and to preach by example.[10] The kind of preaching in which the early Franciscans engaged was what is generally termed *exhortatio,* where the audience was advised on morals and called to repentance. The subject matter of the *exhortatio* is more or less laid out in the First Rule of 1221—praise of God, the imminence of death, hence the necessity to confess and do penance, and the eternal punishment that would be incurred if the sinner died in a state of sin.[11] This kind of preaching did not require much learning or study of theology. Nor did, of course, the Franciscan

10. RNB, chap. 17.
11. RNB, chap. 21.

"preaching" par excellence—that is, preaching by example. The significance of preaching by way of living an impeccable life of penance among the people was well-known and the idea disseminated to the friars through the *First Life* of Celano, who explicitly wrote that Francis did not preach "in the persuasive words of human wisdom but in the learning and virtue of the Spirit."[12] The final and papally approved Rule of 1223 does not particularly urge any kind of preaching. Rather it tries to regulate and control it, but in doing so it evidently assumes that Franciscans were engaged in preaching to the public.[13] Below is the section on preaching quoted in its entirety:

> The brothers may not preach in the diocese of any bishop when he has opposed their doing so. And let none of the brothers dare to preach in any way to the people unless he has been examined and approved by the general minister of this fraternity and the office of preacher has been conferred upon him. Moreover, I admonish and exhort those brothers that when they preach their language be well-considered and chaste for the benefit and edification of the people, announcing to them vices and virtues, punishment and glory, with brevity, because our Lord when on earth kept his word brief.[14]

What is worth noticing here is the necessity to examine would-be preachers and the introduction of the "office of preacher," both of which were absent in the Rule of 1221. The difference on this point between the two Rules has already been noted.[15] It is quite likely that the general minister performing this examination required a reasonable knowledge of theology from the friar under examination, and that consequently a demand arose among the friars for some training in theology. Unfortunately, there is no evidence to inform us concerning the nature of this examination. Gieben, rightly, calls to our attention the passage from Salimbene where a friar pleads with the general minister of the time, John of Parma, to receive the office of preacher in 1248, and obtains the reply that such a grant can be conceded only after a tough examination, for which purpose the general minister calls a lector of the convent and asks him to examine the friar along with Salimbene.[16] Salimbene and other friars aspiring to this office listened to the *lectiones* of the lectors who generally read from a book that presented a commentary on a certain part of the Bible. This constituted the most basic form of theological study in the Order.

---

12. I Celano, 36. See also Berg, "Das Studienproblem," 17.

13. That preaching was not presented in the Rule as a Franciscan ideal has been noticed by other historians, notably Moorman, *History of the Franciscan Order,* 29; and Nimmo, *Reform and Division,* 21.

14. RB, chap. 9; translation in Armstrong, Hellman, and Short, *Francis of Assisi,* 1:104–5.

15. Gieben, "Preaching in the Franciscan Order, " 9.

16. Ibid., 10.

It is tempting to think that Franciscans sought theological knowledge to preach against heresies, as the Dominicans did. The evidence tells a different story. Unlike the Dominicans, the early Franciscans had not taken up the specific mission of fighting against heresy. Francis himself never mentioned heretics in his work. The principal scholar who has worked on the Franciscan relationship with heresy, Mariano d'Alatri, remarkably observed that "we do not know any sermon collection that carries the title *Sermones pro inquisitoribus* or *Sermones contra haereticos,* the type that was directed toward preachers against heresy."[17] D'Alatri explains this lacuna with a hypothesis that the Franciscans were fighting a battle against heresy "by positively asserting the truth of faith."[18] Thus, it is difficult to make a serious case for the introduction of learning with a view to preach against heresies.

Initially, learning and learned men were probably sought more for confession than preaching. It is quite conceivable that penitential preaching, which in itself did not necessitate much learning, did nevertheless create the need for learned clergy in the Order as a result of the increased need for confessors. Preaching and confession were organically linked in the Middle Ages;[19] people often confessed after they heard a moving sermon, which indeed had often urged them to. Without this prerequisite sermon it was difficult to induce the laity to confess. The whole point of an effective sermon was to bring people to a point of crisis, which involved an urgency to repent and confess. A prominent and charismatic preacher like Francis of Assisi, through simple preaching that did not necessitate any study of theology, could and did induce people to repent and seek to make confession in their hundreds. The sinner would come to admit that divine intervention was necessary for his salvation, and the divine intervention in the Catholic Church is sacramental. Formal repentance required confession and therefore the presence of a confessor who could determine the form and degree of the necessary penance for the sinner and absolve him from his sins. The problem essentially lay here. To whom would the enthusiastic crowd turn? The Fourth Lateran Council imposed the obligation on the laity to confess at least once a year to their parish priest, who was thus regarded as the normal confessor.[20] There were practical problems with this, however. In reality, secular priests often lacked the education to hear confessions and impose appropriate penances. Also, at least in some cases, the laity appeared reluctant to confess to their own priests, as Matthew Paris stated in explaining why Franciscans

---

17. Mariano d'Alatri, "La predicazione francescana nel due e trecento," *Picenum seraphicum* 10 (1973): 21.

18. Ibid., 22.

19. David d'Avray, *The Preaching of the Friars: Sermons Diffused from Paris before 1300* (Oxford: Clarendon Press, 1985), 51.

20. Hefele and Leclercq, *Histoire des conciles,* 5:1350.

received confessions.[21] People might not feel comfortable in confessing to someone who lived among them, as opposed to confessing to an outsider. It is known that successful Franciscan preachers, when they were also priests, had to listen to many confessions after their sermons. So it is said of Haymo of Faversham that he had to listen to confessions for three days after his first sermon as a Franciscan in 1225.[22] Salimbene tells us that Humilis of Milan preached and heard confessions for many days.[23] Not that the secular clergy were always happy about this. In 1231, some German bishops complained to the pope that the friars "were invading the ancient and indisputable right of the clergy by coming into their parishes and hearing confessions of their parishioners."[24]

The Link between Preaching and Schools

One reason why historians have readily accepted the medieval friars' explanation linking study of scholastic theology and preaching concerns contemporary developments with regard to preaching in the Parisian schools. These developments have been extensively documented by an exceptional group of historians.[25] What they outline is that starting from the second half of the twelfth century, a new art of preaching was in the making in the schools of Paris. This new style of sermon, known as "the school sermon," or *sermo modernus,* differed from the kind of sermons that had been produced in the period when monks had usually been the dominant intellectual force in the Church, a period that was coming to an end during the twelfth century.[26]

Two questions arise here concerning the Franciscan move to the university centers and their involvement in the intellectual milieu if their purpose was to master the techniques of this new style of preaching. Was this new technique

---

21. "Confessiones etiam, quia multi sacerdotibus suis in pluribus casibus confiteri renuentes periclitabantur, recipiendi" (Matthew Paris, *Matthei Parisiensis historia Anglorum,* 397).

22. Eccleston, 28.

23. Salimbene, 411.

24. Moorman, *History of the Franciscan Order,* 181.

25. See Louis-Jacques Bataillon, *La predication au XIIIe siècle en France et Italie: Études et documents* (Aldershot: Variorum, 1993); Nicole Bériou, *L'avénement des maîtres de la parole: La prédication à Paris au XIIIe siècle,* 2 vols., Collection des études augustiniennes. Série Moyen-Age et temps modernes (Paris: Institut d'études augustiniennes, 1998); d'Avray, *Preaching of the Friars;* Richard H. Rouse and Mary A. Rouse, *Preachers, Florilegia and Sermons: Studies on the Manipulus Florum of Thomas of Ireland,* Studies and Texts (Toronto: Pontifical Institute of Mediaeval Studies, 1979); Jacqueline Hamesse et al., eds., *Medieval Sermons and Society: Cloister, City, University; Proceedings of International Symposia at Kalamazoo and New York,* Textes et études du moyen âge (Louvain-la-Neuve: Fédération Internationale des Instituts d'études médiévales, 1998).

26. For examples of the sermons in these two styles, see Louis-Jacques Bataillon, "Early Scholastic and Mendicant Preaching as Exegesis of Scripture," in *Ad Litteram: Authoritative Texts and Their Medieval Readers,* ed. Mark D. Jordan and Kent Emery Jr., 165–98 (Notre Dame: University of Notre Dame Press, 1992).

of preaching sufficiently developed in the early 1220s to attract the friars' attention, and would this new technique be of benefit in preaching to the laity, the
only kind of preaching on the table for the early Franciscans? Neither of these
questions can be answered in the affirmative.

For the early thirteenth century, a connection between the theology education offered at the University of Paris and the clerical responsibility for
pastoral care was nothing more than wishful thinking: "The distinction
between *clerici scholastici* who attended the schools and *clerici ecclesiastici* who
served in parish churches—a distinction that Peter the Chanter himself
recognized—continued to prevail."[27] "School sermons at the end of the
twelfth century and beginning of the thirteenth seem to be still quite fluid in
structure, with much informal sequence from one idea to another, by word association, which remind one rather of the monastic homily," wrote Richard and
Mary Rouse.[28] The production of *pastoralia,* a term coined by Leonard Boyle to
refer to the literature related to pastoral care, was in its infancy in the schools of
Paris in the early thirteenth century.[29] Insofar as it existed, its audience was not
parish priests, but instead the students in the schools, who may or may not have
had the care of souls.[30] The application of scholastic learning to *pastoralia* was a
slow process that reached its maturity only in the late thirteenth century, not at
the time that friars moved to the circles of the schools. The earliest articulation
of the link between university instruction and pastoral care is to be found in a
letter written by Gregory IX in 1237 to the Victorine canons in Paris, conceding
them the right to have a theology master teaching in their monastery "because
your brothers... are often required to dispense the nourishment of the Word of
God in parish churches which pertain to your monastery."[31]

There was quite a gap between university preaching and preaching
directed toward pastoral care for the laity in the early thirteenth century. The
terminology used in academic circles here can be misleading. It is true that
praedicatio was a part of medieval scholastic teaching, but it was intended as a
technical and sophisticated scholarly exercise.[32] In fact, one suspects that the
university sermon, relying "on the techniques of instruction—organization,

---

27. Marshall E. Crossnoe, "Education and the Care of Souls: Pope Gregory IX, the Order of
St. Victor, and the University of Paris in 1237," *Mediaeval Studies* 61 (1999): 137–72, at 154.

28. Rouse and Rouse, *Preachers, Florilegia and Sermons,* 68.

29. Leonard E. Boyle, "The Fourth Lateran Council and Manuals of Popular Theology," in *The
Popular Literature of Medieval England,* ed. Thomas J. Heffernan (Knoxville: University of Tennessee Press,
1985), 31.

30. Joseph W. Goering, *William de Montibus (c. 1140–1213): The Schools and the Literature of Pastoral
Care,* Studies and Texts (Toronto: Pontifical Institute of Mediaeval Studies, 1992), 62–65.

31. Crossnoe, "Education and the Care of Souls," 137, 156.

32. For a discussion of *praedicatio,* see John W. Baldwin, *Masters, Princes, and Merchants: The Social Views
of Peter the Chanter and His Circle* (Princeton, 1970), 1:107–16.

signposts, documentation and example"—was often used as a means to show off scholarly prowess to an audience made up of peers, as there are several references to the vanity of the scholar-preachers and their adorning of sermons with sophisticated phrases to impress others. Nicole Bériou, who studied the *reportationes* as a particular genre within the new *artes praedicandi* of the schools, wrote that it was not possible to identify any sermons that were directed even to ordinary parish priests, let alone laymen.[33]

This comes as no surprise given the sentiments concerning pastoral work among the Paris scholars. For the educated clergy who were studying and teaching in the great intellectual centers, pastoral care was a kind of "donkey work," which they shunned. Thus Robert Grosseteste conveys with powerful rhetoric the general dislike for pastoral work among the clergy in a letter he sent to a priest, who resisted leaving the schools to take up pastoral work:

> We have received your letter, dear friend, saying that, since you do not wish both to lecture at the University of Paris and bear the cure of souls, right now you would rather lecture than carry the burden of pastoral care. So for the moment you have put off accepting the cure of souls to which we summoned you so that souls could be saved.... We certainly believe that you do not throw off this weight like a mule bucking against its burden; but we also realize that no one taking on this task looks upon it as a prize, and that, dragging and kicking, you agree to undertake it unwillingly because it is onerous and full of dread. Yet when it has been undertaken it can be borne tirelessly and with strength.[34]

Grosseteste expressed similar ideas in a letter addressed to a renowned scholar of theology, Thomas of Wales. Grosseteste tries to convince Thomas to decline the opportunity to teach at Paris and accept the pastoral office he assigned to him. "If you love saving souls... you should not reject the shepherd's burden, you should not run away from the task, and you should not be wearied by these cares once you have taken them on."[35] Grosseteste is, however, well aware of the two major arguments to challenge his invitation. "A great many people will tell you that you should not forsake wisdom for riches, and the good you will be able to do by your teaching in the schools for high office." Even though the bishop too seems to think that Thomas can do a lot of good in the schools, he

---

33. Bériou, *L'avénement des maîtres,* 125.

34. Shinners and Dohar, *Pastors and the Care of Souls,* 13.

35. Robert Grosseteste, *The Letters of Robert Grosseteste, Bishop of Lincoln,* ed. Frank A. C. Mantello and Joseph W. Goering (Toronto: University of Toronto Press, 2010), 177, letter 51.

still suggests that it is a greater good to take up "such an important cure of souls humbly and painstakingly than to teach wisely from a master's chair."[36]

Although it is undisputed among historians that in the Middle Ages there was a severe shortage of educated clergymen who could adequately carry out pastoral care, it has been perhaps insufficiently noted that the educated clergy were frequently unwilling to perform pastoral duties, and often studying or being part of the schools was far more preferable. And in fact, this was the prevailing clerical culture in Paris in the early thirteenth century. The unwillingness to carry out pastoral care seems to be so commonplace that the famous Bolognese rhetorician Buoncompagno da Signa (d. 1240) produced model letters for recalling studying priests from schools. The fate of the abandoned parish people is dramatically expressed in this letter. "The Church of Maguntina (Mainz) keeps on waiting for her most venerable Lord father and pastor but he does not return. She is in tears and cannot desist mourning, because she is orphaned by all her guards... wild wolves have invaded his flock."[37] We can add to this the testimony of the Franciscan John of Rupella, who, in a sermon he preached on Anthony of Padua, contrasted the saint to those "who always wish to preach to the clergy and the good," and do not preach unless the audience is made up of "clerics of enlightened minds."[38] Bériou, who has extensively studied the sermons originating in the Parisian schools, observed that, from the end of the twelfth century onward, the sermons preached in Paris denounced the career ambitions that prevented the fulfillment of pastoral commitments. The preachers complained that the clerics were abandoning their flocks to incompetents in the hope of social promotion and for money. In general, the sermons preached to the synods and to the scholars were both preoccupied, along with concern about clerical ignorance, with the indifference of clerics to their pastoral duties.[39] If such indifference to pastoral care was seen to be permeating the world of scholars, we can hardly expect Franciscan scholars to have been immune to it, particularly those scholars who took the habit at the schools. We should then concede that a fair number of scholars who entered the Order would be unlikely to have been eager to become preachers to the laity. Perhaps unwillingness to preach rather than sheer laziness made some friars with the office of preacher abstain from fulfilling their offices. A statute ordained by

---

36. Ibid.

37. Buoncompagno da Signa, *Testi riguardanti la vita degli studenti a Bologna nel sec. XIII: Dal Boncompagnus 1, Biblioteca di "Quadrivium,"* ed. Virgilio Pini (Bologna: Testi per esercitazioni accademiche, 1968), 50.

38. "Item, dirigit ambulantes in tenebris vitiorum, et hoc contra quosdam, qui semper vel bonis vel religiosis predicant et predicare volunt qui sunt in die gratie, non peccatoribus... quidam, qui non predicant nisi clericis illuminate mentis" (de Amsterdam, "Tres sermones inediti," 47).

39. Bériou, *L'avénement des maîtres de la parole,* 122.

the provincial chapter of Padua in 1295 stated that "those friars who have the office of preacher and who are suitable to preach but do not want to preach shall be deprived of the office of preacher."[40] What is rather unexpected here is that the only punishment for such friars was deprivation of office. If, as is generally suggested, the Franciscans saw pastoral care as the central objective of their educational organization, why then did they not impose a harsher punishment on these unwilling preachers in order to deter others?

The clerical unwillingness to serve laypeople is not on the whole a surprising sentiment. Clerics once entering the community of scholars did not wish to abandon that community and the collegial lifestyle to go back to a life among the predominantly uneducated laypeople, whom they considered their inferiors: hence the centuries-old discourse on "knowledge puffs up" (1 Cor. 8:1). Of course the mendicant convents in university towns actually pioneered that "collegial" environment, which must indeed have been one of the attractions for the student, something he could not yet find among the secular student community. It is only from the second half of the thirteenth century onward that we see a new and strengthened effort among the leading members of the university to establish a strong link between school learning and pastoral care. The foundation of the college of Sorbonne, which was initiated between 1254 and 1255, was finalized in 1257, and is perhaps the most definite example of this new sense of urgency among the members of the university to channel intellectual resources toward the much-neglected sphere of pastoral care. Around 1260 Robert de Sorbonne put down a set of rules concerning members of the college. He sought to oblige them to undertake preaching to the laity in the parishes as a virtue of their privilege and in the spirit of charity, as well as frequenting their theology classes and disputations.[41] In her research on the *reportationes,* Bériou finds three members of this college who were particularly receptive to the idea of employing their theological training for the benefit of preaching to the laity. Pierre de Limoges, writing around 1260–1264, Raoul de Châteauroux, and Jean d'Essômes, writing around 1270, seem to be the earliest to engage in the vulgarization of university sermons.[42]

What is to be noted here is precisely the chronology. The argument for the desirability of the study of theology by those who were destined to pastoral offices was already formed in the episcopal circles in the twelfth century. In 1219, the secular masters of the University of Paris scored a professional success

---

40. "Item quod illi fratres, qui habent predicationis officium, et ydoneitatem habent ad predicandum, et tamen predicare nolunt, priventur per ministrum officio predicationis." Andrew G. Little, ed., "Statuta provincialia provinciae Franciae et marchiae Tervisinae," *AFH* 7 (1914): 464.

41. Bériou, *L'avénement des maîtres,* 85–86.

42. Ibid., 86–87, 125–31.

in recruitment of scholars when Honorius III issued *Super Speculam* and allowed for nonresidence up to five years for any secular clerk destined to pastoral office and wishing to study theology in Paris. But at that time yet no one argued that the study of theology was an obligation and a requirement for the acquisition of pastoral office (the decision to send pastors to schools was still left to the discretion of the bishops), nor were the emerging mendicants yet charged with the care of souls. Mendicants took up this link between preaching and study of theology in a university setting and made it the central point of their justification to be in the schools, when faced with questions concerning why they strive to be masters. Thence onwards, the relation between study and pastoral office moved speedily from desirability to obligation. Robert de Sorbonne decided to establish his college and make preaching to the laity a condition for its membership exactly at the time when the mendicants defended their existence in the university principally in terms of their Order's involvement in preaching, that is, at the height of the mendicant-secular dispute of 1253–1256. In fact, wishing to attack the justification used by the mendicants for their academic presence, the secular masters advanced the counterargument that if the mendicants truly cared for the pastoral well-being of the laity, then they should voluntarily give up their magisterial chairs to the seculars, since it is the secular clergy who actually has the responsibility of the care of souls.[43]

When we move further on in time, the connection between preaching and theology moved from one of desirability to one of strict obligation on pain of damnation. And it was none but a Franciscan master of the late thirteenth century who voiced it in a quodlibetal question. The question is whether those who accept the office of preaching and confession despite being ignorant and inapt to execute it sin mortally if they have the means to study and become apt but simply do not care to or disdain to learn.[44] This quodlibetal question, authored with great probability by Raymond Rigaud, was written sometime between 1286–1292 either in Paris or Toulouse.[45] Raymond's answer to the question is rather blunt. Those who accept this position and do not prepare themselves to execute it sin. They sin even more if they disdain such a preparation. And he who adventurously assumes the office in ignorance and indiscretely and puts himself

---

43. A. G. Traver, "Rewriting History? The Parisian Secular Masters' Apologia of 1254," *History of Universities* 15 (1997–1999): 14.

44. Todi, Biblioteca Comunale, 98, f. 6v: "Utrum suscipiens officium predicationis et confessionis ignarus et insufficiens ad executionem potens tamen per studium perficere et ydoneus fieri, peccet mortaliter si non curet vel contempnat addiscere. Et videtur quod sic: quia suscipiens officium obligat se ad executionem officii."

45. Sylvain Piron, "Franciscan *Quodlibeta* in Southern *Studia* and at Paris, 1280–1300," in *Theological Quodlibeta in the Middle Ages: The Thirteenth Century,* ed. Chris Schabel (Leiden: Brill, 2006), 423–25.

in danger sins most gravely.[46] An incumbent of this office is "held to do whatever he can to acquire sufficient learning for the purpose of teaching, just as he is held to live an exemplary life."[47] We can only imagine the horror of a friar who heard that he might be facing eternal damnation if he does not study sufficiently before taking on the office of preaching. Preaching by an uneducated friar, even with a disposition for holiness is simply out of question.

Considering, however, that the Franciscans moved to Paris in 1219, at a time when they did not formally have the charge of pastoral care, and at a time when there was as yet hardly any discernible connection between university education and the pastoral mission, and considering that the general clerical culture in the university tended toward a disregard of and dislike for pastoral responsibilities, it does not seem to be a satisfactory explanation to say that the friars' initial interest in scholastic education and recruits from scholarly circles concerned exclusively the improvement of their preaching to the laity, or more generally their pastoral care. Bonaventure, in his enthusiasm to defend Franciscan presence in the universities, might have explained that presence with a view to preaching, but would the majority of the Franciscan lectors explain their enthusiasm about taking the office of lector in terms of improving their own preaching or that of their fellow friars? The evidence to be presented in the chapter 4 sheds serious doubts on this. We need to take into account the likely spread to the rest of the Order of this highly intellectual culture that shunned pastoral work. The educational organization of the Franciscans had at its origin and core the University of Paris. The first known lectors of the Order were all scholars from the University of Paris, and they further trained the would-be lectors, preachers, and confessors. In the pre-1260 constitutions, the studium at the Paris convent was designated as the only school in the Order for training friars to be lectors. The majority of the lectors of the Order must have breathed in the air of Paris, where learning was often pursued for reasons other than saving souls. The centrality of Paris in the Franciscan educational organization must have facilitated the spread of intellectual-cultural trends in the University of Paris to the rest of the Order.

Furthermore, how to explain the high-level involvement of many Franciscans in the intellectual activities that had no bearing on preaching? From very early times onward, both Franciscans and Dominicans strived to keep a chair of theology in Paris, and later Oxford, the second-greatest seat of scholastic theology in Europe. It is true that the majority of the clerical Franciscans who followed the

---

46. Todi, Biblioteca Comunale, 98, f. 6v: "Suscipiens igitur officium simul voluntarius simul compulsus peccat, si ad executionem officii se diligenter non preparat. Peccat quidam si negligat. Peccat gravius, si contempnat. Peccat gravissime si ignarus et indiscretus temerarie se intromittat et periculo se committat."

47. "Sicut igitur tenetur ad vitam ratione exempli sic tenetur quod potest facere, ut habeat sufficientem scientiam ratione doctrine" (ibid).

theology classes in the various provincial schools of the Order took the offices of preachers and confessors. However, the more intellectually gifted among them were sent to the studia generalia of the Order and continued their studies beyond the requirement for preaching in order to become lectors. In the studia generalia they generally listened to the lectures of lectors trained in Paris. The provincial constitutions of Umbria published in 1985 reveal that some lectors, at a later point in their teaching career, had the opportunity of going to Paris for further study of two years.[48] A smaller group still, the crème de la crème, was selected from among the lectors to incept at Paris and Oxford, and thence to teach as masters of theology, usually after teaching for some time as lectors in their home province.[49] To become a bachelor or a master at a university like Paris, Oxford, or later Cambridge was the highest position a friar could reach on the intellectual ladder. These bachelors and masters of theology engaged in high-level involvement in learning and study, which should be distinguished from the low-level involvement of the friars who studied theology at an intermediary level, just enough to pass their examinations as preachers and confessors. This is also true for the Dominicans: there seems to be no explicit evidence that a formal integration of the Order with the University of Paris was among founder Dominic of Guzman's intentions.[50] In fact, Thomas Aquinas himself suggested that a man destined for the *cura animarum* did not need to have any great learning.[51] Pierre Mandonnet, a prominent historian of the Dominican Order, wrote that the Dominicans considered teaching in the schools an activity akin to preaching since the Church was in a grave crisis with regard to the provision of teachers of theology.[52] However, this theory that Dominicans saw a need of the Christian people and were enthusiastic to fill it falls short of explaining why the Dominicans launched such a persistent recruitment strategy in Paris and other university or school towns. Most students in the schools whom the Dominicans, along with the Franciscans, tried to attract into their Order were clergy on benefices and expected to go back to their canonical residences to fulfill pastoral duties. The friars thus deprived many bishops of suitable candidates who could preach and teach. Furthermore, the Dominicans supported this recruitment strategy with a theology that claimed the regular religious to be superior to the parish priests, reminiscent of the way canons regular argued

---

48. "Ordinazioni dei capitoli provinciali Umbri dal 1300 al 1305." *CF* 55 (1985): 5–31. For the wording of the relevant statute, see chap. 5, n. 103.

49. The details and selection procedures are explained in chap. 5.

50. Crossnoe, "Education and the Care of Souls," 156.

51. Leonard E. Boyle, "Aspects of Clerical Education in Fourteenth-Century England," in *Pastoral Care, Clerical Education and Canon Law, 1200–1400* (London: Variorum, 1981), 19–20.

52. Mandonnet, "La crise scolaire," 43.

their spiritual superiority against the monks in the twelfth century.[53] Thomas Aquinas, in his *Perfection of the Spiritual Life*, claimed men in religious orders to be in a higher state of perfection than the archdeacons and parish priests, and refuted contrary arguments posed by the secular clergy.[54]

Besides their teaching duties, these friars were responsible for an impressive intellectual output in the thirteenth and fourteenth centuries: they disputed questions, wrote theological treatises and commentaries, and introduced new concepts and theories that contributed greatly to the disciplines of theology and philosophy. As John van Engen rightly observed, the scholastic works of the universities replaced the letters of the earlier century as a vessel through which a medieval scholar demonstrated his learning. "The *consilium* or the *quodlibet* replaced the letter as a means of formulating ideas and addressing public realities."[55] The majority of these works were not related in any direct way to preaching. Scholars have already observed that the copying of books was an integral activity of Franciscan convent life, one that set the Franciscans apart from the Dominicans.[56] Pre-Narbonne constitutions designated for the first time *scribere* as an obligatory activity for friars.[57] This in time led to the production of autographs, books authored by Franciscans and written in their own hand, instead of being dictated to another friar acting as scribe.[58] Bonaventure formed a hierarchy in ascending order of the four professions associated with writing: *scriptor, compilator, commentator,* and *auctor.*[59] For the thirteenth century and beyond, the evidence for Franciscans writing books is overwhelming, as we have many works by prominent Franciscan academics such as John of Rupella, William of Meliton, Bonaventure of Bagnoregio, Matthew of

53. Caroline Walker Bynum, *Jesus as Mother: Studies in the Spirituality of the High Middle Ages* (Berkeley: University of California Press, 1982), 29.

54. "Rursusque considerandum est quod in presbyteris et diaconibus curam animarum habentibus duo sunt consideranda: scilicet officium curae et dignitas ordinis. Manifestum est autem quod officium curae suscipientes perpetuam obligationem non habent, cum multotiens curam susceptam dimittant, sicut patet de illis qui dimittunt parochias vel archidiaconatus et religionem intrant. Patet autem ex supra dictis quod status perfectionis non habetur nisi cum perpetua obligatione. Manifestum est igitur quod archidiaconi et parochiales sacerdotes, et etiam electi, ante consecrationem, statum perfectionis nondum sunt adepti, sicut nec novitii in religionibus ante professionem." Thomas Aquinas, *De perfectione vitae spiritualis* (Rome: Ad Santa Sabinae, 1970), chap. 20, http://www.corpusthomisticum.org/oap.html.

55. John van Engen, "Letters, Schools and the Written Culture in the Eleventh and Twelfth Centuries," in *Dialektik und Rhetorik im früheren und hohen Mittelalter: Rezeption, Überlieferung und gesellschaftliche Wirkung antiker Gelehrsamkeit, vornehmlich im 9. und 12. Jh.,* ed. J. Freed, 97–132 (Munich, 1997), 132.

56. Attilio B. Langeli, "I libri dei frati: La cultura scritta dell'Ordine dei Minori," in *Francesco d'Assisi e il primo secolo di storia francescana,* ed. Maria Pia Alberzoni (Turin: Einaudi, 1997), 296–98.

57. "Fratres tam clerici quam laici compellantur per suos superiores in scribendo et in aliis sibi competantibus exerceri" (Pre-Narbonne, 91).

58. Langeli, "I libri dei frati," 299.

59. Ibid.

Aquasparta, John Peckham, Roger Bacon, Peter John Olivi, Duns Scotus, and Francis of Marchia.

Along with works of high-scholastic culture, Franciscans also produced books that were particularly relevant to the Order's character and mission. Bartholomeus Anglicus, who was one of the earliest recruits of the Paris convent, completed his famous encyclopedic work *De proprietatibus rerum* sometime before 1245.[60] In the epilogue, he wrote that he had composed this work especially with a view to making the complex terms in the Bible and patristic works understandable to the less educated friars in the Order. He added, however, that those who understand these things completely should move on without delay to investigating subtler things in the writings of the doctors.[61] Similarly, the third Franciscan regent master in Paris, William of Meliton, wrote a short work in order to explain the basics of liturgy to the "simplices clericos praesertim et sacerdotes."[62] John of Rupella, the second Franciscan master of theology at Paris, who died in 1244, apparently wrote a book on Aristotle's *Predicaments* that was practically the textbook of Aristotelian old logic, now lost, which the friars of Todi had in their possession in the early fourteenth century.[63] It is not possible to know the nature of this book, but it is conceivable that John's aim was to make Aristotelian logic accessible to friars.

Casting doubt on the argument that preaching was the prevailing motive for seeking out schools and learned men should not be taken as undermining the enormous contribution of the Franciscans to the "preaching revival" of the thirteenth century. The libraries and archives of Europe present indisputable evidence of the sermon cycles and preaching aids, whose authors were evidently men trained in theology. However, certain points require attention. The first of these is the chronology: the Franciscan intellectual enterprise started in 1219 with the early settlement in Paris, and the first step in the establishment of an educational structure 1228. This is too early for the scholastic milieu of Paris to be associated with the production of the pastoral genres such as *distinctiones* or *concordances*. Second, David d'Avray has shown successfully that although Paris was the center par excellence for the diffusion of preaching materials, "the

---

60. Michael C. Seymour et al., *Bartholomaeus Anglicus and His Encyclopaedia* (Aldershot: Variorum, Ashgate, 1992), 11.

61. "Simplicia siquidem sunt et rudia, quae excerpsi, utilia tamen mihi rudi et mei consimilibus eadem iudicavi...sed cum haec plenius intellexerint, ad subtiliora intelligenda et investiganda ad maiorem et doctorum industriam recurrere non different neque omittant." Bartholomaeus Anglicus, *De proprietatibus rerum* (Frankfurt: Minerva, 1601), 1261. See also Seymour, *Bartholomaeus Anglicus*, 15.

62. "Et sic Opusculum nostrum considerandum est tamquam libellum ad propagandam vitam liturgicam apud simplices clericos praesertim et sacerdotes." William of Meliton, *Opusculum super missam*, ed. A. van Dijk, *Ephemerides Liturgicae* 53 (1939): 306–7.

63. "Scriptum super librum predicamentorum secundum magistrum ioannem ropelle." Todi, Biblioteca Comunale, 185, f. 41v.

best-known component of intellectual life in thirteenth-century Paris, scholasticism, would only have helped preachers in rather round-about ways. The important connections between Paris as university and Paris as centre for mass communication are not obvious, the most interesting being the development of an ideology of the preacher's role, the exposure of young friars to living paradigms in the form of university sermons, whose forms of thought were closer to those of popular preaching than of scholastic exercises, and finally the oral culture of student friars."[64] It still remains unclear to what degree scholastic education was beneficial to the making of a good and effective preacher. Therefore, we need to reflect on why, once they had decided that some theological training was desirable for the purposes of preaching, the friars did not devise an alternative, perhaps humbler system of education and intellectual involvement like that of the nonmendicant religious orders in Paris, without insisting on having regent masters and without spending their time on the production of highly sophisticated theological treatises.

Why Franciscans Embraced Scholastic Learning

What follows below is a consideration of motives Franciscans had for embracing scholarly learning in the crucial period of 1228–1244, other than that of improving their preaching and pastoral care. It is likely that none of these other motives should be seen as exclusively responsible; nor do they altogether supplant the objective of having learned preachers and confessors.

Learning as Social Leverage

A very significant motive that pushed the first generation of ministers to recruit learned men and introduce learning into the Order's structure was their preoccupation with the friars' prestige and respectability within society. It is important to emphasize that the reasons for the Order's effort to enlist learned men can hardly be separated from its reasons for establishing an educational system. The preoccupation with prestige must not be understood in a cynical sense or a mere outcome of the friars' vanity, because it was, rather, in many ways a consequence of the particular character of the early Franciscan Order. As shown in the previous chapters, in the early days Francis's fraternity had expanded quite rapidly owing to its lack of a policy on recruitment, its acceptance of laity on equal terms with clergy, and its short, three-month novitiate that remained in place until 1219. The result was a religious community of men from all social

---

64. David d'Avray, *Preaching of the Friars,* 203.

classes, many of them uneducated and lacking religious discipline, as outside observers such as Jacques de Vitry observed. Unlike the Dominican Order, the Friars Minor had a large lay membership. The dignity associated with the traditional religious orders was hard to see in the early Franciscans, whom the chroniclers reported to be wandering barefoot with unshaven faces and ragged clothes. Such absence of dignity could appear sympathetic in a figure of obvious sanctity like Francis, but not all friars had his charisma to help make themselves amiable.

One can argue that holiness or prestige was crucial for the success of any religious order, but the traditional monastic orders like the Benedictines, Cluniacs, or Cistercians could draw on their social and political influence from the high social status of their members and their large initial endowments. In the case of a mendicant order like the Franciscans, social leverage was all the more crucial since the Franciscans relied completely on local support for their sustenance unlike the monks who could provide for their livelihood from substantial estates. People were not likely to join the Franciscans, nurture them in towns, go hear their sermons, and make donations if they did not see something particular in the members of this Order. Nor would the local bishops grant them permission to preach in their diocese or stretch out a helping hand to them. Sanctity or the holy life of the friars would be that "something particular," and groups like the Cathar *perfecti* did gain quite a following and support among the people without being men of learning. It was the sanctity of his brothers, Francis of Assisi hoped, that would bring success and endurance to his Order, rather than their respectability. However, it would have been too much to hope that most members of this Order, who amounted to some five thousand in 1221, could live in as saintly a way as Francis might have liked. The illiteracy of most friars, combined with their low social status, must have been a particular concern for ministers, especially as the Rule discouraged the illiterate brothers from learning their letters. Probably it was this concern with respectability that pushed the first ministers to try to convince Francis to adapt an existing monastic Rule, and it was this concern that made them incorporate learning, perhaps the only medieval means to social mobility for the lowborn, into the mission of the Order. The road to social mobility was closed to the illiterate, but for those lowborn clergy who were at least minimally lettered, the pursuit of learning was the means to acquire an authority while preaching and hearing confessions among the uneducated laity. This was precisely the upper hand that the Franciscans would have over parish priests, who often lacked prestige and were objects of ridicule because of their lack of morals and education. In fact, in his study of the forms of sainthood, André Vauchez finds that from the second half of the thirteenth century onward, cults of parish priests appear in places like western France and Tuscany. Such "saint-priests" like Thomas Hélye (d. 1257) and Yves

Hélory of Kenmartin (d. 1310) were highly educated men, having studied at Paris. Vauchez correctly observes that, despite their excellent education, they chose voluntarily to perform pastoral work as an "act of voluntary abasement" that contributed to the aura of sanctity around them.[65] Similarly, in the case of Franciscans coming from families who were not wealthy, their association with the universities and with men of higher learning would be precisely the leverage that showed their religious life as a voluntary abasement. If, therefore, there was a link between learning and preaching, it was not so much in the sense that learning improved the effectiveness of the friars' preaching, but more that the Order's involvement with schools and high-flying scholars made the preaching of the friars, even those who were not associated with schools, worthy of the laity's attention.

The easiest and fastest way to increase the prestige of an order like the Friars Minor was to attract men of great learning. We have already seen that all the extant constitutions of the thirteenth century include the statute concerning the recruitment of learned men, and have quite good reasons to suspect that the desire to recruit the *litterati* dates from much earlier than the first extant set of constitutions, those of 1239–1241. One might suggest that it was the major reason why the vicars Gregory of Naples and Matthew of Narni rushed Brother Pacifico to Paris as early as 1219. There were several advantages to recruiting educated men. The entry of a scholar added to the prestige of the Order; the more prestige the scholar had, the better the publicity. Thus Franciscan Roger Bacon in his *Opus minus* described the entry of the first Parisian regent master, Alexander of Hales, in 1236: "When he entered the Order of Friars Minor he was God's greatest friar not because of his praiseworthy condition but because of this: in those times, the Order of Friars Minor was neglected by the people, and he edified the people and exalted the Order. On account of his entry into the Order, friars exalted him to the Heavens and gave him the authority over all studies."[66]

Francis himself pointed to the fact that the entry of famous scholars would be generally considered a triumph and an occasion for joy: "A messenger arrives and says that all the Masters of Paris have entered the Order. Write: this isn't true joy!"[67] "True joy" of course, for Francis, lay in a humble imitation of Christ and

---

65. André Vauchez, *Sainthood in the Later Middle Ages* (Cambridge: Cambridge University Press, 1997), 312–13.

66. "Nam quum intravit ordinem Fratrum Minorum fuit Deo maximus Minor non solum propter suas conditiones laudabiles sed propter hoc. Novus fuit Ordo Minorum et neglectus a mundo illis temporibus et ille aedificavit mundum et ordinem exaltavit. Ex suo ingressu fratres et alii exaltaverunt in caelum et ei dederunt auctoritatem totius studii." Roger Bacon, *Opus minus*, in *Fr. Rogeri Bacon opera quaedam hactenus inedita,* ed. John S. Brewer (London: Longman, Green, Longman and Roberts, 1859), 1:325–26.

67. Armstrong, Hellman, and Short, *Francis of Assisi,* 1:166.

his sufferings, but he sets that against a number of occasions for joy that were genuinely desirable even while not matching Francis's idea of "true joy."

Once in the Order, scholars could transfer their knowledge to other friars by way of formal teaching or through informal conversations. We know that already in Francis's time, before the office of lector was introduced, someone like Anthony of Padua was teaching theology to friars, and that this received Francis's blessing. After 1228, when the first lectors were appointed, there was all the more reason for the ministers to encourage the entry of scholars and learned men into the Order to fill the openings for lectors in the provinces. As we saw in the discussion concerning the statutes of recruitment, there was also increasingly the issue of functionality. The learned men in the Order could fill various offices, such as minister or preacher or confessor. They could be used in negotiations and correspondence with the secular clergy, monks, or papacy. They would also, of course, serve to balance the numbers of the uneducated lay brothers, of which there were many in the early years of the Order. The learned men enjoyed prestige in the society: the public would have been more interested in listening to a sermon from an educated priest than from an uneducated lay-man, particularly if that layman lacked the holiness of Francis.

The ministers' interest in attracting the educated was not a particularly Franciscan phenomenon. Throughout the centuries, religious orders had both attracted and nurtured the learned, no matter how much the sanctity of simplic-ity and devotion was praised, and however cautiously *scientia* was approached. In the twelfth century, the monks and canons regular attracted numerous students and masters from the urban schools into a life that was cloistered to a greater or lesser extent.[68] When the fashion for the new learning hit Europe in the late twelfth century, this task became more difficult. Cistercians tried to attract recruits from the schools by arguing for the superiority of the contemplative knowledge of the cloister over the seductive academic knowledge of schools.[69] Contemporary observers also mentioned that the lack of opportunity for learn-ing discouraged many people who were considering life in a religious commu-nity. "Many good and great persons would never enter a religious order, if there is no study there," wrote Humbert of Romans, the Dominican master general, while explaining the uses of study in his Order. According to Humbert, study-ing was a priority for all orders, since the study of the sacred was a good thing. It helped the recruitment of good people, and it brought greater devotion, since

---

68. Jean Leclercq, *Cultura umanistica e desiderio di Dio: Studio sulla letteratura monastica del medio evo* (Florence: Sansoni, 1988), 255–56.

69. This is the general theme found in many letters written by Cistercians advertising the monastic life to potential converts. Stephen C. Ferruolo, *The Origins of the University: The Schools of Paris and Their Critics, 1100–1215* (Stanford: Stanford University Press, 1985), 68.

people tended to show more devotion and greater honor to the educated than to the uneducated.[70] Members of nonmendicant orders observed similarly that the religious orders that did not offer the new learning to their members witnessed a decline in the number of distinguished new recruits. "For the last thirteen years, no famous person learned in theology has joined our Order, and those who are already in the Order are aging and dying," lamented the Cistercian Stephen of Lexington around 1233.[71] The implication was that theology masters stopped entering the Cistercian Order around the 1220s, the time when the Dominicans and Franciscans settled in Paris and other university towns. While considering why the Humiliati did not achieve the same status as the Dominican and Franciscan Orders, Frances Andrews suggested that it might have been as a result of *their failure* to move into the universities and to attract some of the great minds of their generation.[72]

We must remember that the earliest extant statutes of the Order, dating from 1239–1241, reveal a distinct interest in attracting men who taught in the schools and men who were famous and reputable in general, whereas the later statutes moderated this imperative to recruit learned men by not requiring them to already be teachers. This is understandable since greater prestige was necessary in earlier times. The ministers who drafted the early statutes were not content with having just moderately educated men to preach, even though that might have been all that was necessary if preaching were the only ultimate objective. They sought those who preached laudably, but even famous preachers were not their priority. Instead, their primary target was men who were teachers at the universities. Twenty years later, at the time of the Narbonne constitutions of 1260, the Order had set up its educational network, consolidated its chairs in the universities of Paris and Oxford, and had received the privileges that secured its position among the local bishops, clergy, and universities.

In fact, the friars' insistence on having a magisterial chair, even at the cost of entering into conflict with the secular masters, can be explained in terms of their desire to attract scholars into the Order. The secular students who listened to the lectures of a friar-*magister*, or were attracted to his fame, might end up taking the Franciscan habit themselves. Besides, having a theology master in the Order was a great source of prestige not just in order to attract the learned but for the reputation of the Order in general. Furthermore, the prospect of a

---

70. Humbert of Romans, *Expositio regulae beati Augustini*, in *Opera de vita regulari*, ed. J. J. Berthier (Paris, 1888; repr., Turin: Marietti, 1956), 1:433–34.

71. "Iam timendum est, ne verbum cuiusdam de maioribus in numero predicatorum lacrimabiliter de nobis verificetur, videlicet quod ante decennium completum oportebit ipsos regere et corrigere ordinem nostrum, eo quod a retroactis iam annis XIIIIcim nullus famose litteratus precipue in sacra pagina ad nos se transtulerit." Bruno Griesser, ed., "Registrum epistolarum Stephani de Lexinton abbatis de Stanlegia et de Savisniaco," *Analecta sacri ordinis Cisterciensis* 2 (1946): 117.

72. My emphasis. Andrews, *Early Humiliati,* 224.

magisterial chair, although very difficult to attain, highly competitive, and destined only to a few, was nevertheless a great attraction in itself for an ambitious
scholar. Certainly, very few clerical friars who entered the Order ended up
incepting in theology, and afterward went on to become regent masters. We
have independent proof, however, that the promise of a magisterial chair constituted a strong attraction to the students when they made career choices. This
is implied in a letter written by the masters of the University of Paris in 1254,
when they tried to prevent the regulars—those in the religious orders, such as
friars—from having two magisterial chairs. "The student embraces studying so
much more when he sees a chance of reaching the teaching chairs."[73] To increase
that chance for secular students, the secular masters wanted to limit the chairs of
regulars to one only. Perhaps other religious orders, once they made their debut
into the world of the universities, also succumbed to the general enthusiasm for
magisterial chairs. It might not be a coincidence that the Premonstratensians
bought their first house in Paris on June 15, 1252, four months following the
statute of the University of Paris in February 1252 declaring that "no religious
would be promoted in the faculty of theology, unless he had a college in Paris."[74]

The development of the particular theological stand that saw learning as part
of evangelical perfection and the early Franciscan interest in enrolling teachers
must be understood within the medieval context of the high prestige associated with teaching, particularly teaching in a university or other famous school.
Indeed, medieval schools were dominated by a mentality that saw the teaching
of theology as an activity superior to caring for the pastoral needs of the laity.
Discussing the question of "whether someone is bound to give up the study of
theology, even if he is suited to teaching others, in order to devote himself to
the salvation of souls," Thomas Aquinas made it clear that he was no friend of
bishops like Robert Grosseteste who wished to call the teachers back to pastoral duty.

> However, we must consider that in any art the one who arranges the art
> and is called the architect is absolutely better than any manual laborer
> who carries out what is arranged for him by another. . . . But in a spiritual

---

73. "Nos igitur diligentius attendentes sacrarum eminentiam litterarum magis necessariam esse
secularibus clericis, qui ad curam animarum et ecclesiarum regimen frequencius evocantur, quam regu-
laribus viris, qui ad ea rarius promoventur; attendentes etiam, quantum intendat scolaris studio si se speret
quandoque ad docendi cathedram perventurum: diligenti deliberatione prehabita duximus statuendum
ut nullus regularium conventus in collegio nostro duas simul sollempnes cathedras habere valeat actu
regentium magistrorum, non intendentes per hoc statutum eos arctare quominus liceat eis inter fratres
suos extraordinarios multiplicare sibi lectores, secundum quod sibi viderint expedire" (CUP, 1, nos.
230, 254).

74. ". . . ordinaverunt, ut de cetero religiousus aliquis non habens collegium et cui est a jure publice
docere prohibitum, ad eorum societatem nullatenus admittatur" (CUP, 226, no. 200). Astrik L. Gabriel,
"The Role of Canons of Prémontré in the Intellectual Movements of the Twelfth and Thirteenth Centuries," in Gedenkboek Orde van Prémontré, 1121–1971, ed. R. J. Maes (Averbode, 1971), 219.

building there are the manual workers, as it were, who particularly pursue the direction of souls, e.g., by administering the sacraments or by doing some such thing in particular. . . . And likewise teachers of theology are like principal artificers who inquire and teach how others ought to procure the salvation of souls. Therefore, it is absolutely better to teach theology and more meritorious if it is done with good intention, than to devote particular care to the salvation of this one or that.[75]

In many ways, the evolution of the office of lector and its rise to dominance within the administrative structure of the Franciscan Order furnishes proof that Franciscan scholar–clerics indeed partook in the medieval idea of the superiority of teaching to preaching to the laity and providing pastoral care.[76]

We need also to think of this prestige attached to teaching in connection with Franciscan discourse concerning the superiority of Franciscan life over other forms of religious life. Franciscan scholars discussed in the previous chapter, John of Rupella, Bonaventure, John Peckham, and Peter John Olivi, perceived it to be a superior form of religious life. Bonaventure and Hugh of Digne wrote that a Franciscan dedicated to the perfection of evangelical life was a superior teacher compared to a teacher who did not take up the Franciscan life.[77] Looked at from this angle, it is only natural that Franciscan friars were better off if they were taught by Franciscans rather than by the secular masters, who would be inferior teachers.

The Authority of the Masters and Paris's Growing Leadership in Christian Theology

The insistent desire of the Franciscans to keep a master of theology among their ranks, who would also be officially part of the board of masters of theology of a university, is of particular importance in explaining the complex relationship between the Order and the schools. In this particular matter, there is a very strong parallel with the Dominican case. In 1229, the Dominican friar Roland of Cremona incepted at Paris under a secular master, John of St. Giles, who himself took the Dominican habit the next year.[78] Thus, within a year, two chairs in the theology faculty were Dominicans. A master of theology would normally promote his own best student for inception, but the inception would

---

75. Shinners and Dohar, *Pastors and the Care of Souls,* 11; Thomas Aquinas, Quodlibetal Questions 1, ques. 7, art. 2.

76. For a full exploration of the dominant role the Franciscan lectors played in the Order's administration, see chap. 4.

77. See above chap. 2, nn. 170 and 173.

78. Mulchahey, "*First the bow is bent,*" 364.

have to have the approval of other masters as well. Strikingly, the Dominicans insisted on continuing to select the successors to these chairs from among the Dominicans.

We observe the same insistence from the Franciscans. In both Paris and Oxford, Franciscans made a strong effort to have their own masters of theology. However, there was also a considerable cost, quite literally, to the Order, in having a friar incept as a master. Franciscans who incepted as a *magister* had to pay fees to the university and were obliged to hold a large banquet and buy presents for the regent masters of the theology faculty, just as would any secular scholar who incepted.[79] Such an expense was something of a challenge to the Order's creed of absolute poverty, yet this did not deter them. This desire of the Franciscans and Dominicans to have a magisterial chair attracted a critical response from outsiders. One of the questions raised by the Unnamed Master and addressed to Bonaventure around 1254 was why friars were venturing to become masters, while Christ, whom the friars were supposed to imitate, clearly prohibits the use of this title.[80] During the secular-mendicant controversy of the 1250s, the same point was part of the ammunition used by William of Saint-Amour against the mendicants.[81]

It is quite difficult to explain this mendicant enthusiasm for magisterial chairs solely from the point of view of a desire to improve the education of friars who were to preach. Discussing why the Dominicans tried to attract a doctor of theology to their Order, Mulchahey points to the decrees of a church council in 1212. That year the Council of Paris under the apostolic legate Robert Courçon issued a decree that forbade the *claustrales* (the cloistered religious) to leave their cloisters in order to go to school. If they wished to study, they could do so inside the cloister.[82] Such a decree, with exactly the same wording, was repeated at the 1214 Council of Rouen, again summoned under Robert Courçon.[83] Mulchahey argues that since this decree prohibited the regular religious from leaving their convents to go to the schools, the Dominicans had to attract doctors of

---

79. Little, *Grey Friars in Oxford,* 50–52, gives a list of all expenses that were incurred on the inception of a friar.

80. "Nec tibi videtur tante humilitatis professoribus posse competere nomen 'magistri,' cum hoc nomen videatur Dominus in Evangelio suis discipulis inhibere, quorum non dicimus imitatores tanquam professores Evangelii Jhesu Christi" (Delorme, "Textes Franciscains," 213).

81. "Si ergo desiderent et procurent se magistros fieri, vel magistros vocari (quod est contra Evangelicam Christi doctrinam praedictam) videntur facere contra suam perfectionem et regulam beati Francisci." William of Saint-Amour, *Opera omnia* (Constantiae, 1632), 399, cited by Maranesi, "I commenti alla Regola francescana," 49.

82. "Prohibemus etiam, ne quis, postquam intrat claustrum causa religionis, exeat causa eundi ad scholas, sed in claustro, si voluerit, addiscat. Et qui modo sunt in scholis, intra duos menses ad claustrum redeant" (Mansi, *Sacrorum conciliorum,* 22:838). *CUP,* 1:78, no. 19, dates the decree to 1213.

83. The same decree was repeated in 1215. Mansi, *Sacrorum conciliorum,* 22:916.

theology to teach in their own convents.[84] However, certain objections might be raised. Both of these councils had met before the foundation of the Dominican Order in 1215, and the decree in question was directed at keeping monks in their monasteries not friars in their convents. Ever since the foundation of their Order, Dominicans, like Franciscans, had adopted the itinerant way of life, unlike the monks. We know that in Oxford, Franciscan friars, who did not have anybody to teach them in their convent, were going barefoot to the schools before Robert Grosseteste agreed to teach them in 1235, which is proof that the decree of the 1212 and 1214 Church councils mentioned above was either not enforced or did not apply to mendicants.[85] The latter is likely since there is evidence that the members of the mendicant orders were not considered *claustrales*. In fact, mendicants whom contemporary authors often designated "new orders" (*novi ordines*) were distinguished from *claustrales* in a sermon preached by Guiard de Laon around 1230–1231, where the Parisian master made a reference to the competition between the old and new orders: "But now the *claustrales* are so envious that they regard the new orders with envy and they judge the other orders so insignificant that they believe that no one can be saved except in their order. They are not ashamed to say, no indeed they say, that there are so many orders that in the end all will be ruined."[86]

It is much more likely that the Franciscan and Dominican interest in Paris and the insistence on having one of their own instated as a doctor of theology lay in the special status of the University of Paris, and the immense prestige associated with it. When mendicant orders emerged, Paris had already become the most noted place for theological disputation. Peter Biller has shown that, before the mendicants, even Cathars in the twelfth and early thirteenth centuries had proceeded to Paris and were actively producing theological treatises there.[87] Alexander Neckam wrote in his *De laudibus divinae sapientiae* that Paris was

---

84. Mulchahey, *"First the bow is bent,"* 33.

85. "Licet autem fratres summae simplicitati et conscientiae puritati summopere studerent in omnibus, in audienda tamen lege divina et scholasticis exercitiis ita fuerunt ferventes, ut scholas theologiae, quantumcumque distarent, adire quotidie nudis pedibus in frigoris asperitate et luti profundidate non pigritarentur" (Eccleston, 27).

86. "Sed jam ita invidi sunt claustrales quod etiam novis ordinibus invident et ita parvi pendunt alios ordines quod non credunt aliquem posse salvari nisi in suo ordine. Unde dicere non erubescunt, imo dicunt, quod tot sunt ordines quod totum in fine annihilabitur" (Davy, *Les sermons universitaires,* 236–37). Guiard de Laon was master in theology from 1226 to 1229, and the chancellor of Paris University from 1236/early 1237 until 1238. Palémon Glorieux, *Répertoire des maîtres en théologie de Paris au XIIIe siècle,* 1 (Paris: Librairie philosophique J. Vrin, 1933), no. 133, 299.

87. Peter Biller, "Northern Cathars and Higher Learning," in *The Medieval Church: Universities, Heresy and the Religious Life; Essays in Honour of Gordon Leff,* ed. Peter Biller and Barrie Dobson, 25–51 (Woodbridge: Boydell Press, 1999). For the later period, see Ian P. Wei, "The Masters of Theology at the University of Paris in the Late Thirteenth and Early Fourteenth Centuries: An Authority beyond the Schools," *Bulletin of the John Rylands University Library of Manchester* 75 (1993): 37–63.

"the fountain of doctrine."[88] Already in 1206, Paris was described by the author of *Historia Albigensis,* the Cistercian Peter of Vaux-de-Cernay, as "fons scientie et religionis christianae."[89] The admiration for the masters of Paris ran so high that popes did not hesitate to describe them in terms of heavenly elements. It is probably no coincidence that the first such enthusiastic papal endorsement came at the same time Franciscans took to the road to Paris. In 1219, Honorius III likened the masters to the stars of the firmament. Later, Alexander IV likened the University of Paris to "the Tree of God's Paradise and to the light of thunder in the House of God."[90] Theology was not the only faculty at the University of Paris, but it was the most prestigious one from the viewpoint of the university administration. In an official letter of the university dated February 4, 1254, theology, law, medicine, and arts, in descending order of importance, were likened to the four rivers of paradise.[91]

There can be little doubt that the emerging status of masters of theology in matters of religion, particularly the Parisian masters, fueled Franciscan ambition to acquire their own university theology master. It has even been argued that the most distinguishing mark of scholastic theology was the creation of a new type of authoritative voice: that of the "Masters." With the transformation of theology into a science, or an *ars fidei,* the schoolmasters of the twelfth century and university masters of the thirteenth century became "guildmasters."[92] During the twelfth century, the masters had increased their authority in matters of faith. In the words of Marie-Dominique Chenu, "They were giving private and public counsels (like the case of Thomas Becket and Henry II), taking positions in debates by way of official declarations (their intervention in 1241 concerning the beatific vision), and finally in the thirteenth century forming a common opinion on matters of faith ('via magistorum communis est... nobis autem videtur... ')."[93] A new social group was emerging at the university, a scholarly community that

88. Quoted in Astrik L. Gabriel, "English Masters and Students in Paris during the Twelfth Century," in *Garlandia: Studies in the History of the Mediaeval University,* ed. Astrik L. Gabriel (Frankfurt am Main, 1969), 19.

89. Quoted in Biller, "Northern Cathars," 50.

90. Astrik L. Gabriel, "The Ideal Master of the Mediaeval University," *Catholic Historical Review* 60 (1974): 7–8.

91. Jacques Verger, "Rapports hiérarchiques et amicitia au sein des popolations universitaires médiévales," in *Hiérarchies et services au moyen age: Séminaire sociétés, idéologies et croyances au moyen age,* ed. Claude Carozzi and Huguette Taviani-Carozzi, 289–307 (Aix-en-Provence: Publications de l'Université de Provence, 2001). Verger is careful to note, however, that although this hierarchy of faculties was adopted by the universities of northern Europe, in the southern universities civil law tended to be the faculty with the most prestige.

92. Marie-Dominique Chenu, *La teologia nel dodicesimo secolo,* trans. Paolo Vian (Milan: Jaca Book, 1986), 365–94. For the particular argument concerning the *Magistri* as guildmasters, see 371.

93. Ibid., 370–71.

motivated and encouraged its members on their chosen path.[94] By the time mendicants emerged then, Paris had become the center of theological debates, and an institution to which theological problems would be delegated. It had begun to shape the concept of the Roman Church, indeed becoming to a degree an intellectual branch of the Curia. No doubt the mendicant friars made very significant contributions and strengthened the central role of Paris in debating and defining Catholic doctrine, but the phenomenon itself precedes the mendicants.

The growth to prominence of the secular schools in the course of the twelfth century left monastic education and theology in the shade and meant that the monks largely lost their authority in theological debates. It was arguably neither desirable nor sensible for a religious order to be without links to the theological faculty of Paris, which by the 1230s was even teaching several future cardinals and popes. Such was the conviction of James John, the historian of the Premonstratensian Order. John observed that the Premonstratensians moved to Paris because they felt obliged to keep up with contemporary theological thought, if not to further it themselves. While in the twelfth century this could be done in the monasteries and priories, in the thirteenth century "a greater integration of effort, a more abundant assemblage of books were necessary merely to maintain and much more so to advance on what had already been achieved. It was precisely this function of integration that was filled by the University of Paris."[95]

In fact, in the twelfth century, long before the mendicants arrived on the scene, the priory of the canons of Saint Victor had become the first regular religious to be integrated into the intellectual life of Paris. Figures such as Hugh and Richard of Saint Victor were among the noted theologians. However, several historians have remarked on a subsequent distancing of the famous school of Saint Victor from the university's intellectual life in the early thirteenth century, even though the members of the Order remained active in providing pastoral care to the scholars at Paris.[96] Perhaps the administration of the mendicant orders acknowledged the fact that Paris represented the most acute and up-to-date theological thought at a considerably earlier date than those of the monastic orders and canons regular, whose only chance to establish ties with the University of Paris was to found study houses there, since the aforementioned decree of the Council of Paris prohibited monks from leaving their cloisters to go to the schools. The decree, when read as a response to an ongoing practice, suggests that there were monks who wished to follow the courses at Paris. As the mendicant orders were new, and they were mobile from the very beginning,

94. Arno Seifert, "Studium als soziales System," in *Schulen und Studium im sozialen Wandel des hohen und spaeten Mittelalters* (Sigmaringen, 1986), 609–11.

95. James John, *The College of Prémontré in Mediaeval Paris,* ed. Astrik L. Gabriel and J. N. Garvin (Notre Dame, IN: Mediaeval Institute, University of Notre Dame, 1953), 6–7.

96. Crossnoe, "Education and the Care of Souls," 137–72.

it was easier for them to make the move to the universities, whereas the monks had to change a centuries-old tradition, and understandably it took them some time to come to terms with these changes.

If we look at the intellectual heritage of the thirteenth-century Franciscans, we can see how much they indisputably contributed to and, in fact, determined the major subjects of the theological thought of their time. The friars' intellectual interest and enthusiasm in absorbing and advancing theological thought went far beyond the level of knowledge necessary for preaching or even beyond that necessary to teach the teachers of preachers. A great many friars who selected advanced studies at Paris were already preachers and, in some cases, lectors.[97] They certainly did not go to Paris to learn how to preach effectively. In fact, the pursuit of high-level theology was not just restricted to the Paris studium. Franciscans wrote theological treatises and disputed questions in all the studia generalia of the Order. The Dominicans did likewise. Late thirteenth-century Franciscan *quodlibeta* were produced by lectors at a variety of *studia*.[98] In fact, the studia generalia that were not part of universities, such as those of Florence or Montpellier, also became important theological centers.

Why the Franciscans Were Successful in Attracting Scholars

When seeking the motives behind the Franciscans' desire to have a strong presence in the great intellectual centers of Europe it is imperative to consider the general medieval attitudes toward these centers and toward scholastic education. The educational organization of the Franciscan Order owed its existence to the initiatives of the first ministers, who based this initiative on scholastic theology and university-style education. The success of this initiative owes a lot to the general attitude toward learning among the clergy. The Franciscan initiative would have been doomed to failure if the friars resented the idea of studying, or if the Order had failed to attract the scholars already in the university towns to the idea of becoming Franciscans. It is important that we recognize the formation of a circular evolution. Once the ministers with a mentality that favored educated clergy over the uneducated lay friars made a silent pledge to establish an educational system, the Order started to attract men who wished to live a religious life but also not abandon the intellectual life they pursued in the schools. The entry of such scholars into the Order, drawn to what they perceived to be

---

97. d'Avray, *Preaching of the Friars,* 180. See also chap 5.

98. See Sylvain Piron, "Franciscan *Quodlibeta* in Southern *Studia* and at Paris (1280–1300)," in *Theological Quodlibeta in the Middle Ages: The Thirteenth Century,* ed. Chris Schabel, 403–38 (Leiden: Brill, 2006). *Quodlibeta,* or quodlibetal questions, literally means "questions about anything" and was a form of academic exercise prevalent from 1230 to 1330 in some universities and mendicant *studia.* For further discussion, see the introduction in Schabel, *Theological Quodlibeta,* vol. 1.

the Franciscan way of life, allowed the initial commitment of the ministers to be put in practice and be expanded. The scholars started to serve as lectors and masters of theology, as in the case of the first Parisian master of the Order, Alexander of Hales. The question of why the friars embraced and clung to a strong intellectual presence in the medieval world converges with the question of why men of education and learning thought it a good idea to become Franciscans. Those reasons should be considered as distinct from what is to be found in the discourses of the learned Franciscans as they articulated their own Franciscan identity, as has been discussed in the previous chapter.

Evidence points to the phenomenal success of the mendicant Orders in attracting scholars. In a sermon delivered at sometime between 1238 and 1244, the chancellor of the University of Paris stated that many scholars had entered the Franciscan and Dominican Orders.[99] Thomas Eccleston discusses at length some of the masters that entered the Franciscan Order, "who have amplified the fame of the brothers."[100] Among the myriad of scholars that joined the Order in Paris and Oxford in the first half of the thirteenth century we can list Haymo of Faversham, Bartholomeus Anglicus, Alexander of Hales, Eudes Rigauld, Bonaventure of Bagnoregio, Richard Rufus of Cornwall, Roger Bacon, John Peckham, and Bartholomeo of Bologna, several of whom, with the exception of the first two, went on to become regent masters of theology in the universities of Paris and Oxford. Toward the end of 1223, the Dominican master general, Jordan of Saxony, wrote to Sister Diana, founder of Saint Agnes nunnery in Bologna, asking her to advise the sisters to pray for the students in Paris to enter the Dominican Order.[101] On April 14, 1224, Jordan again wrote to let the sister know that, within four months, around forty novices, the majority of them masters, had joined the order.[102] This was followed by yet another letter at the end of March of 1226, announcing that within the previous four weeks twenty-one new people had taken the habit, six of them masters of arts.[103] The particular mention in these letters of the number of masters among the recruits no doubt signifies the joy and pride that Jordan had in having these learned people wear the Dominican habit.

---

99. "Vere vacaverat et quieverat haec civitas [Parisius] a malo, tempore regis Ludovici et Joannis de Vineis.... Duo ordines Praedicatorum et Minorum eam mundaverant, maxime quoad scolares, quorum quamplurimi hos ordines intraverunt, alii honestatem amplexati sunt." Hauréau, *Notices et extraits,* 2:119, citing Paris, BnF Ms lat. 12423, 152.

100. "Post hos intraverunt quidam magistri, qui famam fratrum magnificaverunt" (Eccleston, 15).

101. "Saluta sorores, filias in Domino dilectas, et orare moneas pro scholaribus Parisiensibus, ut Dominus adaperiat corda ipsorum, ut ad conversionem efficiantur faciles, et hii, qui bone voluntatis propositum conceperunt, inveniantur in opera efficaces et ad vitam perseveranter proficiant sempiternam" (*CUP,* 1, no. 47, 104–5).

102. Ibid., 1, no. 49, 106.

103. Ibid., 1, no. 51, 108.

This new fashion for mendicancy among the scholars was not welcomed by the parents of students or by secular university masters. In a sermon preached to the students and masters of the University of Paris, an anonymous mendicant preacher warned the students against their parents and friends who tried to prevent them from joining the mendicant orders:

> One will come before his death to the friars, when he is fifty and will say: "When I was young I would have gladly entered your Order, but I had a master or a friend who stopped me." Will he be saved in this way, he who committed such an evil, who not only himself sinned but made others sin and kept them away from a good resolution?...Be careful, you, young men, and you, masters who have young men to guide! When they send them to Paris, parents say to the masters of their sons: "Don't let our boys go to the Franciscans and Dominicans. They are thieves, and will quickly snatch our sons." They do not say to them: "Don't let them go the brothel or the tavern."[104]

The reader will also recall the sermon cited in chapter 2 that complained of clerics who were impeding students from entering a religious order pursuing poverty.[105] Despite this evident opposition from secular clerks and parents, diverse testimonies establish the indisputable success of both Dominicans and Franciscans in enlisting scholars. Once it pointed itself in the direction of intellectual and educational prowess, the Franciscan Order became an attractive option for men who were both intellectually inclined and seeking life in a religious community. This success was in part due to the rise of scholasticism.

Enthusiasm for Scholastic Learning

"If I had five or six marks a year to keep me in the schools, I should never have been a monk or an abbot,"[106] said Abbot Samson of Bury of Saint Edmunds,

---

104. "Veniet aliquis in morte ad fratres, quando erit quinquagenarius, et dicet: 'Quando fui juvenis libenter intrassem religionem, sed habui magistrum vel socium qui impedivit me.' Et quomodo salvabitur ille qui tot mala commisit, qui non solum in propria persona peccavit, imo alios peccare fecit et a bono proposito retraxit?...Attendatis, vos pueri, et vos magistri qui habetis tales regere! Dicunt parentes magistris puerorum suorum, quando mittunt eos Parisius: 'Nos permittatis pueros nostros ire ad fratres Predicatores vel Minores, quia ipsi sunt latrones et cito raperent eos.' Non dicunt eis: 'Non permittatis eos ire ad lupanar nec ad tabernam.'" This is from an anonymous sermon preached possibly by a Franciscan or Dominican friar. Paris, BnF Ms lat. 14899, 116, cited by Haureau, *Notices et extraits*, 3:287.

105. "Simus igitur pauperes pro Christo quia et pro nobis factus est pauper. Sed sunt aliqui qui non solum nolunt fieri pauperes sed etiam prohibent aliis ne et ipsi pauperes sint, et ne intrent claustrum; et propter hoc qui vult entrare religionem caveat sibi ne consilium accipiat a talibus quia de mundo sunt et de mundo loquuntur: quia autem non debeat consilium intrandi religionem accipi a mundanis" (Davy, *Les sermons universitaires parisiens*, 385).

106. "Audivi abbatem dicentem, quod si fuisset in eo statu quo fuit antequam monacharetur, et habuisset v. vel sex marcas redditus cum quibus sustentari possit in scholis, nunquam fieret monachus nec

who ruled the famous abbey from 1182 to 1211, to a fellow monk. He was not alone. The twelfth century was a time of literary eloquence and a craze for schools. Young men from all over Europe were attracted to the urban and cathedral schools, and soon afterward to the universities, often far from home, in pursuit of the "new learning."

> A clerk is not much worth
> who has not been to Paris
> to study, and stayed there,
> and studied so much,
> and so much learned that he has become a master
> who there and elsewhere
> are renowned with the best.[107]

This is what Robert of Blois wrote about contemporary perceptions of the clergy educated in Paris. There is no doubt that the new schools, in particular the universities, had become a great and fashionable attraction for many young men in Europe.[108]

We can perhaps pinpoint two major sets of reasons behind this enthusiasm for receiving education in the schools. The first set would be intellectual and psychological reasons such as the appetite for the new learning, the desire for fame, the enthusiasm to be with other young like-minded men, or even the attraction of *la dolce vita* in the university towns. The second set would be socioeconomic reasons, such as the increasing number of jobs open to the learned, offering good salaries and social advancement.[109] Although these points have long been argued, they have not been taken sufficiently into account in explaining why the mendicant orders moved so quickly to university towns. The history of the rise of learning in the Franciscan Order partly belongs to the history of the rise of universities and scholasticism. The cultural and intellectual trends that

---

abbas." Jocelin de Brakelond, *Chronica Jocelini de Brakelonda de rebus gestis samsonis abbatis monasterii sancti edmundi,* ed. John Gage Rokewood (London: Sumptibus Societatis Camdenensis, 1840). See also Helen Waddell, *The Wandering Scholars of the Middle Ages,* 7th ed. (London, 1968), 115.

107. Translation by Gabriel, "English Masters and Students," 2. He cites Robert von Blois, *Sämtliche Werke,* ed. Jacob Ulrich (Berlin, 1895), 3:44. "Que cler ne sont pas de haut pris, / S'ençois n'ont a Paris esté / Pro aprendre, et sejorné, / Et quant il i ont tant estu, / Et tant apris k'il ont leù / Don sont il et la et aillors / Renommé avoc les moillors."

108. See Gabriel, "English Masters and Students," 1–37, on the attraction of English scholars to the University of Paris.

109. Rolf Köhn, "Schulbildung und Trivium im lateinischen Hochmittelalter und ihr möglicher praktischer Nutzen," in *Schulen und Studium im sozialen Wandel des hohen und späten Mittelalters,* ed. Johannes Fried, 203–84 (Sigmaringen: J. Thorbecke, 1986). Ferruolo, *Origins of the University,* 12–13, talks of the increasing demand of the French and English royal houses to employ learned men as administrators.

contributed to the rise of universities also partially explain the increasing importance attached to studying and teaching in the Franciscan Order.

Already in 1957, Herbert Grundmann argued that the emergence and rise of the universities was rooted not so much in the economic and social conditions or state and church initiative but instead in the love of learning that united like-minded men.[110] Alexander Murray also points to this "intellectual interest," though he adds that "not all adherents of the interest were university men, nor were all university men its adherents. But the interest throve round schools, and that is chiefly where it must be studied."[111] Indeed, the intellectual attractions and love of learning are prominently represented in the writings of some of the famous scholars of the twelfth century, men like Peter Abelard, John of Salisbury, Robert of Melun, or the Irish author of the *Life of St. Machulius,* who wrote that "because of the desire I had for learning, I gave all my night to letters."[112]

If we claim the pursuit of study drew men of intellectual inclinations to the mendicant orders, we need to also reply to the hypothetical question of why such men were not drawn to the orders of monks, which allowed studying. It is clear from the passages quoted above that monks and canons regular had difficulty in attracting and keeping scholars, and here perhaps the reasons had to do with a general preference for scholastic type of theology as opposed to monastic-style theological study. The latter was often not in a school setting, based instead on self-study that concentrated on patristics.[113] Given that monks and canons regular could and did preach, an argument that would suggest preaching as the major motive for the Franciscans' involvement in the schools would also have to explain why the study of patristics as pursued by the monks was insufficient or unhelpful for preaching. Referring to the Premonstratensians, Astrik Gabriel wrote that "theological speculation was never very deep among Premonstratensians. Conscientious lining up of *auctoritates* in masterly grouped scriptural quotations satisfied their need to give a scholarly framework to their pastoral activities."[114] Despite the apparent absence of a well-defined educational program, as could be found in the universities, the theological formation of monks and canons regular was good enough for them to be employed on preaching missions. During the better part of the twelfth and early thirteenth

---

110. Herbert Grundmann, *Vom Ursprung der Universität im Mittelalter,* Berichte über die Verhandlungen der Sächsischen Akademie der Wissenschaften zu Leipzig, Philologisch-Historische Klasse, 103, no. 2 (Berlin, 1957), 65; see also 39. Köhn, "Schulbildung und Trivium," 207.

111. Murray, *Reason and Society,* 237.

112. On John of Salisbury, see Gabriel, "English Masters and Students," 7–8; Robert of Melun, ibid., 10–11; the author of *Life of Saint Machulius,* ibid., 6.

113. Clifford Hugh Lawrence, "Stephen Lexington and Cistercian University Studies in the Thirteenth Century," *Journal of Ecclesiastical History* 11 (1960): 164–65.

114. Gabriel, "Role of Canons of Prémontré," 207.

century, when the urban schools and cathedral schools were already established and functioning in the developing scholastic manner, preaching against heresy was entrusted primarily to the Cistercian Order.[115] Under Innocent III, "the Order was made the papal workhorse, utilized in a wide range of missionary and reform efforts, including the preaching of the Fourth, Albigensian and Fifth Crusades."[116]

"The passage from monastic theology to scholastic theology was the beginning of a new era," wrote Marie-Dominique Chenu.[117] The new theology, or scholastic theology, as taught in the urban schools and universities and as it had emerged in the course of the twelfth century was distinct from the type of theology pursued by monks and almost a rival to it. One can hardly overestimate the contribution of the nature of scholasticism in generating this enthusiasm for its pursuit. Scholasticism can be viewed in a way as a literary theory, a way of reading a number of authoritative texts with a view to solving the apparent contradictions found in them. Such a task draws as much on imagination and creative intelligence as on logic and grammar. Not just the form, but also the content of scholastic theology was attractive. For scholastic theologians, the word of God had become an object of analysis beyond religious fervor and experience, and they attempted to analyze and explain what had so far been accepted as the mysteries of faith, such as the human nature of Christ and the essence of God.[118] These were topics into which an enthusiastic scholar could easily integrate much of ancient philosophy, for which there seems to have been a particular love. It is precisely this extended role of the human intellect that gave scholastic theology its greatest charm, made it a mischievously playful discipline, and prompted the fury of conservative figures such as Bernard of Clairvaux.

Scholastic investigation pushed scholars more toward Aristotle, this time to what are called the books of natural philosophy (*libri naturales*) such as *Physics* (*Physica*) and *On the Soul (De anima)*. Perhaps one of the biggest attractions of scholastic theology was precisely this study of the Aristotelian corpus, at times alongside commentaries by Muslim philosophers. The gradual extension of the arts and their integration, as philosophy, into scholastic theology generated a good deal of intellectual enthusiasm among scholars. This is evident in the

---

115. Sebastian C. J. Naslund, "Papal-Cistercian Relations: 1198–1241 with Particular Emphasis on France" (PhD diss., University of Illinois at Urbana-Champaign, 1976), 30–93.

116. Jessalynn Bird, "The Religious's Role in a Post-Fourth-Lateran World: Jacques de Vitry's *Sermones ad status* and *Historia occidentalis*," in *Medieval Monastic Preaching*, ed. Carolyn Muessig (Leiden: Brill, 1998), 216. See also Rouse and Rouse, *Preachers, Florilegia and Sermons*, 55.

117. Chenu, *La teologia nel dodicesimo secolo*, 387.

118. Ibid., 389–92. For discussions comparing the two theologies, see Ermenegildo Bertola, "Teologia monastica e teologia scolastica," *Lateranum* 34 (1968): 237–45; Leclercq, *Cultura umanistica*, 247–305.

following decree of the Council of Paris of 1213 that sought to prevent the clergy responsible for the care of souls from engaging in what had come to be called the "secular sciences":

> We decree that no one who has the care of a parish is allowed to study the secular sciences, from which no benefit can come to the well-being of his parishioners. Indeed, if anyone obtains a license from his superior to go to schools, he should learn nothing except the true book, which is the sacred scripture, for the education of his parishioners. However, if he brings back from all his schools the rubbish of the secular sciences, and no flowers from the meadows of heavenly philosophy, according to the Gospel, he will be repelled as someone who has made a fool of himself and will be despised by everyone.[119]

It is, then, no surprise that when the mendicant orders introduced the study of the arts in their curriculum, many scholars who were keen on studying the arts but could not do so with their benefices or lacking private funds would have a particular interest in taking the mendicant habit. When the news broke out that the Dominican province of Provence was developing an Arts program, there was a surge in the number of people trying to enter the Order in this province over the next few years, so much so that the provincial chapter asked the convents to bluntly tell postulants that admission to the Order was no guarantee that they would be put to the Arts program.[120]

Career Choices

To Grundmann's psychological argument of *amor sciendi* as a motive for the pursuit of study we can also add other motives such as the ambition to rise, the appetite for glory, and the desire for money and praise.[121] In fact, in addition to the love of learning, an equally compelling factor in seeking higher education was the close link between learning and church offices. Alexander Murray wrote, "That love of office was a motive for study is revealed by sources which begin, not in the twelfth-century renaissance, but in the Carolingian," but "the golden age for careerism via the schools nevertheless began with the twelfth

---

119. "Statuimus, ut nulli habenti curam parochialem liceat seculares scientias addiscere, ex quibus nullatenus possit subditorum suorum saluti prodesse. Immo si a prelato suo licentiam adeundi scolas obtinuerit, nihil nisi veram litteram aut sacram paginam ad informationem parochianorum suorum addiscat; si enim de scholis suis omnibus quisquilias secularis scientie attulerit, et nullos flores de pratis celestis philosophie, secundum evangelium tanquam infatuatus rejiciatur et ab omnibus conculcetur" (*CUP*, 1, no. 9, 77).

120. Mulchahey, *"First the bow is bent,"* 220.

121. Seifert, "Studium als soziales System," 605.

century."[122] Murray also cites Bernard of Clairvaux, who accused clergy of avarice and ambition, and John of Salisbury, who discussed the two vices of *elatio* and *cupiditas,* which accompanied *curiositas.* While the aristocracy could rather easily obtain offices, education had become the magic wand that removed the barriers between higher offices and men of low birth. Contemporary observers like Walter Map in the late twelfth century mentioned that it was not the upper class but people of low birth who were more attracted to the schools, since they saw in education a chance to get rich.[123] Clerical office was particularly effective as a social ladder. A contemporary French knight, Philippe de Novare, who counseled youth to consider a clerical career since "through clergie it has often happened, and can happen again, that the son of a poor man becomes a great prelate; and enjoys riches and honours, and is father and lord over the man formerly lord over him and his family; and can govern and rule everyone in the region; nay he may become pope, and be father and lord of all Christendom."[124] The university was a special type of medieval institution where all literate social classes freely mingled. The formation of *nationes* according to the geographical provenance of students, instead of by the social classes of people, was a significant proof of this.[125] Education bridged the gap between the lowborn and high offices. It was perceived as such by contemporaries. During the 1251 peasant revolt in Orléans, known as the rebellion of the Pastoureaux, the peasant leader, in his preaching, attacked the Dominicans and Franciscans as hypocrites.[126] Murray interpreted this attack to be "a general hostility to clerks in the special sense of those who had benefited by education."[127] As the early Franciscan Order largely consisted of men from the middle and low classes, it is easy to understand that in putting themselves on the path of learning, they created for themselves a chance to climb the ecclesiastical, and therefore social and economic, ladder. In fact, Grundmann had already pointed out that the only phenomenon in Europe comparable to the universities was constituted by the new religious orders of Dominicans and Franciscans, where friars from all social strata came together under one order, and where one with a humble

---

122. Murray, *Reason and Society,* 220.

123. Ibid.

124. Murray, *Reason and Society,* 221, quotes from Philippe de Novare, *Les quatre ages de l'homme,* ed. M. Freville (Paris, 1988), 10–11. Murray suggests that what Philip had in mind was the career of Urban IV, who, coming from humble origins, climbed the steps of the ecclesiastical ladder after studying in Laon and was elected pope in 1261. Murray, *Reason and Society,* 226–27.

125. Grundmann, *Vom Ursprung,* 17.

126. "Et in suis praedicationibus a fidei Christianae articulis et a regulis manifestae veritatis duces et magistri eorum, qui quamvis laici praedicare praesumpserunt, enormiter exorbitarunt.... Et cum eorum summus dux praedicaret, stipatus undique armatis, condempnavit reprehendendo omnes ordines praeter eorum conventicula; maxime autem Praedicatorum et Minorum, vocans girivagos et hypocritas." Matthew Paris, *Chronica majora,* ed. H. R. Luard (London, 1880), 5:249.

127. Murray, *Reason and Society,* 244.

social background had the chance of taking the highest office.[128] It is true that a Franciscan coming from a low social background could become a minister general, but only if he had studied theology in Paris.

While trying to explain the anger of secular masters in Paris against the mendicants, Decima Douie wrote the following:

> Doctors of theology, who had always prided themselves on being the teachers of the future bishops of the Church, now saw many of their ablest pupils renounce all future ecclesiastical preferment to enter orders, whose way of life seemed to the holders of rich canonries and benefices precarious and hardly respectable. A modern analogy would be for a brilliant scholar with first class honors and every prospect of a successful academic career to be hippy.[129]

In theory, perhaps, Douie was right, but not so much in practice. The evidence we have from the thirteenth century on the careers of Franciscans tells a strikingly different story. There was no question of "renouncing future ecclesiastical preferment"; just the contrary, "Franciscanism became a career opportunity," as David Burr correctly observed.[130] From the 1230s onward, popes employed Franciscans in a variety of prestigious offices, as chaplains, penitentiaries, legates, inquisitors, and above all, as bishops and archbishops.[131] Thomson's extensive research lists more than forty Franciscan bishops, with a dozen marginal possibilities before 1261.[132] Under Innocent IV, twenty-four Franciscans were promoted as bishops, and at the time of Salimbene there were a hundred Franciscan bishops and 177 Dominican bishops.[133] If someone had an ambition to rise in the Church, they could hardly do better than to join the mendicant orders. It would not be wrong to expect that at least some Franciscans must have been quite eager to study so that they could fill high offices within the Order and in the wider organization of the Church. In fact, this ambition for office makes up an important part of Ubertino da Casale's complaints concerning corruption in the Order, as will be discussed in depth in the next chapter. To all these motives that might have attracted the scholars to the Franciscan Order, we can also add an aversion to the sinfulness of the city and the desire to pursue an intellectual life in a virtuous environment. From student letters and sermons preached in

---

128. Grundmann, *Vom Ursprung,* 20.

129. Douie, "St. Bonaventura's Part," 2:586.

130. Burr, *Olivi and Franciscan Poverty,* 5.

131. Thomson, *Friars in the Cathedral,* 16.

132. Ibid., 20.

133. Antonio Rigon, "Vescovi frati o frati vescovi?" in *Dal pulpito alla cattedra: I vescovi degli Ordini Mendicanti nel '200 e nel Primo '300; Atti del XXVII convegno internazionale Assisi, 14–16 Ottobre 1999* (Spoleto: Centro italiano di studi sull'alto medioevo, 2000), 7.

the universities, we learn that the temptations of student life in the university towns, the taverns, and the promise of mischief with like-minded young men motivated many students to linger in the schools.[134] The pious among them might have wished to escape the life of the town while not abandoning study, and entering a religious order like the Franciscans might have seemed to be the best solution.

A Life of Intellectual Pursuits

Another point of attraction of the mendicant orders to those who opted for the life of the mind was the promise of permanence of the intellectual pursuit, which was very rare in the Middle Ages, as the overwhelming majority of the clergy studied only for a limited time. For some the craze for universities and learning was so great that they did not want to part from it again. Haskins quotes the case of a student who kept putting off entering monastic life since first he wanted to earn his degrees in Paris, Montpellier, and Bologna![135] In this respect, the mendicants were unrivaled. They offered candidates the unique chance of spending a lifetime in study.[136] For men like Roger Bacon or Duns Scotus who wished to dedicate their whole life to the pursuit of the divine truth, there could be hardly any profession better than the office of lector in one of the mendicant orders. The guarantee that the students and masters who joined the Franciscan Order would be able to continue their chosen path was firmly expressed in the letter of Bonaventure to an unknown master sometime around 1254. "For, following the Apostle, St. Francis wished everyone to remain in the condition in which he received his call [1 Cor. 7:24], so that no lay brother should ascend to the clerical state; on the other hand, he did not want clerics to become lay brothers by rejecting study."[137]

There was no equivalent of the mendicant office of "lector" for many of the clerics that had come to Paris to study theology with the help of benefices. A secular theology student sooner or later had to go back to the place of his benefice, engage in pastoral care that was seemingly so unpopular among the learned,

---

134. See, for example, Charles H. Haskins, "The University of Paris in the Sermons of the Thirteenth Century," *American Historical Review* 10 (1904): 1–27.

135. "Clericus quidam Parisius scholaris cum quodam socio suo in una domo et camera manens inspiratus a Deo deliberavit intrare religionem et socium suum ad hoc inducere. Quod renuens socius ait se velle adhuc esse Parisius per triennium et fieri magister, iterum morari apud Montem Pessulanum et fieri magister in medicina, iterum morari Bononie per septennium et fieri dominus legum." MS Tours 468, 78; MS Baluze 77, 175, quoted by Haskins, "University of Paris," 12.

136. Merlo also argued that the mendicant orders offered the masters and students a way out of the sterility of the traditional monastic orders. Merlo, *Nel nome di san Francesco,* 113.

137. Bonaventure of Bagnoreggio, "A Letter in Response to an Unknown Master," in *St. Bonaventure's Writings,* 51.

or undertake various administrative tasks that would hardly leave time for intellectual matters. He might make a successful career in the secular Church, but it was not likely to be focused on intellectual pursuits. However, once a friar had been given the office of lector, he would be teaching in various convents almost until the end of his life, unless he was called on by his superiors or the pope to perform other offices such as being custodian, provincial minister, or even minister general, or to take part in negotiations with the Eastern Church or in missionary activities. Even if they were not elected to go to Paris, probably all clerical entrants to the Franciscan Order received a basic education in theology from the 1240s on, quite a few being sent to provincial schools, some of which were in university cities like Toulouse, Bologna, or Oxford. If a friar with intellectual ambitions were to fail to become a lector, there was always the luxurious compensation of having books at his disposal through the convent libraries that were rapidly expanding in the course of the thirteenth century.

In fact, the opportunity for study that the mendicant orders offered was attractive not just to secular clerks but also to the students of other religious orders. Already in 1233, the Cistercians decreed that any of their monks transferring to the Dominicans or Franciscans were to be considered apostates.[138] In 1237, the Cistercian General Chapter accepted the proposal of Abbot Evrard of Clairvaux to keep monks in the Paris house for the purpose of academic education. The Cistercian monks, lacking a lector of their own, started studying under the mendicant masters. When, however, several of them ended up taking the mendicant habit, the Cistercian General Chapter of 1242 protested to the Dominican and Franciscan superiors against the admission of Cistercian students.[139] An undated letter written by a thirteenth-century Franciscan friar to two Cistercian novices in Milan demonstrates the problem clearly. The novices were intending to leave their Order and join the Franciscans to pursue studies. The friar tried to persuade them to stay in the Order into which they had been called, and not to follow the temptation that in another Order they might excel better in knowledge.[140] In 1233, two Augustinian canons of Dunstable Priory in Bedfordshire fled their priory through a broken window, scaled the walls, and went to Oxford to join the Franciscans, taking books with them.[141] Perhaps the canons were drawn to the fame of Grosseteste, who was teaching at that time to

---

138. F. Donald Logan, *Runaway Religious in Medieval England c. 1240–1540* (Cambridge: Cambridge University Press, 1996), 44.

139. Lekai, *White Monks,* 60.

140. "Unusquis vestrum in qua vocatione, id est in quo Ordine vel monasterio seu domo, vocatus est, in ea permaneat. Nec vos moveat temptatio aliqua suggerens vobis quod in alio Ordine melius in scientia profecissetis" (Delorme, "Textes Franciscains," 207).

141. Logan, *Runaway Religious,* 47.

the Oxford Franciscans. They must have thought that the books they brought would serve as an incentive for the Franciscans to accept them.

Furthermore, by entering a mendicant Order, a scholar was entering a community where education and study were highly valued, and this appreciation was demonstrated quite clearly by the granting of the high offices in the Order, along with several privileges, to the educated. Lectors, for example, would have a *socius,* a younger friar who would help with administrative and practical matters, similar to a private secretary.[142] The *socii* would also undertake the copying of books. In a letter addressed to the provincial minister, Adam Marsh asks for a replacement for his *socius,* Adam of Hereford, since he thinks that Adam should continue his studies instead.[143] In another letter, he tries to attract the attention of the provincial minister to the case of the lector Walter de Maddele, who, unlike the other lectors, did not have books and the assistance of a *socius* to help him.[144]

While the Narbonne constitutions prohibited meat to all friars, Bonaventure declared that he did not wish to extend this prohibition to the lectors actively teaching on the grounds that they were performing very hard, continuous, and useful work.[145] In some provinces, the lectors seem to have been exempt from the Divine Office, while elsewhere they were at least excused from the Compline.[146] For the lectors teaching in the studia generalia, the privileges were even greater, since they also enjoyed the luxury of having a room of their own.[147] The masters of the Order continued to enjoy privileges even after their death.

---

142. Little, *Grey Friars in Oxford,* 33–34.

143. "Carissimum fratrem A. de Hereford, quem mihi pia vestrae circumspectionis sedulitas assignavit pro socio, inveni benignum. . . . Quamobrem indubitanter credi debet quod. . . si eidem de continuitate studii provideatur, laudabiliter proficiet ad praedicationem Verbi Dei" (Adam Marsh, *Epistolae,* no. 174, 314–16).

144. "Et quid est quod caeteris fratribus officio legendi deputatis, praesertim quibus successit, in magnis provisum est voluminibus, et in sociorum subventuum adjutoriis, iste solus videtur non curari" (ibid., no. 197, 355).

145. Delorme, "Explanationes constitutionum generalium Narbonensium," *AFH* 18 (1925): 519, no. 27. The Narbonne edict itself reads as follows: "Querimus hic, utrum hec prohibitio ad lectores et fratres artifices in edificiorum structura laborantes se extendat et pro quanto debilitas ad esum carnium sufficiat, utrum scilicet debilitas capitis, etas tenella, etas decrepita?—Respondeo, quod ad lectores nolo, quod se extendat, dum sunt in actu legendi, et hoc propter laborem eorum magnum, utilem et continuum, propter quem ipsi excepti fuerunt in capitulo generali" (Narbonne-Assisi-Paris, 55, no. 4).

146. "Omnes fratres, tam clerici quam laici et forenses, post recreationem acceptam secundum exigentiam itineris et laboris, veniant ad completorium" (Narbonne-Assisi-Paris, 58, no. 18). "Item, utrum lectores, qui mane lecturi sunt, debeant singulis diebus licentiam remanendi petere, cum causam habeant legittimam remanendi?–Respondeo, quod, cum mane debeant legere, non obligantur ad completorium conventus; debent tamen servare silentium." Delorme, "Explanationes constitutionum," 521, no. 42. Geroldus Fussenegger, ed., "Statuta provinciae Alemanie superioris annis 1303, 1309 et 1341 condita," *AFH* 53 (1960): 259.

147. "Nullus frater habeat cameram clausam [vel a dormitorio sequestratam, Ministris exceptis et lectoribus in generalibus Studiis constitutis]" (Narbonne-Assisi-Paris, 57, no.16).

The *definitiones* of the 1260 Narbonne constitutions order that one Divine Office was to be celebrated for William of Meliton, the regent master in Paris between 1248–1253;[148] Adam Marsh, the regent master in Oxford from 1247 to 1252;[149] Friar Bertramo; as well as other friars who were named in the chapter.[150]

While the Order was giving all these privileges to the lectors, the statutes say nothing about any kind of privilege given to those holding the office of preacher. In these lectors' privileges then, we can clearly detect a mentality that valued them above the rest of the friars.

Financial Aspects

For a scholar keen on pursuing his intellectual interests, one of the most significant advantages of joining a mendicant Order was that he would receive an advanced education free of charge. "By far the largest element in the correspondence of mediaeval students consists of requests for money," wrote Haskins in his study of medieval student letters.[151] Indeed, the greatest barrier that stood between a young man and a university education was the high cost. A student who wished to attend a secular studium generale had to cover both the cost of studying and the cost of living. Although these costs varied from one university to another, the cost of studying included the fixed payments of the enrollment fee in the university, the registration fee for the faculty, and ongoing payments such as course fees paid to masters and doctors as well as costs related to books and stationery.[152] It should be noted that the cost of studying was directly proportional to the level of studies, and getting a degree was particularly expensive since examinations, graduation, and related ceremonies meant exorbitant costs, and such a road was open to only a very few.[153] The costs of books could amount to quite a significant sum, even when one did not own the books. The costs of renting the books or, whenever available, *peciae*—copying fees paid to the scribes and pledges left for books—could amount to large sums. The fees paid to university masters were also considerable, and fees paid to the theology masters

---

148. Palémon Glorieux, "D'Alexandre de Hales a Pierre Auriol: La suite des maîtres franciscains de Paris," *AFH* 26 (1933): 268.

149. Little, *Grey Friars in Oxford,* 136, 139.

150. "Pro fratre Wilhelmo de Melitona, pro fratre Berchtramo, pro fratre Adam de Marisco, adiunctis eis aliis fratribus in capitulo nominatis, fiat semel officium sicut pro uno fratre." Ferdinand Delorme, "Definitiones capituli generalis OFM Narbonensis 1260," *AFH* 3 (1910): 504.

151. Charles H. Haskins, "The Life of Mediaeval Students as Illustrated by Their Letters," in *Studies in Medieval Culture* (Oxford: Clarendon Press, 1929), 7.

152. Rainer Christoph Schwinges, "Student Education, Student Life," in *History of the University in Europe,* vol. 1, *Universities in the Middle Ages,* ed. Hilde de Ridder-Symoens (Oxford: Clarendon Press, 1992), 235–36.

153. Ibid., 235.

were no exception. In theory, beneficed theology masters were not supposed to demand fees from the students, since sacred learning was thought to be a gift of God to be given to others freely. In practice, however, they often did accept or demand fees to compensate for their insufficient income.[154]

The available means of finance for a university student who did not belong to a religious order consisted of private financing through family and relatives, ecclesiastical benefices, college grants, flying grants (such as a scholarship foundation set up by a wealthy individual), royal patronage, or institutional patronage such as that of a town commune or charitable institution.[155] Apart from private financing, none of these grants provided for all the expenses of a university student. Instead, they were generally intended to cover only the cost of living.[156] Besides, for the first half of the thirteenth century, there were no colleges (the first college, the Sorbonne in Paris, was founded in 1257). Flying grants and other sources of patronage were rather scarce. Ecclesiastical benefices that allowed nonresidence, thus permitting the secular clergy to reside outside of their prebends while continuing to receive the revenues for the purpose of attending a school of theology, were introduced in 1219 by Honorius III. Yet although they were technically available to all students who were clerks, in reality the process of petition took a lot of time and could be speeded up only through the intervention of an institution or an individual of high position. Theoretically, the official duration of this nonresident prebend was five years, but in practice the financial subsidy was paid only for a year or two; the intention was usually to make the clerk educated in the basics of theology, not to train him to engage in high-level studies.[157] Often the aspiring clerks had difficulties securing the permission of their bishops for nonresidence, and papal interference was required to let the candidate benefit from Honorius's bull.[158] It was not until 1298, with the papal bull *Cum ex eo* of Boniface VIII, that the need for the parochial clergy to study was fully realized and measures taken to make it more practical.[159] Even at a later period, in the fourteenth century, when arguably

154. This point has been argued convincingly by Gaines Post in his "Masters's Salaries and Student-Fees in the Medieval Universities," *Speculum* 7 (1932): 181–98. See also G. Post, K. Giocarinis, and R. Kay, "The Medieval Heritage of a Humanistic Ideal: 'Scientia donum dei est, unde vendi non potest,'" *Traditio* 11 (1955): 195–210.

155. Paul Trio, "Financing of University Students in the Middle Ages: A New Orientation," *History of Universities* 4 (1984): 1–24.

156. Ibid., 2, 4, 10. See also Pearl Kibre, *Scholarly Privileges in the Middle Ages: The Rights, Privileges, and Immunities of Scholars and Universities at Bologna, Padua, Paris, and Oxford* (London: Mediaeval Academy of America, 1961), 227, for the financial difficulties of clerks with benefices.

157. Kibre, *Scholarly Privileges*, 228–29.

158. Frank Pegues, "Ecclesiastical Provisions for the Support of Students in the Thirteenth Century," *Church History* 26 (1957): 309.

159. On this, see Leonard E. Boyle, "The Constitution 'Cum ex eo' of Boniface VIII: Education of Parochial Clergy," *Mediaeval Studies* (1962): 263–302.

there were more benefactors, obtaining patronage was still quite a complex affair and very difficult for those who were not well connected.[160] Those who were unskilled in flattery would find it particularly difficult to get such a benefice, since many times the masters who had some influence with certain bishops would try to secure benefices for their favorite students.[161]

Getting a degree in theology was quite out of question for the vast majority of enthusiasts, as it required at least eight years of study, which could be financed only through private means or the grace of a wealthy benefactor. Even if fortunate enough to obtain a prebend that allowed nonresidence, the five-year limit was insufficient for such a prolonged course of study. Even while it lasted, a single benefice seldom covered the cost of living and education, and pluralism—that is, holding multiple benefices—seems to have been the only viable solution for some masters, such as Peter the Chanter. In 1213, the papal legate Robert Çourcon prohibited the holding of multiple benefices. The prohibition was relaxed by the Fourth Lateran Council with exceptions allowed in certain situations.[162] In any case, after 1213 it must have become even more difficult for a secular clerk without independent funds to sustain himself in Paris more than a few years, to get a degree in theology, and hence to become a university master. The situation was grim also for those who had nonecclesiastical funds such as family money, since theology education was not a favorite with the families who often sent their sons off to university in the hope that they might learn something of practical value with a prospect of temporal gain. After all, the majority of the students financed by their families in medieval universities were of intermediate social status, that is, from artisan or merchant families.[163] A letter written around 1250 by a student from Orléans demanding money from his father for a Bible illustrates this point. The father praises the good intentions of his son but declines the request on the ground that the theological course required a great sum, as he was told, and the son should turn to more practical sciences.[164]

A Franciscan scholar did not have to worry about any such financial matters. He did not have to pay a fee to his master, who was, like himself, a Franciscan. Moreover, he had the luxury of having frequent access to his master outside of lecture hours. His books were provided by the Order; he had access to an adequate library; he had free lodgings. The direst problems of a secular student

160. Guy Fitch Lytle, "Patronage Patterns and Oxford Colleges c. 1300–c. 1530," in *The University in Society,* ed. Lawrence Stone, 1:111–49 (Princeton, NJ: Princeton University Press, 1975).

161. Haskins, "University of Paris," 10.

162. Ferruolo, *Origins,* 304.

163. Cobban, *Medieval English Universities,* 198.

164. Haskins, "Life of Mediaeval Students," 25.

were thus solved.[165] If he proved himself apt and hardworking enough to be designated for the office of lector, he had the chance of spending four years in Paris, perhaps returning later on to get his degree and join the ruling class of Parisian masters.

All this might still be little incentive for a layperson with intellectual interests to become a mendicant, just so that he could study, if he was not already predisposed to the religious life. But we are here comparing the advantages of becoming a mendicant for men of intellectual ambitions, as opposed to becoming a monk, or becoming or remaining a secular clerk. All these opportunities would be attractive to a young scholar at the beginning of his career, as well as to a mature scholar who wished to advance his intellectual career and continue his work. Taking into consideration the difficulties involved in financing a university education, or even just a modicum of education in theology or arts, it would not be unrealistic to suggest that many clerics and scholars joined the mendicant orders for a chance to further their education. For the secular clerical student who could not secure an ecclesiastical benefice, and who did not have a wealthy benefactor, the mendicant orders were perhaps the only chance to get an education in the arts or theology. In fact, it has been suggested that the purpose of founding the College of Sorbonne was to provide for secular clergy working conditions equivalent to those already possessed by the Dominicans at Saint Jacques and the Franciscans in Cordeliers, so that the clergy who wished to study did not have to take the habit.[166]

Against such a thesis, it can be argued that only a few students were sent to Paris or other studia generalia to study and take the office of lector. However, for the students who could procure some money from outside—from a living wealthy relative, for example—the chance of obtaining a good education with the Franciscan Order was not at all a small possibility. This was as a result of the particular system developed in the Order with regard to financing students. While the education of a highly restricted number of students of each province, called *studentes de debito,* was financed by the general treasury of the Order, the provinces were allowed to send extra students, *studentes de gratia,* if they were able to pay for their living expenses in the convents they were sent to. Such a system opened the way to Paris and other studia generalia for the students who could procure the amount needed to be sent by the province to a foreign studium. The amount paid would still be significantly lower than the expenses of a secular student, since friars did not have to pay masters fees and lodging costs.[167]

---

165. Ibid., 21–22.

166. Traver, "Rewriting History?" 15.

167. For details concerning the students who went to the studia with the help of secular relatives, see chap. 5.

The scholarly class of thirteenth-century Europe—the *clerici scholastici*, to use Peter the Chanter's description—were men governed by a number of passions, career expectations, and aspirations, some of which, if not all, have been discussed above as fully as possible. When Franciscans moved to the university towns in the 1220s, they tapped into this distinct class of society and attracted many of them into their Order. This interest in recruiting from among scholars seems to have had much to do with a concern for the prestige of the Order and with a need to have men to fulfill the Order's various offices, including but not limited to preaching. These men, who took the Franciscan habit during their studies, brought into the Order their own vision of the world and blended it with the version of Franciscanism they had received. The result was the formation of a new class of friars. Serving as lectors in the Order, these *fratres scholastici* stood between two distinct categories described by Peter Chanter: the *clerici scholastici* and the *clerici ecclesiastici*. If the schools of Paris in the thirteenth century increasingly became an arena of intellectual output that was related to pastoral care, as argued admirably in the works of David d'Avray and Nicole Bériou,[168] this owed a lot to the friars' presence, their gradual fusion of study with the pastoral needs of the clergy, their influence on and competition with the secular clergy, and their mobilization by the papacy. Being a part of what was an evangelization movement made the friars interested in applying their scholarly talents and energy in the much neglected field of pastoral care, but the most intellectually inclined of them remained interested for the most part in the production of theological and philosophical works rather than works concerned with pastoral care.

Preaching and other activities related to pastoral care were not the main occupation of these scholastic friars. They usually left the task of preaching to their fellow friars who were not as focused on learning. Instead, they chose to teach those who were to fulfill the office of preacher. These *fratres scholastici*—the lectors of the Franciscans—were a minority in relation to the rest of the Order. The majority was still made up of lay friars and clerical friars who did not study beyond the requirements of being a *socius*, or the office of preacher or confessor. However, the small numbers of scholastic friars should not mislead us into thinking that their influence in defining medieval Franciscanism was not significant. A particularly important development was the gradual absorption of all political power in the Order by the lectors. The lectors made up almost the entire administrative body of the Order, as provincial and general ministers were almost exclusively lectors during the second part of the thirteenth century, and as such they were responsible for the entire legislative activity of the Order.

---

168. Cited by Crossnoe, "Education and the Care of Souls," 153–54.

This legislation, embodied in the general and provincial constitutions of the Order, was responsible for the perpetuation of a mentality that exalted lectors above the rest of the friars, including preachers, by giving them considerable privileges. It is in the next chapter that we will see how the powers and privileges of this lector class of friars came to be abused, and created tension within the Order.

🦢 CHAPTER 4

Paradise Lost

When scholars from Paris joined the Franciscan Order and, to the best of their conviction, integrated the study of theology into the Franciscan mission, they made a genuine effort to emphasize at every stage the importance and necessity of humility and charity. This was a significant part of the discourse of the Franciscan scholars who reflected on the Order's association with learning. This emphasis on humility was there precisely to act as a counterweight to the general association of learning in the medieval world with prestige, respectability, and pride. However, the culture of the Order, which was affected by social norms, allowed and encouraged practices such as giving privileges to lectors and showing obvious preference for lectors when making appointments to ministerial positions. Even when these things were done with good intentions, the social and political culture in the Order that resulted from the pursuit of learning and the preference for learned ministers was not conducive to the essential Franciscan virtues of humility, *minoritas,* and simplicity. Both some friars and outsiders saw these problems, and either tried to propose solutions or denounced them outright.

The first instance of an openly and publicly articulated criticism of the Franciscans' chosen way of life was the publication by the Parisian secular master William of Saint-Amour of *De periculis novissimorum temporum* in 1255. William attacked the theoretical basis of some Franciscan premises such as absolute poverty, begging, and the absence of manual labor. By the late thirteenth century, however, this was followed by other types of criticism heard from different

189

quarters, even from Franciscans themselves. These later criticisms were not con-cerned with the evangelical legitimacy of the tenets of Franciscanism, but rather with the failure of the friars to observe these tenets. Also, while earlier external testimonies were generally in praise of the Franciscans, later ones adopted a more skeptical tone toward the Friars Minor, as toward those who preach high ideals but do not live up to them. The famous French poet Rutebeuf, at the begin-ning of his career around 1248, wrote in favor of the Franciscans, but displayed a change of heart in his later work, *Chanson des ordres,* suggesting that the Francis-cans had turned out to be like the Dominicans, whom he criticized harshly.[1] In England, Matthew Paris's *Chronica majora* reflects the changing reputation of the friars. Although initially Matthew Paris was quite impressed by the friars' ideals, from the 1240s onward he criticized friars, after witnessing or hearing of many occasions when friars had violated their vows of humility and poverty.[2] This criticism of friars, particularly with regard to their perceived hypocrisy—their failure to put into practice the high ideals they preached—is also well known from Chaucer's *Canterbury Tales* in the fourteenth century.

There was no shortage of friars who agreed with these critics. A perceived fall from the high standards that the Rule set out disturbed many friars in the Order. In the early 1250s, in a letter he sent to his provincial minister, we find the famous English Franciscan theology master Adam Marsh lamenting bitterly the grandiosity of friars' buildings and the worldliness of the novices.[3] Roger Bacon complained of the fall of the new religious orders from their initial dignity, and he did not exclude his own.[4] In 1257, in the first circular letter he wrote after his election as minister general, Bonaventure made a list of all the scandalous practices in the Order and pleaded for them to stop:

> So get the lazy brothers to work; restrain the ones who are wandering. Call a halt to the importunate begging. Put down the ones who want to put up big houses. Send off to a hermitage those looking for suspicious familiarities. Bestow the offices of preaching and hearing confessions with great care. See to it that the old constitutions on wills and burials are observed more strictly. Do not allow anyone to change the site of a friary before the general chapter. In this last matter, taking the advice of discrete

---

1. See J. Batany, "L'image des Franciscains dans les 'revues d'états' du XIIIe au XIVe siècle," in *Mouvements franciscains et société française XIIe–XXe siècles: Études présentées à la table ronde du CNRS 23 Octobre 1982,* ed. A. Vauchez (Paris: Beauchesne Religions, 1984), 64, which presents the image of Franciscans in the French-speaking part of Europe.

2. Thomson, "Image of the Mendicants," 3–34, where Thomson shows by using other evidence that Matthew of Paris's testimony should not be easily discounted as biased, and that many things he says have some truth in them.

3. Adam Marsh, *Epistolae,* 361–63.

4. "Consideremus religiosos; nullum ordinem excludo. Videamus quantum ceciderunt singuli a statu debito, et novi ordines jam horribiliter labefacti sunt a pristina dignitate" (*Compendium Studii Philosophiae,* in Bacon, *Opera hactenus inedita,* 1:399).

men regarding prevention of scandals, I am following what was laid down by my predecessor and reserving it to myself.[5] Therefore, I command under obedience that henceforth no one may change the location of a friary without my specific permission. And have the brothers learn to be content with few things.[6]

In the first General Chapter after his election, in 1260 at Narbonne, Bonaventure published in an orderly fashion the statutes made in the previous general chapters, sectioned under rubrics. To the third section, which came after the sections concerning recruits and the Franciscan habit, Bonaventure and his ministers gave the title *De observantia paupertatis.* Throughout the thirteenth and fourteenth centuries, constitutions, both general and provincial, kept this section with the same title, and even a rudimentary reading of the statutes placed in this section proves both the presence of scandalous practices in the Order and the administrative effort to stop them. Such practices had to do with the lifestyle of friars, buildings, money, and the use of books and all other goods the Franciscans used or consumed, some of which had come to be regarded as violations of the vow of poverty.

Neither Bonaventure's admonitions nor the orderly Narbonne constitutions succeeded in allaying these concerns. In 1266, Bonaventure was still lamenting bitterly, referring to how the reputation of the Order was being hurt:

> Until recently, the height of evangelical perfection we practiced captured both the attention and hearts of the world, making us worthy of every respect and honour. But now, what do we see?—large numbers of brothers on a downward trend, an ever-increasing laxity towards these tendencies by those in charge, abhorrent deviations springing up like briars. These are the things that are causing many people to see this holy and venerable

---

5. Already before Bonaventure, John of Parma had issued a mandate forbidding any convent to move to new premises without first obtaining a special license from him (Brooke, *Early Franciscan Government,* 261). These unauthorized changes of convent sites seem to have caused great trouble in the Order. Angelo Clareno also complains of this. "Videntes igitur, se nihil proficere et considerantes, quod ex verbis eorum peiores fiebant, et quod pro vera et pura observantia regulari introducebantur quaestus enormes, mutationes locorum et aedificationes intra civitates et castra cum scandalo cleri et populi." Angelo Clareno, *Historia septem tribulationum,* ed. A. Ghinato (Rome, 1959), 90.

6. *St. Bonaventure's Writings,* translated by Monti, 61. "Otiosos stimuletis ad laborem; vagantes compescatis ad quietem; importune petentibus imponatis silentium; intentos exaltandis domibus profundius deprimatis; familiaritates quaerentes arceatis ad solitudinem; officia praedicationis et confessionis cum multo examine imponatis; constitutionem olim factam de testamentis et de novo des sepulturis faciatis arctus observari; locorum vero mutationem nullatenus concedatis alicui ante Capitulum generale. Nam de consilio Discretorum propter scandala vitanda iuxta praedecessoris mei mandatum hoc mihi reservo, districte per obedientiam iubendo, ut nullus deinceps locum mutet sine mea licentia speciali. Discant etiam fratres modicis esse contenti, quia vehementer a sapientibus et rationaliter formidatur, quod oportebit, eos modicis esse contentos, velint nolint" (Bonaventure of Bagnoregio, *Epistolae officiales,* in *Opera omnia,* 8:469).

brotherhood as something despicable, burdensome, and odious, turning into a stumbling block what ought to be a pattern for all to follow.[7]

Eight years later, in 1274, at the General Chapter of Lyons, there was no sign of improvement:

> In those provinces where up to now the vicious custom has existed of receiving alms, the ministers are ordered to take firm action to eradicate this practice; in addition, all strong boxes and tables for offerings are to be removed. Again lay servants are to be barred from serving in the infirmary and the kitchen. Also, the constitution forbidding private rooms is to be strictly enforced; all barriers creating such chambers, whether they be doors or curtains, are to be removed from the study houses. And nowhere shall women be permitted to eat in the brothers' residences. All the regulations in this paragraph are commanded under obedience.[8]

It was not different interpretations of the Franciscan Rule but scandalous practices heard of in this or that province that ignited the first sparks of inner conflict within the Order. The trouble was not just about the observance of the Rule, but also the general failure to observe the very statutes made in successive general chapters, as we see Bonaventure repeatedly exhorting friars to observe the statutes. The statutes themselves constitute testimony that the General Chapter, as the main legislative body, attempted to stop scandalous practices, but without apparent success. An effort to understand the unrest in the Order that prompted such letters from its general minister has to investigate what was considered scandalous and to whom it was scandalous; what was a matter of interpretation as opposed to downright violation of a Rule or statute; and most important, in which ways the Order's internal culture was conducive to the commitment of such acts that at the same time made enforcement of its own statutes difficult.

The difficulties inherent in defining the spiritual standards, expressing them in a legal language, and enforcing them are not inconsiderable. However, certain practices, such as the buying and selling of things or dealing with money, seem to have been regarded as unambiguously criminal. In 2004, Cesare Cenci found in a thirteenth-century Toledo manuscript of Franciscan provenance a list of sixty-six practices that constituted the crime of appropriating things (*crimen*

---

7. Translation by Monti in *St. Bonaventure's Writings*, 226. "Sane cum evangelici culminis observata perfectio hactenus spectabiles et amabiles nos mundo reddiderit omnique favore ac reverentia dignos; ecce, iam nunc multitudine in proclivia tendente, et remissius agentibus his qui praesunt, vitiorum quaedam sentes cernuntur succrescere, quae dum sacrum hoc venerandumque collegium despicabile, onerosum et odibile reddunt plurimis, convertunt in scandalum quod cunctis esse debuerat in exemplum" (Bonaventure of Bagnoregio, *Epistolae officiales*, in *Opera omnia*, 8:470).

8. Translation by Monti in *St. Bonaventure's Writings*, 257.

proprietariorum).[9] This list, of course, is also testimony to what friars were doing wrong. They were buying and selling things (number 1 on the list), depositing money (number 2), making agreements with scribes on prices and paying them (number 21), threatening people when asking for alms (number 23), going on pilgrimages with purses (number 29), selling the wood or the fruits of trees belonging to the convent (number 37), claiming certain bits of the lakes and rivers for fishing (number 45), and asking for money from the convent for the treatment of their illnesses even when they had already received alms (number 51). These practices are quite similar to those Bonaventure complained of. The existence of such an exhortatory list, which was probably distributed to other provinces as well, is additional proof that the administration was trying as a legislative body to combat corruption among the friars but was failing terribly in its capacity as an executive body.

Bonaventure saw the problem in the failure of individual friars, or of the occasional provincial minister, to observe the statutes, and believed that it could be solved by means of horizontal pressure, with friars correcting each other:

> Although there are many friars who are not guilty of the aforesaid [corrupt practices], this malediction involves everyone unless those innocent stand against those who commit these errors. It is quite clear that everything mentioned above is damaging the Order greatly and cannot be ignored. Yet, to the lukewarm brothers who are lacking devotion, wise in the ways of the world, such practices seem normal, excusable, and unpreventable, as they point to custom and the high number of friars.[10]

One of these "lukewarm" brothers was the anonymous Franciscan author of the probably late thirteenth-century *Determinations of Questions Concerning the Rule*.[11] David Burr gives an excellent and concise analysis of the author's stance regarding the decline in the Order. The three different explanations the author of *Determinations* offered for the spiritual decline were centered around the failings of individual friars; institutional changes within the Order that tended to feed the decline by leading to such results as greater contact with the world or a greater

---

9. From the document "Contractus, a quibus fratres abstinere tenetur ne crimen proprietariorum incurrant, sunt hii," published in appendix I of Cenci, "Vestigia constitutionum," 95–97.

10. "Licet autem plurimi reperiantur, qui non sunt culpabiles in aliquo praedictorum, tamen omnes involvit haec maledictio, nisi a non facientibus his qui faciunt, resistatur; cum luce clarius omnia supradicta in maximum et nullo modo dissimulandum vergant nostri Ordinis detrimentum, licet tepidis et indevotis et secundum carnem sapientibus, considerantibus consuetudinem et allegantibus multitudinem quasi facilia et excusabilia ac irremediabilia videantur" (Bonaventure of Bagnoregio, *Epistolae officiales,* 469).

11. (pseudo) Bonaventure of Bagnoregio, *Determinationes quaestionum,* 337–74.

number of friars; and a degree of inevitability in the introduction of relaxations for the sake of peaceful cohabitation in the Order.[12]

In the paragraph quoted above, it is particularly remarkable that Bonaventure calls on the innocent friars to stand against those who violate the rules and statutes. After Bonaventure, the situation in the Order seems to have spiraled out of control. The statutes made in the General Chapter and some provincial chapters after 1274 display an obvious concern about certain practices in the Order and seek ways to correct them by ordering the friars to stop certain practices under the pain of punishment.[13] There is a particular concern with the friars' handling of money and their appropriation of things.

Evidently, however, the violations were unstoppable. In 1310–1312, a group of friars under the leadership of Ubertino da Casale made a list of complaints to the pope about the state of affairs in the Order. Ubertino's team included Raymond Gaufridi, who was a popular minister general elected twice, in charge of the Order from 1289 to 1295. The list presented to the pope was long. The nature of their complaints ranged from the disregard of the vow of poverty to the politics of governance. Practices related to learning and books featured prominently on the list. Ubertino was a friar who was alienated from the Order and who was trying to prove a point to the pope. Hence he might have had a tendency to exaggerate or mislead. As I will demonstrate below, however, most of his complaints concerning learning and books were justified, as independent evidence corroborates.

Practices Related to Learning: Abuse or Inevitability?

The Political Dominance of Lectors

According to Ubertino, the educational program was strongly linked to the abusive practices, inasmuch as education had become a prerequisite for the exercise of power and authority in the Order. It is worthwhile trying to pin down the ways in which the existence of an educational organization and the participation of the friars in the scholastic world, coupled with the high value attached to learning, affected the administrative structure of the Order, and what forms of it were related to abusive practices in the Order. Ubertino's criticism compels us to examine the intricate relationship between learning and the administrative positions in the Order:

> Almost all conflicts in many provinces of the Order are on account of the ambition to be promoted to the studia, so that they [friars] become lectors and superiors and rule over others.... So the order is ruled by these, since

---

12. Burr, *Olivi and Franciscan Poverty*, 3–4.
13. For a quick overview, see Moorman, *History of the Franciscan Order*, 187.

almost always the entire bodies of the provincial chapters and after that the General Chapter consists of them.[14]

Ubertino also condemns the administrative mechanism that allowed these men of material ambition to rise in the Order:

> Promotions both to the studium and to the high administrative positions are done carnally and not spiritually, by cunning associations in the chapters, the same way the promotions to these chapters are done, through which those who are unworthy and insufficient are promoted, when they are friends of the mighty. Those who are worthy and able are thought of as rivals and therefore rejected.[15]

Ubertino's accusation focuses on two points: first, many among the lectors were not worthy of the office, and pursued this office in order to lord over the friars. Second, the only people who were in a position to correct, rebuke, or prevent such friars from becoming lectors, the provincial administrators, were themselves lectors who also had perhaps obtained the office in dubious ways. So the system lacked a mechanism to correct itself. Ubertino's claim that the lectors dominated the ministerial positions can be shown from plentiful evidence. Any organization tends to privilege those individuals who are deemed most worthy to advance its main objectives. Within the thirteenth-century Franciscan Order, this privileged group was not made up of simple friars such as Saint Francis had aimed to be, but of the educated—namely, the masters and lectors. Under ideal circumstances, the lectors were chosen from among the best students, or those who were already learned, with the implication that they were considered to be brighter and more intelligent than those who did not obtain this office. The students and lectors were obliged to take an active part in the election of the *discreti* in the provincial and general chapters.[16] As a result, the number of lectors who filled administrative positions in the Order steadily rose. After the death of Albert Pisa in 1240, there was never again a minister general who had not studied at the University of Paris. The work of

---

14. "Et omnes dissensiones quasi, que sunt in provinciis multis ordinis, sunt propter ambicionem promocionis ad studia, ut sint lectores et prelati et aliis dominentur.... Et quia a talibus [lectoribus] ordo regitur, cum quasi semper sint de corporibus capitulorum provincialium et postea generalium" (Ubertino da Casale, *Responsio*, 73–74).

15. "Et promotiones sive ad studium sive ad prelationes carnaliter et non spiritualiter sepe fiunt et per astutas colligationes in capitulis et aliter per promotiones sibi invicem adherentium in via carnis fiunt, per quas promoventur sepe indigni et insufficientes, si sunt amici potentium; et digni et valentes, si reputantur emuli, repelluntur." Ubertino da Casale, *Rotulus iste* in "Zur Vorgeschichte des Councils von Vienne no. 4 Vorarbeiten zur Constitution Exivi de paradiso vom 6. Mai 1312," ed. F. Ehrle, *ALKG* 3 (1887): 117–18.

16. "Lectores etiam extra suam provinciam legentes et similiter fratres extra suam provinciam studentes, in electionibus discretorum tam ad gle quam ad provle capitulum vocem tantum activam habeant, non passivam" (Bihl, "Statuta generalia ordinis," 306).

F. Joyce Mapelli on the English and French administrations shows the extent to which the lectors took over positions of authority in the Order.[17] The case of the province of Strasbourg demonstrates this point. All of the late thirteenth-century provincial ministers of this province were without exception lectors. In 1271, Konrad Probus, who had previously served as the lector at Constance, was elected provincial minister and held the post until 1279 when he became bishop of Toul.[18] That year, the Provincial Chapter in Rutlingen elected Friar Thidericus Golinus (Dietrich Goellin), who at that time was lector at Basel, the new provincial minister. When Thidericus died in 1289, the then lector at Constance, Berthold de Columbaria, was elected as provincial minister. Berthold served until his death in 1297, at which time the Provincial Chapter chose the lector at Speyer, Henry of Otendorf, as the provincial minister. Henry was a master of arts and of canon law. In 1302, the office of provincial minister passed for a third time to a lector at Constance, Henry of Ravensburg. In 1309, when the General Chapter decided that the province of Strasbourg needed a reform, and the *visitatores* absolved Henry of Ravensburg from the ministry, they assigned in his place an Englishman, Peter, who had been the regent master in theology at Paris from 1303 to 1305.[19] Peter kept his new post until 1316.[20]

Careers for sale

In itself the appointment of lectors as administrators was not problematic, but Ubertino talks clearly of the friars' seeing learning and education as steps toward the acquisition of political power and positions of authority in the Order. Although many were not suited for study, they still wanted to have the title of lector in order to be honored.[21] The ambition for schooling did not, according to Ubertino, always arise from *amor sciendi,* because some friars were apparently unwilling to lecture once they actually received the office of lector. "Once they

---

17. F. Joyce Mapelli, *L'amministrazione francescana di Inghilterra e Francia: Personale di governo e strutture dell'Ordine fino al Concilio di Vienne (1311)* (Rome: Pontificio Ateneo Antonianum, 2003), 286.

18. L. Lemmens, ed., "Chronicon provinciae argentinensis O.F.M. circa an. 1310–1327 a quodam fratre minore basileae conscriptum (1206–1325)," *AFH* 4 (1911): 677. It has been suggested that Konradus Probus studied theology in Siena and received a doctor's degree before his entry to the Order. This is highly unlikely, however, since there was no theology faculty in Siena in the thirteenth century. "Der Franziskusorden: Die Franziskaner, die Klarissen und die Regulierten Franziskanerterziarinnen in der Schweiz," ed. K. Arnold et al., *Helvetia sacra,* part 5 (Bern, 1978), 1:59.

19. Glorieux, *Répertoire des maîtres,* 2:196–97.

20. Lemmens, "Chronicon provinciae argentinensis," 678–81; *Helvetia sacra,* part 5, 1:61–62.

21. "Et quia non multi sunt ingeniosi et apti ad subtilia et tamen, ut honorentur, volunt mitti ad studia et habere nomen lectoris, licet parum sciant" (Ubertino da Casale, *Responsio,* 73–74). "Causa autem quare est tanta ambitio et sepe turbe inter fratres propter studia, maxime propter Parisiense, esse videtur, quia quasi ubique per ordinem soli magistri et lectores Parisini dominantur" (Ubertino da Casale, *Rotulus,* 118).

come back from Paris, they care little for studying, and whether they lecture or not, a great many Parisian lectors dominate the Order's administration in the provinces of Italy and elsewhere."[22]

But if Ubertino's claims were true, how did these friars who did not have any love or capacity for learning get to Paris in the first place? The answer to this question uncovers another problem in the educational system of the friars. Friars could be backed financially at the schools by a powerful secular benefactor, or the latter could assist the friar's promotion through proximity to and influence over the administrators of the Order. Prosopographical research on Parisian bachelors and doctors from the mendicant orders supports Ubertino's claims. William J. Courtenay, for instance, wrote that "a large number of them came from prominent, sometimes even aristocratic, families, or had connections with persons of power and privilege."[23]

"Now the study in Paris is bought by many," wrote Ubertino.[24] Theoretically, a student sent to Paris was called de gratia when his expenses were paid by his province, and de debito when his expenses were paid by the central budget of the Order. It appears that when a friar was able to procure some of the money and books for studying from outside—for example, from a living relative—it could be arranged that he be sent to Paris de gratia. This should not be seen as a blatant case of abuse. Probably the provincial administrations did not mind or even encouraged such students, since it meant more lectors for the province without incurring much or any cost.

While the early general chapters seem to have recognized the implications of such a practice, later on the administration gave in. The Narbonne constitutions of 1260 prohibited friars from seeking help from secular people to be sent to a studium generale.[25] In 1279 the Assisi constitutions repeated the same decree.[26] In 1292, two decrees make it certain that the General Chapter chose the path of regulating the practice instead of outright prohibiting it. One of these decrees was an extended version of the Narbonne and Assisi decrees, which ordered

---

22. "Quod autem hiis moveantur pocius quam amore scientie, patet, quia de facto videmus eos invite legere, quando possunt preesse; et postquam habent nomen, quod fuerint lectores, et de Parysius redeunt, parum curant postea de studio, sed sive legant sive non, in provinciis Ytalie et eciam alibi, ut plurimum soli lectores Parysienses dominantur" (Ubertino da Casale, *Responsio,* 73).

23. William J. Courtenay, "The Instructional Programmes of the Mendicant Convents at Paris in the Early Fourteenth Century," in *The Medieval Church: Universities, Heresy, and the Religious Life; Essays in Honour of Gordon Leff,* ed. Peter Biller and R. B. Dobson (Woodbridge: Boydell Press, 1999), 92.

24. "Quale est istud, quod nunc Parisiense studium emitur a pluribus, et dantur XXIIII libre parisienses a quolibet studente de gracia ibi omni anno" (Ubertino da Casale, *Responsio,* 74). "Quod frater emeret sibi studium Parisiense, sicut modo fit" (Ubertino da Casale, *Rotulus,* 111).

25. "Quodsi aliquis se vel alium per saeculares personas procuraverit mitti ad Studium generale, ipso facto omnibus officiis Ordinis sit privatus, quosque per Generalem secum fuerit dispensatum" (Bihl, "Statuta generalia ordinis," 72).

26. Ibid., 78, no. 17.

deprivation of office for those who sought to be promoted to a studium or to the office of lector, bachelor, or master through the help of those outside the Order.[27] The second decree stated that friars who went to studia generalia at the expense of or request of people outside the Order were not to be assigned to the office of lector on their return to the provinces, except at the dispensation of the General Chapter. Nor were such friars in the schools to enjoy the liberty of the students.[28] These decrees meant that friars who could fund themselves independently could go to the studium and get an education, but there was no guarantee that this education would result in the procurement of an office. It seems that the General Chapter tried to stop precisely the practice that Ubertino complained about: friars using education as a means to rise to positions of power. By 1296, the practice of securing outside funds for students seems to have become acceptable in the provinces. That year, the chapter of the province of Saint Anthony decreed that those who were at, or who could be sent to, studia generalia through the intervention of laypeople were to receive no provision from the province.[29]

This practice and the related decrees are proof of the tremendous complexity of the situation, where the "right path" is so elusive. The legislators in the 1292 General Chapter might have had in mind the benefit of having more friars educated by not blocking the path of education to those who could afford it without having recourse to the Order's funds. The more educated friars the Order had, the better. The recruitment policy established in the 1240s was based on this assumption. The problem, as the legislators saw it, was to break down the causal connection between education and office, so that friars would not seek education as a way to positions of power but for its own sake. Yet the allowance for such a practice as letting friars finance their own education must have indirectly bred a culture of envy and inequality. More gifted and intelligent students who could not procure financial support from outside did not have the chance of becoming lectors, while they watched others with lesser intellectual capabilities but greater access to funds rising in the Order. The Friars Minor were, after

---

27. "Quod si aliquis se vel alium per personas extra Ordinem procuraverit mitti ad Studium quodcumque [sive ad lectoriam, bacchalariam, magisterium vel quodcumque Ordinis officium promoveri] ipso facto omnibus officiis Ordinis sit privatus, quosque per generalem Ministrum secum fuerit dispensatum" (ibid., 79, no. 20b).

28. "Inhibet autem generale capitulum, ne fratres, qui per personarum extra Ordinem procurationes et preces generalia ad Studia transmittuntur, revocati ad suas provincias, assignentur alicubi pro officio lectionis, sine dispensatione capituli generalis, nec in studiis gaudeant studentium libertate" (ibid., no. 20c).

29. "Ad obviandum periculose abusioni contra illos, qui per procurationem secularium mediate vel immediate ad generalia studia transmittantur, vel possent fortasse transmitti, preter illud quod super hoc statuit capitulum generale, ordinat et vult minister et diffinitores cum consensu totius capituli provincialis Verone celebrati anno Domini MCC nonagesimo VI, intrante Augusto, quod talibus sic transmissis nullo modo detur provisio per provinciam" (Little, "Statuta provincialia," 465).

all, to enjoy the privileges of poverty not of wealth. Furthermore, when such a practice was allowed, the provinces would have little incentive to allocate funds from their budgets to sustain worthy candidates for lectorship at the studia. In the end, it was such small adjustments, giving in here and there to ongoing practices, even when done with good intentions, that created little by little a whole new culture, one which bred discord among the friars and gave rise to abuse.

Lectors and the Abuse of Privileges

The lectors in their capacity as administrators were held responsible by Ubertino for what he considered the Order's state of decline, but he further accused them with respect to their extensive privileges and the abuse of these. Such privileges, already discussed at length in the previous chapter, included the permission to eat meat, exemption from divine office, and the right to have a *socius* and a private room. Initially these privileges were intended to compensate for the heavy tasks of teaching and writing that the lectors shouldered. However, when certain lectors who did not actually teach still enjoyed these privileges, it was a clear case of abuse.

> In many provinces, whether they teach or not, [the lectors] are exempt from the Divine Office and the communal labors of the friars. They eat and drink as they like in the infirmaries and in the guesthouses, consuming those things that are supposed to be distributed to the poor. And then they wander about between the convents of the province, having a friar to serve them and everywhere they are received with reverence as if they are lords. Rarely do the prelates dare to deny them something they want, or to disagree with them, but commonly try to please them.[30]

The privilege of having a *socius* was also abused in that lectors treated their *socii* as personal servants.[31] Most important of all, the lectors were accused of serious violations of the Order's constitutions on issues of poverty. According to Ubertino, contrary to the constitutions that ordered all traveling friars to beg and not to carry money, the lectors took with them secular boys who carried their purses

---

30. "Et in multis provinciis, sive legant sive non, sunt exempti a divinis officiis et communibus laboribus fratrum et comedunt et bibunt in forestariis et infirmariis sicut volunt, quod deberet pauperibus compartiri. Et discurrunt per terras et per loca provincie, habentes unum fratrem servitorem et ubique recipiuntur egregie sicut domini. Et raro prelati audent eis negare, quod volunt vel eos redarguere, sed student eis communiter complacere" (Ubertino da Casale, *Rotulus,* 118).

31. "Ideo postea fastiditi de studio efficiuntur ociosi et vagi et aridi et indevoti nec curant chorum sequi, sed uno socio habito servitore discurrunt, ut volunt, et stant in terris propriis ceteris fratribus dominantes" (Ubertino da Casale, *Responsio,* 73–74).

while traveling between provinces since they were ashamed of begging.[32] "It is not a miracle, therefore," wrote Ubertino, "that such lectors, masters, and prelates hate the doctrine of *usus pauper*, since it is a great disturbance to their lives."[33] Indeed, many French satires invoked the Parisian convent of the Franciscans, the crown jewel in the Order's educational organization, to refer to the hypocritical practices in the entire Order.[34]

The 1309 Provincial Chapter of Strasbourg, which was summoned under the new provincial minister assigned by the General Chapter, issued a series of decrees that verify Ubertino's complaints and that are aimed at reforming the province. The chapter ordered the lectors and other prelates to hold food, drink, and clothing in common with others; exercise their offices in humility; and be an example to other friars. Just like other friars, they were obliged to go begging for alms.[35] Furthermore, the Provincial Chapter ordered that the lectors who lectured infrequently be deprived of their office.[36] Those deprived of the office were to attend the choir just like the rest. The existence of such a statute is enough evidence that, just as Ubertino complained, some friars holding the office of *lectio* were not willing to lecture, and that lectors, whether teaching or not, were often exempt from liturgical activities. We come across a similar decree from the chapter of the province of Saint Anthony celebrated in Vicenza in 1294. The lectors were asked to continue their lectures as scheduled, and to finish the books they had started according to the statutes of the General Chapter. Those who did otherwise were to be deprived of their *socius,* and obliged to attend the Divine Office without exception.[37]

---

32. "Item dicebant constituciones, quod fratres euntes per viam extra loca fratrum nullo modo bursarium secum ducerent pro expensis, sed more pauperum mendicarent. Nunc vero quasi communiter fratres, qui possunt, habent quilibet sua deposita apud depositarios et faciunt fratres suas expensas per eos. Et vix etiam intra suas provincias volunt ire sine bursario; et quomodo expendant, sciunt tabernarii et pueri, qui pecuniam portant. Et quia istud est vicium maiorum prelatorum, lectorum et sollempnium predicatorum et confessorum, qui quasi nullas volunt sustinere penurias, immo certe semper nituntur multi ex eis procurare delicias; et victum temperatum mendicare, quod est eorum proprium, erubescunt" (ibid., 71). The statutes that prohibited traveling friars from carrying purses or from having secular boys carry their purses date from around 1239. Pre-Narbonne, 84, no. 55.

33. "Non est mirum, si tales lectores et magistri et prelati odiunt doctrinam de usu paupere, quia nimis ab eorum vita discordat" (Ubertino da Casale, *Responsio,* 71).

34. Batany, "L'image des Franciscains," 61–74. "Aux yeux du public, l'image des Franciscains (sous le nom de 'Frères Mineurs' ou de 'Cordeliers') avait prise dans l'image globale de la société." (ibid., 61).

35. "Item praelati, Lectores ac alii maiores in victu communi quod cibum, potum atque vestitum, in humilitatis officiis exercendis se praebeant aliis fratribus exemplares, vadantque pro eleemosyna sicut alii fratres de conventu" (Fussenegger "Statuta provincie Alemanie," 258).

36. "Lectores autem, qui parum legunt, tenatur Minister in Capitulo privare officio lectionis. Privati autem vadant ad chorum sicut ceteri de conventu" (ibid., 259).

37. "Ordinat et vult minister et provinciale capitulum, quod lectores iuxta statutum capituli generalis suas ordinarie continuent lectiones, et libros inceptos perficiant fideliter, sicut possunt. Quod si contrarium fecerint, priventur socio, et vadant continue ad officium, et nihilominus provinciali capitulo accusentur" (Little, "Statuta provincialia," 464).

The Problem of Books

Although today books are generally considered an everyday item to be bought at reasonable prices, in the Middle Ages they were luxury goods that only the wealthy could afford. The ownership of books was in itself a sign of prosperity, and individual book collectors of the early thirteenth century were none other than the high-ranking clergy, kings, and other nobility with intellectual tastes. Cathedrals and monasteries kept their positions as the principal communal book owners. In this context, it was rather striking that the Franciscans, who were supposed to be the poorest of the poor, collected and preserved many books. When the Order decided to move into the world of scholastic theology, books became indispensable. Bonaventure's syllogism was all too simple: the Rule conferred the authority and office of preaching on the friars. If friars were to preach, they should not tell fables, but instead expound the Bible. They could not know the Bible if they did not read it; they could not read if they did not have access to books. So it very much went along with the perfection of the Rule to have books.[38] However right Bonaventure was in his own terms, unfortunately Franciscans also kept books for reasons other than study.

In 1220, one of the first statutes of the Order had prohibited the friars from having books. At that time there were no lectors, no schools, and no organized education, though somehow book donations to the Order started soon after. The first known substantial book donation came in 1224 when a certain Bartholomew de Bruyères donated ten books to the Paris convent.[39] During the same year, a canon of Padua Cathedral, Master Aegidius, donated a manuscript containing the sermons of Saint Anthony of Padua to the Franciscan convent of Padua, which housed one of the earliest Franciscan schools.[40] We find evidence of many book donations to the Order in these early years.[41] Donations did not remain the only means of book acquisition for long. In 1230, the papal bull *Quo elongati* categorized books as "necessary items" for Franciscans, and this practically meant that now friars could arrange the purchase of books with money bequeathed to them through the assistance of secular individuals referred to as *amici spirituali*. The guardians were to supply books for the convent library. For example, Brother Guido de Fraxia, the guardian of the Florentine convent,

---

38. "De libris et utensilibus qui sentiam, audi. Clamat Regula expresse imponens Fratribus auctoritatem et offcium praedicandi, quod non creado in aliqua Regula alii reperiri. Si igitur praedicare non debent fabulas, sed verba divina; et haec scire non possunt, nisi legant; nec legere, nisi habeant scripta: plurissimum est, quod de perfectione Regulae est libros habere sicut et praedicare" (Delorme, "Textes Franciscains," 214).

39. Beaumont-Maillet, *Le grand couvent*, 12.

40. Giuseppe Abate and Giovanni Luisetto, *Codici e manoscritti della Biblioteca Antoniana col catalogo delle miniature* (Vicenza: N. Pozza, 1975), 1:xxvii.

41. For a detailed discussion of the donations, see Neslihan Şenocak, "Book Acquisition in the Medieval Franciscan Order," *Journal of Religious History* 27 (2003): 14–28.

bought the *Decretum* of Gratian in 1246 for nineteen Pisan lire from a layman in Florence for the use of the friars in the convent of Florence. The papal procurators of the Franciscans carried out the transaction.[42]

Books as Money

Even though, as mentioned in the introduction, scholars have identified books as a point of conflict between the "Spirituals" and the "Conventuals," the presence of books in the Order was not in itself problematic for Ubertino da Casale. He agreed fully with Bonaventure on the necessity of books. He conceded that celebrating Divine Office necessitated a Breviary, and that learning to preach called for the use of books.[43] Not only did he raise no objections to study and books, he even went so far as to say that Francis and his brothers from the beginning of the Order held books in common in order to study and to say the Divine Office.[44] For Ubertino, the problem was not that the friars studied books, but that they appropriated them. He even quoted episodes concerning a conversation between Francis and a clerical friar called Richard of Marchia, who asked Francis whether the clerical friars can keep their books. Francis told the friar that friars were not supposed to have anything except their clothing.[45] Ubertino's interpretation is that Francis opposed the appropriation of books, not the use of books in common.[46]

For Ubertino the problem was that friars bought books individually, and these were not really treated as the common property of the convent until the friar died. Being the only commodity of commercial value that a friar could collect and keep, books replaced money in the Order. "Very expensive and unnecessary books acquired through various ways multiply in the Order. There is a great deal of appropriation of books; that is, only a few would share the books with his brothers freely. Many have too many books, and many do not

---

42. "Istum librum emit Frater Guido de Fraxia tunc temporis Guardianus Florentinus anno Domini millesimo CCXLVI. Fuit autem emptus pro libris XIX Pisanorum et dimidia ab Ugone Florentino filio. Instrumentum vero factum fuit inde a Domino Bono de Arlotto Bentivenni de Arlotto recipienti procuratorio nomine pro Domino Episcopo Ostiensi ad usum, et utilitatem Fratrum Minorum Conventus Florentini." Florence, Bibliothecae Medicea-Laurenziana, Santa Croce, Plut. I Sin. cod. 1, 339.

43. "Licet igitur offitium divinum supponat usum breviariorum et predicatio scientiam et scientia studium et studium usum librorum, non tamen propter hoc sequitur librorum appropriatio et sic in tanto excessu multiplicatorum per singulos fratres, sed solum usum talium in locis fratrum pro communitate conservatorum" (Ubertino da Casale, *Declaratio,* 176).

44. "Quod a principio fuit per beatum Franciscum et sotios observatum, qui in libris communi usui deputatis dicebant offitium et studebant" (ibid., 176).

45. Ubertino di Casale, *Declaratio,* 177. See Brooke, *Scripta Leonis,* 206.

46. For a brief summary of Ubertino's position on books, see Burr, *Spiritual Franciscans,* 123–24.

even know how to use them."[47] Similarly, Angelo Clareno also categorized the unnecessary accumulation of books as one of the evils in the Order.[48]

The evidence from books used by and the statutes of the Order supports Ubertino's testimony. Among the surviving manuscripts of Franciscan origin, there are quite a few books elaborately illuminated. Some of these had been commissioned specifically by the Franciscans from the professional scribal ateliers. One example is an illuminated Franciscan missal commissioned from the Johannes Grusch atelier in Paris between 1254 and 1261.[49] Some humble manuscripts were in fact adorned with illuminations after they came into the Franciscans' possession, in some cases with gold.[50] Ubertino's observation that friars collected books for reasons other than studying was also correct. The 1310 General Chapter, which met in Padua, decreed that no friar was to be allowed to have the duplicate of a book, and no friar could have a book that he could not use.[51] In 1285, the provincial chapter of Aquitaine decreed that custodians and guardians had to compel friars who were in debt to other friars and secular people to pay their debts. If the friars did not pay, then their books and other possessions were to be confiscated and sold within the Order, so that the debt could be paid and great scandals avoided.[52] Similarly, the thirteenth-century provincial constitutions of Provence decreed that if a friar who was in debt to his convent was transferred to another convent, the guardian or vicar of the original

---

47. "Hinc multiplicantur salme librorum preciosorum et curiosorum superflue acquisite diversis viis a quolibet taliter qualiter; et tanta est apropriacio librorum, quod valde pauci inveniuntur, qui de accomodacione sint suis fratribus liberales. Et multi superfluos libros habent, et multi, qui nesciunt eis uti. Et multi de eis faciunt thesaurum dicentes: 'Si ego infirmabor, ego michi providerem de libris meis'; et vendunt et emunt ea intus ordinem et extra, melius quam possunt, et multi suis fratribus carius quam emant, more mercatorum." Ubertino da Casale, *Sanctitas vestra*, in "Zur Vorgeschichte des Councils von Vienne no. 4: Vorarbeiten zur Constitution Exivi de paradiso vom 6. Mai 1312," ed. F. Ehrle, *ALKG* 3 (1887): 73.

48. "Ignorantes enim demonum astutias et suarum affectionum inclinationes ad malum non precaventes, confidenter dicent, quod non est contra regule puritatem pro confessionibus audiendis et predicationibus magis libere faciendis et ecclesiis hedificandis et fratribus multiplicandis et infirmis fovendis et personis devotis sepeliendis et studiis et libris multiplicandis et pro aliis, que ad utilitatem et firmitatem et spiritualem statum totius religionis faciunt, privilegia a summo pontifice impetrare." Angelo Clareno, *Expositio Regulae Fratrum Minorum*, ed. L. Oliger (Florence: Ad Claras Aquas, 1912), 53.

49. Robert Branner, *Manuscript Painting in Paris during the Reign of Saint Louis: A Study of Styles* (Berkeley: University of California Press, 1977), 82.

50. Sabina Magrini, "Production and Use of Latin Bible Manuscripts in Italy during the Thirteenth and Fourteenth Centuries," *Manuscripta* 51 (2007): 248, nn. 102–3.

51. "Item iniungitur ministris omnibus ut nullum fratrem permittant habere librum aliquem duplicatum, nec aliquem fratrem permittant habere librum quo uti non possit." Cenci, "Le costituzioni Padovane del 1310," 535.

52. "Item custodes et gardiani fratres sibi subditos compellant ad solutionem debitorum, que debent fratribus vel aliis personis, assignato ad solvendum termino competenti. Post quem, si solutum non fuerit, accipiant libros et res alias fratrum non solventium eo modo quo dictum est, et inpignorent vel vendant intra ordinem, ut sic debita persolvantur, cum ex huiusmodi magna scandala oriantur. Qui vero solvere non poterunt, graviter puniantur." Michael Bihl, ed., "Statuta provincialia provinciarum Aquitaine et Franciae (saec. XIII–XIV)," *AFH* 7 (1914): 478.

convent was to keep the friar's books as a pledge to his creditors. Eventually, the friar would be deprived of his books and other things in return for his accumulated debts.[53] The fact that the convent would confiscate a friar's books to pay his debts is proof enough that friars in practice individually owned books.

Another practice that went against the Franciscan Rule was the sale of books within and outside the Order. It is interesting to note that Franciscans were not scrupulous about such transactions. They left records of the sale of books, even on official documents like library inventories, a sign that they did not generally regard it as inappropriate.[54] As early as 1245 David of Augsburg mentions friars selling books to each other in his Rule commentary. He adds, however, that when a friar sells a book to another friar, this is not exactly called a "sale" or "purchase" since everything is in common; instead it is said that the book is assigned to him by the license of his superior.[55] From the very beginning, when it was necessary to explain how friars could keep books despite their vow of poverty, the usual response would be that friars only had the use of books, but they could not claim the right of ownership, which would mean the right to sell or exchange books.[56] Legally speaking, individual friars never had permission to sell their books without permission. The general and provincial chapters discouraged the practice but to no avail. The chapter of the province of Saint Anthony decreed in 1290 that no friar was to sell, mortgage, or exchange any book without receiving special permission from the minister or custodian and the approval of *discreti* of the convent.[57]

The transformation of books into a currency in the Order—a means by which the friars could trade—gave way almost naturally to another controversial practice, the use of books as a means of investment: "Many make a treasure out of their books, saying, 'When I get sick, I will provide for myself by selling my books.' And they sell and buy books within the Order or, better, outside

---

53. "Item, si frater debitis obligatus ad conventum transferatur aliquem, gardianus conventus, unde recesserus est, seu eius vicarius libros eius et suppellectilem aut pignus habundans retineat, unde possit plenarie satisfieri creditoribus; et omnis viciosus in contrahendis debitis, custodis iudicio, libris et rebus privetur aliis, donec sufficienter apparuerit emendatus." F. Delorme, ed., "Constitutiones provinciae provinciae (saec. XIII–XIV)," *AFH* 14 (1921): 422.

54. See, for example, Neslihan Şenocak, "The Earliest Library Catalogue of the Franciscan Convent of St. Fortunato of Todi (c. 1300)," *AFH* 99 (2006): 475.

55. "Si frater vendit fratri librum vel simile non dicitur proprie venditio vel emptio ubi sunt omnia communia, sed de licentia superioris assignat ei librum commissum." David Flood, "Die Regelerklärung des David von Augsburg," *Franziskanische Studien* 75 (1993): 217.

56. Particular stress was put on the point that friars could not sell books. Bonaventure's letter to the unnamed master is representative. See Delorme, "Textes Franciscains," 214.

57. "Item ordinat, quod nullus frater vendat, impignoret seu commutet librum aliquem, calicem, seu paramenta, sine ministri licentia speciali vel custodis cum discretorum loci consilio. Et ad hoc per obedientiam firmiter teneantur. Et qui contrafecerint, provinciali capitulo accusentur" (Little, "Statuta provincialia provinciae," 462).

the Order, whenever they can. Many sell the books to their own brothers at a higher price than they bought, following the custom of merchants."[58] Once again Ubertino is not exaggerating. In the fourteenth-century manuscript that contains the inventory of the Franciscan convent in Pisa, there is a memo written in 1344 concerning what the convent had done with the books of a deceased friar, Pietro Bottari. A large volume of the Bible was sold, the convent receiving half of the proceeds from its sale to cover the friar's debt to the convent, while the other half was used to pay for expenses incurred during the friar's illness.[59] Some of Pietro's other books were sold to other friars in the convent. The use of books as a provision for old age was obviously a violation of one of the silent yet most powerful Franciscan—in fact, Christian—principles: reliance on divine providence. The transformation of books into an insurance investment provides a perfect example of how far some developments could be taken, and how difficult it was to prevent and eradicate such controversial practices once they crept into common use. To combat the accusations of Ubertino concerning books during the preparations for the Council of Vienne, the administrative party of the Order simply repeated Bonaventure's justification, which was cited earlier: in order to preach, friars needed books; and they did not possess the books, but only had the use of them.[60] This was true in theory, but not in practice, as the statutes of the Order make it clear that friars did engage in commercial transactions involving books, selling and pledging books, and investing in books that they could not read. Still, they were warned by the administration not to use words that indicate ownership.[61]

---

58. "Hinc multiplicantur salme librorum preciosorum et curiosorum superflue acquisite diversis viis a quolibet taliter qualiter; et tanta est apropriacio librorum, quod valde pauci inveniuntur, qui de accomodacione sint suis fratribus liberales. Et multi superfluos libros habent, et multi, qui nesciunt eis uti. Et multi de eis faciunt thesaurum dicentes:'Si ego infirmabor, ego michi providerem de libris meis'; et vendunt et emunt ea intus ordinem et extra, melius quam possunt, et multi suis fratribus carius quam emant, more mercatorum" (Ubertino di Casale, *Responsio,* 73).

59. "Una biblia magni voluminis fuit vendita pro florenis viginti quinque de qua pecunia partim pro debito quod habebat recipere a conventu, partim fuerunt exspense in infirmitate sua." Pisa, Archivio di Stato di Pisa, Archivio del Comune Divisione-D, no. 1386, 3r.

60. "Et ideo cum secundum regulam fratres debeant populo predicare et eis immineat secundum regulam hec necessitas; si non predicare fabulas debeant, sed divinam scripturam, et hanc scire non possunt sine aliarum scientiarum peritia nisi cum multis libris; restat, quod sicut de perfectione regule est predicare, sic et multos habere libros, in quibus studeat, quid debeat predicare, precipue cum eos nullus frater habeat ut proprios, sed nec ut perpetuos, quod ad licteram servatur per totum ordinem, ut libros unusquisque reputet se habere ad usum tantum simplicem studii, et non ad proprietatem nec in perpetuum. Quod patet, quia ministri cotidie auferunt eos fratribus et aliis dant usum, quod non possent, si essent proprii fratrum vel etiam ad perpetuum concessi." "Zur Vorgeschichte des Councils," 148. See also Aniceto Chiappini, ed., "Communitatis responsio 'Religiosi viri' ad Rotulum Fr. Ubertini," *AFH* 7 (1914): 654–75.

61. "Pecuniam meam vel tunicam meam, librum meum aut quamcumque rem meam etiam ore dicere, nisi peccatum proprium, vel etiam nostram, nisi intelligendo de usu nudo; quod res quecumque sit ordinis, nisi solum usum, asserere aut mente credere." From the document "Contractus, a quibus fra-

Another controversial aspect of the presence and use of books in the Order was the assignment of books to individual friars. When friars were given permission to keep books, it was understood that all books in the Order were to be held in common. However, soon some books were assigned to individual friars for exclusive usage for a certain period of time. One reason for this was the medieval habit of taking notes on the books themselves rather than in a separate notebook. A lector who lectured on the Bible or a master who was writing a commentary on Peter Lombard's *Sentences* had to keep his own copies of the Bible and the *Sentences,* which he would have glossed himself. In this sense, the assignment of books for individual use was justified, and even inevitable. Toward this end, the Order made some arrangements to assign, with the permission of prelates of the Order, certain books to individual lectors and students.[62]

This privilege was badly abused. Some friars took convent books with them when they ventured into apostasy.[63] Other friars used books as pledges when they borrowed money from outsiders, despite the repeated statutes of the Order prohibiting this practice.[64] Hence, when the friar could not pay his debt, the book would be lost to the convent. To prevent such losses, convents started to assign books to friars in return for a monetary pledge to cover the cost of the book if it was lost; this also meant that poorer friars who could not afford such pledges had restricted or no access.[65] The early fourteenth-century inventory of the Franciscan convent of Gubbio contains the names of five friars who were holding a book in return for a pledge.[66]

Furthermore, many friars held books from their convents that were designated for their use throughout their lifetime.[67] The team that responded to Ubertino's accusations in 1310–1312 denied the existence of the practice of conceding books for life, arguing that friars did not appropriate books, nor did

---

tres abstinere tenetur ne crimen proprietariorum incurrant, sunt hii," published in appendix 1 of Cenci, "Vestigia constitutionum Praenarbonensium," 95–97.

62. I have discussed the details of the system of book assignment in the Franciscan Order in Nesli-han Şenocak, "Circulation of Books in the Medieval Franciscan Order: Methods, Attitude and Critics," *Journal of Religious History* 28 (2004): 146–61.

63. See *BF,* 1:578, n. 375. A letter of Innocent IV from 1251 addressed to the magister of the Order of Humiliati in Lombardy mentions the Franciscan friar Salvus of Papia, who joined the Humiliati and took with him convent books.

64. "Nec libros communes vel alicui fratri deputatos ad usum, aliquo modo pignorari obliget, sine expressa et speciali licentia ministri, qui nulli det licentiam, nisi pro necessitatibus et utilitatibus fratrum. Nec aliquis frater alienet aut commutet sine ministri expressa licentia. Et si quis contra fecerit tanquam proprietatibus a ministro vel custode puniatur" ("Statuta provincialia provinciarum Aquitanie," 472). For a detailed discussion of pledges and books, see Şenocak, "Circulation of Books," 157–59.

65. Şenocak, "Circulation of Books," 156–59.

66. Michele Faloci Pulignani, "La biblioteca Francescana di Gubbio," *MF* 9 (1902): 160, no. 46; 161, no. 77; 162, nos. 120, 127.

67. Şenocak, "Circulation of Books," 153–55.

they have the use of books perpetually.[68] The manuscript evidence contradicts them. Notes for lifetime concessions are to be found in the flyleaves of many Franciscan manuscripts and in library inventories.[69] Some friars who held convent books became possessive about them and refused to share them with other friars.[70] This in turn forced the convent libraries to acquire several copies of the same work, which obviously violated the principle established by the 1230 papal bull *Quo Elongati* that friars could purchase goods through the mediation of spiritual friends only in cases of sheer necessity. Once again, the reforming ministers had attempted to prevent such abuses through legislation. The convents were ordered to keep library inventories and record on them all the movements of books.[71] Friars who had permission to remove books from the library were asked to show them at regular intervals to the guardian or the librarian. Friars were also asked not to take books with them if they were leaving the convent for a long time, and never to give them as a pledge to outsiders. The General Chapter of 1307 condemned what is called "the communities of books"—that is, the private possession of books by a group of friars who shared among themselves books assigned to them and who denied other friars the use of these books.[72]

As with the privileges of lectors, the assignment of convent books for private use was intended in the beginning to facilitate the work of students and lectors. However, abuses made the system of book assignments a major point of conflict, as it became a means through which the evangelical poverty of the Order was violated. Ubertino stated that neither the Rule nor the papal bulls contained

---

68. "Restat, quod sicut de perfectione regule est predicare, sic et multos habere libros, in quibus studeat, quid debeat predicare, precipue cum eos nullus frater habeat ut proprios, sed nec ut perpetuos, quod ad licteram servatur per totum ordinem, ut libros unusquisque reputet se habere ad usum tantum simplicem studii, et non ad proprietatem nec in perpetuum." F. Ehrle, "Zur Vorgeschichte des Concils von Vienne no. 4 Vorarbeiten zur Constitution Exivi de Paradiso vom 6. Mai 1312," *ALKG* 3 (1887): 148.

69. In the early fourteenth-century library inventory of Todi, eleven books were noted as given to friars for life. Todi, Biblioteca comunale, 185, ff. 2r–31r.

70. "Nam senes et decrepiti et fratres sepe otiosi et in aliis quam studiis occupati habent magnas salmas, quos tenent clausos et sibi appropriatos; et vix unus liber ab alio fratre potest haberi mutuo ab eisdem, nisi sicut haberetur ab alio extranei status" (Ubertino da Casale, *Declaratio,* 180).

71. "Item unus liber habeatur in qualibet sacristia in quo scribantur omnes res notabiles loci et omnia que licite deponuntur in locis fratrum et nomina deponentium et tempus. Et nullus liber vel res notabilis extra ordinem comodetur sine consilio discretorum, et tunc redigantur in scriptis libro prefato." Andrew G. Little, ed., "Constitutiones provinciae Romanae, anni 1316," *AFH* 18 (1925): 365–66.

72. "Revocat Generalis Minister omnes successiones personales sive per generales, sive per provinciales Ministros, aut alios quoscumque inferiores concessas, tam de libris, quam de elemosyna, seu aliis quibuscumque rebus; et prohibet tales concessiones fieri in futurum. Revocat etiam communitates librorum, idest non vult, quod aliqui fratres libros eis concessos inter se communes habeant, quod eos, quasi pro indiviso possideant sive teneant, vel quod uno eorum defuncto, libri eius alteri cedant." Giuseppe Abate, ed., "Memoriali, statuti ed atti di capitoli generali dei Frati Minori dei sec. XIII e XIV," *MF* 33 (1933): 30.

anything that favored the private use of books by the individual friars.[73] It was true that the papal bull *Exiit qui seminat* had given the general and provincial ministers license to dispose of books within the Order.[74] "Perhaps," wrote Ubertino, "some therefore wish to conclude that canon law gives permission to ministers to appropriate the use of books. But this seems wrong."[75]

Ubertino's claim that friars in effect owned books instead of only using them is proved by another type of evidence found in the medieval Franciscan manuscripts—a wide variety of book curses against potential thieves. Placing a curse on the book is one of the oldest methods of book protection, and it was often used by Western monks, who generally threatened the potential book thief with excommunication.[76] In 1212, a Church council in Paris prohibited the use of book curses, declaring them to have no effect.[77] Despite this decree, however, Franciscans seem to have believed in the discouraging nature of book curses and used them without giving much thought to their incompatibility with the Franciscan Rule. Several thirteenth- and fourteenth-century manuscripts that once belonged to the Franciscan convent of Padua bear versions of the following note on their flyleaves: "This book belongs to the convent of Padua and should remain there. Whoever takes it away shall be cursed and excommunicated." Individual friars sometimes took it to extremes. On a fourteenth-century book from the same convent, the following threat was written in Latin: "This book was given for the use of friar John Cruzania of Padua. Whoever steals it shall be hanged by the neck."[78]

---

73. "Nam nunquam dicit, quod frater aliquis habeat aliquem librum suis usibus spetialiter assignatum, sed dicit, quod ordo et fratres possunt habere usum facti librorum, qui sunt ad divinum cultum et sapientiale studium oportuni" (Ubertino da Casale, *Declaratio,* 178).

74. "Item infra dicit, quod generali et ministris coniunctim et divisim de dispositione usus librorum et aliarum rerum, quarum usum licet fratribus habere, ordinare concedit" (ibid., 179). The relevant passage in *Exiit qui seminat* is "Et ad eas res quarum usum Fratribus licet habere, de Generalis et Provincialium Ministrorum in suis administrationibus conjunctim, vel divisim auctoritate procedat; quibus etiam de dispositione usus talium rerum concedimus ordinare." *BF,* 3:412.

75. "Ex quo forsitan vellent concludere aliquid, quod talem modum appropriandi sibi usum librorum decretalis concederet auctoritatem generali et provintialibus fratribus concedendi. Sed hoc videtur falsum" (Ubertino da Casale, *Declaratio,* 179).

76. On medieval book curses, see M. Drogin, *Anathema! Medieval Scribes and the History of Book Curses* (Totowa-Montclair: A. Schram, 1983), 52–58.

77. "Interdicimus inter alia viris religiosis, ne emittant juramentum de non commodando libros suos indigentibus, cum commodare inter praecipua misericordiae opera computetur. Sed adhibita consideratione diligenti, alii in domo ad opus fratrum retineantur, alii secundum providentiam abbatis, cum indemnitate domus, indigentibus commodentur. Et amodo nullus liber sub anathemate teneatur & omnia praedicta anathemata absolvimus." Mansi, *Sacrorum concilium,* 22, 1166–1225, col. 832.

78. "Iste liber est ad usum fratris Johannis de Cruzania de Padua. Et si quis furabitur per gulam suspendatur." MS. 291, 1, described in Abate e Luisetto, *Codices,* 1:277.

The Study of Philosophy

One other issue related to the pursuit of learning that caused controversy in the Order was the study of philosophy. This particular criticism is, however, best understood within the context of the general suspicion in some clerical circles toward the incorporation of the Aristotelian corpus into the study of theology. In the course of the thirteenth century, the study of Aristotelian philosophy became increasingly popular among scholars in the faculty of arts as well as theology. Studying philosophy meant basically studying Aristotle, who was a pagan. Some of Aristotle's works were only available together with the commentaries of Muslim philosophers like Averroes and Avicenna. As such, many clerical authorities did not welcome the idea of Christian scholars studying the books of pagans and Muslims that did not have a clear and direct contribution to the understanding of Christian theological points. The suspicion surrounding the *libri naturales* of Aristotle can be most clearly observed by their two successive condemnations, in 1210 and 1215, by ecclesiastical authorities who prohibited any public and private lecturing on these books.[79] This was prompted by the spread of intellectual heresy as found in the works of the Parisian masters, David Dinant and Amalric of Bène. In 1228, Pope Gregory IX asked the masters in the theology faculty at Paris specifically not to be inclined to make use of natural philosophy in their theology lectures. He described such an inclination as reckless and impious.[80] In 1231, he ordered all masters of the university not to use the books of natural philosophy that had been condemned at the Council of Paris unless they had been examined and purged of all heretical errors. He further asked the masters and scholars of theology not to "present themselves as philosophers."[81]

The chancellor of the University of Paris in the years 1238–1244, Eudes de Chateauroux, expressed his reservations concerning the penetration of philosophy into the domain of theology in a sermon preached in Paris:

> It is reprehensible that the faculty of theology, which is called the city of sun, truth, and intelligence, strives to speak the language of the philosophers. That is, those who study and teach in the faculty of theology try to submit to the authority and the sayings of the philosophers, as if this would not be betraying all wisdom, from which comes every other

---

79. Monika Asztalos, "The Faculty of Theology," in *A History of the University in Europe*, vol. 1, *Universities in the Middle Ages*, ed. H. de Ridder-Symoens (Cambridge: Cambridge University Press, 1992), 420–21.

80. *CUP,* 1:115.

81. Ibid., 1:138.

wisdom. . . . Many who know almost nothing of the words of theology
or the sayings of the saints have an excellent knowledge of philosophical
discourses and the sayings of the pagans, and they sell themselves as the
sons of Greeks, that is, philosophers.[82]

Despite this reaction against philosophy, in the second half of the thirteenth
century, philosophical books became part of the theology curriculum for those
who planned to pursue the career all the way to the top. This happened in two
stages; first, by 1250–1251, the University of Paris passed a statute making the
regency in arts a prerequisite for inception in theology; this statute was followed
by a similar statute at Oxford University in August.[83] Then, in 1254–1255,
the faculty of arts in the University of Paris officially revised its curriculum to
include Aristotle's books on natural philosophy such as the *Physica, Metaphysica,*
and the *Liber de animalibus.*[84]

The friars who held chairs of theology in Paris and Oxford no doubt felt
pressure to respond to this new development. The Franciscans had some kind of
an arts school in some provinces before 1260, as the term *studia artium* is used in
a Franciscan document that was discovered and published in 2004.[85] Whether
the study of arts entailed only logic, as was the case with the Dominicans, or
whether it included philosophy as well is unknown. Judging by the trends
observed in the intellectual output of prominent Franciscan scholars, the Order
probably set out to incorporate philosophical works into the curriculum of the
friars. Both Angelo Clareno and Ubertino da Casale criticized the introduction
of philosophy into the friars' studies. According to Angelo Clareno, it was for
the first time during the minister generalship of Crescentius of Jesi, 1244–1247,
that "the infertile art of Aristotle," was introduced in the Order.[86] To prepare for
a union with Christ, one must avoid reading the books of pagans and instead
focus on sacred scripture and particularly the life and rules of the holy fathers.[87]

---

82. "Reprehensibile est quod facultas theologiae, quae est et vocatur civitas solis veritatis et intel-
ligentiae, nititur loqui lingua philosophorum, id est illi qui in facultate theologiae student et docent
conantur ei praebere auctoritatem e dictis philosophorum, ac si non fuerit tradita a summa sapientia, a
qua est omnis alia sapientia. . . . Multi, verba theologica et verba sanctorum quasi nihil habentes, verba
philosophica, verba ethnicorum optima arbitrantur, et seipsos vendunt filii Graecorum, id est philosophis."
Eudes de Chateauroux in Paris, Mazarine, n. 356, 214rv, cited in Hauréau, *Notices et extraits,* 4:215–16.
83. Rashdall, *Universities of Europe,* 3:68.
84. "Statutum facultatis artium de modo docendi et regendi in artibus, deque libris qui legendi
esserit" (ibid., 3:277–79).
85. The relevant incipit talks of "Ordinarie scole artium." Cenci, "Vestigia constitutionum praenarbonensium," 93.
86. ". . . et quod oratione relicta, Aristotelis curiosam et sterilem sapientiam divinae praeferebant, et
naturales et dialecticos magistros audire avidius sitiebant, et scholas scientiarum harum habere et multiplicare ardenter procurabant" (Angelo Clareno, *Liber Chronicarum,* 338).
87. "Preparantia vero [ad] Christi Iesu habitationem et mansionem ineffabilem et divinam in nobis,
secundum exterioris hominis mores sunt ista: . . . fuga et evitatio familiaritatis et colloquii hereticorum

He complained that friars took up the study of pagan works directly after the novitiate, and studied too little the works of the saints and the text of the Bible, thereby killing the spirit of piety.[88] Similar to Angelo, Ubertino of Casale wrote in 1310–1312,

> We are founded in the most innocent simplicity, which Christ calls a dove. But this simplicity shuns prolonged pagan studies, and cunning curious words with duplex meanings, sophistical contentions of useless opinions, and the appearance of the false name of science, as the apostle says, but it studies with total devotion the sacred pages and the sayings of the saints.[89]

It is worth noting that Ubertino construed the study of philosophy as a violation of simplicity in a line of argumentation offered by Thomas of Celano and the companions, who saw education essentially as a threat to an important Franciscan trait, simplicity. The reaction against the inclusion of philosophy into theology was neither particularly Franciscan nor "Spiritual," however. One of the famous lectors and preachers of the Order, Thomas of Pavia, was not happy to see philosophy gaining a foothold in the Order. He wrote around 1254 in his *Distinctiones* that in order to comment on Scripture, which was a matter of faith, one did not have to know anything philosophical.[90] Thomas further reproached those whom he called "modern preachers," since they tried to reinforce their sermons from the sayings of philosophers rather than by quoting the Bible.[91]

The general defense for the study of philosophy was that it assisted understanding of the Bible and theology in general, an argument that drew its strength from the *De doctrina christiana* of Augustine.[92] This was in fact a major trend

---

et lectionis librorum paganorum, lectio sacrarum scripturarum et spetialiter in vitis et regulis sanctorum patrum." From an undated letter addressed to "reverendis et diligendis fratribus in Christo Iesu," in Ronald G. Musto, "The Letters of Angelo Clareno (c. 1250–1337)" (PhD diss., Columbia University, 1977), 160, letter 9.

88. "Et quia statim post noviciatum student in scripturis paganicis et postea in questionibus, ut plurimum magis curiosis quam devotis, et parum in dictis sanctorum et textu biblie comparative, spiritum devocionis extinguunt" (Ubertino da Casale, *Responsio*, 73).

89. Ibid., 72.

90. "Vinum philosophiae maxime cavere debemus in intelligentia divinae Scripturae; et ideo Lev. X 9, praecipitur Aaron et filiis eius ut non bibant vinum quando intrant tabernaculum testimonii, quia in exponendo Scripturam, quae fidei est, non debemus sapere quidquam philosophicum" (Longpré, "Les 'Distinctiones," 22).

91. "Haec omnia [verba Domini] oportet acuere contra peccatores, sed tempus malum quando Israelitae vadunt ad acuendum huiusmodi ad Philisthiim, quod fit quando moderni praedicatores nituntur roborare verba sua non secundum sacram Scripturam sed secundum verba philosophorum" (Longpré, "Les 'Distinctiones,'" 21–22).

92. S. Brown, "The Intellectual Context of Later Medieval Philosophy: Universities, Aristotle, Arts, Theology," in *Routledge History of Philosophy*, vol. 3, *Medieval Philosophy*, ed. John Marenbon (London: Routledge, 1998), 189.

in the intellectual world of the thirteenth century, as can be observed in the curricular developments. One of its most influential Franciscan advocates was Bonaventure. In his *On the Reduction of the Arts to Theology,* he used a technique that combined rational/philosophical arguments with arguments based on revelation to prove theological points.[93] Beryl Smalley wrote that Bonaventure set an example by "making the widest possible use of the *Libri naturales*" of Aristotle in his writings.[94] Furthermore, Bonaventure claimed that "if one studies the books of the heretics so that one can understand the truth better by avoiding their arguments, then this is neither curiosity, nor heresy, but orthodoxy (lat: *catholicus*)."[95]

Olivi largely agreed with Bonaventure on this subject. He acknowledged the potential hazards of the study of philosophy, but nevertheless regarded it as an inseparable part of the study of theology. On the one hand, he noted that it was harmful and superfluous to study the auxiliary sciences extensively.[96] Yet while discussing the argument that the study of arts made one garrulous, headstrong, proud, and disobedient, he defended it, asserting that these sciences did not lead to such evil, but that they make the will prone to such bad things as were already found abundantly among the young.[97] He noted that the young were more willing to take up the study of these sciences than the science of theology. However, "even though the corrupt will assumes evil easier from these sciences, we cannot stop learning them," wrote Olivi, "for without these, especially without logic, no one can penetrate fully to the investigation and understanding of sacred scripture."[98]

Despite endorsement from such eminent contemporary scholars, the Franciscan legislation toward philosophy remained cautious. The general and provincial

---

93. Bonaventure, *De reductione artium ad theologiam,* in *Opera omnia* (Quaracchi: Ad Claras Aquas, 1882–1902), 5:317–25.

94. Beryl Smalley, *The Study of the Bible in the Middle Ages,* 3rd ed. (Oxford: Blackwell, 1983), 312.

95. "Si quis enim studeret in dictis haereticorum, ut eorum sententias declinando magis intelligeret veritatem; nec curiosus, nec haereticus, sed catholicus esset" (Delorme, "Textes Franciscaines," 217).

96. "Studere ergo in Sacra Scriptura est perfectivum et viro perfecto competens, informatum conditionibus et circumstantiis supradictis; et etiam studere in aliis scientiis, quantum est necessarium et utile ad praedicta. Amplius autem in ipsis studere, superfluum est et novicum." Olivi's discussion of the question "an studere sit opus de genere suo perfectum" is edited by A. Emmen and F. Simoncioli, in Olivi, "La dottrina dell'Olivi sulla contemplazione, la vita attiva e mista," *Studi Francescani* 61 (1964): 141–59, 151.

97. See objection 14 ibid., 144.

98. "Ad decimum quartum dicendum quod, sicut dictum est, studere in logicis et in aliis scientiis non inducit per se illa mala, quae ratio supponit; sed illorum causa per se est voluntatis perversitas et pronitas voluntatis ad illa mala, quae potissime abundat in iuvenibus. Verum est tamen quod facilius accipit occasionem omnium malorum ex istis scientiis et studio earum, quam ex studio sacrae Scripturae; et ideo tales multa repressione et exercitatione sui indigent, tam per se quam per alios. Licet autem voluntas corrupta ex istis occasionem mali faciliter sumat, non tamen propter hoc sunt nobis non addiscendae; quia sine eis, et specialiter sine logica, nullus potest ad profundam venire, maxime cum voluntas ardens proficiendi in divina perfecte possit ista vitare" (ibid., 157).

constitutions of the late thirteenth century gave the impression that logic and philosophy were regarded as risky occupations, and therefore the young friars and even the lectors who were studying in the schools of arts had to be watched carefully. The provincial constitutions of Tuscany included a decree that in order to be sent to an arts school a friar had to be virtuous, have a fundamental knowledge of grammar and an aptitude for study, should spend at least two years in the Order after his profession, and know how to sing psalms.[99] The same constitutions further decreed that no friar was to teach grammar or logic without the permission of the provincial minister.[100] It was also forbidden for friars to attend the lectures of the seculars in any faculty.[101] Similar to the Tuscan constitutions, the Umbrian constitutions of 1300 ordered that no one should be sent to a studium of arts as a lector or as a student without the permission of the provincial minister. Even more remarkable in this respect is the decree in the provincial statutes of Aquitaine toward the end of thirteenth century, which ordered that young, insolent friars who did not correct themselves despite being warned would be removed from all study of philosophy and be assigned to the study of theology.[102] Finally, the 1313 Barcelona constitutions felt the need to condemn friars' involvement with alchemy and necromancy, occupations closely linked to natural philosophy.[103] These statutes suggest that the Order's administration approached the study of philosophy with caution and tried hard to keep it to the role originally intended for it, as an auxiliary for the study of theology. In this sense, the reactions within the Franciscan Order to the study of philosophy were not much different from those of the medieval intellectual world at large.

Consideration of the complaints made to the pope by a group of Franciscans in 1310–1312, together with a reading of the provincial and general constitutions, reveal the gradual emergence of a culture within the Order that made it very difficult to observe the Order's creed of poverty and humility. From the 1250s onward, the central administration struggled to make sure that provinces

---

99. "Item statuimus quod nullus iuvenis studio loicali deputetur, nisi de cuius vita laudabili constet et de cuius ingenio et fundamento grammaticae et aptitudine ad scientiam profectus laudabilis praesumatur. Ita tamen quod post professionem in ordine egerit duos annos, et sciat competenter cantare, si habet aptitudinem ad cantandum, nisi monistro videatur circa aliquem vel aliquos, propter bonam idoneitatem, quantum ad secundum annum aliter faciendum." C. Cenci, ed., "Costituzioni della provincia Toscana tra i secoli XIII e XIV," *Studi Francescani* 80 (1983): 188–89.

100. "Nullus frater doceat in grammatica vel loica sine ministri licentia" (ibid., 190).

101. "Nullus frater audiat aliquem lectionem ab aliquo saeculari in aliqua facultate" (ibid., 187).

102. "Item iuvenes insolentes, si moniti non se correxerint, ab omni philosophie studio amoveantur et theologie studio assignentur" (Bihl, "Statuta provincialia provinciarum Aquitaine," 481).

103. "Item, vult Minister Generalis de voluntate et assensu Capituli Generalis, quod in constitutione edita contra alchimistas, nigromanticos, et ceteros maleficos, immediate post illud 'nisi per Generalem' ponatur sic. 'vel Provinciale Ministrum de consilio discretorum, sive per eum, cui ipsi in speciali duxerint committendum'" (Abate, "Memoriali, statuti ed atti," 33).

observed the Order's official legislation and the Rule, but perhaps too much was still left to the discretion of provincial ministers. When we look at what went on in the Order on a day-to-day basis, the controversy about Olivi's theory of *usus pauper* seems to fade into the background, when much more clear-cut violations, such as the appropriation of books, come across as epidemic among the friars. It is difficult to see, however, how the Order could exalt learning and make the learned its leaders, and yet forcefully convince the friars not to spend their alms on books. The complaints considered above are selected for being particularly related to the rise of learning in the Order. Even though the statutes have been often cited to place these complaints in context, without a proper appreciation of the Franciscan system of education and the management of books in the Order an understanding of these complaints will be incomplete. What kind of an educational organization did the friars establish over the years that allowed for these abuses to occur? Consideration of the particulars of this organization, along with the features of the Order's management of books, will also help reveal the considerable success of Franciscan scholars in the intellectual arena of medieval Europe, highlighting the many advantages a Franciscan scholar enjoyed over his secular colleagues.

❦ CHAPTER 5

The Educational System around 1310

Franciscan educational organization experienced rapid change throughout the thirteenth century paralleling the Order's spectacular expansion in both recruits and new provinces, changes in the university curricula, and the diverse roles the friars assumed in the ecclesiastical world. This change was so rapid that a general description of the Franciscan educational organization in the Middle Ages would be confusing and misleading. What follows, therefore, is something of a snapshot of the educational framework around 1310, tracing the steps of a virtual friar from novitiate all the way to the master of theology in Paris. The choice of 1310 as the date for this snapshot is not arbitrary but rather complements the story narrated in the previous chapter.

The Novitiate

Innocent III had determined the minimum age of entry into a religious Order as fourteen.[1] It is safe, then, to assume that until 1260, when the General Chapter of Narbonne fixed the earliest age of entry for the Franciscan Order at eighteen,[2] the earliest formal age of entry into the Franciscan Order must have been fourteen. Neither the Rule nor the pre-Narbonne constitutions regulated the age of

---

1. Livarius Oliger, "De pueris oblatis in ordine minorum (cum textu hucusque inedito fr. Ioannis Pecham)," *AFH* 8 (1915): 393.
2. Narbonne-Assisi-Paris, 39.

entry; hence it seems that the Order relied on the relevant statute of canon law.[3] In fact, we know from a variety of sources that candidates even below fourteen were received into the Order.[4] After the minimum age was set at eighteen, exception was still made for those who had an excellent education or physical constitution, so that they could be accepted once they were fifteen years old.[5] The Order did not want to miss the chance to recruit those young students of the arts faculty who were predisposed to lead the life of a regular. Probably not wishing to lose good students to the Franciscans, in 1265 Dominicans followed this lead and they too reduced the age of entry from eighteen to fifteen in exceptional cases where a candidate was well educated.[6]

In practice, not much changed with the introduction of the minimum age of eighteen, since the decision about the reception of minors was left in the end to the initiative of local administrators. The concern about an age requirement might have had to do as much with the candidates' proficiency in Latin as with their spiritual maturity. As education in the thirteenth century was exclusively in Latin, sufficient knowledge of Latin was a prerequisite to follow the lectures. A Dominican subprior was punished by his Order for recruiting ill-educated boys by making him personally teach them Latin.[7] The Franciscans insisted on knowledge of grammar or logic as a condition for recruitment.[8] For them, teaching basic Latin in the convent would be a clear violation of the Rule, which explicitly forbade the illiterate to learn their letters.[9] Only in the last decade of the thirteenth century do we come across the term *studium of arts* (*studium in artibus*) in the Franciscan constitutions, specifically intended for the young and perhaps offering an advanced grammar education as well as logic.[10] The first mention of a specific education in grammar is as late as 1316, when the

---

3. Bert Roest seems to think that eighteen was the earliest age of entry even before the Narbonne constitutions. Roest, *History of Franciscan Education,* 240; and Roest, "Franciscan Educational Perspectives: Reworking Monastic Traditions," in *Medieval Monastic Education,* ed. George Ferzoco and Carolyn Muessig (London: Leicester University Press, 2000), 170. Yet I could not find statutory evidence to support the theory that prior to 1260 the OFM had fixed a different age of entry other than that specified in canon law.

4. Roest, *History of Franciscan Education,* 66.

5. "Ordinamus etiam, ut nullus recipiatur citra XVIII annum, nisi per robur corporis vel industriam sensus seu per excellentem aedificationem, a XV anno et supra, aetas secundum prudentium iudicium supleatur" (Narbonne-Assisi-Paris, 39).

6. Mulchahey, *"First the bow is bent,"* 84. In fact, Mulchahey does not give any clear evidence when exactly the earliest age of entry was fixed at eighteen. She says that the practice was introduced between 1232 and 1235 without citing any statutes. Ibid., 76, n. 8.

7. Ibid., 85.

8. "Quod nullus recipiatur in Ordine nostro, nisi sit talis clericus qui sit competenter instructus in grammatica vel logica" (Narbonne-Assisi-Paris, 39, no. 3).

9. "Non curent nescientes litteras litteras discere" (RB, chap. 10, 235).

10. "Item, vult Generale Capitulum, quod Ministri in suis provinciis ordinent Studia in artibus pro iuvenibus provincie instruendis" (Abate, "Memoriali, statuti ed atti," 28).

Roman province ordered that *studia grammaticalia, logicalia, et philosophica* should be instituted in various convents—borrowing the clause of the General Chapter of 1292—"for the education of the young."[11] A few scholars have argued that the Franciscans provided or needed grammar education in the thirteenth century, but there is no solid normative or practical evidence to support this.[12] The argument that grammar schools were needed is not a strong one, since the entry age, fourteen or fifteen, was not a young age to be competent in Latin grammar—the normal age to start Latin grammar in the Middle Ages was between seven and nine.[13]

How much Latin, then, was necessary to take the Franciscan habit? When asked a similar question, Bonaventure said: "It suffices if the candidate knows enough grammar to enable him to go on to become a confessor or preacher or lector, lest through a lack of such knowledge he be unable to carry out these offices."[14] Those who were destined for the office of lector had to possess a reasonable knowledge of Latin grammar to be able to follow subtle scholastic arguments, not to mention the complex system of abbreviations in scholastic manuscripts.[15] Probably for this reason the Narbonne constitutions decreed that friars should not be sent to the Paris studium before having studied for three or four years in some other studium in their province or nearby. An exception was made for those who were already sufficiently learned; they could be sent right after the novitiate.[16] In the early years, it was thus the schoolmasters, or masters and students of arts who were sent to Paris for the advanced study of theology. A student in the Paris studium and the author of the *Introduction to the Eternal Gospel,* Gerard of Borgo di San Donnino, had been a grammar teacher in Sicily before he joined the Order.[17] John of Parma was a renowned logician before

---

11. "Item ordinentur per ministrum studia grammaticalia, logicalia et philosophica in locis diversis, ad que gradatim mittantur iuvenes secundum capacitatem et aptitudinem ipsorum." A. G. Little, ed., "Constitutiones provinciae Romanae, anni 1316," *AFH* 18 (1925): 368.

12. Roest, *History of Franciscan Education,* 137–38; and Roest, "Franciscan Educational Perspectives," 178, n. 7. Alfonso Maierù suggested that Franciscans "needed grammar schools." Alfonso Maierù, *University Training in Medieval Europe* (Leiden: Brill, 1994), 10.

13. Lynn Thorndike, "Elementary and Secondary Education in the Middle Ages," *Speculum* 15 (1940): 405.

14. Monti's translation, in Bonaventure of Bognoregio, *Works of St. Bonaventure,* 5:206.

15. On the difficulty of scholastic Latin, see Thorndike, "Elementary and Secondary," 406.

16. "Item mittendi Parisius ad studentum, primo exerceantur tribus vel duobus annis post novitiatum in aliquo Studio suae provinciae vel vicinae, nisi adeo fuerint litterati, quod post novitiatum continuo possint mitti. Non mittantur tamen nisi de auctoritate Ministri, cum consilio et assensu capituli provincialis" (Narbonne-Assisi-Paris, 12, no. 72).

17. "Et nota quod iste qui fecit istum libellum dictus est frater Ghirardinus de Burgo Sancti Donini, qui in Sicilia nutritus fuit in seculo et ibi docuit in gramatica. Et cum intrasset Ordinem fratrum Minorum, processu temporis missus fuit Parisius pro provintia Sicilie et factus est lector in theologia" (Salimbene, 660).

he took the habit.[18] And the early regent masters Adam of Marsh, Thomas of York, and Bonaventure were all students in the arts faculty when they joined the Order.[19]

Types of Studia

Once the year of the novitiate was over and the novice had made his profession, he could be sent to a studium provided that he knew the Divine Office quite well and had been instructed in singing the psalms.[20] The course of studies that a friar followed after the novitiate depended on his level of education. If the newly professed already had an advanced level of theology, as was the case for the students who joined the Order while studying theology in the universities, he could be directly given the office of lector without further education. If he had been a student of arts, then he would be sent to one of the studia generalia of the Order to become a lector, provided that he could satisfy the character requirements. These were rare cases, however. Generally, if the friar had only a working knowledge of Latin, then he would be sent to a studium in the province to receive introductory theology classes.

Studium is never defined in the Franciscan constitutions. The first time that we come across the term is in the 1239 constitutions, where it designates a physical place in the convent, probably the place where the friars had their classes and perhaps where they studied outside of lecture hours. The relevant statute requires silence from both residents and visitors when they are in a cloister, choir, studium, dormitory, or refectory.[21] Dominican constitutions routinely used two terms to designate the schools in the Order. One is *schola,* which existed in every convent and simply stood for the convent school,[22] and the other is *studium,* which stood for a *schola* bigger in size, which existed therefore only in some convents and where the level of teaching was higher than in a *schola*. Because of the lack of information on early Franciscan convent education, scholars have used the Dominican term *schola* and applied it to Franciscan cases.[23] However, unlike in

---

18. "Revera magister Iohanninus dicebatur frater Iohannes, cum in secula docebat in loyca" (ibid., 297).

19. Ibid., 237.

20. "Item nullus ad professionem per aliquem ministro inferiorem recipi valeat, nisi sciat divinum officium in breviario dicere; nec mittantur professi ad studium, nisi competenter divinum sciverint officium et in cantu aliqualiter sint instructi" (Delorme, *Constitutiones provinciae provincie,* 421).

21. Pre-Narbonne, 83, no. 52.

22. Mulchahey, "Dominican Studium System," 302. Heinrich Denifle has argued that for school localities and *Hörsäle, scholae* was used. For a discussion of the terms *studium, schola,* and *studium generale,* see Denifle, *Die Entstehung der Universitäten des Mittelalters bis 1400* (Graz: Akademische Druck-u. Verlagsanstalt, 1956), 9.

23. Attilio B. Langeli wrote about the Franciscans that their bigger *scholae* were called *studia:* "Tali scholae erano di tipi e livelli diversi; le maggiore erano dette studia, e ne esistevano di generalia, provincialia, specialia" (Langeli, "I libri dei frati," 284).

the Dominican case, not every Franciscan convent had a classroom or a study place simply because there was not a lector in every convent.[24] The only Franciscan statute that mentions *scholae* is from the province of Provence, where all friars were compelled to frequent *scholae* and to show an interest in the repetition of the lectures.[25] *Studium* appears to be the main Franciscan term used to indicate both a place of a study in an ordinary convent and also a convent that was indentified with its school, as in the "Paris studium."

The level of education offered by a studium varied, but unlike the Dominicans, Franciscans were not in the habit of distinguishing their studia as particular types. The substitution of Dominican terminology and the extrapolation backward of late fourteenth-century terms have prompted historians to assign names like *studia solemnia* and *studia generalia principalia*. This has created confusion when it comes to exploring the thirteenth-century educational organization of the Order. In reality, Franciscans used only three terms in the thirteenth and early fourteenth century: *studium, studium generale,* and *studium provinciale.* The Franciscan system of studia, however, was more complicated than the terminology would lead us to believe.

Theology Schools

Constitutional evidence suggests the presence of four different kinds of theological studia in the Order with varying levels of theology education. At the bottom lies what is simply referred to as *studium* or *studium theologiae,* such as the studia found in the custodies of a province. In these studia, generally a commentary on a book of the Bible would be read cursorily by a lector. One degree above these studia are the studia provincialia. In 1303, for the first time, in the provincial constitutions of Strasbourg, we find this new term, *studium provinciale.* The relevant statute orders the foundation of two "studia provincialia," which will be provided with a sufficient number of lectors. "These lectors," the decree goes on, "will lecture and dispute as it is customary in studia." To these studia every custody will send one student, and only these students would then be eligible to be sent to the studium of Strasbourg, unless a student was so learned that he could be sent to the Strasbourg studium directly by virtue

---

24. That not every convent had a studium is evident also from the provincial constitution of Aquitaine in the thirteenth century, which refers to "those convents where there is a *studium theologiae*": "In quocunque autem conventu, ubi est *studium* theologie, duo paria indumentorum aurifrigiata habera valeant, pro solempnitatibus maioribus" (Bihl, "Statuta provincialia provinciarum Aquitaine," 476).

25. "Item compellantur fratres frequentare scolas, et lectionum repetitionibus interesse" (Little, "Statuta provincialia provinciae Franciae," 451).

of his own merit.[26] Clearly, the Strasbourg studium offered a higher level of theology education than the studia provincialia. The relevant statute does not give any information about how the teaching in these two studia provincialia differed from that of a custodial school. All we can say for certain is that they offered a higher education than was available in a custodial school, and were preparatory to the studium of Strasbourg. The reason for creating such studia provincialia may have been to provide a buffer against the overcrowding of the Strasbourg studium.

One degree above such studia provincialia were the studia where Peter Lombard's *Sentences* as well as the Bible would be read. Such studia were generally to be found in the large and important friaries of a province. For the sake of convenience, we can call them advanced studia.[27] The lack of evidence does not allow us to know which friaries had an advanced studium around 1310; the earliest evidence we have is from 1336. The constitutions of 1336 listed the convents that were not called studia generalia in the Order, but where Peter Lombard's *Sentences* were read: Rouen, Reims, Metz, Bruges, London, York, Norwich, Newcastle, Stamford, Coventry, Exeter, Bordeaux, Narbonne, Marseilles, Asti, Oradea, Prague, Pisa, Erfurt, Rimini, and Todi.[28] As we see from this list, while some provinces—Dacia, for example—did not have such a studium, the province of England had seven studia where the *Sentences* were read (London, York, Norwich, Newcastle, Stanford, Coventry, Exeter). England is generally an exception in the Franciscan Order, since it uniquely possessed two university faculties of theology (Oxford and Cambridge) within its borders. It was also probably the province with the highest number of lectors per friar in the Order. To this fact we need to add that the provinces of Ireland and Scotland, for which there is no recorded studium in the thirteenth century, relied heavily on the English province for their educational needs.

These advanced studia would accept students from outside their province, a feature they shared in common with the studia generalia of the Order. In fact, failure to take this point into consideration has led to many erroneous

---

26. "Item ordinamus quod duo studia provincialia in nostra Provincia habeantur, quibus de Lectoribus sufficienter provideatur, qui legant et disputent secundum quod in studiis est consuetum. Ad quae studia quaelibet Custodia studentem unum mittat, quem etiam vestire teneatur. Nec aliquis studens mittatur in Argentinam, qui non fuerit in praedictis studiis exercitatus, nisi adeo intelligens fuerit, quod merito statim mitti possit" (Fussenegger, "Statuta provinciae Alemanie," 250).

27. The reader can find a more detailed analysis and more ample documentary evidence on the advanced studia and the studia generale of the Franciscan Order in Neslihan Şenocak, "The Franciscan Studium Generale: A New Interpretation," in *Philosophy and Theology in the Studia of the Religious Orders and at Papal and Royal Courts,* ed. K. Emery Jr., W. J. Courtenay, and S. M. Metzger, 221–36 (Turnhout: Brepols, 2012). What follows summarizes some of the arguments given there.

28. M. Bihl, "Ordinationes A Benedicto XII Pro Fratribus Minoribus Promulgatae Per Bullam 28 Novembris 1336," *AFH* 30 (1937): 356.

identifications of Franciscan studia as studia generalia, since scholars have assumed that only the studia generalia would admit students from outside their respective provinces, an idea once again based on the assumption that Franciscan educational organization resembled that of the Dominicans. There is, however, enough evidence to show that it was not only studia generalia that accepted students from outside the studium's own province.[29] The 1292 provincial of Tuscany, in response to the request of the general chapter summoned the same year, asked all custodies to provide for the friars they had *in generalibus studiis et in aliis studiis extra provinciam.*[30] The 1292 general chapter of Paris ordered that during the long summer holiday, when the lectures had stopped, the foreign students in Oxford should be distributed between Cambridge and London in proportion with the number of foreign students that were already in these two convents.[31] The existence of foreign students in London suggests that the convent offered advanced-level theology training, but it was certainly not a studium generale.[32]

Above the advanced studia were the studia generalia.[33] These offered the highest possible level of theology training. To become a lector, it was necessary to study at a studium generale.[34] In the thirteenth century, the studia generalia of Paris and Oxford, and later on of Cambridge, were distinguished from the rest. The studia in these towns were incorporated into the university, which meant that the Franciscan master teaching there was also member of the board of regent masters in the theology faculty of the university. This also meant that the student-friars studying with such a master of theology had the right to incept—that is, to graduate from the university and have the title of doctor of theology. The studia generalia did not offer only this highest level of training. In a studium generale like Paris or Florence, there would be theological training at the general, custodial, and provincial levels as well.[35] To determine which convents in the Order featured a studium generale is rather difficult; intuitively, however,

---

29. "Item quaelibet provincia induat suos studentes, quos mittit ad provincias alienas, illis exceptis, qui ex debito mittuntur Parisius, et exceptis studentibus provinciae Franciae, qui ad alias mittuntur provincias, et exceptis etiam provinciae Romanae studentibus, qui mittuntur ex debito ad Studia aliena" (Narbonne-Assisi-Paris, 79, no. 20g).

30. Cenci, "Costituzioni della provincia Toscana" (1983), no. 27.

31. "Ut tempore vacationis maioris onus conventus Oxonie aliqualiter relevetur, ordinat generale capitulum, quod studentes ibidem de provinciis inter ipsam Oxoniensem et Londonensem et Cantebrigiensem conventus pro tertia parte, connumeratis aliis studentibus extraneis, qui in prefatis Londonensi et Cantebrugiensi conventibus fuerint, ad ministri provincialis arbitrium dividantur." Franz Ehrle, ed., "Memorialia ministro Anglie," in "Die ältesten Redaktionen der Generalkonstitutionen des Franziskaner Ordens," *ALKG* 6 (1892): 63.

32. In the 1336 constitutions of Benedict XII, London is counted among the advanced studia of the Order, where Sentences was read: it was therefore not a studium generale.

33. For a more in-depth analysis of the studia generalia, see Şenocak, "Franciscan Studium Generale."

34. This is implied in the Narbonne-Assisi-Paris, 72, nos. 12–16.

35. For Paris, see William J. Courtenay, "The Parisian Franciscan Community in 1303," *FS* 53 (1993): 164–65. For Florence, see Şenocak, "Franciscan Studium Generale," 232–34.

the following factors—especially if more than one factor is present—increase the likelihood of a convent hosting a studium generale: the existence of a university in the town of the convent; the presence of masters of theology or Parisian-educated lectors or the presence of several lectors; and the presence of a substantial library and any significant spatial enlargement of sufficient size to host a general chapter. Based on these factors and taking into account the advanced studia listed above for the year of 1336, I have come up with a list of likely studia generalia by 1336. These were Paris, Oxford, Cambridge, Bologna, Toulouse, Cologne, Curia Romana, Rome, Milan, Montpellier, Padua, Florence, Strasbourg, Assisi, Perugia, Barcelona, and Lyon.[36]

Philosophy and Arts Schools

Our understanding of the study of arts and philosophy in the Franciscan Order is to this day incomplete due to confusion with regard to terminology. The first time a school of arts was mentioned in an official Franciscan document, around the 1250s, the term used was *studium artium*.[37] The constitutions use a number of terms: in 1292, the General Chapter of Paris ordered the ministers to open *studium in artibus* in their provinces for the education of the young, which might mean that these studia were to provide education in advanced grammar and logic.[38] The Provincial Chapter of Tuscany in the same year decreed that no young friar was to be sent to the *studium loicale* unless he had led a praiseworthy life and had a fundamental knowledge of grammar and an aptitude to learning.[39] The singular—studium—indicates that there was only one such school in the Tuscan province, one that had probably just been founded following the decree of the General Chapter. The chapter of the province of Saint Francis in 1300 uses the term *studia artium* when it orders the foundation of schools of arts, more than one in this case, in the province.[40] Some provinces appear to have been keener on education in the arts than others. In 1303, the province

---

36. For the documentary evidence to support the factors listed here, and the reasons of the inclusion of individual studia in this list, please see Şenocak, "Franciscan studium generale," 225–32.

37. The relevant incipit talks of *"ordinarie scole artium."* Cenci, "Vestigia constitutionum praenarbonensium," 93.

38. "Item, vult Generale Capitulum, quod Ministri in suis provinciis ordinent Studia in artibus pro iuvenibus provincie instruendis" (Abate, "Memoriali, statuti ed atti," 28).

39. "Item statuimus quod nullus iuvenis studio loicali deputetur nisi de cuius vita laudabili constet et de cuius ingenio et fundamento grammaticae et aptitudine ad scientiam profectus laudabilis praesumatur." C. Cenci, ed., "Costituzioni della Provincia Toscana Tra I Secoli XIII e XIV," *Studi Francescani* 80 (1983), 188–89.

40. "Item ordinentur studia artium in provincia, in quibus nullus ponatur lector vel studens, nisi per ministrum fuerit assignatus; et de eis bona sollicitudino et cura diligens habeatur." C. Cenci, ed., "Ordinazioni dei Capitoli Provinciali Umbri dal 1300 al 1305," *CF* 55 (1985): 22.

of Strasbourg decreed that each custody should have at least one *studium philosophiae vel artium*.[41] Assuming that *"vel"* is used to designate a synonym rather than two distinct types of studium, we have then a third term, *studium philosophiae*, to designate a studium of arts. As mentioned earlier, around 1316 the Roman province ordered that *studia grammaticalia, logicalia, et philosophica* should be founded in various convents for the education of the young.[42] The Latin is slightly ambiguous, but it seems most likely that this concerned schools that would offer training in all three disciplines, rather than three different types of schools. In the mid-fourteenth century, there was a studium for logic in Cortona that trained friar-students of the province of Tuscany.[43]

How to interpret this scattered evidence? In the 1250s there might have been only a few schools in the Order that formally taught the arts. By 1292, however, at least one school teaching the arts was made obligatory for each province. The Narbonne constitutions of 1260 do not make any mention of the study of philosophy or the natural sciences. The 1279 General Chapter of Assisi decreed that during the holidays, philosophy and law should not be taught in the schools of theology, or by the lector of theology, but at some other time and in another place, whenever there was a chance.[44] This suggests that the teaching of arts was done on an irregular basis and according to the availability of suitable teachers. Such a construction also fits with Roger Bacon's perpetual complaints to the papacy that many Franciscans studied theology without a knowledge of philosophy and logic. In his *Compendium studii philosophiae*, written in 1271–1272, Bacon complained about the lack of philosophical knowledge among novices.[45] He argued that the young novices who entered the Order started immediately with the study of theology, without having a proper knowledge of philosophy first, and whenever friars studied philosophy, they did it alone and without an instructor.[46]

---

41. "Habeat etiam quaelibet Custodia studium unum philosophiae vel artium ad minus, quo studentes sufficienter instructi ad memorata studia provincialia transferantur" (ibid.).

42. See n. 11 above. Roest (*History of Franciscan Education,* 67) suggests that these arts schools were called *studia particularia* in many sources. However, I have not found any Franciscan document dating from before 1310 where such a term was used.

43. "Ista loyca est ad usum fratris Iohannis...de florentia ordinis sancti Francisci quam emit 6 florenis....studentus in loycalibus apud cortona." Florence, Biblioteca Laurenziana Medicea, Plut XXII Sin II, f. 213v.

44. "Iura vero et philosophica in scholis theologiae ab eodem lectore et eodem tempore non legantur, sed alibi et alias, ubi fuerit opportunum" (Narbonne-Assisi-Paris, 76, 11d).

45. For the dating of the work, see Jeremiah Hackett, "Roger Bacon: His Life, Career and Works," in *Roger Bacon and the Sciences: Commemorative Essays,* ed. Jeremiah Hackett (Leiden: Brill, 1997), 22.

46. "Unde plura millia intrant qui nesciunt legere Psalterium nec Donatum; sed statim post professionem ponuntur ad studium theologiae. Et a principio ordinis, scilicet a tempore quo primo floruit studium in ordinibus, primi studentes fuerunt tales, sicut posteriores. Et dederunt se illi studio theologiae, quod omnem sapientiam desiderat humanam. Et ideo oportuit quod non proficerent ullo modo, paecipue cum non procuraverunt se instrui ab aliis in philosophia, postquam ingressi sunt. Et maxime quia

The Dominican Order also introduced training in the arts into its official curriculum in the 1250s. In 1259, the Order made the decision to have one studium of arts in every province.[47] As the Dominicans had twelve provinces then, as opposed to the thirty-two provinces of the Franciscans, it was probably more feasible for the Dominicans to have one such school in each province. As Michèle Mulchahey has significantly stressed, this was not arts in the Parisian sense, where the arts faculty was overrun by Aristotelian philosophy.[48] Arts education in the Dominican Order meant logic and logic alone.[49]

There is no good evidence to know what exactly was taught in the Franciscan arts schools, and how it was done. Although they are called, in some instances, *studium loicale,* this does not necessarily suggest that only logic was taught. It might be useful to take a look at the library inventory of the Gubbio convent that housed a custodial school,[50] and the library inventory of the Todi convent that housed an advanced theology studium. In the Gubbio inventory, which around 1300 shows roughly two hundred books, only two volumes concern natural philosophy, one called *Libri naturales* and the other *Liber de animalibus.*[51] On the other hand, we find around thirteen logic and grammar books. The Todi convent presents a different picture. Its earliest surviving library inventory dates from the first decade of 1300 and has separate sections for the books of philosophy and the books of logic. The philosophy books number nineteen, including Aristotle's books on natural philosophy, his ethics and metaphysics, and commentaries written on these by Thomas Aquinas, Adam of Buckfield, and Aegidius Romanus. In the logic section twelve books are listed that include the *Logica nova* and *Logica vetus* of Aristotle, along with commentaries on various other books by Aristotle that are related to logic.[52] The presence of books of

---

praesumpserunt in ordinibus investigare philosophiam per se sine doctore; ita quod facti sunt magistri in theologia et philosophia antequam fuerunt discipuli; et ideo regnat apud eos error infinitus, licet non appareat propter causas certas, Deo permittente et diabolo procurante." Roger Bacon, *Compendium studii philosophiae,* in *Opera,* 1:426.

47. Mulchahey, *"First the bow is bent,"* 220–23.

48. In 1252, the faculty of arts was proclaimed to be the faculty of rational, natural, and moral philosophy. For an excellent discussion of the domination of philosophy in the faculty of arts, see Mary Martin McLaughlin, *Intellectual Freedom and Its Limitations in the University of Paris in the Thirteenth and Fourteenth Centuries* (New York: Arno Press, 1977), 40–45.

49. "Dominican studia *artium* did not solve the problem of university arts equivalency, because the teaching of natural philosophy, Aristotelian or otherwise, was not a part of their mandate. Dominican studia artium were logic schools" (Mulchahey, *"First the bow is bent,"* 224).

50. The reader will find that the Gubbio inventory in Pulignani, "La biblioteca Francescana di Gubbio," actually lists 234 books, but this number includes the later additions to the library. Gubbio was the head convent of the custody of Gubbio in the Umbrian province. On this particular inventory, see also Neslihan Şenocak, "Early Franciscan Library Catalogues: The Case of the Gubbio Catalogue (c. 1300)," *Scriptorium* 59 (2005): 29–50.

51. Pulignani, "La biblioteca Francescana di Gubbio," 163.

52. See Şenocak, "Earliest Library Catalogue," 499–503.

grammar and philosophy alongside the books of logic is a possible indication of the diversity of material covered in the schools of arts in the Order.

The Number of Studia in the Order

One of the striking differences between the Dominican and Franciscan educational organizations is the number of studia. While no Dominican convent would be founded without a *schola,* there was no such condition for the establishment of Franciscan convents. The number of studia in the Franciscan Order increased gradually and slowly. By 1240, many provinces had only one or two studia. Around 1241–1242, the four masters wrote in their commentary that there were students "only in a few places compared to the rest."[53] By 1310, in most urbanized provinces, there might have been a studium in every custody.[54] This was the case even before 1260 in the province of England and in the province of Marches of Treviso by 1280. In this province, the head convent was Padua, whose studium was probably a studium generale by 1280. In the custody of Padua, there was also a lector present in the convent of Vicenza.[55] In the custody of Venice, lectors were present in the convents of Venice and Treviso, in 1273 and 1285 respectively.[56] In the custody of Verona, a lector was recorded in the Verona convent for the year of 1286.[57] Finally, a lector was present in the convent of Udine in 1292, which belonged to the custody of Friuli.[58] It is important to note here that the presence of a lector in a convent did not necessarily make it a studium, since, as Ubertino complained, some lectors did not teach despite having the office.[59] One of the possible indications for the presence of a studium in a convent is the physical size of a convent, since

---

53. This comes up in the third chapter on discussion of the Divine Office: "Item cum levitas sit in nobis maxime reprobanda, et fratres multi proniores sint ad otium quam ad orationem et in paucis locis comparatione partis residuae sint studentes, et fratres clerici ad faciendum officium sanctae romanae ecclesiae teneantur, mutatio facta officii multos gravat" (Oliger, *Expositio quatuor magistrorum,* 138).

54. Franciscan provinces were divided into custodies. In each custody, there were often four to ten convents. We do not know when this division into custodies was introduced. For the custodial breakdown of all provinces, see Conrad Eubel, ed., *Provinciale ordinis Fratrum Minorum vetustissimum secundum Codicem Vaticanum Nr. 1960* (Florence: Ad Claras Aquas, 1898), 62–63.

55. The earliest date when a lector was recorded in Vicenza was 1285. Antonio Sartori, *Archivio Sartori: Documenti di storia e arte Francescana,* vol. 3/1, *Evoluzione del Francescanesimo nelle Tre Venezie. Monasteri, contrade, località abitanti di Padova Medioevale,* ed. Giovanni Luisetto (Padua: Biblioteca antoniana, 1988), 352.

56. Ibid., 354.

57. Ibid., 352.

58. Antonio Sartori, *Archivio Sartori, 2/2, La Provincia del Santo dei Frati Minori Conventuali,* ed. Giovanni Luisetto (Padua, 1986), 1737.

59. William J. Courtenay, "Academic Formation and Careers of Mendicant Friars: A Regional Approach," in *Studio e studia: Le scuole degli Ordini Mendicanti tra XIII e XIV secolo* (Spoleto: Centro italiano di studi sull'alto Medioevo, 2002), 204–5, 210.

the convents with a studium had to have additional space for a classroom, a library, and cells to accommodate visiting student friars from other convents or custodies. In general, the convents with a studium would have been physically the largest ones in a custody. In fact, in the first half of the thirteenth century we witness a rebuilding and enlargement program for several convents in England. It is no coincidence that the convents that were enlarged were often those with a studium. Eccleston tells us that during the time when Albert of Pisa was the provincial minister, the convents of Northampton, Hereford, and Gloucester were altered.[60] All of these convents hosted a school. In 1258, King Henry III granted timber to the Northampton convent for the building of the school there.[61]

Assignments of Studia to Provinces and Vice Versa

The decision regarding which province would send students to which studia, and from which provinces to admit students, was made by the General Chapter. The centralization of this decision probably resulted from the uneven distribution of studia, which was a unique feature of the Franciscan educational organization. By 1290, only six Dominican provinces had a studium generale, which exclusively served the students of that province, Paris being an exception.[62] The Franciscan case was drastically different because not all thirty-two provinces had a studium generale or even an advanced studium, while a province like England enjoyed an embarrassment of riches with more than one studium generale and several advanced studia. Thus we find the 1285 General Chapter of Milan deciding that the province of Aquitaine could send one student to each of the studia of Oxford, Assisi, and Bologna, and it could accept one student to its own studium in Toulouse from each of these provinces: Dacia, Austria, Cologne, Touraine, France, Burgundy, Castille, Santiago, Saint Francis, and Rome.[63]Apparently, sometimes provincial administrations did not necessarily follow the decisions of the General Chapter, and in some provinces, ministers took matters into their own hands. Thus, the 1292 provincial constitutions of Tuscany order that the provincial minister cannot admit any student

---

60. Eccleston, 44.

61. Moorman, *Grey Friars in Cambridge,* 21.

62. Mulchahey, "*First the bow is bent,*" 351, 355n.

63. "Item provintie, que possunt mittere studentes ad studium Tholose Dacia, Austria 1, Colonia, Turonia 1, Francia 1, Burgundia unum, Castella 1, provintia sancti Jacobi 1, provintia sancti Francisci 1, provincia Romana.—Provintia Aquitaine potest mittere unum studentem Oxonie, Assisii unum, Bononie unum." André Callebaut, "Acta capituli generalis mediolani celebrati an. 1285," *AFH* 22 (1929): 290.

from outside the province to a studium in Tuscany without the consent of the Provincial Chapter.[64]

This situation seems to have gotten out of hand, since the General Chapter of 1295 specifically asked all the provincial ministers to call back their students who were studying in other provinces, particularly those that had already completed their fourth year in the study of theology. Those who had not were to be transferred to the studia assigned to their province.[65] Examples similar to the studia and student assignments of Aquitaine survive also from 1307 and 1310 for the province of Milan.[66] In the General Chapter of 1307, it was decided that the province of Milan could send students to four studia: Oxford, Bologna, Perugia, and Strasbourg.[67] Among these, Oxford and Bologna were definitely studia generalia. It is difficult to say with certainty whether the studia of Perugia (in the province of Saint Francis) and of Strasbourg (in the province of Germany Superior) had the status of studia generalia or were simply advanced studia by 1307.[68] In the next General Chapter of 1310, the province of Milan was this time assigned the studia of Oxford, Montpellier, Padua, Florence, and Rome.[69] We know for certain that the studium of the Rome convent was not a studium generale in 1310, since the same chapter ordered that in the Roman province, at the main convent of Rome or anywhere else where the Provincial Chapter thought suitable, a studium generale should be founded.[70] The *memoralia* also recorded which provinces could send students to the Milan studium. In 1307, the number of such provinces were seven: the two geographically close provinces of Saint Anthony and Tuscany, and then others further afield—Aquitaine, Bohemia, and the southern Italian

64. "Item, minister nullum studentem de extraneis provinciis recipiat in aliquo studio nostrae provinciae sine capituli provincialis assensu" (Cenci, "Costituzioni della provincia Toscana" [1983]: 190).

65. "Mandat autem generalis minister ministris omnibus omnes fratres suos in studiis existendes, qui compleverint tempus studii a quadriennio supra, debeant in proximo provinciali capitulo ad suas provincias revocare; aut si tempus praedictum non compleverint; transferre eos debeant ad studia nunc suae provinciae assignata. Et si aliquis ultra ordinationem praedictam in studiis propriis assignatis remanserit, quod super collocationem illius loqui debeat generali." C. Cenci, "Le Costituzioni Padovane del 1310," *AFH* 76 (1983): 520.

66. Abate, "Memoriali, statuti ed atti," 29–32.

67. "Provinciae Mediolanensi assignantur studia Oxonie, Bononnie, Perusinum, Argentinense" (ibid., 30).

68. By 1300, Perugia appears to be a studium provinciale, where every custody in the province of Saint Francis sent one student de debito (Cenci, "Ordinazioni dei capitoli provinciali Umbri," 20). By 1327 it was an advanced studium where a bachelor as well as a lector was present. *Francesco d'Assisi: Documenti e archivi, codici e biblioteche, miniature,* ed. F. Porzio (Milan, 1982), 49.

69. "Provincia Mediolanensis mittet ad Studia Oxonie, Montempessulanum, Paduam, Florentiam, Romam" (Abate, "Memoriali, statuti ed atti," 31).

70. "Tertium est, quod per Generalem Ministrum et Generale Capitulum ordinatum est, quod in Romana Provincia, videlicet, in Conventu Romano Maiori, vel in alio loco competenti prout ordinaverit Provinciale Capitulum eiusdem Provincie, de cetero generale studium habeatur" (ibid., 30).

provinces of Rome, Apulia, and Calabria.[71] In 1310, the same list included the provinces of Bologna and Saint Anthony, the province of France, Aquitaine, the Holy Land, Hungary, and Penna.[72]

Selection of Students

The novice's knowledge of theology at the time of his profession would determine the type of studium to which he would be sent. For a clerical friar who was merely literate the usual course was for him to enroll at an ordinary studium for a couple years and then be sent to one of the advanced studia in his province or in a neighboring province. A novice who before joining the Order had already spent a few years in theology schools could be sent directly to a studium generale. Different offices within the Order required different durations of theological study. In the late thirteenth century, to become eligible for the office of preacher, one had to have attended theology lectures at least for four years.[73] The students were closely watched by their lectors and other superiors during the first stages of their studies. Ideally, students well suited for intellectual studies were designated to become preachers and lectors, while the rest would be destined for positions that did not require a high level of theology education, such as becoming a *socius* (practically an assistant) to a lector. Here we should recall the previously cited case of Adam Marsh and his *socius*.[74] In a letter written to the provincial minister, the famous English lector Adam of Marsh expressed his regret at the assignment of Adam of Hereford as his *socius*, since this friar had been forced to quit his studies to take this assignment.[75] Adam of Marsh thought very highly of him, and believed that he could successfully proceed to the office of preacher if he were given the opportunity to continue his studies. He lamented the fact that students inferior to Adam of Hereford had been designated to teach theology, and requested that another friar be assigned to him as *socius*, and that Adam of Hereford be sent back to London to study.[76]

---

71. "Provincia Mediolanensis habet studentes de Provinciis Aquitaine, Calabrie, Boemie, Apulie, Sancti Antonii, Tuscie, Romanie" (ibid., 31).

72. "Ad studium Mediolanense mittent Provincie Francie, Aquitanie, Terre Sancte, Ungarie, Pennensis Calabrie, Bononie, et Sancti Antonii" (ibid.).

73. Such was the decree of the province of Aquitane. "Item ordinamus, quod nullus de cuius sufficientia, moribus sive scientia dubitatur, mittatur ad capitulum provinciale pro suscipiendo predicationis officio, nisi minister expresse et nominatim licentiam concederet talem mittendi. Item nullus mittatur, nisi audierit ad minus theologiam per quatuor yemes" ("Bihl, Statuta provincialia provinciarum Aquitanie et Franciae, 479). *Yem (p) es* literally means "winters." As Franciscan lectures started at the beginning of October and continued until Pentecost, perhaps here *yemes* stood for "academic years."

74. See chap. 3.

75. Adam of Marsh, *Epistolae,* 314–16, letter 174.

76. "Etiam nonnulli longe inferiores ad officium eruditionis impendendae, ut opinor, in Sacra Scriptura sunt designati de discretorum consilio" (ibid., 314). A. G. Little translates *designati* as "those who are

It was the Provincial Chapter's duty to choose the students to be sent to other provinces. The selected student would be provided with books along with a letter from his provincial minister recommending him to the new province and explaining that the student was sent in accordance with the general chapter's assignments. An example of such of a recommendation letter is found in the formulary of Bologna province:

> Letter from..., for the student to be sent to the studium outside of the province.
>
> As you know very well, dear Father, in the Chapter General celebrated in..., it was decided that the Province of Bologna can have one student, beloved in Christ, the bearer of the present letter, young and by all means honest and holy and apt for studying, by the pleasure and counsel of our provincial chapter, to be transferred to the said studium.[77]

Students sent to study outside the province would be provided with books by their home province. Exemplary evidence comes from a note on a Padua manuscript containing the first part of the *Summa theologica* of Thomas Aquinas:

> This book, which is the first part of the *Summa* of friar Thomas of Aquinas, belongs to the friar Bartholomeo of Padua a Sancto Andrea de Mascaris, lector of the Order of Friars Minor. He conceded this book to friar Peter of Padua of the same order, when he went to the Milan studium for the love of God and his mother Virgin.[78]

Friar Bartholomeo de Mascara was the lector in the Padua convent in 1281 and in Verona in 1286. In 1291 he was made the provincial minister of Padua.[79] The book in question had come into the possession of Bartholomeo de Mascara in 1286.[80] Since, in the first note, Bartholomeo is referred to as lector not as

---

appointed"; however, the usual word for appointment seems to be *ordinatio* (Eccleston, 33). "Remittere dignemini praefactum fratrem A. Londinum ad studentum" (Adam of Marsh, *Epistolae,* 315).

77. "Lictera de eodem, pro studente ituro ad studium extra Provinciam.... Cum, sicut bene scitis, karissime Pater, ordinatum fuerit in Capitulo Generali, celebrato..., quod Provincia Bo[nonie] unum studentem possit habere, dilectum in Christi Fratrem, exhibitorem presentium, iuvenem utique honestum et sanctum et ad studium bene aptum, de beneplacito et consilio Provincialis nostri Capituli, ad dictum Studium transmittendum duxi de obedientia salutari; quem ex multa confidentia reverende Paternitate vestre, quo affectuosius valeo, in Domino recommendo. Valete. Data" (De Luca, "Un formulario di cancelleria," 243).

78. "Iste liber qui est prima pars Summae fratris Thomae de Aquino est fratris Bartholomaei de Padua a Sancto Andrea de Mascaris lectoris de ordine Fratrum Minorum quem concessit fratri Petro de Padua eiusdem ordinis quando ivit Mediolanum ad studium pro amore Dei et Virginis matris eius." Padua, Biblioteca Antoniana, MS 304, f. 1r. as described in G. Abate and G. Luisetto, *Codici e manoscritti della Biblioteca Antoniana col catalogo delle miniature,* 2 vols. (Vicenza, 1975), 1:283.

79. Sartori, *Archivio Sartori,* vol. 1, *Basilica e convento del santo,* ed. P. Giovanni Luisetto (Padua, 1983), 1264.

80. This we know from another note on the same manuscript: "Iste liber est concessus ad usum fratris Bartholomaei de Padua a S. Andrea... post eius obitum conventui paduano... in testamento patrui

provincial minister, we can conclude that the book was then given to Peter of Padua sometime between 1286 and 1291.

Toward the Office of Lector: The Studium Generale

Friars who had shown an aptitude for study were selected at the end of two to three years of study in the schools to be sent to a studium generale as candidates for the office of *lectio*. Formally, the decision to choose these students was made by the Provincial Chapter, and a selected student would then be sent along with a letter of recommendation from the provincial minister.[81] For example, Salimbene was chosen to go to Paris on behalf of the province of Bologna in 1249.[82] The Narbonne constitutions of 1260 required that a friar sent to Paris should be able, eloquent, morally strong, and not argumentative, but kind and of a peaceful disposition. The provinces were warned not to send those who did not possess these traits, since those who recommended an unsuitable candidate could face a penance of three days of bread and water.[83] It was the responsibility of the province to provide these friars with books and the assistance of a *socius*. In a letter written in 1240–1249, Adam Marsh informs the provincial minister, William Nottingham, that the two friars chosen to study in Paris—Walter de Maddele and John of Westun—had not been sufficiently provided for, although other friars designated for the office of lector received large volumes and the assistance of *socii*.[84] The general administration would pay the living expenses of two friars from each province that were going to Paris (*studentes de debito*), but for any other students sent to Paris or any other studia generalia, it was the province's responsibility to pay the living expenses (*studentes de gratia*).

---

sui magistri Manfredi de Mascaris cuius animam... anno Domini M.CC.LXXXVI" (Padua, Biblioteca Antoniana, MS 304, f. 140r).

81. A letter collection of the thirteenth to fourteenth centuries from the Bologna province includes a letter that was addressed by a provincial minister to the Paris convent asking for them to recommend the student of their choice: "Reverendis in Christo Patribus, Fratri... Custodi... Guardiano parisiensi... Frater Minister salutem in recommendatione, sincere dilectionis affectum. Fratrem, exhibitionem presentium, in Christo karissimum, meo ac Diffinitorum et aliorum fratrum nostri Provincialis Capituli judicio pro studio ydoneum reputatum, ad vos pro studente transmitto, de obedientia salutari... rogo... confovere" (De Luca, "Un formulario di cancelleria francescana," 243).

82. "Et dixit mihi frater Rufinus minister (Bononie): 'Ego te misi in Franciam, ut studeres pro provincia mea, et tu ivisti ad conventum Ianuensem, ut habitares ibi?'" (Salimbene, 322).

83. "Circa mittendos autem attendatur, quod sint ad proficiendum habiles, fortes corpore, eloquentiae bonae et conversationis honestae, non contentiosi, sed 'mites et pacifici' inter fratres.... Teneantur autem fratres mittere illos quos iudicaverint magis idoneos secundum conditiones praemissas. Si autem aliquem miserint, qui propter defectus notabiles sit indignus, tribus diebus tantum in pane et aqua ieiunent, illi scilicet quorum consilio est transmissus" (Narbonne-Assisi-Paris, 72, no. 14).

84. Adam Marsh, *Epistolae,* 353–55, letter 197.

After the Studium Generale: The Conferral of the Office of Lector

According to the Narbonne constitutions, a candidate for the office of lector had to spend a minimum of four years in a studium generale, unless he was judged adequate to be assigned as a lector before that time.[85] The students who were sent to Paris or any other studium generale were expected to return to their province and start teaching. Thus, at the end of the required sojourn, they would be sent back to their province together with a testimonial letter from the custodian and the lector of the convent where they had studied.[86] This letter would give the opinion of the prelates of the studium about the aptitude of the student for the office of lector.[87]

Once the students had returned to their province, the office of lector would be conferred on them by the provincial diffinitors,[88] and they would be appointed to their teaching posts. In some cases, even before their return they would be allocated to convents. Eccleston tells us that the provincial minister William of Nottingham was assigning one of the friars studying in the universities to each convent, in case of the removal or death of the lector of that convent.[89] It has

---

85. "Taliter autem missi studeant quattuor annis ad minus, nisi adeo fuerint provecti, quod merito iudicentur idonei ad lectoris officium exsequendum" (Narbonne-Assisi-Paris, 72, no. 13). The practice of studying for four years probably existed before 1260, as Gerard of San Donnino had studied four years in Paris to become a lector on behalf of the province of Sicily. "Frater Ghirardinus Parisius missus fuit, ut studeret pro provincia Sicilie, pro qua receptus fuerat; et studuit ibi IIIIor annis": Salimbene, 239.

86. "Item teneantur studentes in generalibus studiis reportare secum, cum ad suas provincias redeunt, litteras testimoniales gardiani et lectoris loci, in quo studuerunt de sua conversatione et profectu in scientia, quas suis ministris ostendere teneantur" (Callebaut, "Acta Capituli Generalis Mediolani Celebrati an. 1285," 288). "Item ordinat minister de consensu provincialis capituli, quod quilibet frater missus ad studia generalia theologie intra provinciam, naturalium seu logice, debeat dum revocabitur secum, ferre testimoniales litteras custodis, si tempore sui recessus presens fuerit, aut gardiani, lectoris theologie et duorum discretorum ad hoc per custodem assignatorum; quod si non ferens litteras predictas recesserit, non possit promoveri in aliquo gradu scientie, donec per ministrum secum fuerit dispensatum" (Delorme, "Constitutiones provinciae provinciae," 423–24).

87. An example of this kind of letter has survived in the Franciscan letter formulary that dates from the thirteenth to fourteenth centuries: "Reverendo etc. Noveritis, tenore presentium, Fratrem..., qui aliquot tempore fuit studens...a Provincia vestra, fuisse inter nos honeste et pacifice conversatum. Et quantum scire possum, credo eum aptum ad officium Lectorie. Valeatis, etc." (De Luca, "Un formulario di cancelleria francescana," 244).

88. Under chapter 10, titled *De capitulo provinciali*, the duties of provincial definitors are explained as follows: "Quae sunt haec: Collatio super transmissis ad capitulum, correctio eorum quae provli capitulo corrigenda notificabuntur; ordinatio eorum quae ad necessitatem vel honestatem morum provinciae videbuntur pertinere, cum diversae provinciae diversis consuetudinibus varientur; divisio custodiarum, ordinatio lectorum, receptio, mutatio vel dimissio locorum, assignatio librorum notabilium fratrum decedentium vel ab Ordine recedentium. Et dicimus librum notabilem valentem dimidiam marcam argenti et supra.—Definitoribus vero tempore suae definitionis nihil de huiusmodi libris erogetur" (Bihl, "Statuta generalia ordinis," 303).

89. "Assignaverat enim in universitatis pro singulis locis studentes" (Eccleston, 50).

been already mentioned that Albert of Pisa, the provincial minister of England, appointed lectors to custodial schools in England.[90]

Generally, then, a lector taught in his own province, though he could be assigned to another province if there was a shortage of lectors there. Whenever a province did not have a lector to teach in a certain studium, it was the responsibility of the General Chapter to provide the lector.[91] Since the General Chapter was summoned every three years, often the minister general had to step in to provide lectors. According to Salimbene, Thomas of Pavia served as lector in Parma, Bologna, and Ferrara, all of which belonged to the province of Bologna.[92] However, Thomas of Pavia also served in Lucca, which belonged to the neighboring province of Tuscany.[93] In Salimbene's chronicle, we meet an English lector called Stephen in the year 1248. When John of Parma visited England, he promised to send Stephen to Rome, but when two friars of the Genoa convent appealed to him for a good lector, he assigned Stephen there as lector.[94] However, as will be seen below, sometimes a lector who had already served a few years in his province would be sent to Paris for further study, or if he was exceptional, he would be chosen by the General Chapter to teach as a bachelor or doctor of theology. In such cases, he would be appointed to one of the studia generalia of the Order, often to those that were incorporated into a university. For example, Ralph de Colebruge had entered the Order in 1250 while he was a regent master in Paris.[95] The same year he was appointed to Oxford by the minister general to teach theology as regent master.

Paris: A Unique Studium Generale

Among all the studia generalia of the Order, Paris had a unique status. In the first place, it accepted students from *all* provinces, whereas all other studia generalia were accepting students only from the provinces assigned to them. Furthermore, while the other studia generalia generally accepted only one friar from each

---

90. Eccleston, 49.

91. The first statute about this arrangement comes from the Narbonne 1260 constitutions. See chap. 11, *De capitulo generali:* "Provideatur de lectoribus, predicatoribus, de mittendis 'Inter Saracenos et alios infideles,' de mittendis de una provincia in aliam ad manendum, de novis provinciis capiendis et ministrationibus distinguindis et huiusmodi" (Bihl, "Statuta generalia ordinis, 313).

92. Salimbene, 429.

93. "Actum ad domum fratrum Minorum de Luca im posteriori claustro propeque dormentorium, coram fratre Thomasio de Papia lectore dicti loci." Vito Tirelli and Matilde T. Carli, eds., *Le Pergamene del convento di S. Francesco in Lucca (secc. XII–XIX)* (Rome: Ministero per i beni culturali e ambientali, 1993), 110.

94. Salimbene, 296.

95. "Secundus frater Radulfus de Colebruge, qui Parisiis, ubi prius laudabiliter rexerat—siquidem actu regens in theologia intravit—Oxoniam, ut regeret a generali ministro destinatus est, ubi et legit novicius existens" (Eccleston, 50).

province assigned to them, whose expenses were paid by the sending province, Paris would have at least two *de debito* students from each province, whose expenses were paid by the general administration of the Order.[96] If provinces wanted to send more students to Paris, the provinces had to pay for their living expenses. Naturally, the cost of providing for two students from each province for four years was a very serious burden on the Order's finances. Precautions were taken to provide the Paris convent with a steady income. The *definitiones* of the 1266 constitutions asked all friars who were consulted by the laity on the subject of alms, or who would be present at the preparation of wills, to advise people to bequeath alms to the Paris convent.[97] The provincial constitutions of this period passed similar decrees to support the Parisian convent.[98] A list of cardinals in the thirteenth century bequeathing money to the Paris convent shows that the 1266 decree did not remain a dead letter. Ottobono Fieschi, in his testament dated September 28, 1275, at Valencia, asked to be buried in the Franciscan church in Genoa, and left money to the Franciscan convents in Genoa, Clavaro, Paris, and Reims, and to the Franciscan General Chapter. Another cardinal, Hugh of Evesham, in his testament dated November 15, 1286, at Rome, left forty marks to be divided equally between the Franciscans and Dominicans studying in Paris. The Franciscan cardinal Bentivegna Bentivegni, in his testament dated June 1286 at Rome, left to the Parisian convent ten *livres tourainnes* for a pittance. Cardinal Giovanni Cholet, in a testament dated between 1289 and 1292, left two hundred *livres parisiennes* to the Paris convent of Franciscans for his anniversary to be celebrated.[99]

Paris differed from other studia generalia in the Order in another way: it was the only studium in the Order where Franciscans who were already lectors could go on to further study at a later point in their career. The related evidence comes from the 1300 Umbrian constitutions:

> He wishes and commands with the consent of the same chapter that friars who are sent to Paris for study should be chosen from among those who have studied in a studium generale and have already taught in the province. And these should stay in Paris only two years unless for some

---

96. "Possit autem quaelibet provincia habere duos studentes Parisius sine aliqua provisione; quibus provideatur in libris secundum arbitrium provlis capituli et Ministri" (Narbonne-Assisi-Paris, 72, no. 19).

97. "Diffinimus, quod ministri dicant fratribus omnibus, ut in testamentis et aliis consiliis recommendatam habeant domum Parisiensem, cum ibi Fratres adiscant, unde alii fratres totum mundum erudiuntur." Andrew G. Little, "Definitiones capitulorum generalium ordinis Fratrum Minorum 1260–1282," *AFH* 7 (1914): 678.

98. "Item fratres sint solliciti et attenti in testamentis et alibi, ut conventiu Parisiensi alique elemosine erogentur" (Little, "Statuta Provincialia Provinciae Franciae et Marchiae Tervisinae," 452).

99. Agostino Paravicini-Bagliani, *I testamenti dei cardinali del Duecento* (Rome: Presso la Società, 1980), 142–63, 210, 237.

reason the provincial chapter [minister], with the consent of the chapter, dispenses more time.[100]

Here the statute uses the term *pro studio* for this advanced-study group, while those who are sent to Paris to become lectors are referred to in the same constitutions by the phrase *pro lectore*.[101] Generally, even in the most recent historiography, it has been suggested that friars were sent to Paris—or Oxford and Cambridge for that matter—either to train as lectors or to obtain university qualifications as bachelors and masters.[102] What the statute above suggests is that there was a third group of friars, at least after 1300, who went to the Paris studium simply to advance their knowledge by pursuing higher studies in theology for two years. The two-year limit would have made it impossible for them to obtain a degree.

Becoming a Bachelor and a Regent Master

The highest steps in the career ladder of a medieval Franciscan lector were the positions of bachelor and master at Paris, Oxford, or Cambridge. The tradition of having Franciscan university masters dated back to 1236, when a regent master at the University of Paris, Alexander of Hales, decided to take up the Franciscan habit. The event would have been of little importance if, after the resignation or death of Alexander, his magisterial chair had reverted to the committee of secular masters to be filled. Instead, Alexander's entry meant that from 1236 onward, the Franciscan Order claimed one magisterial chair for its own members. At Oxford, Adam Marsh was the first Franciscan to become a theology master at the university in 1247. However, when he left his position in 1253, the university was asked to allow his pupil Thomas of York to incept in theology.

Naturally, the office of *magisterium* existed only in the studia generalia that were incorporated into a university, and not in other studia generalia of the Order. One could only be made a *magister* either by a board of regent masters of the faculty or by a special license from the pope.[103] By 1336, promotion to

---

100. "Item voluit et ordinavit, de consensu eiusdem capituli, quod fratres mictendi Parisius pro studio eligantur de illis qui studuerunt in aliquo studio generali et qui in provincia iam legerunt. Et hi tantum duobus annis commorentur ibidem, nisi aliquando ex causa aliqua videatur provinciali capitulo [ministro], de consensu ipsius capituli, de maiori tempore dispensandum" (Cenci, "Ordinazioni dei capitoli provinciali Umbri," 20).

101. "Item provideatur cuilibet fratri studenti Parisius pro lectore in septuaginta libris ravennatum" (ibid., 21).

102. Courtenay, "Parisian Franciscan Community," 157–58; Maierù, "Formazione culturale," 23; Roest, *History of Franciscan Education,* 89; Courtenay, "Academic Formation," 201.

103. This is derived from the objection by Benedict XII to the decision of the chancellor of Toulouse University to promote a Franciscan friar. "Sicut facultas sacre pagine alias quascunque precellit, sic debet honorari pre ceteris, et diligentius precaveri ne in ea, qua universalis illuminatur ecclesia et fides dirigitur

the *magisterium* in theology was possible only in Paris, Oxford, and Cambridge. Generally, before assuming the title of a *magister,* a student had to become a bachelor (*baccalarius*). In medieval academic terminology, a bachelor was a student of an advanced level who gained the right to teach before becoming a *magister.* However, the specific function and job description of a bachelor differed from one university to another. Olga Weijers suggested that in the mendicant terminology, *bachelor* meant simply one who seconded the lector.[104]

Both the bachelors and the masters teaching in a studium generale incorporated in a university would be nominated by the minister general,[105] and most often the university administration duly accepted the candidates.[106] The candidate for the *magisterium* would be chosen from among those who had already served as bachelors.[107] The lector who was promoted to this position would carry the title of *magister sacrae theologiae.* As a general rule, both the bachelors and the masters were chosen from among the lectors who had taught in the provincial schools for several years, and not from among those who had just completed their studies to be a lector.[108] The provincial minister of France and other ministers could also recommend to the minister general those from their provinces who were suitable for reading the Sentences.[109] Salimbene referred to the year 1248 when John of Parma gave Bonaventure of Bagnoregio permission to teach at the University of Paris, although he had never taught in any other place, since he was still bachelor and not a *cathedratus.*[110]

Incepting as a master of theology was the crowning achievement for a friar who wished to have a scholarly career. The story of Richard Rufus of Cornwall, who was the fifth regent master at Oxford in 1255, is a good example of a

---

et defensatur catholica, indigni sedem et magisterium promovendi ad tante magisterium facultatis per plures professores ipsius examinari diligenter et stricte, ut illi et non alii cathedram in eadem facultate magistralem ascenderet, qui reperti sufficientes existerent, scirentque stabilire domum Domini et resistere ascendentibus ex adverso" (*CUP,* 2:451).

104. Olga Weijers, *Terminologie des universités au XIIIe siècle* (Rome: Ateneo, 1987), 173, 175–76.

105. "Item statuit et diffinit capitulum generale, quod minister generalis provideat tam de eo, qui debet ad magisterium presentari Parisius quam de illo, qui ad legendum ibidem Sententias assumetur" (Geroldus Fussenegger, ed., "Definitiones capituli generalis Argentinae celebrati anno 1282," *AFH* 26 [1933]: 137); "Item de fratribus lecturis Sententias et ad Magisterium praesentandis Parisius Minister provideat generalis" (Bihl, "Statuta generalia ordinis," 77).

106. Concerning the relationship of mendicant schools to the universities, see Rashdall, *Universities,* 1:376–78, for Paris; 2:66–68, for Oxford.

107. Roest, *History of Franciscan Education,* 97–108.

108. Courtenay, "Academic Formation," 200–201.

109. "Et ut via sibi pateat utilius providendi, minister Francie et ministri alii et discreti capituli generalis teneantur per obedientiam ei nominare in scriptis illos et non alios, quos de provinciis suis pro lectione Sententiarum Parisius tam ratione vite quam scientie iudicabunt idoneos de presenti; et istud preceptum in quolibet generali capitulo renovetur." Fussenegger, "Definitiones capituli generalis Argentinae celebrati anno 1282," 137.

110. Salimbene, 435.

Franciscan lector's quest to become a regent master. It is believed that Richard took the Franciscan habit in 1238 in Paris, probably when he was a student of arts.[111] He was sent to the English province to spend his novitiate. Probably after his novitiate, Richard started his studies in theology with the intention of becoming a lector. After about ten years, he received permission to go to Paris, probably in 1248 during John of Parma's visit to England.[112] John of Parma was a bachelor and was reading the *Sentences* in Paris at the time when he was elected minister general. It might have been his intention to send Richard of Cornwall to Paris to read the *Sentences* to fill the gap that arose from his own election. However, for some reason not known to us, Richard remained in England. In order to become a regent master in theology, one had to incept either at Oxford or Paris. In both of these universities, there was room only for one Franciscan regent master at a time. The chances of becoming a regent master at Paris probably seemed small to Richard, since in May 1248, William of Meliton had already succeeded Eudes Rigaud as the fourth regent master in Paris.[113] The reason why Richard chose to stay in Oxford may have been that he had seen his chances of incepting and becoming a regent master higher there, with less competition than at Paris.[114]

In 1250, we find Richard reading the *Sentences* in the Oxford convent. However, he failed to achieve his ambition of becoming a regent master, since the Oxford convent promoted Thomas of York for inception in 1253.[115] On this occasion, Richard decided to make use of his permission to go to Paris. Raedts suggests that his irreversible decision to go to Paris stemmed from his disappointment and jealousy at seeing a friar younger and less experienced than himself being promoted to the magisterial chair.[116] It may also have been due to the fact that in 1253, the University of Oxford passed a decree not allowing anyone to incept in theology unless he had graduated first from a school of arts.[117] In 1254 we find Richard once again in Paris, reading the *Sentences* under the regent master Bonaventure, using Bonaventure's commentary on the *Sentences*. He did not incept at Paris,

---

111. The date of Richard's entry into the Order is disputed. For this dispute and the latest conclusion on this issue, see Peter Raedts, *Richard Rufus of Cornwall and the Tradition of Oxford Theology* (Oxford: Clarendon Press, 1987), 2–4.

112. We have the letter of Adam Marsh to the provincial minister William of Nottingham concerning the letter of concession by the minister general to Richard. See Adam of Marsh, *Epistolae*, 365–66; Raedts, *Richard Rufus*, 5.

113. Glorieux, "D'Alexandre de Hales," 268.

114. Raedts suggests that Richard stayed in England because of poor health. Raedts, *Richard Rufus*, 5.

115. For the carrier of Thomas of York, see Little, *Grey Friars in Oxford*, 141.

116. Raedts, *Richard Rufus*, 7–8.

117. Little, *Grey Friars in Oxford*, 141.

but finally became a regent master at Oxford in 1256, when Thomas of York transferred to the lectorship at Cambridge.[118]

Seculars in the Franciscan Schools

Initially founded with the intention of teaching theology to friars, mendicant schools in towns were soon obliged to welcome another class of students: the secular clergy. The papacy had been particularly keen on educating the clergy since the twelfth century, but for this it had to rely on the cathedral schools and the theology faculties of Paris and Oxford. Thus instruction progressed at a slower pace than desired. Roger Bacon pointed to the ignorance of the prelates and wrote that they were forced to borrow the notes of the young friars for their sermons.[119] When the friar-lectors started to give instruction in theology at their convents, it probably seemed to the papacy a welcome opportunity to provide more education to the clergy. To this purpose Franciscans served in two ways: they opened their convent schools to the public and sent their lectors to teach in the cathedral schools. Victor G. Green asserted, based on Roger Bacon's testimony, that the schools of the friars in England and elsewhere contributed to a great extent to the proper theological education of the clergy.[120] Felder argued that the Minorite schools were divided between public (*öffentliche*) and private schools.[121] Teaching outsiders probably started quite early in the convent schools. Dominican constitutions talk about public lectures being held as early as 1228.[122] The earliest evidence for the attendance of the secular clergy at Franciscan schools I have been able to find dates from the year 1236. Archbishop Tedericus promised indulgences to those who would contribute to the building of a new convent for the Franciscans in Bologna. The new building was to be constructed in a more suitable place for the sake of people who went to the friars for confessions and the scholars and clergy who went to the Franciscan school.[123] In the 1240s, the papacy actively encouraged the attendance

---

118. Raedts, *Richard Rufus,* 9.

119. "Saeculares a quadraginta annis neglexerunt studium theologiae et philosophiae secundum veras vias illorum studiorum, occupati appetitu deliciarum, divitiarum et honorum" (Bacon, *Compendium studii philosophiae,* in *Opera,* 1:428–29). "Et quia prelati, ut in pluribus, non sunt multum instructi in theologia, nec in praedicatione dum sunt in studio, ideo postquam sunt praelati, cum eis incumbit opus praedicandi, mutuantur et mendicant quaternos puerorum, qui adinvenerunt curiositatem infinitam praedicandi" (Bacon, *Opus tertium,* in *Opera,* 1:309).

120. Victor G. Green, *The Franciscans in Medieval English Life (1224–1348)* (Paterson, NJ: St. Anthony Guild Press, 1939), 132.

121. Felder, *Geschichte,* 328.

122. Heinrich Denifle, ed., "Die Constitutionen des Predigerordens von Jahre 1228," *ALKG* 1 (1885): 223.

123. "Tedericus divina miseratione S. Ravent. Ecclesie archiep.... Cum igitur domus S. Marie de Puliola Fratrum Minorum Bononie a civitate ita remotus (sic) esset quod clerici et scolares ad scolas et

of secular clergy at the Franciscan schools. In a letter to the clergy of Dijon in 1246, Innocent IV conferred on the clergy pursuing theological studies in the schools of the Friars Minor the privilege of continuing to receive their benefices as if they were attending the theology faculty in Paris.[124] In another letter dated to 1249, the same pope informed the provincial minister, Brother Rufino, that the clergy who frequented the theology faculty of the Friars Minor in Bologna were to receive their benefices, just like those in Paris did.[125] It is of particular importance that several candidates for canonization from among the secular clergy in the thirteenth and early fourteenth century had studied at the studia of the Franciscans. Among these we can count Saint Yves (d. 1310, canonized 1347), a well-educated secular priest who had ardently taken on pastoral work; Thomas Cantilupe, bishop of Hereford (d. 1282, canonized 1320); and Louis of Anjou (d. 1297, canonized 1297).[126]

Although embraced by the papacy as a means of raising the educational level of the clergy, the Franciscan schools became a rival to the existing institutions of theological education. In a letter from 1254, the Parisian masters complained about the scarcity of students in the theology faculty, since now "they are taught in cities and other major universities by the friars."[127] The masters were indeed justified in their fear of losing students: in 1258 the provost and chapter of Imola refused permission to two canons to go to Paris for study on the grounds that there was a school of theology in Imola at the Franciscan convent.[128] Other evidence for these open theology schools comes from Naples. In 1302, the

---

sermones, et generaliter omnes civitatis eiusdem tam ad confessiones faciendas quam ad verbum Domini audiendum et cetera que ad salutem pertinent animarum, temporibus oportunis, quomode ad predictum locum accedere non valebant; placuit summo pontifici, ad quem spectat omnium ecclesiarum provisio, d. episcopo Bononien. Dare suis litteris in mandatis, ut praedictam domum in loco honesto et apto ad omnia superdicta salubriter permutaret." Bonaventura Giordani, ed., "Acta Franciscana e tabulariis Bononiensibus deprompta," *AF* 9 (1927): 4.

124. "Ducis Burgundiae, auctoritate vobis praesentium indulgemus, ut quicumque vestrum in Scholis Fratrum Minorum Divionen. Lingonen Diocesis studio institerint Theologiae facultatis, beneficiorum suorum proventus integre percipiant, ac si Parisius in eodem studio morarentur" (*Inclinati precibus,* June 22, 1246, *BF* 1:416, no. 137).

125. "Tuis devotis supplicationibus inclinati universis clericis intrantibus scholas Fratrum administrationibus tuae pro audienda Theologica facultate auctoritate praesentium indulgemus, ut quoad perceptionem beneficiorum suorum illa Indulgentia gaudeant, quam studentes in eadem facultate Parisiues habere noscuntur" (ibid., 1:529, no. 300).

126. Vauchez, *Sainthood in the Later Middle Ages,* 314, 401–2.

127. "Propter scolarium apud nos in theologia studentium raritatem, cum jam in civitatibus et aliis locis majoribus universis per fratres eosdem et alios non sine grandi periculo dicte littere doceantur" (*CUP,* 1:253–54, no. 230).

128. "Significant sanctitati vestre prepositus et capitulum Imole, quod cum presbiter Raynerius et canonicus eorum peteret ab eis licentiam eundi Parisius ad studentum in theologia, dictus prepositus denunciavit eidem quia Imolensis Ecclesia paciebatur defectum in ordine sacerdotali ad presens, cum ipsa Ecclesia teneatur celebrare divina in duabus suis ecclesiis de novo constructis, et in dicta civitate teneatur solempne studium in scientia predicta in domo Fratrum Minorum, quod non potuerant ei licentiam dare." Serafino Gaddoni, ed., "Documenta ad historiam trium ordinum S. Francisci in urbe Imolensi," *AFH* 5 (1912): 57.

king of Naples, Charles II, gave the Franciscans, Dominicans, and Augustinian hermits a share of the taxes collected in the city for having schools of theology in their convents.[129] This privilege was respected by Charles's successors during the entire fourteenth century.[130] This grant most probably meant that the friars accepted the secular clergy in their theology schools and were rewarded for providing a public service. In Pisa too the friars held open theology classes for secular clergy. In a sermon preached to the clergy in 1260–1261, Federico Visconti, the bishop of Pisa, recommended the clergy learn from the Dominican and Franciscan theology masters, who, he said, teach the New and the Old Testament "gratis et sine pecunia."[131]

Bishops indeed welcomed this opportunity for a variety of reasons. They no longer had to send clergy for one or two years to a far-away university and deal with the difficult task of filling the vacancies left by such absentees. By attending a local mendicant theology school, the clergy could receive instruction without the problem of nonresidence. Remarkable in this respect is the exemplary letter found in the *Formelbuch* of the bishops of Breslau. This letter, which bears the name of Nankerus, bishop of Breslau from 1326 to 1341, asked the provincial minister to allow the Franciscan lector to continue teaching in Breslau, because of his praiseworthy character, his scientific merits, and the fruits of his works.[132] It is not clear whether the lector was teaching in his convent, with his classes open to the secular clergy, or perhaps teaching elsewhere in the city, but what is important is that the bishop sees the Franciscan lector as an important resource. It should be noted that although the clergy were admitted

---

129. "Carlo II d'Angiò re assegna ai conventi di S. Domenico, S. Lorenzo e S. Agostino della città di Napoli per il mantenimento degli Studi di teologia esistenti nei loro conventi, 150 once da ricavarsi dalla gabella del ferro, della pece e dell'acciaio della stessa città, così distribuite: 80 once ai frati Predicatori, 40 once ai frati Minori e 30 once ai frati Eremitani di S. Agostino." Rosalba di Meglio, *Il convento Francescano di S. Lorenzo di Napoli: Regesti dei documenti dei secoli XIII–XV* (Salerno: Carlone, 2003), 7, no. 9 The original of this grant is in ASN, Diplomatico, Pergamene del convento di S. Agostino Maggiore di Napoli, 9.

130. For Robert of Anjou, see di Meglio, *Il convento Francescano*, 9, no. 12. (May 15, 1314); Joanna I of Anjou, ibid., 12, no. 18 (January 31, 1344); Louis of Anjou and Hungary, ibid., 9, no. 19 (March 14, 1348); Louis and Joanna I of Anjou, ibid., 15, no. 25 (February 1, 1360).

131. "Et ideo dedit vobis Deus doctores iustitie, scilicet magistros theologie de ordine fratrum predicatorum et minorum, qui ad vos existentes in terra vestra gratis et sine pecunia descendere facient *imbrem serotinum et etiam matutinum,* Ioelis 2, id est vos docebunt Testamentum vetus et novum vel que ad humanitatem et divinitatem Christi pertinere noscuntur, vel que apta sunt simplicibus et provectis. Non ergo sitis, Karissimi, pigri vel negligentes habere scientiam Dei." Celestino Piana, "I sermoni di Federico Visconti, Arcivescovo di Pisa (d. 1277) (Cod. Laurenz. Plut. 33 sin.1)," *Rivista di Storia della Chiesa in Italia* 6 (1952): 238–39.

132. "Ven. et religioso fratri… ministro fratrum minorum provincie… Nankerus dei et apostolice sedis providentia Ep. Wrat…. virum fratrum… lectorem fratrum… ob sue laudabilis et honeste conversacionis atque sciencie sue merita prosequimur specialiter, necnon et fructus commendabiles ex eius provenientes operibus nos multipliciter inducebant, quod nuper dum essetis nobiscum Wrat. pro eodem lectore, videlicet quod in ipso lectoratus officio nobiscum Wrat. remaneret, circumspeccioni vestre votivas porreximus cum instancia preces nostras." Wilhelm Wattenbach, *Das Formelbuch des Domherrn Arnold von Protzan* (Breslau, 1862), 278.

to Franciscan theology classes, their admittance to philosophy classes was prohibited by the Franciscan constitutions.[133]

Teaching by Franciscans outside their convent started as a result of the demand from other religious orders. It has already been argued that the intellectual activities of both Franciscans and Dominicans in Paris and elsewhere, and their increasing popularity among the young students in the university towns, had an impact on the traditional monastic orders. The Cistercian Order was the first order to make an attempt to follow the path of the mendicant orders by opening a studium in Paris. Similarly, the Benedictines realized the need to adopt to the changing times through a bigger emphasis on studying.[134] When the mendicants set about implementing an educational network, they set out to university towns that allowed them to recruit from among the scholars who could perform the office of lector. Benedictines, on the other hand, did not have an active presence around Paris and Oxford to attract theology recruits. Finding lectors was therefore a serious problem for them. The solution was to appeal to secular or mendicant lectors of theology, just as in the 1230s the Franciscans at Oxford, without a lector of their own to teach them, had appealed to Robert Grosseteste. In 1247 the Benedictine General Chapter at Northampton decreed that in all abbeys and priories, a *lectio* of theology or canon law was to be given in a suitable place. The lectors for this purpose were to be gathered from among seculars or regulars.[135] William Pantin points to the significance of this decree since it is the first decree leading to the establishment of the Benedictines at the universities.[136]

It was probably after this date that the Franciscans started to teach Benedictines. The earliest evidence I have been able to find is from 1275, when the cathedral priory of Christ Church, Canterbury asked the Franciscan William of Everel to teach theology to the monks.[137] From a series of letters in the chapter library and register of Christ Church, we can tell that for the next

---

133. "Iura vero et philosophica in scholis theologiae ab eodem lectore et eodem tempore non legantur, sed alibi et alias, ubi fuerit opportunum.—Saeculares autem ad huiusmodi lectiones nullatenus admittandur" (Bihl, "Statuta generalia ordinis," 76).

134. Joan Greatrex, "Monk Students from Norwich Cathedral Priory at Oxford and Cambridge, c. 1300 to1530," *English Historical Review* 106 (1991): 555.

135. "Statuit[ur], ut in singulis abbaciis et prioratibus, quibus [facultas] suppetit [ac fratrum multitudo] suffragatur, iuxta providenciam prelati, [saltim] una leccio de theologia vel de [sacris can]onibus, in loco decenti [et] honesto, singulis diebus, fratribus ad hoc deputatis ab aliquo [religioso vel seculari in] divina lege perito legatur." William A. Pantin, ed. *Documents Illustrating the Activities of the General and Provincial Chapters of the English Black Monks, 1215–1540,* Camden Third Series (London: Royal Historical Society, 1931–1937), 3:28, no. 9.

136. Ibid., 3:27.

137. The evidence is from the continuation of the chronicle of Gervase of Canterbury; Charles Cotton, *The Grey Friars of Canterbury 1224 to 1538: A Contribution to the 700th Anniversary of Their Arrival in England* (Manchester: Manchester University Press, 1924), 34.

forty years the Franciscan Provincial Chapter continued to appoint a lecturer at the request of the monks.[138] From a series of letters between 1286 and 1298, we learn that Friar R. de Wodehaye remained as lecturer to the monks of the priory of Christ Church, and he was reappointed every year by the Franciscan Provincial Chapter. Among his successors, the only name surviving is that of the Franciscan Robert of Fulham, who kept the post until 1314.[139] A similar occasion is recorded in 1285, in Worcester. The bishop of Worcester, Godfrey Giffard, wrote to Friar William of Gainsborough, vicar of the Friars Minor, asking him to appoint Friar Robert de Crull as lector to the Benedictine monks of the cathedral church of Worcester.[140]

Franciscan masters also taught at the papal studium in Rome, which should not be confused with the Franciscan studium generale in the Roman Curia, which was founded as late as 1313.[141] The *studium curiae* was founded in 1244 by Innocent IV.[142] Matthew of Aquasparta was teaching there at the time when he was elected minister general in 1287. In 1288, we find the English Franciscan John Peckham teaching in the *studium curiae*.[143] Somewhat distinct from these activities, some odd evidence points to the probability that the Franciscans loaned their classrooms to lay masters for their lectures. In the year 1288, in Venice, a certain Master Peter was holding his classes in the Franciscan convent in Chà da Monte.[144]

What the overall picture presented here shows is a striking difference between the Franciscan educational organization and that of the Dominicans. The number of Franciscan studia, both absolutely and in relation to the numbers of convents and provinces, was very different from the number of Dominican studia. The assignment of advanced studia and studia generalia to take students from other, particular provinces, a system that necessitated extreme mobility from the Franciscan friars, had no equivalent among the Dominicans, who tended to remain within a province-based system. The assignment of friars to

---

138. Four letters between the prior and convent of Christ Church and the provincial minister of England, William of Gainsborough, have been published in *CF*, ed. C. L. Kingsford (Manchester, 1914–1922), 2:4–8.

139. Cotton, *Grey Friars of Canterbury*, 36.

140. A. G. Little, "Franciscan School at Oxford in the Thirteenth Century," *AFH* 19 (1926): 821.

141. "Item determinatum est per Generale Capitulum, quod de cetero habeat Ordo in loco Curie Studium Generale, ubi per Generalem Ministrum provideatur de Magistro et Bachalario et XII studentibus, sicut viderit expedire" (Abate, "Memoriali, statuti ed atti," 34).

142. On the foundation of *studium curiae*, see Agostino Paravicini-Bagliani, *Medicina e scienze della natura alla corte dei papi nel Duecento* (Spoleto: Centro italiano di studi sull'alto Medioevo, 1991), 363–90.

143. Ibid., 398.

144. "1288, Feb. 10, testes..et *magister* Petrus, qui tenet scollas apud fratres minores in domo de chà da Monte." E. Bertanza and G. dalla Santa, eds., *Maestri, scuole e scolari in Venezia fino al 1500* (Venice: Deputazione di Storia Patria per le Venezie, 1907), 1:1.

Paris late in their career for further education even after serving as lectors elsewhere was peculiar to the Franciscans. All of this further weakens the notion that the Franciscans can be assumed, in the absence of evidence, to have copied the Dominicans. It is evident, however, that the Franciscan educational system and terminology was often borrowed, though modified in the process of adoption, from the secular university system. This is certainly not surprising since many of the early lectors, who were the true founders of the educational system, were scholars from the universities.

The Franciscan contribution to the totality of clerical and monastic education in the Middle Ages appears to have been quite substantial, a point undeservedly ignored so far. It is quite conceivable that by way of directly training the secular clergy and monks in many cities and towns, the Franciscans might have transferred, consciously or not, their own particular understanding of evangelical doctrine to their audience. This phenomenon might also explain the interest in Franciscan life and poverty by religious men outside the Order.[145] This is a phenomenon that certainly needs further study.

---

145. See, for example, the analysis of a vita of Francis, *Legenda s. Francisci monacensis,* written by a Benedictine monk around 1275. Ramona Sickert, "Armut im Vergleich: Überlegungen zur zeitgenössischen Wahrnehmung franziskanisher Armut im 13. Jahrhundert," in Melville and Kehnel, *In proposito paupertatis,* 108–9.

Conclusion

When Francis prohibited his brothers the owner-
ship of individual and communal property, he did not just adopt a principle of
the apostolic life as he understood it. He also tried to remove from the path
of the friars one of the most common means by which people were ranked in
society. People's respectability and society's valuation of them normally reflected
the degree of their wealth and property. What the very early Franciscan Order
aimed to be was a brotherhood in which all were valued equally and all saw
one another as such. That is why there was no recruitment policy in the early
period, and that is why Francis would ask no man aspiring to the gray habit
how much he or his parents could give to the Order. Holding property, even
communally, would destroy this fabric of equality, and would carry the profane
conventions of outside society into the spirituality of the Order. The act of selling off one's entire property and distributing it to the poor, just like Francis's
symbolic act of stripping naked in the piazza of Assisi, was an initiation rite of
great significance, which made all men economic equals at the moment of their
entry into the Order. It was to serve this vision of brotherhood and equality
that Francis defied the hierarchy based on the superiority of the *ordo clericus*
over the *ordo laicus*, a hierarchy so enthusiastically supported by the Church
from the Gregorian reforms onward. Francis received clergy and laity into his
Order with the same enthusiasm, and without any hint of partiality. This is the
essential point on which the Franciscan Order diverged in its mission and fabric
from the purely clerical Dominican Order. Wealth and ecclesiastical standing

were certainly not the only factors that could lead to inequality of status. There was of course the inevitable fact that some friars came from noble families and some did not, a distinction that may go beyond one simply of wealth. Parentage could not be erased, but its social consequences could certainly be fought by making such noble friars work and beg, by making them subject to ministers who might come from lesser families, and by admonishing them constantly to poverty and humility.

It is precisely in this context that we need to understand the problem that the integration of the study of theology into the Order caused. Learning or education is a form of wealth in the way it exalts its possessor above those of his peers who lack it and creates another form of hierarchy of value and respectability. In the Middle Ages, doctor of theology was considered superior to a bachelor of theology; a cleric who had spent two years studying in Paris was deemed superior to one who had spent two years in the school of an ordinary city or town. When the learned friars introduced the systematic study of theology into the Order's mission, they thus rendered the Order's extraordinary fabric of equal brotherhood vulnerable and prone to transformation into a socially hierarchical structure. One can argue that this developing hierarchy was a product of institutionalization and based on the offices that friars assumed, but even these offices themselves were essentially founded on degrees of learning. To become a preacher, one had to study four years, whereas to become a lector six or seven years' study was necessary. Lectors could assume all other offices on account of having fulfilled the requisite years of learning. It was intellectual prowess that came to decide the function of a friar within the Order. Ultimately, therefore, it was the pursuit of learning that shaped the nature of the institution rather than the other way around. Similarly, the form of the relationship of the Franciscans with the papacy and the nature of their contributions to the institutional Church were determined largely by the gradual integration of a systematic educational organization into the Order and the supply of trained personnel this provided to the Church.

The pursuit of learning affected more than the administrative hierarchy, however. Ultimately, it created a spiritual hierarchy as well. Those friars who were successful in the schools were soon deemed "better" Franciscans. By statute, friars celebrated masses regularly for the souls of Franciscan doctors of theology. From the late thirteenth century onward, Franciscans along with Dominicans presented the learning of candidates for canonization as partial proof of their sanctity, but the incorporation of learning as an integral part of what Franciscans saw as the true evangelical life followed a particular path, as we can see from the Order's written discourses on the subject.

In the early period of intellectualization, the major argument in favor of learning involved a simple syllogism. The evangelical life the Friars Minor vowed to follow included preaching. Preaching necessitated the study of theology. Therefore, friars had to study. At the beginning of the mendicant-secular conflict, when the secular masters questioned the appropriateness of the presence of friars in the universities, the Franciscans had recourse to this syllogism. It was a convincing argument to make, since Franciscan friars indeed did preach, and often more effectively than most of the secular clergy. Even better, the preaching card was an ace that led the friars to win many privileges and continuous support from the papacy in their disputes with the university masters. The spearhead of the secular masters, William of Saint-Amour, criticized this entire line of argument, insisting that preaching was the responsibility of the secular clergy, and that the preaching mendicants were trespassing on the territory of the local clergy. To him it was an unmistakable sign of the friars' arrogance masked by a false humility: friars were false apostles. Some secular masters, on the other hand, more readily accepted that the friars had a point, and that indeed many even of the learned clergy lacked either the skill or the desire to preach. This gave the friars the upper hand when they sought papal support. A more realistic secular remedy than writing angry treatises was taking action. When founding the first college in Paris for secular clergy in 1259, a college to rival those of the mendicants, Robert de Sorbonne made preaching in the parishes a condition for membership.

However effective, the argument that learning was necessary to support a preaching mission was not without problems when looked at more deeply. Many Franciscan friars, and particularly those set for advancement within the Order, pursued learning more rigorously than was necessary for preaching. This is observable in their insistence on teaching and studying at a university level and on having permanent chairs in the theology faculties of Europe, and in some of the topics they studied. Much of this advanced education was not immediately tied to preaching, and many of those who studied and taught at a higher level never really engaged in popular preaching, or were quite bad at it when they did venture to deliver sermons to the laity. The possibility was there to decide that education was necessary for preaching, but that it could be provided by the university secular masters, or by making more generally such arrangements as the Oxford Franciscans made with Grosseteste. This did not happen. Franciscans chose not only education, but to be the educators themselves as well, and at the very highest level too. It is the adoption of this particular form of educational system that makes the argument from the preaching mission more of a justification than the actual reason for what happened. Also, precisely the form of their educational system allowed the arguments for learning devised at the high end of the educational scale to be spread to the lectors and through them to the rest of the clerical friars who had become their pupils in the convent schools. Had the Franciscans chosen to adopt a system in which they were instructed by men from outside the Order, it would not have been possible for a Franciscan theology of learning to get a firm hold within the Order and be transmitted from generation to generation.

The case for learning gradually moved beyond the argument from preaching. John of Rupella claimed Anthony to be a perfect disciple of Christ, since Anthony not only lived as Christ had but also taught like him. Bonaventure, in his *Journey of the Mind to God,* presented learning as an essential step in the contemplation of God. In the writings of influential theologians like Peter John Olivi and Matthew of Aquasparta, study was said to be an element of evangelical perfection in its own right and therefore a natural activity for Franciscan friars. Its benefits no longer limited to learning to preach, or even teaching others to preach, study was celebrated for taking one's mind away from worldly things, effecting a better understanding of virtue and vice, and thereby contributing directly to the salvation of one's soul. By this time it was being openly argued that the study in question was not only the study of sacred scripture but also the study of all other subjects, such as philosophy and the arts, that could aid in the understanding of sacred scripture.

It is unclear how aware the learned friars—the architects of this integration of learning into the evangelical life—were of its potential to destroy the uniform social structure of the Order. It may have been quite difficult for them to see this. Friars such as Haymo of Faversham and Bartholomeus Anglicus came to the Order from universities with a distinct scholastic culture where erudition and subtlety reigned as prime virtues. It is imperative to take into account the particular traits of the intellectual world of the early thirteenth-century universities that shaped men such as these before they took the gray habit. It was a world of men bent on living the life of the mind, racing each other in the display of scholastic subtleties, collecting and reading books, and in general caring little for pastoral duties. When it was time to leave the university, they often did everything, after years spent among like-minded pursuers of knowledge, to delay their return to an outside world that must have seemed quite alien and inferior. And at least for those who joined the Franciscan Order, leaving the university eventually could scarcely be avoided. When the first generation of university men joined the Franciscans, they may well have considered that their comprehension and appreciation of the perfection of the Franciscan life and Rule, and their consequent decision to embrace the gray habit, were in effect a result of their intellectual formation and capacity. And intellectual capacity could certainly be encouraged and enhanced through study. It is understandable if they tried to make their new world, the Franciscan Order, then at its infancy and therefore pliable, a little bit like the university world they were destined to leave behind. Once the Order became known for its embrace of the pursuit of learning, it really must have seemed an attractive option for many scholars, men who wished to combine a religious life with intellectual pursuits, who truly believed in the necessity of study in the making of a good Christian, and who saw learning as a ladder to lead to the Church offices of high income and prestige.

Even the very first generation of friars from the universities had had little or no contact with Francis and his companions. Yet at the core of these scholars' Franciscanism lay the concept of a life of penance in apostolic poverty and humility. We should be careful not to underestimate the passion with which these men clung to their Franciscan identity; had they been less disposed to observe the ideal of apostolic poverty under the direction of a "novel" Rule written by a man of mediocre education, they could have easily picked the Dominicans, as indeed some scholars did. The silence of the Franciscan Rule on the clerical pursuit of study, in contrast to its explicit discouragement of the lay pursuit of study, was in their mind proof that Francis had no objection to study with respect to clerical brothers. After all, the saint himself had not objected to Anthony of Padua's teaching of theology to friars. As long as one studied with charity and humility and with the objective of saving one's soul and the souls of others, the pursuit of learning and teaching after their profession of the Franciscan Rule did not constitute for them a conflict with their identity as Franciscans.

It is precisely the combination of study with charity and humility that became problematic. The friars who argued for the necessity of study knew as well as anyone that learning could make men boastful and vain. And in their sermons to the other friars they did in fact insist on the importance of humility and poverty as the necessary virtues that one who pursued learning must cultivate. However, it was their intellectual interests that let loose the Joachimist prophecies on to the impressionable minds of the young Franciscan scholars, something that did more harm than anything else to the Order's creed of humility. The spread of the prophecies of Joachim of Fiore in the early 1240s struck a brand-new chord with these Franciscan scholars. Their reading of these apocalyptic prophecies, and of the tripartite history of the world found in Joachim's corpus, formed in their minds a new understanding of Franciscanism. Franciscanism was no longer just another form of evangelical life: it was "evangelical perfection." The stigmata of Francis, authenticated by the papacy, constituted the ultimate and rock-solid proof of Francis's status as the *alter Christus*. Joachimism emboldened the scholarly friars and imbued their Franciscan identity with a new rigor. The idea that the friars were the spiritual men who had come to save the world in the third and last era of life on earth circulated among prominent Franciscan scholars and was spread in the convent schools and adopted by many Franciscan lectors and new recruits. The magnitude of the damage to Franciscan humility soon became obvious: a Franciscan student at Paris, Gerardo of Borgo di San Donnino, publicized this apocalyptic stance, with its implications that Franciscan friars were superior to the rest of the institutional Church and that the Franciscan Rule was an improvement on the existing Gospels. It proved a huge embarrassment to the Order, but even this did not sound a loud enough alarm. The Joachimist strand of Franciscan thought lingered on in the minds of scholars who read or heard the prophecies, and was transmitted from one generation of friar-scholars to the next. From Bonaventure it passed to Peter John Olivi, and from him to Ubertino da Casale.

To the secular masters in the universities, the presence of mendicants was already irksome, and this Joachimist conviction of the friars made the Franciscans' claim to *minoritas* a joke in bad taste. The secular masters demanded answers as to why Franciscans, as followers of the Gospel, insisted on becoming masters when the Gospel explicitly discouraged the seeking of this title. When the Franciscan scholars defended their intellectual pursuits against the secular masters, there was hardly any trace of humility in the way they were adamant on the point of mendicant life as evangelical perfection. They may have said all the right things in the evening sermons to the friars, but during the day when they took up their pens to write treatises against the secular masters, they hardly set an example of men whose learning was crowned with humility. It is impossible not to remember here the wisdom of Francis who, with such clarity, saw the futility of a message not supported by example. Given this failure of the Order to create a culture in which the pursuit of theology would marry happily with the quintessential Franciscan virtues of *minoritas* and simplicity, it is no great surprise that the lectors increasingly came to be associated with arrogance, abuse of constitutional privileges, and the pursuit of power.

Naturally, not all friars were under the spell of the pursuit of learning that was characteristic of medieval universities. Particularly those friars who did not belong to the university circles and who had lived through the early days of the Order could quite clearly see the destructive effect of learning on the unity of the Order. To them the justification for study that relied on the preaching mission was a dangerous point of view. It potentially undermined the validity of the preaching of the uneducated friars who, through rigorous prayer and spiritual devotion, could sometimes preach more effectively than a learned brother. There was certainly a widespread conviction that Saint Francis himself was precisely this kind of devout, unlearned preacher, and encouraged his brothers to be likewise. An argument that made learning a necessary prerequisite for preaching ruled out the simple friars as unfit for preaching. This threatened to divide the Order, to destroy its fabric as a lovingly harmonious brotherhood of men from all classes of society. The Order as a whole was meant to preach, standing as an example of the perfect Christian community, where all lived in mutual respect for one another. Not only were the lay to have respect for the clergy, but the clergy too had to hold the simple illiterate brothers in respect, appreciate their contribution to the Order's spirituality, and in fact imitate them. However, the early simplicity of the friars, and the appreciation shown for it, was in decline and seen to be so. The discontent of some friars and their worries with regard to the future of the Order can be read at times openly, and at times between the lines of the early Franciscan texts authored by friars outside university circles: texts such as the *Second Life* by Thomas of Celano or the Leonine texts. In the course of the thirteenth century, however, learning came to be so well integrated into the Order's life, and its place in the evangelical life was elaborated with such rigor by influential men like Olivi, that the later criticism of men like Ubertino da Casale was no longer directed against learning per se but against the abuses and deviations that resulted from this integration. The objections largely concerned the inappropriateness for friars of the study of arts, the incompatibility of the Franciscan vow of poverty with the enthusiasm for collecting books for study both by convents and individual friars, and the interest in study for the sake of higher offices.

The integration of study and learning into the Order may have damaged irreparably the initial uniformity and unity of the Franciscans. However, its tangible benefits to the society outside can hardly be denied. Franciscans not only educated the members of their own Order but opened their schools to the secular clergy and instructed them on matters of faith, as well as instructing the laity through sermons. In spite of the consensus of scholars on the significant role played by the friars in the religious and social milieu of Europe, their doctrinal influence on both higher and lower clergy has not been sufficiently studied or emphasized. The Franciscans not only established a network of schools of theology that grew speedily during the thirteenth century, but they also accepted secular clergy into these schools with the blessing and encouragement of the papacy and local bishops. It is here that friars transmitted their own particular values, stances, and biblical exegeses to the priests. Their teaching in the studium of the Roman Curia, and as regent masters in the theology faculties of Europe, was a means of further influence on the high-ranking secular clergy. And Franciscan scholars had their own particular messages to give. They strike us as quite vocal defenders and promoters of Franciscanism as the true evangelical life, one where both learning and poverty had important places. It was indeed through their teaching activities and the example of their own persons that they advocated learning as an integral part of the evangelical life—men like Oxford-trained John of Peckham, who taught the secular clergy at the studium of the Roman Curia from 1277 to 1279, and who, like Bonaventure before him, composed an *Apologia paupertatis*.

It is through this infrastructure of schools that Franciscans eventually were successful in spreading the conviction that learning was important in Christian spirituality. As mentioned briefly before, this is best illustrated in the canonization processes of the papacy. In his magisterial study of sainthood in the Middle Ages, André Vauchez called the friars' promotion of learning as a criterion for sainthood from the 1300s onward a radical innovation, "since, in the hagiographical literature prior to the thirteenth century and in the early process of canonization, intellectual activities did not rate highly."[1] Vauchez linked this innovation to the decline of the evangelical ideal. Medieval Franciscan scholars like John of Rupella, Bonaventure, John of Peckham, or Olivi would have objected to this; they saw and promoted learning precisely as a part of the evangelical ideal, and through their studia the Franciscans transmitted this ideal both in discourse and in practice to the clergy of the Middle Ages.

A striking example of this Franciscan use of erudition as a proof of sanctity is the canonization process of Louis of Anjou in 1307, "the first intellectual saint."[2] One of the points the Franciscans emphasized was that the young prince's learning was too great to be of human origin. This is, of course, quite reminiscent of Bonaventure's argument some fifty years before. Bonaventure was well aware that if one were to argue that learning was an essential element of evangelical perfection, then one would need to explain how a saint like Saint Francis, regarded by the Franciscans as the saint of evangelical perfection *par excellence,* was not a man of learning. Bonaventure's solution was to claim Francis to be a man of superior learning, though in a special sense. Francis's learning was not acquired in the conventional way, by receiving education from human teachers; instead he was taught directly by God. In fact, this in itself was proof of his sanctity. The exact same argument was used in the case of Louis of Anjou some fifty years later. Commenting on this Vauchez wrote, "The theme of innate—as opposed to acquired—learning was very popular in the fourteenth century in processes of canonization; it made it possible to reconcile the learning which was increasingly common among the saints, as a result of the spread of education, with the conventions of traditional hagiography."[3] One may argue that this glorification of the learning of divine origin, as opposed to learning acquired through human means, might have had the effect of discouraging men from seeking the learning provided by educational institutions. It plainly did not. Divine instruction outside of the written revelation was not available on demand, and the written revelation might be better studied in the schools. What is important here is the way an organic link was constructed between learning and sanctity. Once learning was made into an attribute of sanctity, men had

---

1. Vauchez, *Sainthood in the Later Middle Ages,* 397.
2. Ibid., 402.
3. Ibid.

the best of incentives to seek learning, and the most practical way to achieve learning was to go to the universities and the studia of the friars. Of course those saints whose school learning had thus been assimilated to traditional hagiography by these means were precisely from among those men who had been taught in the schools of the friars. It is ironic that although the Friars Minor began with a creed of apostolic poverty rather than a creed of learning, they were eventually much more successful in making a case for study as an element of sanctity than they were in making the case for absolute poverty. Because of the disputes over poverty between some Franciscans and John XXII, poverty came no longer to be represented as a test of sainthood.[4] This certainly had a lot to do with the fierce dispute over the definition of apostolic poverty between the Order and the papacy, as well as within the Franciscan Order itself. Learning, on the other hand, had been integrated remarkably smoothly into the fabric of the Order. The early criticism of the Leonine group did not circulate, except in the more muted form of Thomas of Celano's *Second Life*. Later critics such as Ubertino da Casale did not formulate the abuses related to lectors and books as a consequence of the Order's pursuit of learning in itself, nor did they demand a total withdrawal from the study of theology. Rather they saw these abuses as a failure of the general and provincial administration.

This book attempts to make a step toward understanding how and why, during the course of the thirteenth century, scholastic learning and study were increasingly incorporated into the life of the regular religious. In this, the Franciscans were preceded by the Victorines and accompanied by the Dominicans, subsequently to be followed by other religious orders such as the Cistercians, Premonstratensians, and Benedictines. Did these Orders too experience distinctive troubles and tensions in making scholastic learning part of their members' religious and spiritual development, given that their origins and rules were quite different from the Franciscans? It would be interesting to know. And how exactly was the link between learning and sanctity articulated in the writings of the secular clergy? To what extent was the increased attention and attachment to learning among the professed religious a consequence of the prestige of the learned within a largely illiterate society, and to what extent did it influence the lay attitude toward learning and the learned clergy? We need to investigate further the exact role of the gradual but relentless incorporation of systematic learning and study into the religious and spiritual life of both the secular and regular clergy, and the sacred aura that came to be attached to learning in the development of the religious doctrine and practice of the fourteenth and

---

4. Ibid., 396.

fifteenth centuries, a notable example being the importance attached to studying as a devotional exercise in late medieval religious movements such as the
Brethren of the Common Life.[5] These are interesting questions and, in my view,
they promise a scholarly journey as exciting as tracing the development of the
discourse of medieval Franciscans from an emphasis on the saintliness of simplicity to one on the sacred nature of learning.

---

5. John van Engen, *Sisters and Brothers of the Common Life: The Devotio Moderna and the World of the Later Middle Ages* (Philadelphia: University of Pennsylvania Press, 2008), 275–76.

❧ SELECT BIBLIOGRAPHY

Primary Sources

Manuscripts

Paris, BnF Ms lat. 14952
Perugia, Archivio di Stato, Pergamena, 20
Pisa, Archivio di Stato di Pisa, Archivio del Comune Divisione-D, no. 1386
Todi, Biblioteca Comunale, 185
Todi, Biblioteca Comunale, 43
Todi, Biblioteca Comunale, 98

Edited Sources

Abate, Giuseppe, ed. "Costituzioni provinciali inedite dell'Umbria del secolo XIV." *MF* 31 (1931): 126–34, 194–95, 263–67.

———, ed. "Memoriali, statuti ed atti di capitoli generali dei Frati Minori dei sec. XIII e XIV." *MF* 33 (1933): 15–74.

Adam Marsh. *Epistolae.* In *Rerum Britannicarum medii aevi scriptores.* Vol. 1, *Monumenta Franciscana,* edited by T. Brewer, 77–489. London, 1859.

———. *The Letters of Adam Marsh.* 2 vols. Edited and translated by C. Hugh Lawrence. Oxford: Clarendon Press, 2006–2011.

Aegidius Assisiensis. *Dicta beati Aegidii Assisiensis sec. codices mss. emendata et denuo edita.* Quaracchi: Ad Clara Aquas, 1939.

Alberigo, Josepho, Perikle P. Joannou, Claudio Leonardi, and Paulo Prodi. *Conciliorum oecumenicorum decreta.* Basil: Herder, 1962.

Angelo Clareno. *A Chronicle or History of the Seven Tribulations of the Order of Brothers Minor.* Translated by David Burr and E. Randolph Daniel. St. Bonaventure, NY: Franciscan Institute, 2005.

———. *Expositio Regulae Fratrum Minorum.* Edited by L. Oliger. Florence: Ad Claras Aquas, 1912.

———. *Liber chronicarum; sive, Tribulationum ordinis minorum.* Edited by Giovanni M. Boccali. Assisi: Edizioni Porziuncola, 1999.

Armstrong, Regis J., J. A. Wayne Hellman, and William J. Short, eds. *Francis of Assisi: Early Documents.* 3 vols. New York: New City Press, 1999.

Bacon, Roger. *Fr. Rogeri Bacon opera quaedam hactenus inedita.* Edited by John S. Brewer. Vol. 1 (*Opus Tertium, Opus Minus, Compendium Philosophiae*). London: Longman, Green, Longman and Roberts, 1859.

Bartholomaeus Anglicus. *De proprietatibus rerum.* 1601. Frankfurt: Minerva, 1964.

Bihl, Michael, ed. "Statuta generalia ordinis edita in capitulis generalibus celebratis Narbonae an. 1260, Assisii an. 1279 atque Parisiis an. 1292." *AFH* 34 (1941): 13–94, 284–358.

——, ed. "Statuta provinciae marchiae Tervisinae, 1290." *AFH* 7 (1914): 453–65.

——, ed. "Statuta provincialia provinciarum Aquitaine et Franciae (saec. XIII–XIV)." *AFH* 7 (1914): 466–501.

Bonaventura Giordani, ed. "Acta Franciscana e tabulariis Bononiensibus deprompta." *AF* 9 (1927).

Bonaventure of Bagnoregio. *De reductione artium ad theologiam*. In *Opera omnia*, 5: 317–25.

——. *The Disciple and the Master: St. Bonaventure's Sermons on St. Francis of Assisi*. Translated by Eric Doyle. Chicago: Franciscan Herald Press, 1984.

——. *Legenda maior*, in *Fontes Franciscani*, 777–961.

——. *Opera omnia*. 11 vols. Quaracchi: Ad Claras Aquas, 1882–1902.

——. *Quaestiones disputatae de perfectione evangelica*. In *Opera omnia*, 5:117–98.

——. *Selecta pro instruendis Fratribus Ord. Min. scripta S. Bonaventurae una cum libello speculum disciplinae*. 2nd ed. Quaracchi: Ad Claras Aquas, 1923.

——. *St. Bonaventure's Writings concerning the Franciscan Order*. Edited and translated by Dominic Monti. Works of Saint Bonaventure, vol. 5. St. Bonaventure, NY: Franciscan Institute, 1994.

Boncompagno da Signa. *Testi riguardanti la vita degli studenti a Bologna nel sec. XIII: Dal Boncompagnus*. Vol. 1, *Biblioteca di "quadrivium."* Edited by Virgilio Pini. Bologna: Testi per esercitazioni accademiche, 1968.

Brooke, Rosalind B., ed. and trans. *Scripta Leonis, Rufini et Angeli, sociorum S. Francisci: The Writings of Leo, Rufino and Angelo, Companions of St. Francis*. Oxford: Clarendon Press, 1970.

Brufani, Stefano, ed. *Sacrum commercium sancti Francisci cum domina paupertate*. Assisi: Edizioni Porziuncola, 1990.

Callebaut, André, ed. "Acta capituli generalis mediolani celebrati an. 1285." *AFH* 22 (1929): 273–91.

Cenci, Cesare, ed. "Constitutiones prenarbonenses." *AFH* 83 (1990): 50–95.

——, ed. "Constitutiones provinciales provinciae Umbriae anni 1316." *AFH* 56 (1963): 12–39.

——, ed. "Costituzioni della provincia Toscana tra i secoli XIII e XIV." *Studi Francescani* 79 (1982): 369–409.

——, ed. "Costituzioni della provincia Toscana tra i secoli XIII e XIV." *Studi Francescani* 80 (1983): 171–206.

——, ed. "Fragmenta priscarum constitutionum praenarbonensium." *AFH* 96 (2003): 289–300.

——, ed. "Le costituzioni Padovane del 1310." *AFH* 76 (1983): 505–88.

——, ed. "Ordinazioni dei capitoli provinciali Umbri dal 1300 al 1305." *CF* 55 (1985): 5–31.

——, ed. "Vestigia constitutionum praenarbonensium." *AFH* 97 (2004): 61–98.

Chiappini, Aniceto, ed. "Communitatis responsio 'Religiosi viri' ad rotulum Fr. Ubertini." *AFH* 7 (1914): 654–75.

Chronica XXIV generalium Ordinis Minorum. *AF* 3 (1897): 1–575.

Codex redactus legum Fratrum Minorum in synopism cum indice copioso. Ex literis Joannis Cervantes Cardinalis S. Petri ad vincula legati a latere ad XXXVI. Capitulum generale Assisii habito lectis anno MCDXXX. die XXI. Junii in eodem capitulo. ed. Aloysius Perego Salvioni. Rome, 1796.

Costa, Beniamino, Leonardo Frasson, and Giovanni M. Luisetto, eds. *S. Antonii Patavini sermones Dominicales et festivi ad fidem codicum recogniti.* Padua: Centro studi antoniani, 1979.

Dalarun, Jacques et al. *François d'Assise: Écrits, vies, témoignages.* Paris: Le Cerf-Editions franciscaines, 2010.

de Amsterdam, Balduinus. "Tres sermones inediti Joannis de Rupellae in honorem S. Antonii Patavini." *CF* 28 (1958): 33–58.

Delorme, Ferdinand, ed. "Acta et constitutiones capituli generalis Assisiensis (1340)." *AFH* 6 (1913): 251–66.

———, ed. "Constitutiones provinciae provinciae (saec. XIII–XIV)." *AFH* 14 (1921): 415–34.

———, ed. "Definitiones capituli generalis OFM Narbonensis, 1260." *AFH* 3 (1910): 491–504.

———, ed. "Documenta saeculi XIV provinciae S. Francisci Umbriae." *AFH* 5 (1912): 520–43.

———, ed. "Explanationes constitutionum generalium Narbonensium." *AFH* 18 (1925): 511–24.

———. "Textes Franciscaines (lettre de S. Bonaventure innominato magistro)." *Archivio Italiano per la Storia della Pietà* 1 (1951): 209–18.

De Luca, Giuseppe. "Un formulario della cancelleria francescana e altri formulari tra il XIII e XIV secolo." *Archivio Italiano per la Storia della Pietà* 1 (1951): 219–393.

Denifle, Heinrich, ed. "Die Constitutionen des Predigerordens von Jahre, 1228." *ALKG* 1 (1885): 165–227.

———, ed. "Protocoll der Commission zu Anagni." *ALKG* 1 (1885): 99–142.

De Sérent, Antonius. "Bulla inedita Gregorii IX contra Fr. Gregorium Neapolitanum quondam provinciae Franciae ministrum data 28 Iunii 1233." *AFH* 26 (1933): 3–27.

Ehrle, Franz, ed. "Die ältesten Redaktionen der Generalkonstitutionen des Franziskaner Ordens." *ALKG* 6 (1892): 1–138.

Eubel, Conrad, ed. *Provinciale ordinis Fratrum Minorum vetustissimum secundum codicem Vaticanum Nr. 1960.* Florence: Ad Claras Aquas, 1898.

Francis of Assisi. "Testamentum." In *Opuscula sancti patris Francisci Assisiensis,* edited by Kajetan Esser, 305–17. Biblioteca Franciscana ascetica medii aevi, 12. Grottaferrata: Editiones Collegii S. Bonaventure Ad Claras Aquas, 1978.

Fussenegger, Geroldus, ed. "Definitiones capituli generalis Argentinae celebrati anno 1282." *AFH* 26 (1933): 127–40.

———, ed. "Statuta provinciae Alemanie superioris annis 1303, 1309 et 1341 condita." *AFH* 53 (1960): 233–75.

Gaddoni, Serafino, ed. "Documenta ad historiam trium ordinum S. Francisci in urbe Imolensi." *AFH* 5 (1912): 52–73, 544–72, 710–26.

Gamboso, Vergilio, ed. *Vita prima di S. Antonio; o, Assidua (c. 1232).* Fonti agiografiche antoniane, vol. 1. Padua: Edizioni Messagero, 1981.

Gaude, Francesco, ed. *Bullarium diplomatum et privilegiorum sanctorum Romanorum pontificum.* 25 vols. Turin: Seb. Franco et Henrico Dalmazzo, 1858.

Griesser, Bruno, ed. "Registrum epistolarum Stephani de Lexinton abbatis de Stanlegia et de Savisniaco." *Analecta Sacri Ordinis Cisterciensis* 2 (1946): 1–118.

Grosseteste, Robert. *The Letters of Robert Grosseteste, Bishop of Lincoln.* Edited by Frank A. C. Mantello and Joseph W. Goering. Toronto: University of Toronto Press, 2010.

Habig, Marion A., ed. *St. Francis of Assisi: Writings and Early Biographies; English Omnibus of the Sources for the Life of St. Francis.* 2 vols. Chicago: Franciscan Herald Press, 1973.

Hardouin, Jean, ed. *Acta conciliorum et epistolae decretales ac constitutiones summorum pontificum.* 12 vols. Paris: Ex Typographia Regia, 1714–1715.

Hefele, Charles-Joseph, and Henri Leclercq. *Historie des conciles d'après les documents originaux.* 10 vols. Paris: Librairie Letouzey et Ane, 1907–1938.

Hugh of Digne. *Hugh of Digne's Rule Commentary.* Edited by David Flood. Grottaferrata: Editiones Collegii S. Bonaventurae ad Claras Aquas, 1979.

Jacques de Vitry. *Lettres de Jacques de Vitry (1160/1170–1240), évêque de Saint-Jean-d'Acre.* Edited by R. C. B. Huygens. Leiden: Brill, 1960.

Julian of Speyer. *Officio ritmico e Vita secunda.* Fonti agiografiche antoniane, vol. 2, edited by Vergilio Gamboso. Padua: Edizioni Messaggero, 1985.

———. *Vita sancti Francisci. AF* 10 (1941): 333–71.

Lemmens, Leonhard, ed. "Chronicon provinciae Argentinensis O.F.M. circa an. 1310–1327 a quodam Fratre Minore basileae conscriptum (1206–1325)." *AFH* 4 (1911): 671–87.

Little, Andrew G., ed. "Constitutiones provinciae Romanae, anni 1316." *AFH* 18 (1925): 356–73.

———, ed. "Definitiones capitulorum generalium ordinis Fratrum Minorum, 1260–1282." *AFH* 7 (1914): 676–82.

———, ed. "Statuta provincialia provinciae Franciae et marchiae Tervisinae." *AFH* 7 (1914): 447–65.

Longpré, Ephrem. "Les 'Distinctiones' de Fr. Thomas de Pavie, O.F.M." *AFH* 16 (1923): 3–33.

Luard, Henry Richards, ed. *Roberti Grosseteste epistolae.* London: Green, Longman and Roberts, 1861.

Mansi, G. D. Sacrorum conciliorum nova, et amplissima collectio in qua præter ea quæ Phil. Labbeus, et Gabr. Cossartius et novissime Nicolaus Coleti in lucem edidere, ea omnia... exhibentur, quæ Johannes Dominicus Mansi evulgavit. Editio novissima ad eodem Patre Mansi... aliisque item eruditissimis viris... curata... additionibus locupletata... & perfecta. 53 vols. Florence, 1759.

Matthew of Aquasparta. *Quaestiones disputatae: De fide et de cognitione.* Quaracchi, Florence: ex Typographia Collegii S. Bonaventure, 1957.

———. *Sermo de studio sacrae scripturae.* Vol. 1 of *Quaestiones disputatae de fide et de cognitione,* 22–36. Quaracchi, Florence: ex Typographia Collegii S. Bonaventure, 1957.

Matthew Paris. *Chronica majora.* Edited by H. R. Luard. London, 1880.

———. *Matthei Parisiensis historia anglorum.* In *Monumenta Germaniae historica,* 390–434. Scriptores 28. Hannover, 1888.

Menestò, Enrico, and Stefano Brufani, eds. *Fontes Franciscani.* Assisi: Edizioni Porziuncola, 1995.

Moreira de Sá, Artur, ed. *Chartularium Universitatis Portugalensis (1288–1537).* Lisbon: Centro de Estudos de Psicologia e de História da Filosofia anexo à Faculdade de Letras da Universidade de Lisboa, 1966.

Musto, Ronald G. "The Letters of Angelo Clareno (c. 1250–1337)." PhD diss., Columbia University, 1977.

Oliger, Livarius. "De pueris oblatis in ordine minorum (cum textu hucusque inedito fr. Ioannis Pecham)." *AFH* 8 (1915): 389–447.

——, ed. *Expositio quatuor magistrorum super regulam Fratrum Minorum (1241–1242)*. Rome: Edizioni di storia e letteratura, 1950.

——, ed. "Liber Exemplorum fratrum minorum saeculi XIII." *Antonianum* 2 (1927): 207–83.

Olivi, Peter John. "An studere sit opus de genere suo perfectum." In *La dottrina dell'Olivi sulla contemplazione, la vita attiva e mista,* edited by A. Emmen and F. Simoncioli. *Studi Francescani* 61 (1964): 108–67, 141–59.

——. *De usu paupere: The Quaestio and the Tractatus*. Edited by David Burr. Florence: Leonardo S. Olschki, 1992.

Peckham, John. *Quaestiones disputatae*. Edited by Gerard J. Etzkorn, Hieronymus Spettmann, and Livarius Oliger. Quaracchi, Florence: Grottaferrata, 2002.

Piana, Celestino, ed. *Chartularium studii Bononiensis S. Francisci*. *AF* 11 (1970).

Sabatier, Paul, ed. *Actus beati Francisci et sociorum ejus*. Paris: Fischbacher, 1902.

——, ed. *Speculum perfectionis; seu, S. Francisci Assisiensis legenda antiquissima auctore fratre Leone*. Paris: Fischbacher, 1898.

Salimbene of Adam. *The Chronicle of Salimbene de Adam*. Edited and translated by Joseph L. Baird, Giuseppe Baglivi, and John Robert Kane. Binghamton, NY: Medieval and Renaissance Texts and Studies, 1986.

Tirelli, Vito, and Matilde T. Carli, eds. *Le pergamene del convento di S. Francesco in Lucca (secc. XII–XIX)*. Rome: Ministero per i beni culturali e ambientali, 1993.

Tomassetti, R. P. D. Aloysius, ed. *Bullarum diplomatum et privilegium sanctorum Romanorum pontificum*. Vol. 3, *A Lucio III (1181) ad Clementium IV (1268)*. Turin: Seb. Franco et Henrico Dalmazzo editoribus, 1858.

Ubertino da Casale. *Declaratio*. In "Zur Vorgeschichte des Councils von Vienne no. 4 Vorarbeiten zur Constitution Exivi de Paradiso vom 6. Mai 1312," edited by F. Ehrle. *ALKG* 3 (1887): 162–95.

——. *Responsio*. In "Zur Vorgeschichte des Councils von Vienne no. 4 Vorarbeiten zur Constitution Exivi de Paradiso vom 6. Mai 1312," edited by F. Ehrle. *ALKG* 3 (1887): 51–89.

——. *Rotulus iste*. In "Zur Vorgeschichte des Councils von Vienne no. 4 Vorarbeiten zur Constitution Exivi de Paradiso vom 6. Mai 1312," edited by F. Ehrle. *ALKG* 3 (1887): 93–137.

William of Meliton. *Opusculum super missam*. Edited by Aureliano van Dijk. *Ephemerides Liturgicae* 53 (1939): 291–349.

William of Saint-Amour. *De periculis novissimorum temporum*. Edited and translated by G. Geltner. Paris: Peeters Press, 2008.

Secondary Sources

Abate, Giuseppe, and Giovanni Luisetto. *Codici e manoscritti della Biblioteca Antoniana col catalogo delle miniature*. 2 vols. Vicenza: N. Pozza, 1975.

Andrews, Frances. *The Early Humiliati*. Cambridge: Cambridge University Press, 1999.

Asztalos, Monika. "The Faculty of Theology." In *A History of the University in Europe,* vol. 1, *Universities in the Middle Ages,* edited by H. de Ridder-Symoens, 409–41. Cambridge: Cambridge University Press, 1992.

Baldwin, John W. *Masters, Princes, and Merchants: The Social Views of Peter the Chanter and His Circle*. 2 vols. Princeton, NJ: Princeton University Press, 1970.

Barone, Giulia. *Da frate Elia agli spirituali*. Milan: Biblioteca francescana, 1999.

Bataillon, Louis-Jacques. "Early Scholastic and Mendicant Preaching as Exegesis of Scripture." In *Ad Litteram: Authoritative Texts and Their Medieval Readers*, edited by Mark D. Jordan and Kent Emery Jr., 165–98. Notre Dame, IN: University of Notre Dame Press, 1992.

——. *La predication au XIIIe siècle en France et Italie: Études et documents*. Aldershot: Variorum, 1993.

Batany, J. "L'image des Franciscains dans les 'revues d'états' du XIIIe au XIVe siècle." In *Mouvements Franciscains et société Française XIIe–XXe siècles: Études présentées à la table ronde du CNRS 23 Octobre 1982*, edited by A. Vauchez, 61–74. Paris: Beauchesne Religions, 1984.

Beaumont-Maillet, Laure. *Le grand couvent des Cordeliers de Paris: Étude historique et archéologique du XIIIe siècle à nos jours*. Paris: H. Champion, 1975.

Berg, Dieter. *Armut und Geschichte: Studien zur Geschichte der Bettelorden im Hohen und Späten Mittelalter*. Saxonia Franciscana: Beiträge zur Geschichte der Sächsischen Franziskanerprovinz, 11. Münster: Butzon und Bercker, 2001.

——. *Armut und Wissenschaft: Beiträge zur Geschichte des Studienwesens der Bettelorden im 13. Jahrhundert*. Düsseldorf: Schwann, 1977.

——. "Das Studienproblem im Spiegel der franziskanisher Histoiographie." *Wissenschaft und Weisheit* 42 (1979): 11–33, 106–56.

Bériou, Nicole. *L'avénement des maîtres de la parole: La prédication à Paris au XIIIe siècle*. Collection des études augustiniennes. Série Moyen-Age et temps modernes. 2 vols. Paris: Institut d'études augustiniennes, 1998.

Bertanza, Enrico, and Giuseppe Dalla Santa. *Documenti per la storia della cultura in Venezia: Maestri, scuole e scolari in Venezia fino al 1500*. Venice: Deputazione di Storia Patria per le Venezie, 1907.

Bertola, Ermenegildo. "Teologia monastica e teologia scolastica." *Lateranum* 34 (1968): 237–45.

Biller, Peter. "Northern Cathars and Higher Learning." In *The Medieval Church: Universities, Heresy and the Religious Life; Essays in Honour of Gordon Leff*, edited by Peter Biller and Barrie Dobson, 25–51. Woodbridge, Suffolk: Boydell Press, 1999.

Bird, Jessalynn. "The Religious's Role in a Post-Fourth-Lateran World: Jacques de Vitry's *Sermones ad status* and *Historia occidentalis*." In *Medieval Monastic Preaching*, edited by Carolyn Muessig, 209–29. Leiden: Brill, 1998.

Bloomfield, Morton, and Marjorie Reeves. "The Penetration of Joachimism into Northern Europe." *Speculum* 29 (1954): 772–93.

Bolton, Brenda. "Poverty as Protest: Some Inspirational Groups at the Turn of the Twelfth Century." In *Innocent III: Studies on Papal Authority and Pastoral Care*, 1–11. Variorum Collected Studies, vol. 490. Aldershot: Variorum, 1995.

——. "Tradition and Temerity: Papal Attitudes to Deviants, 1159–1216." In *Innocent III: Studies on Papal Authority and Pastoral Care*, 79–91. Variorum Collected Studies, vol. 490. Aldershot: Variorum, 1995.

Bougerol, Jacques-Guy. "La teorizzazione dell'esperienza di S. Francesco negli autori francescani pre-bonaventuriani." In *Lettura biblico teologica delle fonti francescane*, edited by G. Cardaropoli and M. Conti, 247–60. Rome: Pubblicazioni dell'Istituto Apostolico, 1979.

——. "S. François dans les sermons universitaires." In *Francesco d'Assisi nella Storia, secoli XIII–XV: Atti del primo convegno di studi per l'VIII centenario della nascita di*

S. Francesco, 1182–1982, Roma, 29 settembre–2 ottobre 1981, edited by Servus Gieben, 173–99. Rome, 1983.

Boyle, Leonard E. "The Constitution '*Cum ex eo*' of Boniface VIII: Education of Parochial Clergy." *Mediaeval Studies* (1962): 263–302.

——. "The Fourth Lateran Council and Manuals of Popular Theology." In *The Popular Literature of Medieval England,* edited by Thomas J. Heffernan, 30–43. Knoxville: University of Tennessee Press, 1985.

——. "Robert Grosseteste and Pastoral Care." In *Pastoral Care, Clerical Education and Canon Law, 1200–1400.* London: Variorum Reprints, 1981.

Brady, Ignatius. "The Writings of Saint Bonaventure regarding the Franciscan Order." *MF* 75 (1975): 89–112.

Branner, Robert. *Manuscript Painting in Paris during the Reign of Saint Louis: A Study of Styles.* Berkeley: University of California Press, 1977.

Brlek, Michael. *De evolutione iuridica studiorum in Ordine Minorum (ab initio usque ad annum 1517).* Dubrovnik: Jadran, 1942.

Brooke, Christopher Nugent Lawrence. *The Age of the Cloister: The Story of Monastic Life in the Middle Ages.* Mahwah, NJ: Hidden Spring, 2003.

——. *Churches and Churchmen in Medieval Europe.* London: Hambledon Press, 1999.

Brooke, Rosalind B. *Early Franciscan Government: Elias to Bonaventure.* Cambridge: Cambridge University Press, 1959.

——. *The Image of St Francis: Responses to Sainthood in the Thirteenth Century.* Cambridge: Cambridge University Press, 2006.

Burr, David. "The Correctorium Controversy and the Origins of the *Usus Pauper* Controversy." *Speculum* 60 (1985): 331–42.

——. "Franciscan Exegesis and Francis as Apocalyptic Figure." In *Monks, Nuns and Friars in Mediaeval Society,* edited by Edward B. King, Jacqueline T. Schaefer, and William B. Wadley, 51–62. Sewanee, TN: University of the South Press, 1989.

——. *Olivi and Franciscan Poverty: The Origins of the* Usus Pauper *Controversy.* Philadelphia: University of Pennsylvania Press, 1989.

——. *Olivi's Peaceable Kingdom: A Reading of the Apocalypse Commentary.* Philadelphia: University of Pennsylvania Press, 1993.

——. *The Spiritual Franciscans: From Protest to Persecution in the Century after Saint Francis.* University Park, PA: Pennsylvania State University Press, 2001.

Bynum, Caroline Walker. *Jesus as Mother: Studies in the Spirituality of the High Middle Ages.* Berkeley: University of California Press, 1982.

Callebaut, André. "Essai sur l'origine du Premier Convent des Mineurs à Paris." La France Franciscaine 11 (1928): 5–30, 179–206.

——. "Les provinciaux de la province de France au XIII siecle." *AFH* 10 (1917): 289–356.

Campagnola, Stanislao da. *Francesco e francescanesimo nella società dei secoli XIII–XIV.* Assisi (Porziuncola): Società internazionale di studi francescani, 1999.

Casagrande, Giovanna. *Religiosità penitenziale e città al tempo dei comuni.* Rome: Istituto Storico dei Cappuccini, 1995.

Casutt, Laurentius. *Untersuchungen zur Regula Prima sine Bulla.* Graz: Verlag Styria, 1955.

Chenu, Marie-Dominique. *La teologia nel dodicesimo secolo.* Translated by Paolo Vian. Milan: Jaca Book, 1986.

Clanchy, Michael T. *From Memory to Written Record, England, 1066–1307.* Cambridge, MA: Harvard University Press, 1979.

Clark, Andrew, ed. *Anthony Wood's Survey of the Antiquities of the City of Oxford.* Oxford: Clarendon Press, 1890.

Cobban, Alan B. *The Medieval English Universities: Oxford and Cambridge to c. 1500.* Aldershot: Scholar Press, 1988.

Constable, Giles. "The Orders of Society in the Eleventh and Twelfth Centuries." In *Medieval Religion: New Approaches,* edited by Constance H. Berman, 68–94. New York: Routledge, 2005.

Convegni del Centro di Studi sulla Spiritualita Medievale. *Le scuole degli Ordini mendicanti (sec. XIII–XIV), 11–14 ottobre 1976.* Todi: Presso l'Accademia tudertina, 1978.

Cook, W. R., *Images of St. Francis of Assisi: In Painting, Stone and Glass; From the Earliest Images to ca. 1320 in Italy; A Catalogue.* Florence: L. S. Olschki, 1999.

Cotton, Charles. *The Grey Friars of Canterbury 1224 to 1538: A Contribution to the 700th Anniversary of Their Arrival in England.* Manchester: Manchester University Press, 1924.

Courtenay, William J. "Academic Formation and Careers of Mendicant Friars: A Regional Approach." In *Studio e studia: Le scuole degli Ordini Mendicanti tra XIII e XIV secolo; Atti del XXIX convegno internazionale, Assisi, 11–13 ottobre 2001,* 197–207. Spoleto (Perugia): Centro italiano di studi sull-alto Medioevo, 2002.

——. "The Instructional Programmes of the Mendicant Convents at Paris in the Early Fourteenth Century." In *The Medieval Church: Universities, Heresy, and the Religious Life; Essays in Honour of Gordon Leff,* edited by Peter Biller and Barrie Dobson, 77–92. Woodbridge, Suffolk: Boydell Press, 1999.

——. "The Parisian Franciscan Community in 1303." *FS* 53 (1993): 155–73.

Crossnoe, Marshall E. "Education and the Care of Souls: Pope Gregory IX, the Order of St. Victor, and the University of Paris in 1237." *Mediaeval Studies* 61 (1999): 137–72.

Cusato, Michael F. *The Early Franciscan Movement (1205–1239): History, Sources and Hermeneutics,* 1st ed. Spoleto (Perugia): Fondazione Centro italiano di studi sull'alto Medioevo, 2009.

——. "'The Umbrian Legend' of Jacques Dalarun: Toward a Resolution of the Franciscan Question; Introduction to the Roundtable." *FS* 66 (2008): 479–508.

——. "Whence the 'Community'?" *FS* 60 (2002): 39–92.

Cusato, Michael F., and Guy Geltner. *Defenders and Critics of Franciscan Life: Essays in Honor of John V. Fleming.* Leiden: Brill, 2009.

d'Alatri, Mariano, and E. Bonanno. *L'inquisizione Francescana nell'Italia Centrale del Duecento: Con il testo del "Liber inquisitionis" di Orvieto trascritto da Egidio Bonanno.* Rome, 1996.

d'Alatri, Mariano. "La predicazione Francescana nel due e trecento." *Picenum Seraphicum* 10 (1973): 7–23.

d'Avray, D. L. *The Preaching of the Friars: Sermons Diffused from Paris before 1300.* Oxford: Clarendon Press, 1985.

Dalarun, Jacques. "Francesco nei sermoni: Agiografia e predicazione." In *La predicazione dei Frati dalla Meta del '200 alla fine del '300, Atti del xxii convegno internazionale, Assisi, 13–15 octobre 1994,* edited by Edith Pasztor, 339–404. Spoleto: Centro italiano di studi sull'Alto medioevo, 1995.

——. *La malavventura di Francesco d'Assisi: Per un uso storico delle leggende Francescane.* Milan: Edizioni Biblioteca Francescana, 1996.

——. *Vers une résolution de la question Franciscaine: La légende ombrienne de Thomas de Celano.* Paris: Fayard, 2007.

Davy, Marie-Madeleine. *Les sermons universitaires parisiens de 1230–1231: Contribution à l'histoire de la prédication médiévale.* Paris: J. Vrin, 1931.

De legislatione antiqua Ordinis Fratrum Minorum. Vol. 1 of *Legislatio francescana ab an. 1210–1221.* Mostar: Ex Typ. croatica Franciscanae provinciae, 1924.

Denifle, Heinrich. *Die Entstehung der Universitäten des Mittelalters bis 1400.* Graz: Akademische Druck-u. Verlagsanstalt, 1956.

"Der Franziskusorden: Die Franziskaner, die Klarissen und die Regulierten Franziskanerterziarinnen in der Schweiz." In *Helvetia Sacra,* edited by Klemens Arnold et al. Part 5, vol. 1. Bern: 1978.

Desbonnets, Theophile. *From Intuition to Institution: The Franciscans.* Chicago: Franciscan Herald Press, 1988.

Douie, Decima L. "St. Bonaventura's Part in the Conflict between Seculars and Mendicants at Paris." In *S. Bonaventura 1274–1974,* vol. 2, *Studia de vita, mente, fontibus et operibus S. Bonaventurae,* 585–626. Grottaferrata: Editiones Collegii S. Bonaventurae ad Claras Aquas, 1973.

Esser, Kajetan. *Anfänge und Ursprüngliche Zielsetzungen des Ordens der Minderbrüder.* Leiden: Brill, 1966.

———. *Das Testament des Heiligen Franziskus von Assisi: Eine Untersuchung über seine Echtheit und seine Bedeutung.* Münster: Aschendorff, 1949.

Felder, Hilarin. *Geschichte der wissenschaftlichen Studien im Franziskanerorden bis um die Mitte des 13. Jahrhunderts.* Freiburg im Breisgau: Herder, 1904.

Ferrari, Luigi. *L'inventario della biblioteca di San Francesco in Pisa (1355).* Pisa, 1904.

Ferruolo, Stephen C. *The Origins of the University: The Schools of Paris and Their Critics, 1100–1215.* Stanford, CA: Stanford University Press, 1985.

Flood, David. "Die Regelerklärung des David von Augsburg." *Franziskanische Studien* 75 (1993): 201–42.

———, ed. *Poverty in the Middle Ages.* Franziskanische Forschungen, 27. Heft. Werl/Westf.: D. Coelde, 1975.

Forte, Stephen L. *The Cardinal-Protector of the Dominican Order.* Dissertationes Historicae, Fasc. 15. Rome: ad S. Sabinae, 1959.

Freed, John B. *The Friars and German Society in the Thirteenth Century.* Cambridge, MA: Mediaeval Academy of America, 1977.

Frugoni, Chiara. *Francesco e l'invenzione delle stimmate: Una storia per parole e immagini fino a Bonaventura e Giotto.* Saggi. Turin: G. Einaudi, 1993.

Gabriel, Astrik L., ed. "English Masters and Students in Paris during the Twelfth Century." In *Garlandia: Studies in the History of the Mediaeval University,* edited by Astrik L. Gabriel, 1–37. Frankfurt am Main: 1969.

———. "The Ideal Master of the Mediaeval University." *Catholic Historical Review* 60 (1974): 1–40.

Gieben, Servus, ed. *Francesco d'Assisi nella storia: Atti del primo convegno di studi per l'VIII centenario della nascita di S. Francesco, 1182–1982.* 2 vols. Rome: Instituto Storico dei Cappuccini, 1983.

———. "Preaching in the Franciscan Order (Thirteenth Century)." In *Monks, Nuns and Friars in Mediaeval Society,* edited by Edward B. King, Jacqueline T. Schaefer, and William B. Wadley, 1–27. Sewanee, TN: University of the South Press, 1989.

Glorieux, Palémon. "D'Alexandre de Hales a Pierre Auriol: La suite des maîtres franciscains de Paris." *AFH* 26 (1933): 257–81.

———. *Répertoire des maîtres en théologie de Paris au XIIIe siècle.* Paris: Librairie philosophique J. Vrin, 1933.

Godet-Calogeras, Jean François. "Illi qui volunt religiose stare in eremis: Eremitical Practice in the Life of the Early Franciscans." In *Franciscans at Prayer,* edited by Timothy J. Johnson, 307–31. Leiden: Brill, 2007.

Goering, Joseph. *William de Montibus (c. 1140–1213): The Schools and the Literature of Pastoral Care.* Studies and Texts. Toronto: Pontifical Institute of Mediaeval Studies, 1992.

Goetz, Walther Wilhelm. "Die Ursprünglichen Ideale des hl. Franz von Assisi." *Historische Vierteljahrschrift* 6 (1903): 19–50.

Golubovich, Girolamo. *Biblioteca bio-bibliografica della terra santa e dell' oriente francescano.* 2 vols. Quaracchi: Collegio di S. Bonaventura, 1906, 1913.

Gratien, Badin. *Histoire de la fondation et de l'évolution de l'Ordre des Frères Mineurs au XIIIe siècle.* Paris: Société et librairie S. Francois d'Assise, 1928.

Gratien, P. "Sermons Franciscaines d'Eudes de Chatareoux." *Etudes Franciscaines* 30 (1913): 291–317.

Greatrex, Joan. "Monk Students from Norwich Cathedral Priory at Oxford and Cambridge, c. 1300 to 1530." *English Historical Review* 106 (1991): 555–83.

Green, Victor Gerard. *The Franciscans in Medieval English Life (1224–1348).* Paterson, NJ: St. Anthony Guild Press, 1939.

Grundmann, Herbert. "Die Bulle 'Quo elongati' Papst Gregor IX." *AFH* 54 (1961): 3–25.

———. *Religious Movements in the Middle Ages: The Historical Links between Heresy, the Mendicant Orders, and the Women's Religious Movement in the Twelfth and Thirteenth Century, with the Historical Foundations of German Mysticism.* Translated by S. Rowan. Notre Dame, IN: University of Notre Dame Press, 1995.

———. *Vom Ursprung der Universität im Mittelalter.* Berichte über die Verhandlungen der Sächsischen Akademie der Wissenschaften zu Leipzig, Philologisch-Historische Klasse, 103, no. 2. Berlin, 1957.

Hackett, Jeremiah. "Roger Bacon: His Life, Career and Works." In *Roger Bacon and the Sciences: Commemorative Essays,* edited by Jeremiah Hackett, 9–23. Leiden: Brill, 1997.

Hamesse, Jacqueline, et al., eds. *Medieval Sermons and Society: Cloister, City, University; Proceedings of International Symposia at Kalamazoo and New York.* Textes et études du moyen âge. Louvain-La-Neuve: Fédération Internationale des Instituts d'études médiévales, 1998.

Harding, John. *Agnellus of Pisa 1194–1236: The First Franciscan Provincial in England (1224–1236).* Canterbury: Franciscan Study Centre, 1979.

Haskins, Charles H. "The Life of Mediaeval Students as Illustrated by Their Letters." In *Studies in Medieval Culture,* 203–29. Oxford: Clarendon Press, 1929.

———. "The University of Paris in the Sermons of the Thirteenth Century." *American Historical Review* 10 (1904): 1–27.

Hauréau, Barthélemy. *Notices et extraits de quelques manuscrits latins de la Bibliothèque nationale.* 6 vols. Paris: C. Klincksieck, 1890–1893.

Hinnebusch, William A. *The History of the Dominican Order.* Staten Island, NY: Alba House, 1966.

Humphreys, K. W. *The Book Provisions of the Medieval Friars, 1215–1400.* Amsterdam, 1964.

John, James. *The College of Prémontré in Mediaeval Paris.* Edited by A. L. Gabriel and J. N. Garvin. Notre Dame, IN: Mediaeval Institute, University of Notre Dame, 1953.

Johnson, Timothy J. *Franciscans at Prayer.* Leiden: Brill, 2007.

Ker, Neil Ripley, ed. *Medieval Libraries of Great Britain: A List of Surviving Books.* London: Offices of the Royal Historical Society, 1964.

Kibre, Pearl. *Scholarly Privileges in the Middle Ages: The Rights, Privileges, and Immunities of Scholars and Universities at Bologna, Padua, Paris, and Oxford.* Cambridge, MA: Mediaeval Academy of America, 1961.

Kienzle, Beverly M., et al., eds. *Models of Holiness in Medieval Sermons: Proceedings of the International Symposium (Kalamazoo, 4–7 May 1995).* Louvain-la-Neuve: Fédération internationale des instituts d'études médiévales, 1996.

King, Edward B., Jacqueline T. Schaefer, and William B. Wadley. *Monks, Nuns and Friars in Mediaeval Society.* Sewanee, TN: University of the South Press, 1989.

Köhn, Rolf. "Schulbildung und Trivium im lateinischen Hochmittelalter und ihr möglicher praktischer Nutzen." In *Schulen und Studium im sozialen Wandel des hohen und späten Mittelalters,* edited by Johannes Fried, 203–84. Sigmaringen: J. Thorbecke, 1986.

Krüger, Klaus. *Der frühe Bildkult des Franziskus in Italien: Gestalt- und Funktionswandel des Tafelbildes im 13. und 14. Jahrhundert.* Berlin: Gebr. Mann, 1992.

———. "Un santo da guardare: L'immagine di san Francesco nelle tavole del Duecento." In *Francesco d'Assisi e il primo secolo di storia francescana,* edited by Maria Pia Alberzoni 145–61. Turin: Einaudi, 1997.

Lambert, Malcolm. *Franciscan Poverty: The Doctrine of the Absolute Poverty of Christ and the Apostles in the Franciscan Order, 1210–1323.* London: S.P.C.K., 1961.

———. *Medieval Heresy: Popular Movements from the Gregorian Reform to the Reformation.* Cambridge, MA: B. Blackwell, 1992.

Lambertini, Roberto. *Apologia e crescita dell'identità francescana (1255–1279).* Rome: Nella sede dell'Istituto Palazzo Borromini, 1990.

———. *La povertà pensata: Evoluzione storica della definizione dell'identità minoritica da Bonaventura ad Ockham.* Modena, 2000.

Landini, Lawrence C. *The Causes of the Clericalization of the Order of Friars Minor, 1209–1260, in the Light of Early Franciscan Sources.* Chicago: Pontifica Universitas Gregoriana, Facultas Historiae Ecclesiasticae, 1968.

Langeli, Attilio B. "Gli scritti da Francesco: L'autografo di un 'illiteratus.'" In *Frate Francesco d'Assisi: Atti del XXI Convegno internazionale, Assisi, 14–16 ottobre 1993,* 1st ed. *Atti dei convegni della Societa internazionale di studi francescani e del Centro interuniversitario di studi francescani nuova ser. 4,* 101–59. Spoleto: Centro italiano di studi sull'alto Medioevo, 1994.

———. "I libri dei frati: La cultura scritta dell'Ordine dei Minori." In *Francesco d'Assisi e il primo secolo di storia francescana,* edited by Maria Pia Alberzoni, 283–306. Turin: Einaudi, 1997.

Lapsanski, Duane V. *Evangelical Perfection: An Historical Examination of the Concept in the Early Franciscan Sources.* St. Bonaventure, NY: Franciscan Institute, 1977.

Lawrence, Cynthia H. "Stephen Lexington and Cistercian University Studies in the Thirteenth Century." *Journal of Ecclesiastical History* 11 (1960): 164–78.

Leclercq, Jean. *Cultura umanistica e desiderio di Dio: Studio sulla letteratura monastica del medio evo.* Florence: Sansoni, 1988.

Leff, Gordon. "The Bible and Rights in the Franciscan Dispute over Poverty." In *The Bible in the Medieval World: Essays in Memory of Beryl Smalley,* edited by Katherine Walsh and Diana Wood, 225–35. Oxford: Blackwell, 1985.

Lekai, Louis Julius. *The White Monks: A History of the Cistercian Order.* Okauchee, WI: Cistercian Fathers, Our Lady of Spring Bank, 1953.

Lerner, Robert E. "The Vocation of the Friars Preacher: Hugh of St. Cher between Peter the Chanter and Albert the Great." In *Hugues de Saint-Cher ([died] 1263): Bibliste et théologien,* edited by L. J. Bataillon, G. Dahan, and P.-M. Gy, 215–31. Turnhout: Brepols, 2004.

Lesnick, Daniel R. *Preaching in Medieval Florence: The Social World of Franciscan and Dominican Spirituality.* Athens: University of Georgia Press, 1989.

Linehan, Peter. *The Spanish Church and the Papacy in the Thirteenth Century.* Cambridge: Cambridge University Press, 1971.

Little, Andrew G. *Franciscan Papers, Lists, and Documents.* Manchester: Manchester University Press, 1943.

——. "Franciscan School at Oxford in the Thirteenth Century." *AFH* 19 (1926): 803–74.

——. *Grey Friars in Oxford.* Oxford: Clarendon Press, 1892.

——. *Studies in English Franciscan History.* Manchester: Manchester University Press, 1917.

Little, Andrew G., Montague Rhodes James, Henry Marriott Bannister, and Charles Lethbridge Kingsford. *Collectanea Franciscana.* 2 vols. Manchester: Manchester University Press, 1914–1922.

Little, Lester K. *Religious Poverty and the Profit Economy in Medieval Europe.* Ithaca, NY: Cornell University Press, 1978.

Logan, F. Donald. *Runaway Religious in Medieval England c. 1240–1540.* Cambridge: Cambridge University Press, 1996.

Magrini, Sabina. "Production and Use of Latin Bible Manuscripts in Italy during the Thirteenth and Fourteenth Centuries." *Manuscripta* 51 (2007): 209–57.

Maierù, Alfonso. "Formazione culturale e tecniche d'insegnamento nelle scuole degli Ordini mendicanti." In *Studio e studia: Le scuole degli Ordini Mendicanti tra XIII e XIV secolo,* 3–32. Spoleto (Perugia): Centro italiano di studi sull'alto Medioevo, 2002.

——. *University Training in Medieval Europe.* Leiden: Brill, 1994.

Mandić, Dominik. *De protoregula ordinis Fratrum Minorum.* Mostar: Ex Typ. croatica Franciscanae provinciae, 1923.

Mandonnet, Pierre. "La crise scolaire au début du XIIIe siècle et la fondation de l'Ordre des Frères Prêcheurs." *Revue d'Histoire Ecclesiastique* 15 (1914): 34–49.

Manselli, Raoul. *Francesco e i suoi compagni.* Rome: Istituto storico dei Cappuccini, 1995.

——. *Nos qui cum eo fuimus: Contributo alla questione francescana.* Rome: Istituto storico dei cappuccini, 1980.

——. "St. Bonaventure and the Clericalization of the Friars Minor." Translated by P. Colbourne. *Greyfriars Review* 4 (1990): 83–98.

Mapelli, F. Joyce. *L'amministrazione francescana di Inghilterra e Francia: Personale di governo e strutture dell'Ordine fino al Concilio di Vienne (1311).* Rome: Pontificio Ateneo Antonianum, 2003.

Maranesi, Pietro. "I commenti alla Regola francescana e la questione dello studio." In *Studio e studia: Le scuole degli ordini mendicanti tra XIII e XIV secolo: Atti del XXIX Convegno internazionale, Assisi, 11–13 ottobre 2001,* 35–81. Spoleto (Perugia): Centro italiano di studi sull'alto Medioevo, 2002.

——. "L'intentio Francisci' sul rapporto tra minorità e studio nel dibattito del primo cinquantennio dell'Ordine Francescano." In *Minores et subditi omnibus: Tratti caraterizzanti dell'identità francescana,* edited by Luigi Padovese, 273–304. Rome: Edizioni Collegio S. Lorenzo da Brindisi, 2003.

——. "San Francesco e gli studi: Analisi del 'Nescientes Litteras' del X capitolo della Regola Bollata." *CF* 69 (1999): 7–41.

Marrone, Steven P. *The Light of Thy Countenance: Science and Knowledge of God in the Thirteenth Century*. 2 vols. Leiden: Brill, 2000.

McGinn, Bernard. "Apocalyptic Traditions and Spiritual Identity in the Thirteenth Century Religious Life." In *Apocalypticism in the Western Tradition,* 1–26, 293–300. Aldershot: Variorum, 1994.

——. *The Calabrian Abbot: Joachim of Fiore in the History of Western Thought*. New York: Macmillan, 1985.

McLaughlin, Mary Martin. *Intellectual Freedom and Its Limitations in the University of Paris in the Thirteenth and Fourteenth Centuries*. New York: Arno Press, 1977.

Meersseman, Gilles Gérard. *Dossier de l'Ordre de la pénitence au XIIIe siècle*. 2nd ed. rev. ed. Fribourg: Éd. Universitaires, 1982.

Meersseman, Gilles Gérard, and Edvige Adda. "Pénitents ruraux communitaires en Italie au XIIe siècle." *Revue d'Histoire Ecclesiastique* 49 (1954): 343–90.

Meersseman, Gilles Gérard, and Gian Piero Pacini. *Ordo fraternitatis: Confraternite e pietà dei laici nel Medioevo*. 3 vols. Rome: Herder editrice e libreria, 1977.

Melville, Gert, and A. Kehnel, eds. *In proposito paupertatis: Studien zum Armutsverständnis bei den mittelalterlichen Bettelorden*. Münster: Lit Verlag, 2001.

Melville, Gert, and Jörg Oberste, eds. *Die Bettelorden im Aufbau: Beiträge zu Institutionalisierungsprozessen im mittelalterlichen Religiosentum*. Münster: Lit Verlag1999.

Menestò, Enrico, and Stefano Brufani, eds. *Fontes Franciscani: Introduzioni critiche*. Assisi: Edizioni Porziuncola, 1997.

Merlo, Grado G. "Eremitismo nel francescanesimo medievale." In *Eremitismo nel francescanesimo medievale: Atti del XVII Convegno Internazionale, Assisi, 12–13–14 ottobre 1989,* 29–50. Assisi: Università degli Studi di Perugia Centro di Studi Francescani, 1991.

——. *Nel nome di san Francesco: Storia dei Frati Minori e del Francescanesimo sino agli inizi del 16 secolo*. Padua: Editrici Francescane, 2003.

——. *Tra eremo e città studi su Francesco d'Assisi e sul francescanesimo medievale*. Assisi, 1991.

Messa, Pietro. *Frate Francesco: Tra vita eremitica e predicazione*. Assisi (Perugia): Porziuncola, 2001.

Miethke, Jürgen. *Studieren an mittelalterlichen Universitäten: Chancen und Risiken; gesammelte Aufsätze*. Leiden: Brill, 2004.

Moore, Robert Ian. *The Formation of a Persecuting Society: Power and Deviance in Western Europe, 950–1250*. Oxford: B. Blackwell, 1987.

Moorman, John R. H. *The Grey Friars in Cambridge, 1225–1538*. Cambridge: University Press, 1952.

——. *A History of the Franciscan Order: From Its Origins to the Year 1517*. Chicago: Franciscan Herald Press, 1988.

——. *Medieval Franciscan Houses*. St. Bonaventure, NY: Franciscan Institute, St. Bonaventure University, 1983.

——. *The Sources for the Life of S. Francis of Assisi*. Manchester: Manchester University Press, 1940.

Muessig, Carolyn, ed. *Medieval Monastic Preaching*. Leiden: Brill, 1998.

——. *Preacher, Sermon and Audience in the Middle Ages*. Leiden: Brill, 2002.

Mulchahey, Marian Michèle. "The Dominican Studium System and the Universities of Europe in the Thirteenth Century." In *Manuels, programmes de cours et techiques d'enseignement dans les universités médiévales,* edited by J. Hamesse, 277–324. Louvain-la-Neuve: Pontifical Institute of Mediaeval Studies, 1994

——. *"First the bow is bent in study …":Dominican Education before 1350.* Toronto:Pontifical Institute of Mediaeval Studies, 1998.

Murphy, John C. "The Early Franciscan Studium at the University of Paris." In *Studium Generale: Studies Offered to Astrik L. Gabriel,* edited by L. S. Domonkos and R. J. Schneider, 159–203. Notre Dame, IN: Medieval Institute University of Notre Dame, 1967.

Murray, Alexander. *Reason and Society in the Middle Ages.* Oxford: Clarendon Press, 1978.

Nebbiai-Dalla Guarda, Donatella, ed. *I documenti per la storia delle biblioteche medievali (secoli IX–XV).* Rome: Jouvence, 1992.

Nimmo, Duncan. *Reform and Division in the Medieval Franciscan Order: From Saint Francis to the Foundation of the Capuchins.* Rome: Capuchin Historical Institute, 1987.

Oliger, Paul Remy. *Les évêques réguliers: Recherche sur leur condition juridique depuis les origines du monachisme jusqu'a la fin du moyen-âge.* Paris: Desclée de Brouwer, 1958.

Pacheco, M. C., ed. *Le vocabulaire des écoles des Mendiants au moyen age: Actes du colloque Porto (Portugal), 11–12 octobre 1996.* Etudes sur le vocabulaire intellectuel du moyen age, IX. Turnhout: Brepols, 1999.

Padovese, Luigi. *"Minores et subditi omnibus": Tratti caratterizzanti dell'identità Francescana.* Roma: Istituto francescano di spiritualità, 2003.

Pantin, William Abel, ed. *Documents Illustrating the Activities of the General and Provincial Chapters of the English Black Monks, 1215–1540.* Camden Third Series. London: Royal Historical Society, 1931–1937.

Paravicini-Bagliani, Agostino. *I testamenti dei Cardinali del Duecento.* Rome: Presso la Società, 1980.

——. *Medicina e scienze della natura alla corte dei papi nel Duecento.* Spoleto: Centro italiano di studi sull'alto Medioevo, 1991.

Patschovsky, Alexander, ed. *Die Bildwelt der Diagramme Joachims von Fiore: Zur Medialität religiös-politischer Programme im Mittelalter.* Ostfildern: Thorbecke, 2003.

Pegues, Frank. "Ecclesiastical Provisions for the Support of Students in the Thirteenth Century." *Church History* 26 (1957): 307–18.

Pellegrini, Luigi. "Dalla fraternità all'Ordine: Origini e primi sviluppi del Francescanesimo nella società del secolo XIII." In *I Francescani nelle marche: Secoli XIII–XVI,* edited by Luigi Pellegrini and Roberto Paciocco, 12–23. Cinisello Balsamo (Milan): Arti Grafiche Amilcare Pizzi, 2000.

——. *Insediamenti Francescani nell'Italia del Duecento.* Rome: Laurentianum, 1984.

Peters, Edward, ed. *Heresy and Authority in Medieval Europe: Documents in Translation.* Philadelphia: University of Pennsylvania Press, 1980.

Piana, Celestino. "I sermoni di Federico Visconti, Arcivescovo di Pisa (d. 1277) (Cod. Laurenz. Plut. 33 sin.1)." *Rivista di Storia della Chiesa in Italia* 6 (1952): 231–48.

Piazza, Andrea. "Alle origini del coinvolgimento dei Minori contro l'eresia: I frati di Angarano nella Marca di Ezzelino da Romano." *Bullettino dell'Istituto Storico Italiano per il Medio Evo* 107 (2005): 205–28.

Piron, Sylvain. "Franciscan *Quodlibeta* in Southern *Studia* and at Paris (1280–1300)." In *Theological Quodlibeta in the Middle Ages: The Thirteenth Century,* edited by Chris Schabel, 403–38. Leiden: Brill, 2006.

Plasmann, Thomas. "Bartholomaeus Anglicus." *AFH* 12 (1919): 68–109.

Porzio, Francesco, ed. *Francesco d'Assisi, documenti e archivi, codici e biblioteche, miniature: [mostra].* Milan: Electa, 1982.

Potestà, Gian Luca. *Angelo Clareno: Dai poveri eremiti ai fraticelli.* Rome, 1990.

——. *Gioacchino da Fiore nella cultura contemporanea: Atti del 6. Congresso internazionale di studi gioachimiti, San Giovanni in Fiore, 23–25 settembre 2004.* Rome, 2005.

——. *Storia ed escatologia in Ubertino da Casale.* Milan, 1980.

Powell, James M. "The Papacy and the Early Franciscans." *FS* 36 (1976): 248–62.

Protzan, Arnold von. *Das Formelbuch des Domherrn Arnold von Protzan.* Edited by W. Wattenbach. Breslau: J. Max & Komp., 1862.

Prudlo, Donald. *The Origin, Development, and Refinement of Medieval Religious Mendicancies.* Leiden: Brill, 2011.

Raedts, Peter. *Richard Rufus of Cornwall and the Tradition of Oxford Theology.* Oxford: Clarendon Press, 1987.

Rashdall, Hastings. *The Universities of Europe in the Middle Ages.* 3 vols. Edited by F. M. Powicke and A. B. Emden. Oxford: Clarendon Press, 1936.

Ratzinger, Joseph. *The Theology of History in St. Bonaventure.* Translated by Zachary Hayes. Chicago: Franciscan Herald Press, 1989.

Reeves, Marjorie. *The Influence of Prophecy in the Later Middle Ages: A Study in Joachimism.* Oxford: Clarendon Press, 1969.

Richardson, Herbert G. "The Schools of Northampton in the Twelfth Century." *English Historical Review* 56 (1941): 595–605.

Rigon, Antonio. *Dal libro alla folla: Antonio di Padova e il Francescanesimo medievale.* Rome: Viella, 2002.

——. "Vescovi frati o frati vescovi?" In *Dal pulpito alla cattedra: I vescovi degli Ordini Mendicanti nel '200 e nel primo '300; Atti del XXVII Convegno internazionale; Assisi, 14–16 Ottobre 1999,* 3–26. Spoleto: Centro italiano di studi sull'alto medioevo, 2000.

Robson, Michael. *The Franciscans in the Middle Ages.* Woodbridge: Boydell Press, 2006.

Robson, Michael, and Jens Röhrkasten, eds. *Franciscan Organisation in the Mendicant Context: Formal and Informal Structures of the Friars' Lives and Ministry in the Middle Ages.* Berlin: LIT Verlag, 2011.

Roest, Bert. "Franciscan Educational Perspectives: Reworking Monastic Traditions." In *Medieval Monastic Education,* edited by George Ferzoco and Carolyn Muessig, 168–81. London: Leicester University Press, 2000.

——. *Franciscan Literature of Religious Instruction before the Council of Trent.* Leiden: Brill, 2004.

——. "The Franciscan School System: Re-assessing the Early Evidence (ca. 1220–1260)." In *Franciscan Organisation in the Mendicant Context: Formal and Informal Structures of the Friars' Lives and Ministry in the Middle Ages,* edited by Michael Robson and Jens Röhrkasten, 253–79. Berlin: LIT Verlag, 2011.

——. *A History of Franciscan Education (c. 1210–1517).* Leiden: Brill, 2000.

Rouse, Richard H., and Mary A. Rouse. *Manuscripts and Their Makers: Commercial Book Producers in Medieval Paris, 1200–1500.* 2 vols. Turnhout: H. Miller, 2000.

——. *Preachers, Florilegia and Sermons: Studies on the Manipulus Florum of Thomas of Ireland.* Studies and Texts. Toronto: Pontifical Institute of Mediaeval Studies, 1979.

Russo, Francesco. "Gioachimismo e Francescanesimo." In *Joachim of Fiore in Christian Thought; Essays on the Influence of the Calabrian Prophet,* edited by Delno C. West, 129–41. New York: B. Franklin, 1975.

Sabatier, Paul. *Life of St. Francis of Assisi.* Translated by Louise S. Houghton. London: Hodder and Stoughton, 1902.

——. *Vie de S. François d'Assise.* 9th ed. Paris: Librairie Fischbacher, 1894.

Sartori, Antonio. *Archivio Sartori: Documenti di storia e arte Francescana.* Edited by Giovanni Luisetto. Padua: Biblioteca antoniana, 1983–1988.

Schmolinsky, Sabine. *Der Apokalypsenkommentar des Alexander Minorita: Zur frühen Rezeption Joachims von Fiore in Deutschland.* Hannover: Hahnsche Buchhandlung, 1991.

Schmucki, Oktavian. "St. Francis's Level of Education." Translated by P. Barrett. *Greyfriars Review* 10 (1996): 153–70.

Schwinges, Rainer Christoph. "Student Education, Student Life." In *History of the University in Europe,* vol. 1, *Universities in the Middle Ages,* edited by Hilde de Ridder-Symoens, 195–243. Oxford: Clarendon Press, 1992.

Seifert, Arno. "Studium als soziales System."In *Schulen und Studium im sozialen Wandel des hohen und späten Mittelalters,* edited by Johannes Fried, 601–19. Sigmaringen: Jan Thorbecke, 1986.

Şenocak, Neslihan. "Book Acquisition in the Medieval Francisan Order." *Journal of Religious History* 27 (2003): 14–28.

——. "Circulation of Books in the Medieval Franciscan Order: Methods, Attitude and Critics." *Journal of Religious History* 28 (2004): 146–61.

——. "The Earliest Library Catalogue of the Franciscan Convent of St. Fortunato of Todi (c. 1300)." *AFH* 99 (2006): 475, 499–503.

——. "Early Franciscan Library Catalogues: The Case of the Gubbio Catalogue (c. 1300)." *Scriptorium* 59 (2005): 29–50.

——. "The Franciscan Studium Generale: A New Interpretation." In *Philosophy and Theology in the Studia of the Religious Orders and at Papal and Royal Courts.* Acts of the XVth Annual Colloquium of the Société Internationale pour l'Étude de la Philosophie Médiévale, University of Notre Dame, 8–10 October 2008, edited by Kent Emery Jr., William J. Courtenay, and Stephen M. Metzger, 221–36. Rencontres de philosophie médiévale 15. Turnhout: Brepols, 2012.

——. "In the Pursuit of Knowledge: The Franciscan Settlement in England, 1224–1240." *Frate Francesco: Rivista di Cultura Francescana* 71 (2005): 131–48.

——. "Voluntary Simplicity: Attitudes to Learning in the Medieval Biographies of Francis." In *The Cambridge Companion to Francis of Assisi,* edited by Michael Robson, 84–100. Cambridge: Cambridge University Press, 2011.

Seymour, Michael C. et al. *Bartholomeus Anglicus and His Encyclopaedia.* Aldershot: Variorum, Ashgate, 1992.

Shannon, Albert C. *The Popes and Heresy in the Thirteenth Century.* Villanova, PA: Augustinian Press, 1949.

Shinners, John, and William J. Dohar. *Pastors and the Care of Souls in Medieval England.* Notre Dame Texts in Medieval Culture. Notre Dame, IN: University of Notre Dame Press, 1998.

Smalley, Beryl. *The Gospels in the Schools, c. 1100–c. 1280.* London: Hambledon Press, 1985.

——. *The Study of the Bible in the Middle Ages.* 3rd ed. Oxford: Blackwell, 1983.

Società internazionale di studi Francescani. *Chi erano gli spirituali: Atti del III Convegno internazionale, Assisi, 16–18 ottobre 1975.* Assisi, 1976.

——. *Paul Sabatier e gli studi francescani: Atti del XXX Convegno internazionale; In occasione del centenario della fondazione della Società internazionale di studi francescani (1902–2002), Assisi, 10–12 ottobre 2002.* Atti dei convegni della Società internazionale di studi francescani e del Centro interuniversitario di studi francescani, 13. Spoleto: Fondazione Centro italiano di studi sull'alto Medioevo, 2003.

——. *Studio e studia: Le scuole degli ordini mendicanti tra XIII e XIV secolo; Atti del XXIX Convegno internazionale, Assisi, 11–13 ottobre 2001.* Spoleto (Perugia), 2002.

Southern, Richard W. *Robert Grosseteste: The Growth of an English Mind in Medieval Europe.* 2nd ed. Oxford: Clarendon Press, 1992.

Szittya, Penn R. *The Antifraternal Tradition in Medieval Literature.* Princeton, NJ: Princeton University Press, 1986.

Thomson, Williell R. *Friars in the Cathedral: The First Franciscan Bishops 1226–1261.* Toronto: Pontifical Institute of Mediaeval Studies, 1975.

——. "The Image of the Mendicants in the Chronicles of Matthew Paris." *AFH* 70 (1977): 3–34.

Thorndike, Lynn. "Elementary and Secondary Education in the Middle Ages." *Speculum* 15 (1940): 400–408.

Todeschini, Giacomo. *Ricchezza francescana: Dalla povertà volontaria alla società di mercato.* Intersezioni 268. Bologna: Il mulino, 2004.

Traver, Andrew G. "Rewriting History? The Parisian Secular Masters' Apologia of 1254." *History of Universities* 15 (1997–1999): 9–45.

——. "Thomas of York's Role in the Conflict between Mendicants and Seculars at Paris." *FS* 57 (1999): 179–202.

Trio, Paul. "Financing of University Students in the Middle Ages: A New Orientation." *History of Universities* 4 (1984): 1–24.

Van Dijk, Stephen J. P. *Sources of the Modern Roman Liturgy: The Ordinals by Haymo of Faversham and Related Documents (1243–1307).* Leiden: Brill, 1963.

Van Dijk, Stephen J. P., and J. Hazelden Walker. *The Origins of the Modern Roman Liturgy: The Liturgy of the Papal Court and the Franciscan Order in the Thirteenth Century.* Westminster, MD: Newman Press, 1960.

Van Engen, John H. *Educating People of Faith: Exploring the History of Jewish and Christian Communities.* Grand Rapids, MI: William B. Eerdmans, 2004.

——. *Religion in the History of the Medieval West.* Variorum Collected Studies. Aldershot: Ashgate, 2004.

——. *Sisters and Brothers of the Common Life: The Devotio Moderna and the World of the Later Middle Ages.* Philadelphia: University of Pennsylvania, 2008.

Vauchez, André. *Sainthood in the Later Middle Ages.* Cambridge: Cambridge University Press, 1997.

Verger, Jacques. *Les gens de savoir dans l'Europe de la fin du Moyen Age.* Paris, 1997.

——. "Rapports hiérarchiques et amicitia au sein des popolations universitaires médiévales." In *Hiérarchies et services au moyen age: Séminaire sociétés, idéologies et croyances au moyen age,* edited by Claude Carozzi and Huguette Taviani-Carozzi, 289–307. Aix-en-Provence: Publications de l'Université de Provence, 2001.

——. "Studia mendicanti e università." In *Il pragmatismo degli intellettuali: Origini e primi sviluppi dell'istituzione universitaria,* edited by Roberto Greci, 147–64. Turin: Paravia, 1996.

Weijers, Olga. *Terminologie des universités au XIIIe siècle.* Rome: Ateneo, 1987.

West, Delno C., ed. *Joachim of Fiore in Christian Thought: Essays on the Influence of the Calabrian Prophet.* New York: B. Franklin, 1975.

Wolf, Kenneth Baxter. *The Poverty of Riches: St. Francis of Assisi Reconsidered.* New York: Oxford University Press, 2003.

🦋 GLOSSARY

convent Although in modern times *convent* (from Latin, *conventus*) is used to mean the monastery of nuns, in medieval historiography it designates the religious houses of the mendicant orders (friary).

Conventual During the fourteenth century, the Franciscan Order split into two distinct branches. Those who claimed to observe the Rule faithfully were known as the Observants, and those who remained in the existing order took the name O.F.M. Conventuals.

Community Appearing on the historical scene in the early fourteenth century, the term designates the counterpart of Spirituals.

custody, custodian Custody is an administrative division within a province, consisting of several convents. A custodian is the friar assigned to the administration of the affairs of a custody.

diffinitor Friars who are elected specifically to give counsel to the general minister in the governance of the Order.

fidecommissarius A man who is entrusted to secure the proper execution of a testament. Friars often acted as fidecommissarii for medieval laymen.

General Chapter The highest governing and major legislative body of a mendicant Order made up of minister general, provincial ministers, and other representative friars from the provinces. The General Chapter of Franciscans met once in every three years in the Middle Ages.

guardian A friar who administers a convent; also translated into English as warden.

lector Since the major form of teaching in the Middle Ages was literally reading from a text and explaining it, a friar who taught at a convent school was called a lector, literally meaning reader. Lector was an office in the Franciscan Order, which required training in theology and examination by a superior.

minister general The highest executive office in the Franciscan Order and elected by the general chapter.

praedicatio The term, which literally means preaching, takes on multiple meaning in different contexts. In the mendicant Order it is an office that required theological training and examination. Within the medieval university, it is the highest form of academic exercise, in which the student preached to a learned audience.

Provincial Chapter The governing body of a province made up of the provincial minister, custodians, and other representatives from the custodies and convents in a province. During the Middle Ages, a Franciscan Provincial Chapter met annually and passed necessary legislation.

regular clergy Clergy who professes to a monastic or mendicant Rule (see below) and as such is a member of a religious Order.

Rule (*regula*) A set of precepts and counsels delineating the form and purpose of a religious life, a Rule is mostly associated with monastic or mendicant life. The Rule has to be approved by the papacy, and all men and women choosing that particular form of life had to swear an oath (profession) to uphold the Rule in their lifetime.

secular clergy Clergy who did not belong to a religious Order and who had not professed to a Rule.

Spiritual An early fourteenth-century term used to designate the Franciscan friars who criticized the contemporary state of the Order as having lapsed from the original vision of Francis and who wished to observe what they believed to be a genuine Franciscanism.

studium A designated room in a convent where the lector taught the student-friars, or a convent school, such as the Paris studium.

studium generale The school highest in the Franciscan educational organization hierarchy where a friar had to study to become a lector.

studium provinciale The head school in a province, to which all custodies sent students.

zelanti The name given to a group of thirteenth-century friars who wished to have a more rigorous observance of the Franciscan rule against the opposition of the administration. They are considered in the historiography to be the forerunners of Spirituals.

✹ INDEX